Learning Continuous Integration with Jenkins

Second Edition

A beginner's guide to implementing Continuous Integration and Continuous Delivery using Jenkins 2

Nikhil Pathania

Packt>

BIRMINGHAM - MUMBAI

Learning Continuous Integration with Jenkins

Second Edition

First published: May 2016

Second edition: December 2017

Production reference: 1191217

Published by Packt Publishing Ltd.
Livery Place
35 Livery Street
Birmingham
B3 2PB, UK.
ISBN 978-1-78847-935-6

www.packtpub.com

Credits

Author
Nikhil Pathania

Reviewer
Deep Mehta

Commissioning Editor
Vijin Boricha

Acquisition Editor
Prateek Bharadwaj

Content Development Editor
Sharon Raj

Technical Editor
Khushbu Sutar

Copy Editor
Safis Editing

Project Coordinator
Virginia Dias

Proofreader
Safis Editing

Indexer
Rekha Nair

Graphics
Kirk D'Penha
Tania Dutta

Production Coordinator
Melwyn Dsa

About the Author

Nikhil Pathania is currently practicing DevOps at Siemens Gamesa Renewable Energy. He started his career as an SCM engineer and later moved on to learn various tools and technologies in the fields of automation and DevOps. Throughout his career, Nikhil has promoted and implemented Continuous Integration and Continuous Delivery solutions across diverse IT projects.
He enjoys finding new and better ways to automate and improve manual processes and help teams know more about their project's SDLC by bringing valuable metrics. He is also actively working on utilizing Elastic Stack and container technologies efficiently for DevOps.

In his spare time, Nikhil likes to read, write, and meditate. He is an avid climber and also hikes and cycles.

You can reach Nikhil on twitter at `@otrekpiko`.

> *First and foremost, my beautiful wife, Karishma, without whose love and support this book would not have been possible.*
> *Great thanks to Deep Mehta who provided me with valuable feedback throughout the writing process.*
> *Special thanks to the following people who worked hard to make this book the best possible experience for the readers: Sharon Raj, Khushbu Sutar, and the whole Packt Publishing technical team working in the backend.*
> *And finally, great thanks to the Jenkins community for creating such fantastic software.*

About the Reviewer

Deep Mehta is a DevOps engineer who works in CI/CD automation. He is currently working in the San Francisco Bay Area. He helps clients design resilient infrastructure, identifying top microservices patterns and self-healing infrastructure automation. His area of interest is large-scale distributed computing, data science, cloud, and system administration.

I acknowledge my mom, papa, and sister for supporting me to produce this book.

Customer Feedback

Thanks for purchasing this Packt book. At Packt, quality is at the heart of our editorial process. To help us improve, please leave us an honest review on this book's Amazon page at `https://www.amazon.com/dp/1788479351`.

If you'd like to join our team of regular reviewers, you can email us at `customerreviews@packtpub.com`. We award our regular reviewers with free eBooks and videos in exchange for their valuable feedback. Help us be relentless in improving our products!

Table of Contents

Preface 1

Chapter 1: Concepts of Continuous Integration 7

Software Development Life Cycle 7
Requirement analysis 8
Design 8
Implementation 9
Testing 9
Evolution 9
Waterfall model of software development 9
Disadvantages of the Waterfall model 11
Advantages of the Waterfall model 11
Agile to the rescue 12
The twelve agile principles 12
How does the Agile software development process work? 13
Advantages of Agile software development process 14
The Scrum framework 15
Important terms used in the Scrum framework 15
How does Scrum work? 16
Sprint Planning 17
Sprint cycle 17
Daily Scrum meeting 17
Monitoring Sprint progress 17
Sprint Review 18
Sprint Retrospective 18
Continuous Integration 18
Agile runs on CI 19
Types of projects that benefit from CI 20
Elements of CI 21
Version control system 21
Branching strategy 21
GitFlow branching model 23
CI tool 24
Self-triggered builds 25
Code coverage 26
Code coverage tools 27

Static code analysis 27
Automated testing 29
Binary repository tools 30
Automated packaging 31
Benefits of using CI 32
Freedom from long integrations 32
Metrics 32
Catching issues faster 32
Rapid development 32
Spend more time adding features 33
Summary 33
Chapter 2: Installing Jenkins 35
Running Jenkins inside a servlet container 35
Prerequisites 36
Installing Java 36
Installing Apache Tomcat 37
Enabling the firewall and port 8080 39
Configuring the Apache Tomcat server 40
Installing Jenkins on the Apache Tomcat server 42
Installing Jenkins alone on an Apache Tomcat server 43
Setting up the Jenkins home path 44
Installing a standalone Jenkins server on Windows 45
Prerequisites 45
Installing Java 45
Installing the latest stable version of Jenkins 47
Starting, stopping, and restarting Jenkins on Windows 47
Installing a standalone Jenkins server on Ubuntu 50
Prerequisites 51
Installing Java 51
Installing the latest version of Jenkins 52
Installing the latest stable version of Jenkins 53
Starting, stopping, and restarting Jenkins on Ubuntu 54
Installing a standalone Jenkins server on Red Hat Linux 54
Prerequisites 55
Installing Java 55
Installing the latest version of Jenkins 56
Installing the latest stable version of Jenkins 56
Starting, stopping, and restarting Jenkins on Red Hat Linux 57

Running Jenkins behind a reverse proxy 58
Prerequisites 58
Installing and configuring Nginx 58
Configuring the firewall on a Nginx server 59
Starting, stopping, and restarting the Nginx server 62
Securing Nginx using OpenSSL 63
Creating an SSL certificate 63
Creating strong encryption settings 64
Modifying the Nginx configuration 65
Enabling the changes and testing our Nginx setup 68
Configuring the Jenkins server 70
Adding reverse proxy settings to the Nginx configuration 71
Running Nginx and Jenkins on the same machine 73
Running Jenkins on Docker 75
Prerequisites 75
Setting up a Docker host 75
Setting up the repository 75
Installing Docker 76
Installing from a package 78
Running the Jenkins container 78
Running a Jenkins container using a data volume 81
Testing the data volume 82
Creating development and staging instances of Jenkins 85
Prerequisites 85
Creating an empty data volume 85
Copying data between data volumes 86
Creating the development and staging instances 87
Summary 89
Chapter 3: The New Jenkins 91
The Jenkins setup wizard 91
Prerequisites 92
Unlocking Jenkins 92
Customizing Jenkins 93
Creating the first admin user 96
The new Jenkins pipeline job 96
Prerequisite 97
Creating a Jenkins pipeline job 97
The Global Tool Configuration page 101
Jenkins pipeline Stage View 103
Declarative Pipeline syntax 106

Basic structure of a Declarative Pipeline 106
The node block 106
The stage block 106
Directives 107
Steps 107
Jenkins pipeline syntax utility 109
Prerequisite 109
Installing the Pipeline Maven Integration Plugin 110
Creating a Jenkins pipeline using the pipeline syntax utility 111
Multibranch pipeline 117
Prerequisite 119
Adding GitHub credentials inside Jenkins 120
Configuring Webhooks on GitHub from Jenkins 121
Create a new repository on GitHub 124
Using a Jenkinsfile 125
Creating a Multibranch pipeline in Jenkins 126
Re-register the Webhooks 127
Jenkins Multibranch pipeline in action 129
Creating a new feature branch to test the multibranch pipeline 130
Jenkins Blue Ocean 132
Installing the Jenkins Blue Ocean plugin 132
View your regular Jenkins pipeline in Blue Ocean 133
Creating a pipeline in Blue Ocean 136
Summary 147
Chapter 4: Configuring Jenkins 149
The Jenkins Plugin Manager 149
Updating Jenkins plugins 151
Installing a new Jenkins plugin 151
Uninstalling or downgrading a Jenkins plugin 152
Configuring proxy settings in Jenkins 153
Manually installing a Jenkins plugin 154
Jenkins backup and restore 156
Installing the Periodic Backup plugin 157
Configuring the Periodic Backup plugin 157
Creating a Jenkins backup 159
Restoring a Jenkins backup 160
Viewing the backup and restore logs 161
Upgrading Jenkins 162
Upgrading Jenkins running on Tomcat Server 163
Upgrading standalone Jenkins running on Windows 165

Upgrading standalone Jenkins running on Ubuntu 167
Upgrading Jenkins running on a Docker container 169
User administration 171
Enabling/disabling global security on Jenkins 172
Enabling/disabling computers to remember user credentials 172
Authentication methods 173
Delegating to a servlet container 173
Jenkins' own user database 174
LDAP 175
Unix user/group database 176
Creating new users inside Jenkins 176
People page 177
User information and settings in Jenkins 177
Authorization methods 178
Anyone can do anything 179
Legacy mode 179
Logged-in users can do anything 179
Matrix-based security 180
Project-based Matrix Authorization Strategy 181
Summary 184
Chapter 5: Distributed Builds 185
Distributed build and test 185
The Jenkins Manage Nodes page 187
Adding Jenkins slaves – standalone Linux machine/VMs 189
Passing environment variables to Jenkins slaves 192
Passing tools' locations to Jenkins slaves 193
Launching a Jenkins slave via SSH 194
More about the active Jenkins slave 195
Adding Jenkins slaves – standalone Windows machine/VMs 199
Launching a Jenkins slave via Java Web Start 201
Adding Jenkins slaves – Docker containers 204
Prerequisites 204
Setting up a Docker server 205
Setting up the repository 205
Installing Docker using apt-get 206
Installing Docker using a .deb package 207
Enabling Docker remote API 207
Modifying the docker.conf file 208
Modifying the docker.service file 209
Installing the Docker plugin 210
Configuring the Docker plugin 210

Creating a Docker image – Jenkins slave 212
Adding Docker container credentials in Jenkins 215
Updating the Docker settings inside Jenkins 216
Summary 218

Chapter 6: Installing SonarQube and Artifactory 219

Installing and configuring SonarQube 219
Installing Java 220
Downloading the SonarQube package 221
Running the SonarQube application 222
Resetting the default credentials and generating a token 223
Creating a project inside SonarQube 224
Installing the build breaker plugin for SonarQube 226
Creating quality gates 227
Updating the default quality profile 230
Installing the SonarQube plugin in Jenkins 232
Configuring the SonarQube plugin in Jenkins 233
Installing and configuring Artifactory 234
Installing Java 235
Downloading the Artifactory package 236
Running the Artifactory application 238
Resetting the default credentials and generating an API key 240
Creating a repository in Artifactory 241
Adding Artifactory credentials inside Jenkins 244
Installing the Artifactory plugin in Jenkins 245
Configuring the Artifactory Plugin 245
Summary 247

Chapter 7: Continuous Integration Using Jenkins 249

Jenkins CI design 249
Branching strategy 250
The master branch 250
The integration branch 250
The feature branch 250
The CI pipeline 251
Toolset for CI 252
Creating the CI pipeline 252
Creating a new repository on GitHub 253
Using the SonarQube scanner for Maven 253
Writing the Jenkinsfile for CI 254
Spawning a Docker container – build agent 254

Downloading the latest source code from VCS 255
Pipeline code to perform the build and unit test 255
Pipeline code to perform static code analysis 256
Pipeline code to perform integration testing 256
Pipeline code to publish built artifacts to Artifactory 257
Combined CI pipeline code 260
Using a Jenkinsfile 261
Creating a Multibranch Pipeline in Jenkins 263
Re-registering the Webhooks 264
Continuous Integration in action 266
Viewing static code analysis in SonarQube 270
Accessing SonarQube analysis right from Jenkins 272
Viewing artifacts in Artifactory 274
Failing the build when quality gate criteria are not met 275
Summary 277
Chapter 8: Continuous Delivery Using Jenkins 279
Jenkins CD design 279
Branching strategy 280
The release branch 280
CD pipeline 281
Toolset for CD 281
Creating a Docker image – performance testing 282
Adding Docker container credentials in Jenkins 287
Updating the Docker settings inside Jenkins 288
Creating a performance test using JMeter 289
Installing Java 290
Installing Apache JMeter 290
Starting JMeter 291
Creating a performance test case 291
Creating a thread group 292
Creating a sampler 294
Adding a listener 295
The CD pipeline 296
Writing the Jenkinsfile for CD 296
Revisiting the pipeline code for CI 296
Pipeline code to stash the build artifacts 297
Spawning a Docker container – performance testing 297
Pipeline code to start Apache Tomcat 298
Pipeline code to deploy build artifacts 298
Pipeline code to run performance testing 299
Pipeline code to promote build artifacts in Artifactory 300
Combined CD pipeline code 300

CD in action 303
Summary 305
Chapter 9: Continuous Deployment Using Jenkins 307
What is Continuous Deployment? 308
How Continuous Deployment is different from Continuous Delivery 308
Who needs Continuous Deployment? 310
Creating a production server 311
Installing Vagrant 311
Installing VirtualBox 313
Creating a VM using Vagrant 314
Creating a Vagrantfile 314
Spawning a VM using Vagrant 315
Adding production server credentials inside Jenkins 317
Installing a Jenkins slave on a production server 319
Creating a Jenkins Continuous Deployment pipeline 320
A revisit to the pipeline code for CD 321
Pipeline code for a production Jenkins slave 322
Pipeline code to download binaries from Artifactory 322
Combined Continuous Deployment pipeline code 325
Update the Jenkinsfile 327
Continuous Delivery in action 329
Summary 330
Appendix: Supporting Tools and Installation Guide 331
Exposing your localhost server to the internet 331
Installing Git on Windows/Linux 333
Installing Git on Windows 333
Installing Git on Linux 336
Index 339

Preface

In the past few years, the agile model of software development has seen a considerable amount of growth around the world. There is massive demand for a software delivery solution that is fast and flexible to frequent amendments, especially in the e-commerce sector. As a result, the Continuous Integration and Continuous Delivery methodologies are gaining popularity.

Whether small or big, all types of project gain benefits, such as early issue detection, avoiding lousy code into production, and faster delivery, which leads to an increase in productivity.

This book, *Learning Continuous Integration with Jenkins Second Edition*, serves as a step-by-step guide to setting up a Continuous Integration, Continuous Delivery, and Continuous Deployment system using hands-on examples. The book is 20% theory and 80% practical. It starts by explaining the concept of Continuous Integration and its significance in the Agile world, with a complete chapter dedicated to this. Users then learn to configure and set up Jenkins, followed by implementing Continuous Integration and Continuous Delivery using Jenkins. There is also a small chapter on Continuous Deployment, which talks primarily about the difference between Continuous Delivery and Continuous Deployment.

What this book covers

`Chapter 1`, *Concepts of Continuous Integration*, gives an account of how some of the most popular and widely used software development methodologies gave rise to Continuous Integration. This is followed by a detailed explanation of the various requirements and best practices to achieve Continuous Integration.

`Chapter 2`, *Installing Jenkins*, is a step-by-step guide all about installing Jenkins across various platforms, including Docker.

`Chapter 3`, *The New Jenkins*, provides an overview of how the new Jenkins 2.x looks and feels, with an in-depth explanation of its essential constituents. It also introduces readers to the new features added in Jenkins 2.x.

`Chapter 4`, *Configuring Jenkins*, focuses on accomplishing some basic Jenkins administration tasks.

`Chapter 5`, *Distributed Builds,* explores how to implement a build farm using Docker. It also talks about adding standalone machines as Jenkins slaves.

`Chapter 6`, *Installing SonarQube and Artifactory,* covers installing and configuring SonarQube and Artifactory for CI.

`Chapter 7`, *Continuous Integration Using Jenkins,* takes you through a Continuous Integration design and the means to achieve it using Jenkins, in collaboration with some other DevOps tools.

`Chapter 8`, *Continuous Delivery Using Jenkins,* outlines a Continuous Delivery design and the means to achieve it using Jenkins, in collaboration with some other DevOps tools.

`Chapter 9`, *Continuous Deployment Using Jenkins,* explains the difference between Continuous Delivery and Continuous Deployment. It also features a step-by-step guide to implementing Continuous Deployment using Jenkins.

`Appendix`, *Supporting Tools and Installation Guide,* takes you through the steps required to make your Jenkins server accessible over the internet and the installation guide for Git.

What you need for this book

To be able to follow everything described in the book, you will need a machine with the following configurations:

- **Operating systems**:
    - Windows 7/8/10
    - Ubuntu 14 and later
- **Hardware requirements**:
    - A machine with a minimum 4 GB memory and a multicore processor
- **Other requirements**:
    - A GitHub account (public or private)

Who this book is for

This book is aimed at readers with little or no previous experience with Agile or Continuous Integration and Continuous Delivery. It serves as a great starting point for anyone who is new to this field and would like to leverage the benefits of Continuous Integration and Continuous Delivery to increase productivity and reduce delivery time.

Build and release engineers, DevOps engineers, (Software Configuration Management) SCM engineers, developers, testers, and project managers can all benefit from this book.

Readers who are already using Jenkins for Continuous Integration can learn to take their project to the next level, which is Continuous Delivery.

The current edition of the book is a complete reboot of its predecessor. Readers of the first edition can take advantage of some of the new stuff discussed in the current edition, such as Pipeline as Code, Multibranch Pipelines, Jenkins Blue Ocean, distributed build farms using Docker, and more.

Conventions

In this book, you will find a number of text styles that distinguish between different kinds of information. Here are some examples of these styles and an explanation of their meaning. Code words in text, database table names, folder names, filenames, file extensions, pathnames, dummy URLs, user input, and Twitter handles are shown as follows: "This will download a `.hpi` file on your system."

A block of code is set as follows:

```
stage ('Performance Testing'){
    sh '''cd /opt/jmeter/bin/
    ./jmeter.sh -n -t $WORKSPACE/src/pt/Hello_World_Test_Plan.jmx -l
    $WORKSPACE/test_report.jtl''';
    step([$class: 'ArtifactArchiver', artifacts: '**/*.jtl'])
}
```

When we wish to draw your attention to a particular part of a code block, the relevant lines or items are set in bold:

```
stage ('Performance Testing'){
    sh '''cd /opt/jmeter/bin/
    ./jmeter.sh -n -t $WORKSPACE/src/pt/Hello_World_Test_Plan.jmx -l
    $WORKSPACE/test_report.jtl''';
    step([$class: 'ArtifactArchiver', artifacts: '**/*.jtl'])
}
```

The extra "\" used in some of the commands is used to only indicate that the command continues in the next line. Any command-line input or output is written as follows:

```
cd /tmp
wget https://archive.apache.org/dist/tomcat/tomcat-8/ \
v8.5.16/bin/apache-tomcat-8.5.16.tar.gz
```

New terms and **important words** are shown in bold. Words that you see on the screen, for example, in menus or dialog boxes, appear in the text like this: "From the Jenkins dashboard, click on the **Manage Jenkins** | **Plugin Manager** | **Available** tab."

Warnings or important notes appear like this.

Tips and tricks appear like this.

Reader feedback

Feedback from our readers is always welcome. Let us know what you think about this book-what you liked or disliked. Reader feedback is important for us as it helps us develop titles that you will really get the most out of. To send us general feedback, simply email `feedback@packtpub.com`, and mention the book's title in the subject of your message. If there is a topic that you have expertise in and you are interested in either writing or contributing to a book, see our author guide at `www.packtpub.com/authors`.

Customer support

Now that you are the proud owner of a Packt book, we have a number of things to help you to get the most from your purchase.

Downloading the example code

You can download the example code files for this book from your account at `http://www.packtpub.com`. If you purchased this book elsewhere, you can visit `http://www.packtpub.com/support` and register to have the files emailed directly to you. You can download the code files by following these steps:

1. Log in or register to our website using your email address and password.
2. Hover the mouse pointer on the **SUPPORT** tab at the top.
3. Click on **Code Downloads & Errata**.
4. Enter the name of the book in the **Search** box.
5. Select the book for which you're looking to download the code files.
6. Choose from the drop-down menu where you purchased this book from.
7. Click on **Code Download**.

Once the file is downloaded, please make sure that you unzip or extract the folder using the latest version of:

- WinRAR / 7-Zip for Windows
- Zipeg / iZip / UnRarX for Mac
- 7-Zip / PeaZip for Linux

The code bundle for the book is also hosted on GitHub at `https://github.com/PacktPublishing/Learning-Continuous-Integration-with-Jenkins-Second-Edition`. We also have other code bundles from our rich catalog of books and videos available at `https://github.com/PacktPublishing/`. Check them out!

Downloading the color images of this book

We also provide you with a PDF file that has color images of the screenshots/diagrams used in this book. The color images will help you better understand the changes in the output. You can download this file from `https://www.packtpub.com/sites/default/files/downloads/LearningContinuousIntegrationwithJenkinsSecondEdition_ColorImages.pdf`.

Errata

Although we have taken every care to ensure the accuracy of our content, mistakes do happen. If you find a mistake in one of our books-maybe a mistake in the text or the code-we would be grateful if you could report this to us. By doing so, you can save other readers from frustration and help us improve subsequent versions of this book. If you find any errata, please report them by visiting `http://www.packtpub.com/submit-errata`, selecting your book, clicking on the **Errata Submission Form** link, and entering the details of your errata. Once your errata are verified, your submission will be accepted and the errata will be uploaded to our website or added to any list of existing errata under the Errata section of that title. To view the previously submitted errata, go to `https://www.packtpub.com/books/content/support` and enter the name of the book in the search field. The required information will appear under the **Errata** section.

Piracy

Piracy of copyrighted material on the internet is an ongoing problem across all media. At Packt, we take the protection of our copyright and licenses very seriously. If you come across any illegal copies of our works in any form on the internet, please provide us with the location address or website name immediately so that we can pursue a remedy. Please contact us at `copyright@packtpub.com` with a link to the suspected pirated material. We appreciate your help in protecting our authors and our ability to bring you valuable content.

Questions

If you have a problem with any aspect of this book, you can contact us at `questions@packtpub.com`, and we will do our best to address the problem.

1
Concepts of Continuous Integration

We will begin this chapter with an overview of the two primary software development methodologies of the era: Waterfall, and agile. An understanding of their concepts and implications will help us answer how **Continuous Integration** (**CI**) came into existence.

Next, we will try to understand the concept behind CI and the elements that make it. Reading through the topics, you will see how CI helps projects go agile. After completing this chapter, you should be able to:

- Describe how CI came into existence.
- Define what CI is.
- Describe the elements of CI.

Software Development Life Cycle

For those of you who are not familiar with the term: Software Development Life Cycle, let us try to understand it.

The **Software Development Life Cycle**, also sometimes referred to as **SDLC** for short, is the process of planning, developing, testing, and deploying software.

Teams follow a sequence of phases, and each phase uses the outcome of its previous phase, as shown in the following diagram:

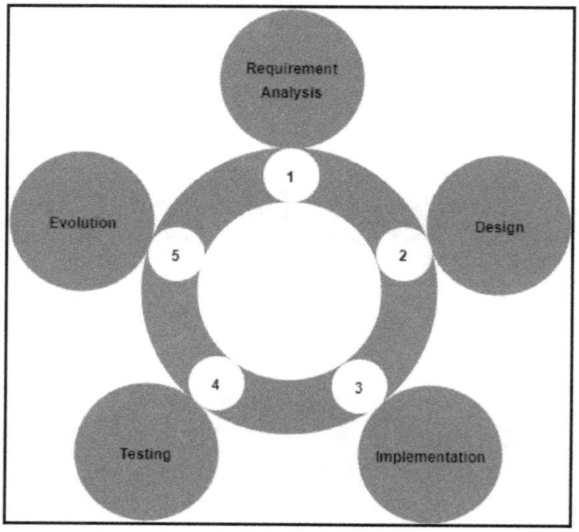

Software Development Life Cycle

Let's take a look at the SDLC phases in detail.

Requirement analysis

This is the first stage of the cycle. Here, the business team (mostly comprised of business analysts) perform a requirement analysis of their project's business needs. The requirements can be internal to the organization, or external, from a customer. This study involves finding the nature and scope of the requirements. With the gathered information, there is a proposal to either improve the system or create a new one. The project cost gets decided, and benefits are laid out. Then the project goals are defined.

Design

The second phase is the design phase. Here, the system architects and the system designers formulate the desired features of the software solution and create a project plan. This plan may include process diagrams, overall interface, and layout design, along with a vast set of documentation.

Implementation

The third phase is the implementation phase. Here, the project manager creates and assigns work to the developers. The developers develop the code depending on the tasks and goals defined in the design phase. This phase may last from a few months to a year, depending on the project.

Testing

The fourth phase is the testing phase. When all the decided features are developed, the testing team takes over. For the next few months, all features are thoroughly tested. Every module of the software is collected and tested. Defects are raised if any bugs or errors occur while testing. In the event of a failure, the development team quickly acts to resolve the failures. The thoroughly tested code is then deployed into the production environment.

Evolution

The last phase is the evolution phase or the maintenance phase. Feedback from the users/customers is analyzed, and the whole cycle of developing, testing, and releasing the new features and fixes in the form of patches or upgrades repeats.

Waterfall model of software development

One of the most famous and widely used software development processes is the Waterfall model. The Waterfall model is a sequential software development process. It was derived from the manufacturing industry. One can see a highly structured flow of processes that run in one direction. At the time of its creation, there were no other software development methodologies, and the only thing the developers could have imagined was the production line process that was simple to adapt for software development.

The following diagram illustrates the Waterfall model of software development:

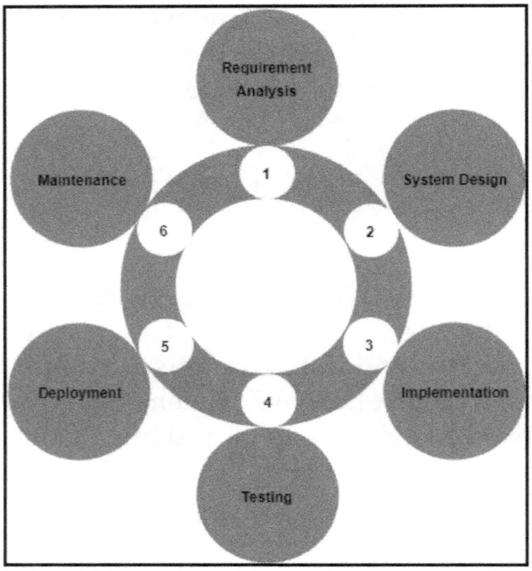

Waterfall model

The Waterfall approach is simple to understand, as the steps involved are similar to that of the SDLC.

First, there is a requirement analysis phase, which is followed by the designing phase. There is a considerable time spent on the analysis and the designing part. And once it's over, there are no further additions or deletions. In short, once the development begins, there is no modification allowed in the design.

Then comes the implementation phase, where the actual development takes place. The development cycle can range from three months to six months. During this time, the testing team is usually free. When the development cycle is completed, a whole week's time is planned for performing the integration of the source code. During this time, many integration issues pop up and are fixed immediately. This stage is followed by the testing phase.

When the testing starts, it goes on for another three months or more, depending on the software solution. After the testing completes successfully, the source code is then deployed in the production environment. For this, a day or so is again planned to carry out the deployment in production. There is a possibility that some deployment issues may pop up. When the software solution goes live, teams get feedback and may also anticipate issues.

The last phase is the maintenance phase. Feedback from the users/customers is analyzed, and the whole cycle of developing, testing, and releasing new features and fixes in the form of patches or upgrades repeats.

There is no doubt that the Waterfall model worked remarkably for decades. However, flaws did exist, but they were simply ignored for a long time. Since, way back then software projects had ample time and resources to get the job done.

However, looking at the way software technologies have changed over the past few years, we can easily say that the Waterfall model won't suit the requirements of the current world.

Disadvantages of the Waterfall model

The following are some of the disadvantages of the Waterfall model:

- Working software is produced only at the end of the SDLC, which lasts for a year or so in most cases.
- There is a huge amount of uncertainty.
- It is not suitable for projects where the demand for new features is too frequent. For example, e-commerce projects.
- Integration is performed only after the entire development phase is complete. As a result, integration issues are found at a much later stage and in large quantities.
- There is no backward traceability.
- It's difficult to measure progress within stages.

Advantages of the Waterfall model

By looking at the disadvantages of the Waterfall model, we can say that it's mostly suitable for projects where:

- The requirements are well documented and fixed.
- There is enough funding available to maintain a management team, a testing team, a development team, a build and release team, a deployment team, and so on.
- The technology is fixed, and not dynamic.
- There are no ambiguous requirements. And most importantly, they don't pop up during any other phase apart from the requirement analysis phase.

Agile to the rescue

The name **Agile** rightly suggests *quick and easy*. Agile is a collection of methods where software is developed through collaboration among self-organized teams. The principles behind agile are incremental, quick, flexible software development, and it promotes adaptive planning.

The Agile software development process is an alternative to the traditional software development processes discussed earlier.

The twelve agile principles

The following are the twelve principles of the agile model:

- Customer satisfaction through early and continuous delivery of useful software.
- Welcome changing requirements, even late in development.
- Working software is frequently delivered (in weeks, rather than months).
- Close daily cooperation between businesses, people, and developers.
- Projects are built around motivated individuals, who should be trusted.
- Face-to-face conversation is the best form of communication (co-location).
- Working software is the principal measure of progress.
- Sustainable development—able to maintain a constant pace.
- Continuous attention to technical excellence and good design.
- Simplicity—the art of maximizing the amount of work not done—is essential.
- Self-organizing teams.
- Regular adaptation to changing circumstances.

To know more about the Agile principles visit the link: `http://www.agilemanifesto.org`.

The twelve principles of Agile software development indicate the expectations of the current software industry and its advantages over the Waterfall model.

How does the Agile software development process work?

In the Agile software development process, the whole software application is split into multiple features or modules. These features are delivered in iterations. Each iteration lasts for three weeks, and involves cross-functional teams that work simultaneously in various areas, such as planning, requirement analysis, designing, coding, unit testing, and acceptance testing.

As a result, no person sits idle at any given point in time. This is quite different from the Waterfall model wherein while the development team is busy developing the software, the testing team, the production team, and everyone else is idle or underutilized. The following diagram illustrates the Agile model of software development:

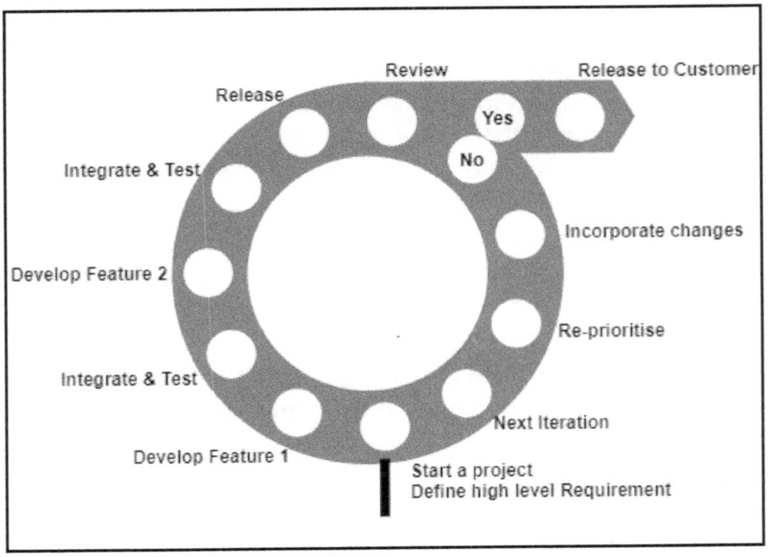

Agile methodology

From the preceding diagram, we can see that there is no time spent on requirement analysis or design. Instead, a very high-level plan is prepared, just enough to outline the scope of the project.

The team then goes through a series of iterations. Iteration can be classified as time frames, each lasting for a month or even a week in some mature projects. In this duration, a project team develops and tests features. The goal is to develop, test, and release a feature in a single iteration. At the end of the iteration, the feature goes for a demo. If the clients like it, then the feature goes live. But, if it gets rejected, the feature is taken as a backlog, re-prioritized, and again worked upon in the consecutive iteration.

There is also a possibility of parallel development and testing. In a single iteration, one can develop and test more than one feature in parallel.

Advantages of Agile software development process

Let us see some of the advantages of the Agile software development process:

- **Functionality can be developed and demonstrated rapidly**: In an agile process, the software project is divided by features, and each feature is called as a backlog. The idea is to develop either a single or a set of features right from its conceptualization till its deployment, in a week or a month. This puts at least a feature or two on the customer's plate, which they can then start using.
- **Resource requirement is less**: In Agile, there are no separate development and testing teams. Neither is there a build or release team, or a deployment team. In Agile, a single project team contains around eight members. Each member of the team is capable of doing everything.
- **Promotes teamwork and cross-training**: Since there is a small team of about eight members, the team members switch their roles in turns and learn from each other's experience.
- **Suitable for projects where requirements frequently change**: In an Agile model of software development, the complete software is divided into features, and each feature is developed and delivered in a short time span. Hence, changing the feature, or even completely discarding it, doesn't affect the whole project.
- **Minimalistic documentation**: This methodology focuses primarily on delivering working software quickly, rather than creating huge documents. Documentation exists, but it's limited to the overall functionality.

- **Little or no planning required**: Since features are developed one after the other in a short period, there is no need for extensive planning.
- **Parallel development**: Iteration consists of one or more features developed in sequence, or even in parallel.

The Scrum framework

Scrum is a framework for developing and sustaining complex products that are based on the Agile software development process. It is more than a process; it's a framework with certain roles, tasks, and teams. Scrum was written by **Ken Schwaber** and **Jeff Sutherland**; together, they created *The Scrum Guide*.

In a Scrum framework, the development team decides on how to develop a feature. This is because the team knows best about the problem they are presented with. I assume most of the readers are happy after reading this.

Scrum relies on a self-organizing and cross-functional team. The Scrum team is self-organizing; hence, there is no overall team leader who decides which person will do which task, or how a problem will be solved.

Important terms used in the Scrum framework

The following are the important terms used in the Scrum framework:

- **The Sprint**: Sprint is a timebox during which a usable and potentially releasable product gets created. A new Sprint starts immediately after the conclusion of the previous Sprint. A Sprint may last between two weeks to one month, depending on the project's command over Scrum.
- **Product Backlog**: The Product Backlog is a list of all the required features in a software solution. The list is dynamic. That is, now and then the customers or team members add or delete items to the Product Backlog.
- **Sprint Backlog**: The Sprint Backlog is the set of Product Backlog items, selected for the Sprint.
- **Increment**: The Increment is the sum of all the Product Backlog items completed during a Sprint and the value of the Increments from all the previous Sprints.

- **The Development Team**: The Development Team does the work of delivering a releasable set of features named Increment at the end of each Sprint. Only members of the Development Team create the Increment. Development Teams are empowered by the organization to organize and manage their work. The resulting synergy optimizes the Development Team's overall efficiency and effectiveness.
- **The Product Owner**: The Product Owner is a mediator between the Scrum Team and everyone else. He is the front face of the Scrum Team and interacts with customers, infrastructure teams, admin teams, everyone involved in the Scrum, and so on.
- **The Scrum Master**: The Scrum Master is responsible for ensuring Scrum is understood and enacted. Scrum Masters do this by ensuring that the Scrum Team follows the Scrum theory, practices, and rules.

How does Scrum work?

The Product Owner, the Scrum Master, and the Scrum Team together follow a set of stringent procedures to deliver the software features. The following diagram explains the Scrum development process:

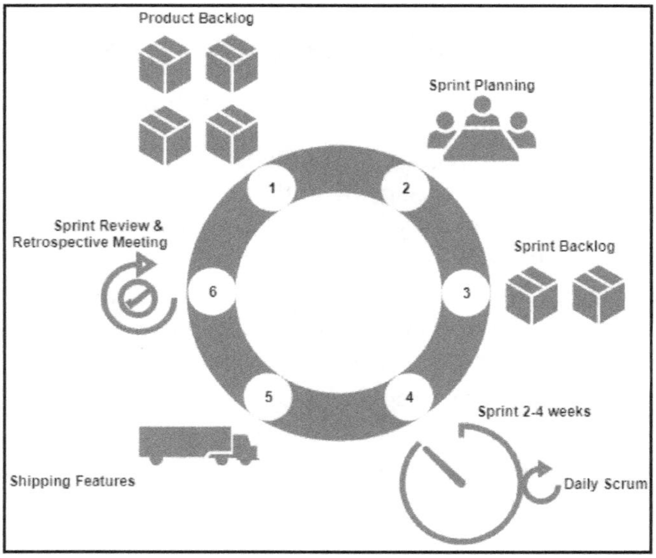

Scrum methodology

Let us see some of the important aspects of the Scrum software development process that the team goes through.

Sprint Planning

Sprint Planning is an opportunity for the Scrum Team to plan the features in the current Sprint cycle. The plan is created mainly by the developers. Once the plan is created, it is explained to the Scrum Master and the Product Owner. The Sprint Planning is a timeboxed activity, and it is usually around eight hours in total for a one-month Sprint cycle. It is the responsibility of the Scrum Master to ensure everyone participates in the Sprint Planning activity.

In the meeting, the Development Team takes into consideration the following items:

- The number of Product Backlogs to be worked on (both new and the old ones from the last Sprint).
- Team performances in the last Sprint.
- Projected capacity of the Development Team.

Sprint cycle

During the Sprint cycle, the developers simply work on completing the backlogs decided in the Sprint Planning. The duration of a Sprint may last from two weeks to one month, depending on the number of backlogs.

Daily Scrum meeting

This happens on a daily basis. During the Scrum meeting, the Development Team discusses what was accomplished yesterday, and what will be accomplished today. They also discuss the things that are stopping them from achieving their goal. The Development Team does not attend any other meeting or discussion apart from the Scrum meeting.

Monitoring Sprint progress

The Daily Scrum is a good opportunity for a team to measure its progress. The Scrum Team can track the total work remaining, and by doing so, they can estimate the likelihood of achieving the Sprint Goal.

Sprint Review

In the Sprint Review, the Development Team demonstrates the features that have been accomplished. The Product Owner updates on the Product Backlog status to date. The Product Backlog list is updated depending on the product performance or usage in the market. Sprint Review is a four-hour activity altogether for a one-month Sprint.

Sprint Retrospective

In this meeting, the team discusses the things that went well, and the things that need improvement. The team then decides the points on which it has to improve to perform better in the upcoming Sprint. This meeting usually occurs after the Sprint Review and before the Sprint Planning.

Continuous Integration

Continuous Integration (CI) is a software development practice where developers frequently integrate their work with the project's Integration branch and create a build.

Integration is the act of submitting your private work (modified code) to the common work area (the potential software solution). This is technically done by merging your private work (personal branch) with the common work area (Integration branch). Or we can say, pushing your private branch to the remote branch.

CI is necessary to bring out issues encountered during the integration as early as possible. This can be understood from the following diagram, which depicts various issues encountered during a single CI cycle.

A build failure can occur due to either an improper code or a human error while doing a build (assuming that the tasks are done manually). An integration issue can occur if the developers do not rebase their local copy of code frequently with the code on the Integration branch. A testing issue can occur if the code does not pass any of the unit or integration test cases.

In the event of an issue, the developer has to modify the code to fix it:

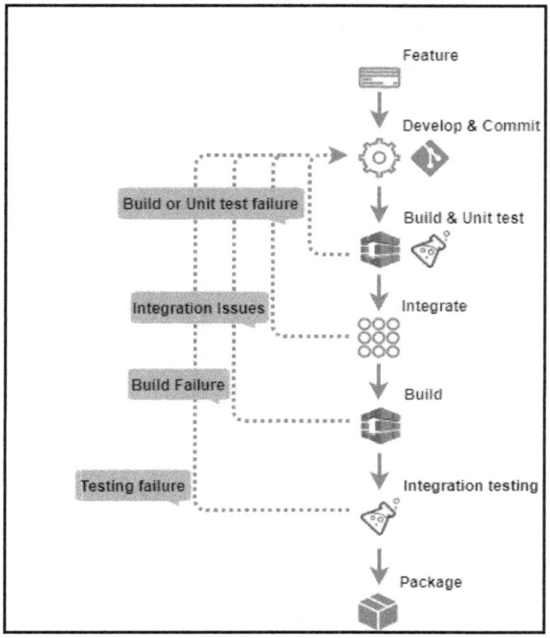

CI process

Agile runs on CI

The Agile software development process focuses mainly on fast delivery, and CI helps Agile in achieving that speed. But how does CI do that? Let us understand by using a simple case.

Developing a feature involves many code changes, and between every code change, there are a set of tasks to perform, such as checking-in the code, polling the version control system for changes, building the code, unit testing, integration, building on the integrated code, integration testing, and packaging. In a CI environment, all these steps are made fast and error-free by using a CI tool such as *Jenkins*.

Adding notifications makes things even faster. The sooner the team members are aware of a build, integration, or deployment failure, the quicker they can act. The following diagram depicts all the steps involved in a CI process:

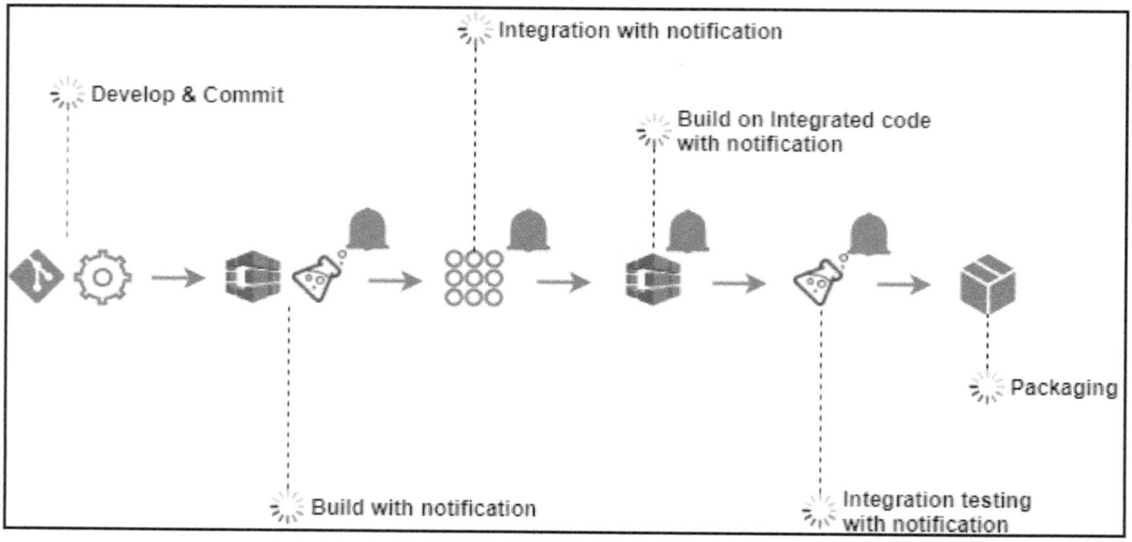

CI process with notifications

In this way, the team quickly moves from feature to feature. In simple terms, the *agility* of the agile software development is greatly due to CI.

Types of projects that benefit from CI

The amount of code written for the embedded systems presents inside a car is more than the one present inside a fighter jet. In today's world, embedded software is inside every product, modern or traditional. Be it cars, TVs, refrigerators, wrist watches, or bikes; all have little or more software-dependent features. Consumer products are becoming smarter day by day. Nowadays, we can see a product being marketed more using its smart and intelligent features than its hardware capabilities. For example, an air conditioner is marketed by its wireless control features, and TVs are being marketed by their smart features, like embedded web browsers, and so on.

The need to market new products has increased the complexity of products. This increase in software complexity had brought the Agile software development and CI methodologies to the limelight, though there were times when agile software development was used by a team of no more than 30-40 people that were working on a simple project. Almost all types of projects benefit from CI: mostly the web-based projects, for example, the e-commerce websites, and mobile phone apps.

CI and agile methodologies are used in projects that are based on Java, .NET, Ruby on Rails, and every other programming language present today. The only place where you will see it not being used is in the legacy systems. However, even they are going agile. Projects based on SAS, Mainframes; all are trying to benefit from CI.

Elements of CI

Let us see the important elements of the CI process.

Version control system

This is the most basic and the most important requirement for implementing CI. A **Version Control System,** sometimes also called a **Revision Control System,** is a tool to manage your code history. It can be centralized or distributed. Some of the famous centralized version control systems are SVN and IBM Rational ClearCase. In the distributed segment, we have tools like GIT and Mercurial.

Ideally, everything that is required to build software must be version controlled. A version control tool offers many features, such as tagging, branching, and so on.

Branching strategy

When using a Version Control System, keep the branching to a minimum. A few companies have only one main branch, and all the development activity happens on that. Nevertheless, most of the companies follow some branching strategies. This is because there is always a possibility that a part of the team may work on one release, while others may work on another release. Other times, there is a need to support the older release versions. Such scenarios always lead companies to use multiple branches.

GitFlow is another way of managing your code using multiple branches. In the following method, the Master/Production branch is kept clean and contains only the releasable, ready-to-ship code. All the development happens on the Feature branches, with the Integration branch serving as a common place to integrate all the features. The following diagram is a moderate version of the GitFlow:

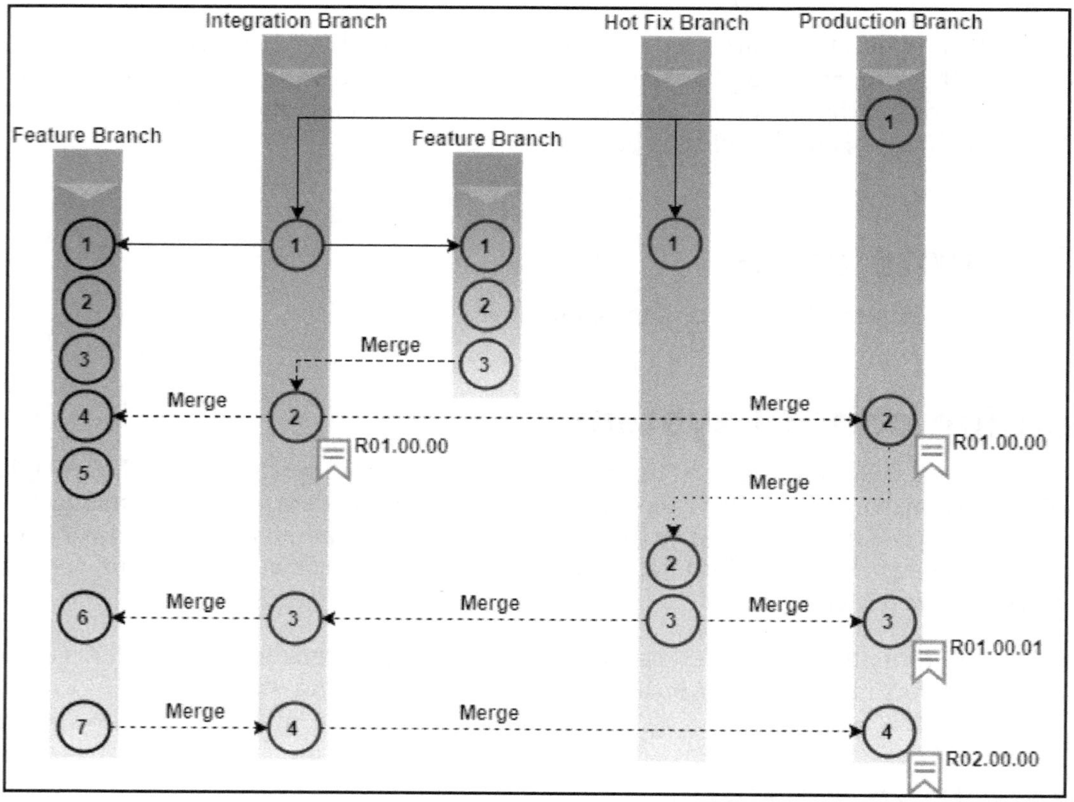

Branching strategy

GitFlow branching model

The following diagram illustrates the full version of GitFlow. We have a Master/Production branch that contains only the production-ready code. The Feature branches are where all of the development takes place. The Integration branch is where the code gets integrated and tested for quality. In addition to that, we have release branches that are pulled out from the Integration branch as and when there is a stable release. All bug fixes related to a release happen in the Release branches. There is also a Hotfix branch that is pulled out of the Master/Production branch as and when there is a need for a hotfix:

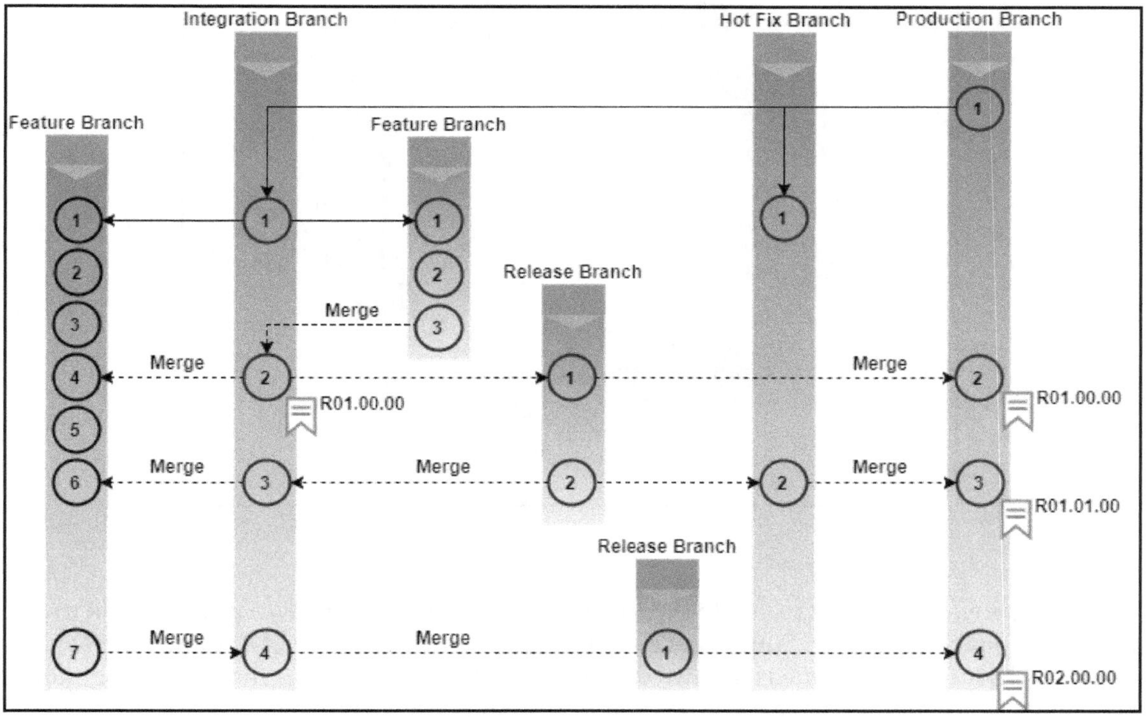

GitFlow branching strategy

CI tool

What is a CI tool? Well, it is nothing more than an orchestrator. A CI tool is at the center of the CI system, connected to the Version Control System, build tools, Binary Repository Manager tool, testing and production environments, quality analysis tool, test automation tool, and so on. There are many CI tools: Build Forge, Bamboo, and TeamCity, to name a few. But the prime focus of our book is Jenkins:

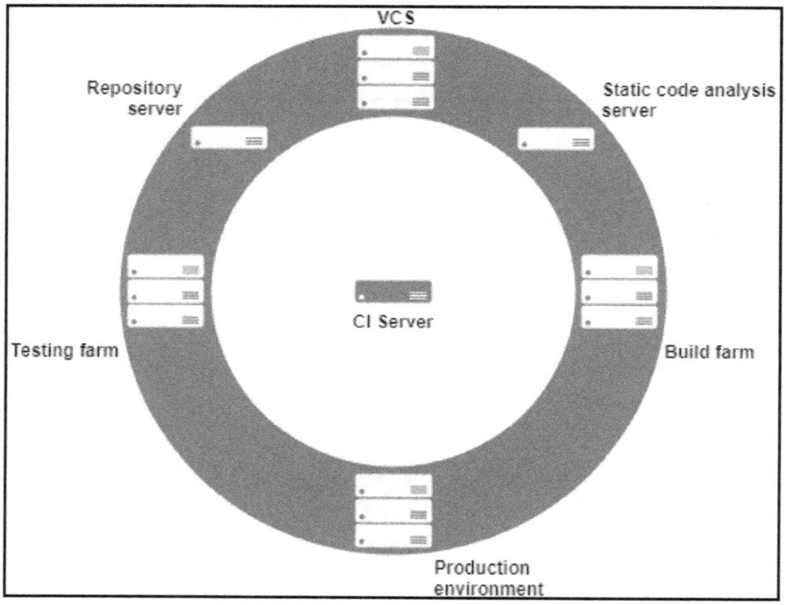

Centralized CI server

A CI tool provides options to create pipelines. Each pipeline has its own purpose. There are pipelines to take care of CI. Some take care of testing; some take care of deployments, and so on. Technically, a pipeline is a flow of jobs. Each job is a set of tasks that run sequentially. Scripting is an integral part of a CI tool that performs various kinds of tasks. The tasks may be as simple as copying a folder/file from one location to the other, or they can be complex Perl scripts to monitor machines for file modifications. Nevertheless, the script is getting replaced by the growing number of plugins available in Jenkins. Now you need not script to build a Java code; there are plugins available for it. All you need to do is install and configure a plugin to get the job done. Technically, plugins are nothing but small modules written in Java. They remove the burden of scripting from the developer's head. We will learn more about pipelines in the upcoming chapters.

Self-triggered builds

The next important thing to understand is the self-triggered automated build. Build automation is simply a series of automated steps that compile the code and generate executables. The build automation can take the help of build tools like Ant and Maven. The self-triggered automated build is the most important part of a CI system. There are two main factors that call for an automated build mechanism:

- Speed.
- Catching integration or code issues as early as possible.

There are projects where 100 to 200 builds happen per day. In such cases, speed plays an important factor. If the builds are automated, then it can save a lot of time. Things become even more interesting if the triggering of the build is made self-driven, without any manual intervention. Auto-triggered build on every code change further saves time.

When builds are frequent and fast, the probability of finding an error (build error, compilation error, or integration error) in the framework of SDLC is higher and faster:

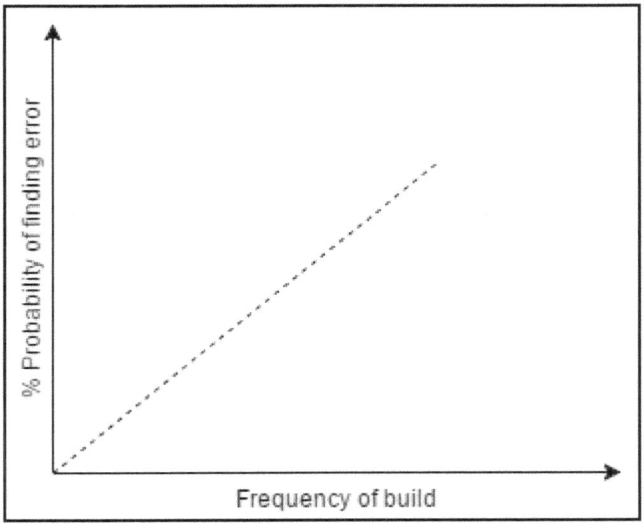

Probability of error versus build graph

Code coverage

Code coverage is the amount of code (in percentage) that is covered by your test case. The metrics that you might see in your coverage reports could be more or less as defined in the following table:

Type of coverage	Description
Function	The number of functions called out of the total number of functions defined
Statement	The number of statements in the program that are truly called out of the total number
Branches	The number of branches of the control structures executed
Condition	The number of Boolean sub-expressions that are being tested for a true and a false value
Line	The number of lines of source code that are being tested out of the total number of lines present inside the code

Types of code coverage

This coverage percentage is calculated by dividing the number of items tested by the number of items found. The following screenshot illustrates the code coverage report from SonarQube:

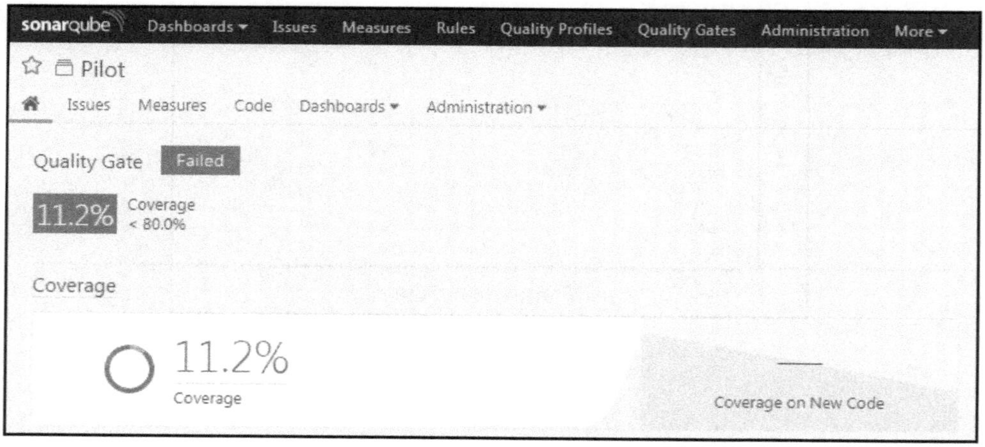

Code coverage report on SonarQube

Code coverage tools

You might find several options to create coverage reports, depending on the language(s) you use. Some of the popular tools are listed as follows:

Language	Tools
Java	Atlassian Clover, Cobertura, JaCoCo
C#/.NET	OpenCover, dotCover
C++	OpenCppCoverage, gcov
Python	Coverage.py
Ruby	SimpleCov

Static code analysis

Static code analysis, also commonly called **white-box** testing, is a form of software testing that looks for the structural qualities of the code. For example, it answers how robust or maintainable the code is. Static code analysis is performed without actually executing programs. It is different from the functional testing, which looks into the functional aspects of software, and is dynamics.

Static code analysis is the evaluation of software's inner structures. For example, is there a piece of code used repetitively? Does the code contain lots of commented lines? How complex is the code? Using the metrics defined by a user, an analysis report is generated that shows the code quality regarding maintainability. It doesn't question the code's functionality.

Some of the static code analysis tools like SonarQube come with a dashboard, which shows various metrics and statistics of each run. Usually, as part of CI, the static code analysis is triggered every time a build runs. As discussed in the previous sections, static code analysis can also be included before a developer tries to check-in his code. Hence, a code of low quality can be prevented right at the initial stage.

They support many languages, such as Java, C/C++, Objective-C, C#, PHP, Flex, Groovy, JavaScript, Python, PL/SQL, COBOL, and so on. The following screenshots illustrate the static code analysis report using SonarQube:

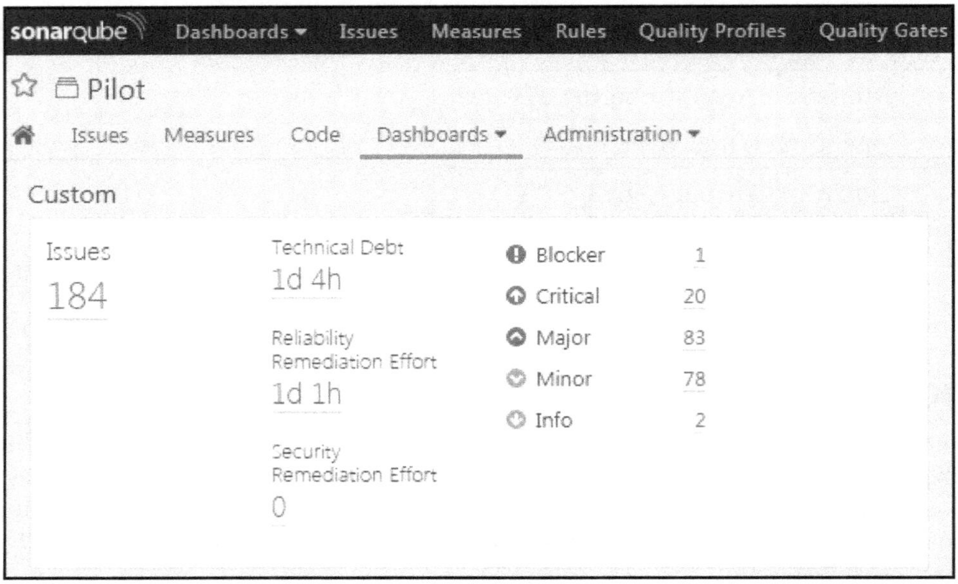

Static code analysis report

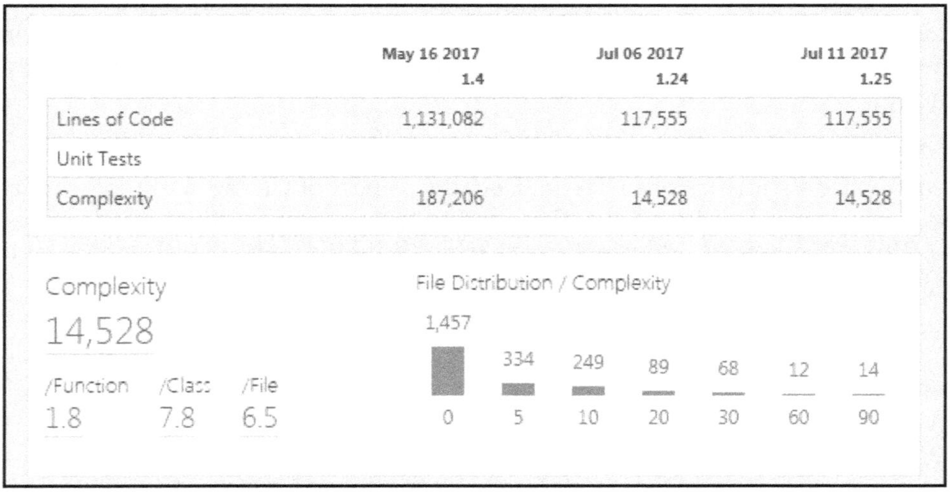

Static code analysis report

Automated testing

Testing is an important part of an SDLC. To maintain quality software, it is necessary that the software solution goes through various test scenarios. Giving less importance to testing can result in customer dissatisfaction and a delayed product.

Since testing is a manual, time-consuming, and repetitive task, automating the testing process can significantly increase the speed of software delivery. However, automating the testing process is a bit more difficult than automating the build, release, and deployment processes. It usually takes a lot of effort to automate nearly all the test cases used in a project. It is an activity that matures over time.

Hence, when beginning to automate the testing, we need to take a few factors into consideration. Test cases that are of great value and easy to automate must be considered first. For example, automate the testing where the steps are the same, although they run with different data every time. Further, automate the testing where software functionality is tested on various platforms. Also, automate the testing that involves a software application running with different configurations.

Previously, the world was mostly dominated by desktop applications. Automating the testing of a GUI-based system was quite difficult. This called for scripting languages where the manual mouse and keyboard entries were scripted and executed to test the GUI application. Nevertheless, today the software world is completely dominated by web and mobile-based applications, which are easy to test through an automated approach using a test automation tool.

Once a code is built, packaged, and deployed, testing should run automatically to validate the software. Traditionally, the process followed is to have an environment for SIT, UAT, PT, and pre-production. First, the release goes through SIT, which stands for system integration testing. Here, testing is performed on an integrated code to check its functionality altogether. If the integration testing is passed, the code is deployed to the next environment, which is UAT, where it goes through user acceptance testing, and then it can lastly be deployed in PT, where it goes through performance testing. In this way, the testing is prioritized.

It is not always possible to automate all the testing. But, the idea is to automate whatever testing that is possible. The preceding method discussed requires the need to have many environments and also a higher number of automated deployments into various environments. To avoid this, we can go for another method where there is only one environment where the build is deployed, and then the basic tests are run, and after that, long-running tests are triggered manually.

Binary repository tools

As part of the SDLC, the source code is continuously built into binary artifacts using CI. Therefore, there should be a place to store these built packages for later use. The answer is, using a binary repository tool. But what is a binary repository tool?

A binary repository tool is a Version Control System for binary files. Do not confuse this with the Version Control System discussed in the previous sections. The former is responsible for versioning the source code, and the latter is for binary files, such as `.rar`, `.war`, `.exe`, `.msi`, and so on. Along with managing built artifacts, a binary repository tool can also manage 3-party binaries that are required for a build. For example, the Maven plugin always downloads the plugins required to build the code into a folder. Rather than downloading the plugins again and again, they can be managed using a repository tool:

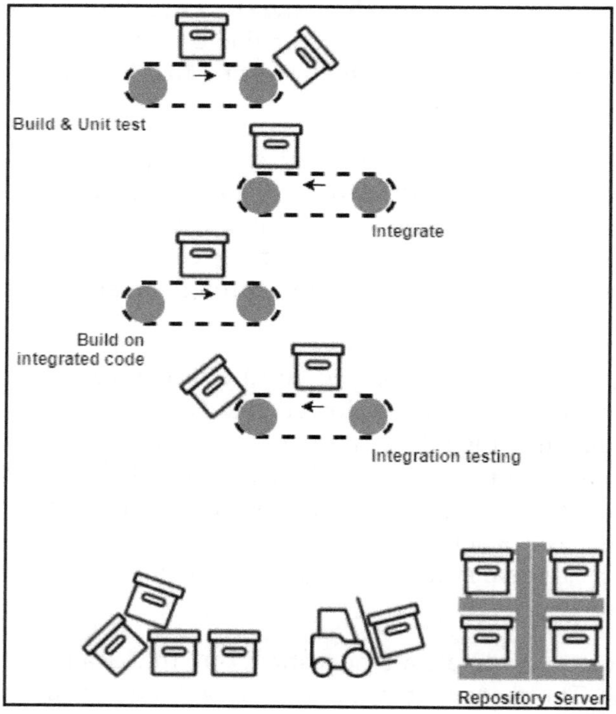

Repository tool

From the above illustration, you can see as soon as a build gets created and passes all the checks, the built artifact is uploaded to the binary repository tool. From here, the developers and testers can manually pick them, deploy them, and test them. Or, if the automated deployment is in place, then the built artifacts are automatically deployed to the respective test environment. So, what're the advantages of using a binary repository?

A binary repository tool does the following:

- Every time a built artifact gets generated, it is stored in a binary repository tool. There are many advantages of storing the build artifacts. One of the most important advantages is that the build artifacts are located in a centralized location from where they can be accessed when needed.
- It can store third-party binary plugins, modules that are required by the build tools. Hence, the build tool need not download the plugins every time a build runs. The repository tool is connected to the online source and keeps updating the plugin repository.
- It records what, when, and who created a build package.
- It provides a staging like environments to manage releases better. This also helps in speeding up the CI process.
- In a CI environment, the frequency of build is too high, and each build generates a package. Since all the built packages are in one place, developers are at liberty to choose what to promote and what not to promote in higher environments.

Automated packaging

There is a possibility that a build may have many components. Let's take, for example, a build that has a `.rar` file as an output. Along with that, it has some Unix configuration files, release notes, some executables, and also some database changes. All of these different components need to be together. The task of creating a single archive or a single media out of many components is called **packaging**. Again, this can be automated using the CI tools and can save a lot of time.

Benefits of using CI

The following are some of the benefits of using CI. The list is brief, and not comprehensive.

Freedom from long integrations

Integrating the code rarely, as seen in the Waterfall model, can lead to *merge hell*. It is a situation wherein teams spend weeks resolving the merge issues.

In contrast to this, integrating every single commit on your Feature branch with the Integration branch and testing it for issues (CI) allows you to find integration issues as early as possible.

Metrics

Tools like Jenkins, SonarQube, Artifactory, and GitHub allow you to generate trends over a period. All of these trends can help project managers and teams to make sure the project is heading in the right direction and with the right pace.

Catching issues faster

This is the most important advantage of having a carefully implemented CI system. Any integration issue or merge issue gets caught early. The CI system has the facility to send notification as soon as the build fails.

Rapid development

From a technical perspective, CI helps teams work more efficiently. Projects that use CI follow an automatic and continuous approach while building, testing, and integrating their code. This results in a faster development.

Developers spend more time developing their code and zero time building, packaging, integrating, and deploying it, as everything is automated. This also helps teams that are geographically distributed to work together. With a good *software configuration management process* in place, people can work on widely distributed teams.

Spend more time adding features

In the past, build and release activities were managed by the developers, along with the regular development work. It was followed by a trend of having separate teams that handled the build, release, and deployment activities. And it didn't stop there; this new model suffered from communication issues and a lack of coordination among developers, release engineers, and testers. However, using CI, all the build, release, and deployment work gets automated. Therefore, the development team need not worry about anything other than developing features. In most cases, even the complete testing is automated. Therefore by using a CI process, the development team can spend more time developing the code.

Summary

> *"Behind every successful agile project, there is a Continuous Integration process."*

In this chapter, we took a glance through the history of software engineering processes. We learned about CI and the elements that make it.

The various concepts and terminologies discussed in this chapter form a foundation for the upcoming chapters. Without these, the coming chapters are mere technical know-how.

In the next chapter, we will learn how to install Jenkins on various platforms.

2
Installing Jenkins

This chapter is all about installing Jenkins across various platforms, and more. After completing this chapter, you should be able to do the following:

- Run Jenkins on a servlet container (Apache Tomcat)
- Run Jenkins as a standalone application on Windows/Ubuntu/Red Hat Linux/Fedora
- Run Jenkins behind a reverse proxy server (Nginx)
- Run Jenkins with Docker
- Leverage the advantages of Docker data volumes
- Run development, staging, and production instance of Jenkins using Docker

Running Jenkins inside a servlet container

Jenkins is available on the following servlet containers:

- Apache Geronimo 3.0
- GlassFish
- IBM WebSphere
- JBoss
- Jetty
- Jonas
- Liberty profile
- Tomcat
- WebLogic

In this section, you will learn how to install Jenkins on an Apache Tomcat server. Installing Jenkins as a service on Apache Tomcat is quite simple. Either you can choose to run Jenkins along with the other services already present on the Apache Tomcat server, or you can use the Apache Tomcat server solely for running Jenkins.

Prerequisites

Before you begin, make sure you have the following things ready:

- You need a system with at least 4 GB of memory and a Multi-core processor.
- Depending on how you manage the infrastructure in your team, the machine could be an instance on a cloud platform (such as AWS, DigitalOcean, or any other cloud platform), a bare metal machine, or it could be a VM (on VMware vSphere or any other server virtualization software).
- The machine should have Ubuntu 16.04 installed on it. Choose an LTS release version.
- Check for administrator privileges; the installation might ask for an admin username and password.

Installing Java

Follow these steps to install Java on Ubuntu:

1. Update the package index:

   ```
   sudo apt-get update
   ```

2. Next, install Java. The following command will install the **Java Runtime Environment** (**JRE**):

   ```
   sudo apt-get install default-jre
   ```

3. To set the `JAVA_HOME` environment variable, get the Java installation location. Do this by executing the following command:

   ```
   update-java-alternatives -l
   ```

4. The previous command will print the list of Java applications installed on your machine along with their installation paths. Copy the Java path that appears on your Terminal:

```
java-1.8.0-openjdk-amd64  1081
/usr/lib/jvm/java-1.8.0-openjdk-amd64
```

5. Open the `/etc/environment` file for editing using the following command:

```
sudo nano /etc/environment
```

6. Add the Java path (the one that you copied earlier) inside the `/etc/environment` file in the following format:

```
JAVA_HOME="/usr/lib/jvm/java-1.8.0-openjdk-amd64"
```

7. Type *Ctrl* + *X* and choose *Y* to save and close the file.
8. Next, reload the file using the following command:

```
sudo source /etc/environment
```

Installing Apache Tomcat

Follow these steps to download and then install Apache Tomcat server on your Ubuntu machine:

1. Move to the `/tmp` directory and download the Tomcat application using the `wget` command, as shown here:

```
cd /tmp
wget https://archive.apache.org/dist/tomcat/tomcat-8/ \
v8.5.16/bin/apache-tomcat-8.5.16.tar.gz
```

To get a complete list of Apache Tomcat versions visit: `https://archive.apache.org/dist/tomcat/`.

2. Create a directory called `/opt/tomcat` using the following command:

```
sudo mkdir /opt/tomcat
```

3. Untar the content of the archive inside `/opt/tomcat`:

```
sudo tar xzvf apache-tomcat-8*tar.gz \
-C /opt/tomcat --strip-components=1
```

4. Next, create a `systemd` service file using the following command:

```
sudo nano /etc/systemd/system/tomcat.service
```

5. Paste the following content into the file:

```
[Unit]
Description=Apache Tomcat Web Application Container
After=network.target

[Service]
Type=forking

Environment=JAVA_HOME=/usr/lib/jvm/java-1.8.0-openjdk-amd64
Environment=CATALINA_PID=/opt/tomcat/temp/tomcat.pid
Environment=CATALINA_HOME=/opt/tomcat
Environment=CATALINA_BASE=/opt/tomcat
Environment='CATALINA_OPTS=-Xms512M -Xmx1024M
-server -XX:+UseParallelGC'
Environment='JAVA_OPTS=-Djava.awt.headless=true
-Djava.security.egd=file:/dev/./urandom'

ExecStart=/opt/tomcat/bin/startup.sh
ExecStop=/opt/tomcat/bin/shutdown.sh

RestartSec=10
Restart=always

[Install]
WantedBy=multi-user.target
```

6. Type *Ctrl* + *X* and choose *Y* to save and close the file.
7. Next, reload the systemd daemon using the following command:

```
sudo systemctl daemon-reload
```

8. Start the Tomcat service using the following command:

```
sudo systemctl start tomcat
```

9. To check the status of Tomcat service, run the following command:

```
sudo systemctl status tomcat
```

10. You should see the following output:

```
● tomcat.service - Apache Tomcat Web Application Container
   Loaded: loaded (/etc/systemd/system/tomcat.service; disabled;
   vendor preset: enabled)
   Active: active (running) since Mon 2017-07-31 21:27:39 UTC;
   5s ago
   Process: 6438 ExecStart=/opt/tomcat/bin/startup.sh (code=exited,
   status=0/SUCCESS)
  Main PID: 6448 (java)
     Tasks: 44
    Memory: 132.2M
       CPU: 2.013s
    CGroup: /system.slice/tomcat.service
            └─6448 /usr/lib/jvm/java-1.8.0-openjdk-amd64/bin/java
-Djava.util.logging.config.file=/opt/tomcat/conf/logging.properties
-Djava.util.logging.manager=org.apache.juli.ClassLoaderLogMan
```

Enabling the firewall and port 8080

Apache Tomcat runs on port `8080`. Follow these steps to enable the firewall, if it's disabled:

1. Enable the firewall using the following command:

```
sudo ufw enable
```

2. Allow traffic on port `8080`:

```
sudo ufw allow 8080
```

3. Enable OpenSSH to allow SSH connections using the following command:

```
sudo ufw enable "OpenSSH"
```

4. Check the firewall status using the following command:

```
sudo ufw status
```

5. You should see the following output:

```
Status: active
To                          Action      From
--                          ------      ----
8080                        ALLOW       Anywhere
OpenSSH                     ALLOW       Anywhere
8080 (v6)                   ALLOW       Anywhere (v6)
OpenSSH (v6)                ALLOW       Anywhere (v6)
```

6. You should now be able to access the Apache Tomcat server page at `http://<IP address of the Apache Tomcat>:8080`.

Configuring the Apache Tomcat server

In this section, we will enable access to the Tomcat Manager app and Host Manager:

1. Open the `tomcat-users.xml` file for editing, which is present inside the `/opt/tomcat/conf` directory:

```
sudo nano /opt/tomcat/conf/tomcat-users.xml
```

2. The file will look something like the following, for simplicity, I have ignored the comments inside the file:

```
<?xml version="1.0" encoding="UTF-8"?>
. . .
<tomcat-users xmlns="http://tomcat.apache.org/xml"
xmlns:xsi="http://www.w3.org/2001/XMLSchema-instance"
xsi:schemaLocation="http://tomcat.apache.org/xml tomcat-users.xsd"
version="1.0">
. . .
  <!--
    <role rolename="tomcat"/>
    <role rolename="role1"/>
    <user username="tomcat" password="<must-be-changed>"
     roles="tomcat"/>
    <user username="both" password="<must-be-changed>"
     roles="tomcat,role1"/>
    <user username="role1" password="<must-be-changed>"
     roles="role1"/>
  -->
</tomcat-users>
```

3. From the previous file, you can see the `role` and `user` fields are commented. We need to enable a role and a user to allow access to the Tomcat Manager app page:

```
<role rolename="manager-gui"/>
<role rolename="admin-gui"/>
<user username="admin" password="password"
 roles="manager-gui,admin-gui"/>
```

4. Finally, the file should look something as shown here (comments removed):

```
<?xml version="1.0" encoding="UTF-8"?>
<tomcat-users xmlns="http://tomcat.apache.org/xml"
xmlns:xsi="http://www.w3.org/2001/XMLSchema-instance"
xsi:schemaLocation="http://tomcat.apache.org/xml tomcat-users.xsd"
version="1.0">
  <role rolename="manager-gui"/>
  <role rolename="admin-gui"/>
  <user username="admin" password="password"
   roles="manager-gui,admin-gui"/>
</tomcat-users>
```

5. Type *Ctrl* + *X* and choose *Y* to save and close the file.
6. By default, you are allowed to access Manager and Host Manager applications only from within the Apache Tomcat server. Since, we will be managing services running on Apache from a remote machine, we would need to remove these restrictions.
7. Open the following two files, `/opt/tomcat/webapps/manager/META-INF/context.xml` and `/opt/tomcat/webapps/host-manager/META-INF/context.xml`.
8. Inside these files, comment the following section:

```
<Context antiResourceLocking="false" privileged="true" >
  <!--<Valve className="org.apache.catalina.valves.RemoteAddrValve"
  allow="127\.\d+\.\d+\.\d+|::1|0:0:0:0:0:0:0:1" />-->
  <Manager sessionAttributeValueClassNameFilter="java\.lang\
  .(?:Boolean|Integer|Long|Number|String)|org\.apache\.catalina\
  .filters\.CsrfPreventionFilter\$LruCache(?:\$1)?|java\.util\
  .(?:Linked)$
</Context>
```

9. Type *Ctrl* + *X* and choose *Y* to save and close the file.

10. Restart the Tomcat server using the following command:

```
sudo systemctl restart tomcat
```

11. Try to access the Manager app and the Host Manager from the Apache Tomcat server home page.

Installing Jenkins on the Apache Tomcat server

You can perform the following steps if you do not wish to have a standalone server for Jenkins master, and want to host it along with other services that exist on the Apache Tomcat server:

1. Move to the `/tmp` directory and download the Jenkins application using the `wget` command, as shown here:

```
cd /tmp
wget http://mirrors.jenkins.io/war-stable/latest/jenkins.war
```

2. The previous command will download the latest stable version of `jenkins.war` file.
3. Move the file from `/tmp` to `/opt/tomcat/`:

```
sudo mv jenkins.war /opt/tomcat/webapps/
```

4. List the content of the `/opt/tomcat/webapps/` directory :

```
sudo ls -l /opt/tomcat/webapps
```

You should see the following output:

```
total 68984
-rw-rw-r--  1 ubuntu ubuntu 70613578 Jul 19 22:37 jenkins.war
drwxr-x---  3 root   root       4096 Jul 31 21:09 ROOT
drwxr-x--- 14 root   root       4096 Jul 31 21:09 docs
drwxr-x---  6 root   root       4096 Jul 31 21:09 examples
drwxr-x---  5 root   root       4096 Jul 31 21:09 manager
drwxr-x---  5 root   root       4096 Jul 31 21:09 host-manager
drwxr-x--- 10 root   root       4096 Jul 31 22:52 jenkins
```

> You will notice that a `jenkins` folder automatically gets created the moment you move the `jenkins.war` package to the `webapps` folder. This is because the `.war` file is a web application archive file that automatically gets extracted once deployed to the `webapps` directory. What we did is a small deployment activity.

5. And that is all you need to do. You can access Jenkins using `http://<IP address of Tomcat server>:8080/jenkins`.

Installing Jenkins alone on an Apache Tomcat server

If you chose to have an Apache Tomcat server solely for using Jenkins, follow these steps:

1. Move to the `/tmp` directory and download the Jenkins application using the `wget` command, as shown here:

```
cd /tmp
wget http://mirrors.jenkins.io/war-stable/latest/jenkins.war
```

2. Rename the downloaded `jenkins.war` package to `ROOT.war`:

```
sudo mv jenkins.war ROOT.war
```

3. Next, delete everything inside the `/opt/tomcat/webapps` directory by switching to the `root` user:

```
sudo su -
cd /opt/tomcat/webapps
sudo rm -r *
```

4. Now move the `ROOT.war` (renamed) package from the `/tmp` directory to the `/opt/tomcat/webapps` folder:

```
sudo mv /tmp/ROOT.war /opt/tomcat/webapps/
```

5. List the contents of the `/opt/tomcat/webapps` directory and you will notice a `ROOT` folder automatically gets created:

```
total 68964
drwxr-x--- 10 root   root       4096 Jul 31 23:10 ROOT
-rw-rw-r--  1 ubuntu ubuntu 70613578 Jul 19 22:37 ROOT.war
```

It's always recommended to have a dedicated web server solely for Jenkins.

6. You can access Jenkins by using `http://<IP address of Tomcat server>:8080/` without any additional path. Apparently, the Apache server is now a Jenkins server.

Deleting the content of the `/opt/tomcat/webapps` directory (leaving behind the `ROOT` directory and `ROOT.war`) and then moving the `jenkins.war` file to the `webapps` folder is also sufficient to make Apache Tomcat server solely for the use of Jenkins.

The step of renaming `jenkins.war` to `ROOT.war` is only necessary if you want to make `http://<IP address of Tomcat server>:8080/` the standard URL for Jenkins.

Setting up the Jenkins home path

Before we start using Jenkins, there is one important thing to configure, the `jenkins_home` path. When you install Jenkins as a service on Tomcat, the `jenkins_home` path is automatically set to `/root/.jenkins/`. This is the location where all of the Jenkins configurations, logs, and builds are stored. Everything that you create and configure on the Jenkins dashboard is stored here.

We need to make it something more accessible, something like `/var/jenkins_home`. This can be done in the following way:

1. Stop the Apache Tomcat server using the following command:

```
sudo systemctl stop tomcat
```

2. Open the `context.xml` file for editing, which is present inside `/opt/tomcat/conf`:

```
sudo nano /opt/tomcat/conf/context.xml
```

3. The file will look like this (comments removed):

```
<?xml version="1.0" encoding="UTF-8"?>
<Context>
  <WatchedResource>WEB-INF/web.xml</WatchedResource>
  <WatchedResource>${catalina.base}/conf/web.xml</WatchedResource>
</Context>
```

4. Add the following line between `<Context> </Context>`:

```
<Environment name="JENKINS_HOME" value="/var/jenkins_home"
type="java.lang.String"/>
```

5. Start the Tomcat service using the following command:

```
sudo systemctl start tomcat
```

Installing a standalone Jenkins server on Windows

Installing Jenkins on Windows is quite simple. Before performing the steps to install Jenkins on Windows, let's have a look at the prerequisites.

Prerequisites

Before we begin, make sure you have the following things ready:

- We need a machine with at least 4 GB of RAM and a Multi-core processor.
- Depending on how you manage the infrastructure in your team, the machine could be an instance on a cloud platform (such as AWS, DigitalOcean, or any other cloud platform), a bare metal machine, or it could be a VM (on VMware vSphere or any other server virtualization software).
- The machine should have any one of the latest Windows OS (Windows 7/8/10, Windows Server 2012/2012 R2/2016) installed on it.
- Check for admin privileges; the installation might ask for admin username and password.
- Make sure port `8080` is open.

Installing Java

Follow these steps to install Java:

1. Download the latest version of Java JRE (x86 or x64 based on your OS) from `https://java.com/en/download/manual.jsp`.
2. Follow the installation procedures.
3. To check that Java has been installed successfully, run the following command using Command Prompt:

```
java -version
```

4. You should get the following output:

```
java version "1.8.0_121"
Java(TM) SE Runtime Environment (build 1.8.0_121-b13)
Java HotSpot(TM) 64-Bit Server VM (build 25.121-b13, mixed mode)
```

5. To set the `JAVA_HOME`, first get the Java installation path on Windows using the following command:

```
where java
```

6. The previous command should output the Java installation path, as shown in the following command. Copy the path without `\bin\java`:

```
C:\Program Files\Java\jdk1.8.0_121\bin\java
```

7. Open the Command Prompt as an administrator and run the following command to set the `JAVA_HOME` path. Make sure to use the Java installation path that appears on your screen:

```
setx -m JAVA_HOME "C:\Program Files\Java\jdk1.8.121"
```

Installing the latest stable version of Jenkins

To install the latest stable version of Jenkins, follow these steps in sequence:

1. Download the latest stable Jenkins package available at the Jenkins official website, `https://jenkins.io/download/`. To install the latest stable version of Jenkins, download the **Long Term Support** (**LTS**) release. Choose the weekly release if you just want the latest version of Jenkins.
2. Unzip the downloaded package, and you will find a `jenkins.msi` file.
3. Run the `jenkins.msi` and follow the installation steps.
4. During the installation, you will get an option to choose your Jenkins installation directory. By default, it will be `C:\Program Files\Jenkins` or `C:\Program Files (x86)\Jenkins`. Leave it as it is and click on the **Next** button.
5. Click on the **Finish** button to complete the installation.

Starting, stopping, and restarting Jenkins on Windows

Jenkins by default starts running when installed. In this section, the commands to start, stop, restart, and check the status of the Jenkins services are shown:

1. Open the **Services** window from Command Prompt using the following command:

   ```
   services.msc
   ```

2. Look for a service named **Jenkins**.
3. Right-click on the **Jenkins** service again and click **Properties**.
4. Under the **General** tab, you can see the Jenkins service name, the path to the executable, the service status, and the start parameters.
5. Using the **Startup type** option, you can choose the way Jenkins starts on the Windows machine. You can choose from **Automatic**, **Manual**, and **Automatic (Delayed Start)**. Make sure it's always set to **Automatic**.

6. In the following service status, there is an option to manually **Start**, **Stop**, **Pause**, and **Resume** the Jenkins service:

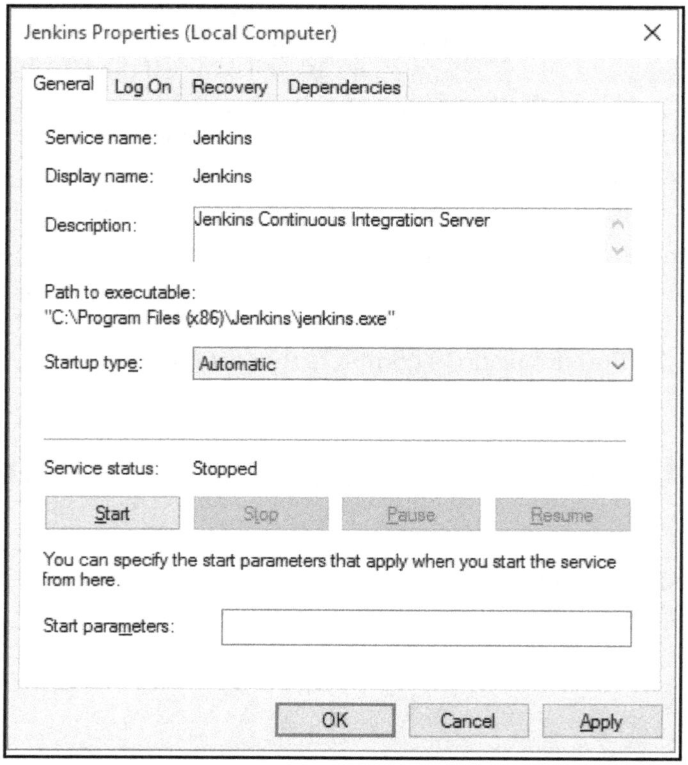

Configuring the Jenkins service startup option

7. Go to the next tab, which is **Log On**. Here, we define the username through which Jenkins start.
8. You can either choose to use the **Local System account** (not recommended) or you can create a special Jenkins user with special permissions (recommended):

An exclusive account for Jenkins is always preferred. The reason is that **Local System account** is not under control; it may get deleted or the password may expire depending on the organization's policies, whereas the Jenkins user account can be set with preferred policies and privileges.

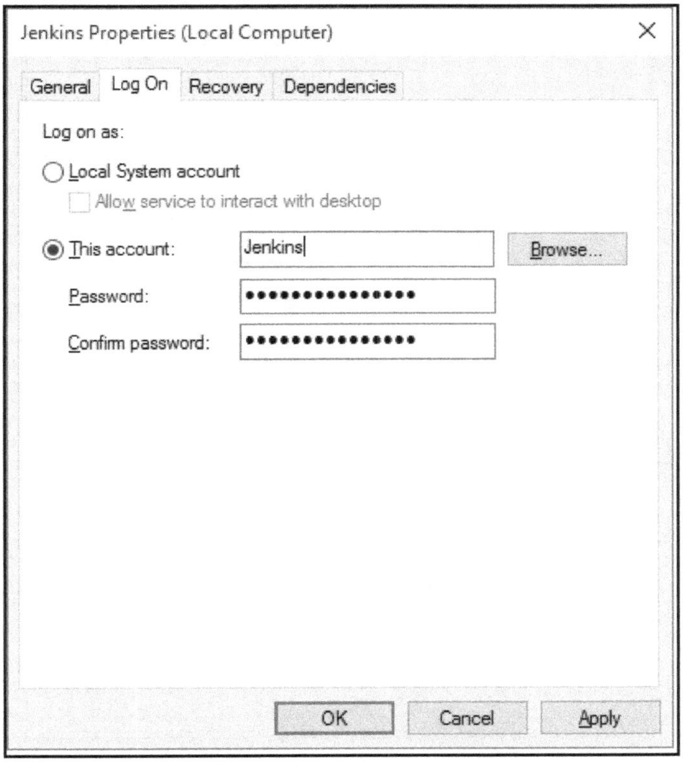

Configuring the Jenkins service Log On option

9. The next tab is **Recovery**. Here, we can specify the action items in case the Jenkins service fails to start.

10. Here is an example. At the first failure, there is an attempt to restart Jenkins, at the second failure an attempt is made to restart the computer. And lastly, at subsequent failures, a program is run to debug the issue, or we can run a script that sends the Jenkins failure log through email to the respective Jenkins admin for investigation:

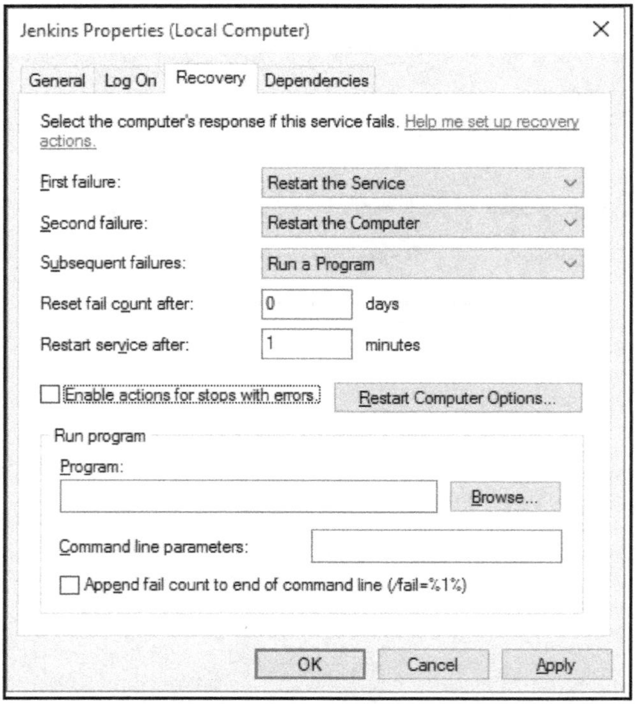

Configuring the Jenkins service Recovery option

Installing a standalone Jenkins server on Ubuntu

Installing a Jenkins server on Ubuntu is quite easy. Before performing the steps to install Jenkins on Ubuntu, let's have a look at the prerequisites.

Prerequisites

Before we begin, make sure you have the following things ready:

- We need a machine with at least 4 GB of RAM and a Multi-core processor.
- Depending on how you manage the infrastructure in your team, the machine could be an instance on a cloud platform (such as AWS, DigitalOcean, or any other cloud platform), a bare metal machine, or it could be a VM (on VMware vSphere or any other server virtualization software).
- The machine should have Ubuntu 16.04 installed on it. Choose a LTS release version.
- Check for admin privileges; the installation might ask for an admin username and password.
- Make sure port `8080` is open.

Installing Java

Follow these steps to install Java:

1. Update the package index using following command:

   ```
   sudo apt-get update
   ```

2. Next, install Java. The following command will install the JRE:

   ```
   sudo apt-get install default-jre
   ```

3. To set the `JAVA_HOME` environment variable, first get the Java installation location. Do this by executing the following command:

   ```
   update-java-alternatives -l
   ```

4. The previous command will print the list of Java applications installed on your machine along with their installation paths. Copy the Java path that appears on your Terminal:

   ```
   java-1.8.0-openjdk-amd64 1081
   /usr/lib/jvm/java-1.8.0-openjdk-amd64
   ```

5. Open the `/etc/environment` file for editing using the following command:

```
sudo nano /etc/environment
```

6. Add the Java path (the one that you copied earlier) inside the `/etc/environment` file in the following format:

```
JAVA_HOME="/usr/lib/jvm/java-1.8.0-openjdk-amd64"
```

7. Type *Ctrl* + *X* and choose *Y* to save and close the file.
8. Next, reload the file using the following command:

```
sudo source /etc/environment
```

Installing the latest version of Jenkins

To install the latest version of Jenkins, follow these steps in sequence:

1. Add the repository key to the system using the following command:

```
wget --no-check-certificate -q -O \
- https://pkg.jenkins.io/debian/jenkins-ci.org.key | \
sudo apt-key add -
```

2. You should get an output of `OK`. Next, append the Debian package repository address using the following command:

```
echo deb http://pkg.jenkins.io/debian binary/ | \
sudo tee /etc/apt/sources.list.d/jenkins.list
```

3. Update the package index:

```
sudo apt-get update
```

4. Now, install Jenkins using the following command:

```
sudo apt-get install jenkins
```

5. See the *Starting, stopping, and restarting Jenkins on Ubuntu* section if you are required to start Jenkins.
6. Jenkins is now ready for use. By default, the Jenkins service runs on port `8080`. To access Jenkins, use `http://localhost:8080/` or `http://<Jenkins server IP address>:8080/` in a browser .

Installing the latest stable version of Jenkins

If you prefer to install a stable version of Jenkins, then follow these step in sequence:

1. Add the repository key to the system using the following command:

```
wget --no-check-certificate -q -O - \
https://pkg.jenkins.io/debian-stable/jenkins-ci.org.key | \
sudo apt-key add -
```

2. You should get an output of OK. Next, append the Debian package repository address using the following command:

```
echo deb http://pkg.jenkins.io/debian-stable binary/ | \
sudo tee /etc/apt/sources.list.d/jenkins.list
```

3. Update the package index:

```
sudo apt-get update
```

4. Now, install Jenkins using the following command:

```
sudo apt-get install jenkins
```

5. See the *Starting, stopping, and restarting Jenkins on Ubuntu* section if you are required to start Jenkins.
6. Jenkins is now ready for use. By default, the Jenkins service runs on port 8080. To access Jenkins, use http://localhost:8080/ or http://<Jenkins server IP address>:8080/ in a browser.

> In order to troubleshoot Jenkins, access the logs file /var/log/jenkins/jenkins.log.
>
> The Jenkins service runs under the user Jenkins, which is automatically created upon installation.

Starting, stopping, and restarting Jenkins on Ubuntu

Jenkins by default starts running when installed. Here are the commands to start, stop, restart, and check the status of the Jenkins service:

1. To start Jenkins, use the following command:

```
sudo systemctl start jenkins
```

2. Similarly, to stop Jenkins, use the following command:

```
sudo systemctl stop jenkins
```

3. To restart Jenkins, use the following command:

```
sudo systemctl restart jenkins
```

4. To check the status of the Jenkins service, use the following `systemctl` command:

```
sudo systemctl status jenkins
```

5. You should see the following output:

```
● jenkins.service - LSB: Start Jenkins at boot time
Loaded: loaded (/etc/init.d/jenkins; bad; vendor preset: enabled)
Active: active (exited) since Wed 2017-07-19 22:34:39 UTC; 6min ago
Docs: man:systemd-sysv-generator(8)
```

Installing a standalone Jenkins server on Red Hat Linux

In this section, we will learn to install Jenkins on Red Hat Linux. The installation process discussed here are also applies to Fedora.

Prerequisites

Before we begin, make sure you have the following things ready:

- We need a machine with at least 4 GB of RAM and a Multi-core processor.
- Depending on how you manage the infrastructure in your team, the machine could be an instance on a cloud platform (such as AWS, DigitalOcean, or any other cloud platform), a bare metal machine, or it could be a VM (on VMware vSphere or any other server virtualization software).
- The machine should have RHEL 7.3 installed on it.
- Check for admin privileges; the installation might ask for an admin username and password.
- Make sure port `8080` is open.

Installing Java

Follow these steps to install Java:

1. Move to the `/tmp` directory and download Java:

```
cd /tmp
wget -O java_8.131.rpm \
http://javadl.oracle.com/webapps/download/AutoDL? \
BundleId=220304_d54c1d3a095b4ff2b6607d096fa80163
```

2. Next, install Java. The following command will install the JRE:

```
sudo rpm -ivh java_8.131.rpm
```

3. To set the `JAVA_HOME` environment variable, first get the Java installation's location. Do this by executing the following command:

```
sudo alternatives --config java
```

4. The previous command will print the list of Java applications installed on your machine, along with their installation paths. Copy the Java path that appears on your Terminal:

```
There is 1 program that provides 'java'.
Selection    Command
-----------------------------------------------
*+ 1           /usr/java/jre1.8.0_131/bin/java
```

5. Add the Java path (the one that you copied earlier) inside the /etc/environment file using the following command:

```
sudo sh \
-c "echo JAVA_HOME=/usr/java/jre1.8.0_131 >>
/etc/environment"
```

Installing the latest version of Jenkins

To install the latest version of Jenkins, follow these steps:

1. Add the Jenkins repository to the yum repository using the following command:

```
sudo wget -O /etc/yum.repos.d/jenkins.repo \
 http://pkg.jenkins-ci.org/redhat/jenkins.repo
sudo rpm --import https://jenkins-ci.org/redhat/jenkins-ci.org.key
```

2. Install Jenkins using the following command:

```
sudo yum install jenkins
```

3. See the *Starting, stopping, and restarting Jenkins on Red Hat Linux* section if you are required to start Jenkins.

Jenkins is now ready for use. By default, the Jenkins service runs on port 8080. To access Jenkins, use http://localhost:8080/ or http://<Jenkins server IP address>:8080/ in a browser.

Installing the latest stable version of Jenkins

If you prefer to install a stable version of Jenkins, then follow these steps:

1. Add the Jenkins repository to the yum repository using the following command:

```
sudo wget -O /etc/yum.repos.d/jenkins.repo \
 http://pkg.jenkins-ci.org/redhat-stable/jenkins.repo
sudo rpm --import https://jenkins-ci.org/redhat/jenkins-ci.org.key
```

2. Install Jenkins using the following command:

```
sudo yum install jenkins
```

3. See the *Starting, stopping, and restarting Jenkins on Red Hat Linux* section if you are required to start Jenkins.

Starting, stopping, and restarting Jenkins on Red Hat Linux

Here are the commands to start, stop, restart, and check the status of the Jenkins service:

1. To start Jenkins, use the following command:

```
sudo systemctl start jenkins
```

2. Similarly, to stop Jenkins, use the following command:

```
sudo systemctl stop jenkins
```

3. To restart Jenkins, use the following command:

```
sudo systemctl restart jenkins
```

4. To check the status of the Jenkins service, use the following `systemctl` command:

```
sudo systemctl status jenkins
```

5. You should see the following output:

```
● jenkins.service - LSB: Jenkins Automation Server
  Loaded: loaded (/etc/rc.d/init.d/jenkins; bad;
  vendor preset: disabled)
  Active: active (running) since Wed 2017-07-19 18:45:47 EDT;
   2min 31s ago
     Docs: man:systemd-sysv-generator(8)
  Process: 1081 ExecStart=/etc/rc.d/init.d/jenkins start
  (code=exited, status=0/SUCCESS)
   CGroup: /system.slice/jenkins.service
           └─1706 /etc/alternatives/java
   -Dcom.sun.akuma.Daemon=daemonized -Djava.awt.headless=true
   -DJENKINS_HOME=/var/lib/j...
```

In order to troubleshoot Jenkins, access the logs in `var/log/jenkins/jenkins.log`.

The Jenkins service runs with the user Jenkins, which automatically gets created upon installation.

Running Jenkins behind a reverse proxy

In this example, we will learn how to position an Nginx server (running on a standalone machine) front of a Jenkins server (running on another standalone machine).

Prerequisites

Before we begin, make sure you have the following things ready:

- We need two machines with at least 4 GB of RAM and a Multi-core processor. One will run Nginx and the other will run Jenkins.
- Depending on how you manage the infrastructure in your team, the machine could be an instance on a cloud platform (such as AWS, DigitalOcean, or any other cloud platform), a bare metal machine, or it could be a VM (on VMware vSphere or any other server virtualization software).
- The machine should have Ubuntu 16.04 or greater installed on it.
- Check for admin privileges; the installation might ask for an admin username and password.
- Both machines should be on the same network. The following setup assumes that your organization has an intranet for all its services.

Installing and configuring Nginx

The installation of Nginx on Ubuntu is simple. Follow these steps to install an Nginx server on Ubuntu:

1. Update the local package index:

```
sudo apt-get update
```

2. Install `nginx` using the following command:

```
sudo apt-get install nginx
```

Configuring the firewall on a Nginx server

We need to configure the firewall on our Nginx server to allow access to the Nginx service. Follow these steps:

1. Check the firewall status using the `ufw` command:

   ```
   sudo ufw status
   ```

   You should see the following output:

   ```
   Status: inactive
   ```

2. If it's enabled, move to *step 3*. But, if you find it disabled, then enable the firewall using the following command:

   ```
   sudo ufw enable
   ```

   You should see the following output

   ```
   Command may disrupt existing ssh connections.
   Proceed with operation (y|n)? y
   Firewall is active and enabled on system startup
   ```

3. List the available configurations using the following command. You should see three Nginx profiles and one OpenSSH profile:

   ```
   sudo ufw app list
   ```

   You should see the following output

   ```
   Available applications:
     Nginx Full
     Nginx HTTP
     Nginx HTTPS
     OpenSSH
   ```

The `Nginx Full` profile opens port `80` (unencrypted) and port `443` (TLS/SSL).

The `Nginx HTTP` profile opens only port `80` (unencrypted).

The `Nginx HTTPS` profile opens only port `443` (TLS/SSL).

The `OpenSSH` profile opens only port `22` (SSH).

It is always recommended to enable the most restrictive profile.

4. To keep things simple, we will enable the `Nginx Full` profile, as shown in the following command:

```
sudo ufw allow 'Nginx Full'
Rules updated
Rules updated (v6)
```

5. Also, enable the `OpenSSH` profile if it's not active, as shown. This will allow us to continue accessing our Nginx machine over SSH:

```
sudo ufw allow 'OpenSSH'
```

You won't be able to log in to your Nginx machine if OpenSSH is disabled.

6. Verify the changes using the following command. You should see `Nginx Full` and `OpenSSH` as allowed:

```
sudo ufw status
```

You should see the following output:

```
Status: active
To                          Action      From
--                          ------      ----
OpenSSH                     ALLOW       Anywhere
Nginx Full                  ALLOW       Anywhere
OpenSSH (v6)                ALLOW       Anywhere (v6)
Nginx Full (v6)             ALLOW       Anywhere (v6)
```

7. Check if the Nginx service is running using the `systemctl` command:

```
systemctl status nginx
```

You should see the following output:

```
● nginx.service - A high performance web server and a reverse proxy
server
   Loaded: loaded (/lib/systemd/system/nginx.service; enabled;
   vendor preset: enabled)
   Active: active (running) since Thu 2017-07-20 18:44:33 UTC;
45min ago
 Main PID: 2619 (nginx)
    Tasks: 2
   Memory: 5.1M
      CPU: 13ms
   CGroup: /system.slice/nginx.service
           ├─2619 nginx: master process /usr/sbin/nginx
   -g daemon on;                   master_process on
           └─2622 nginx: worker process
```

8. From the previous output, you can see that our Nginx service is running fine. Now try to access it using the browser. First, get the IP address of your machine using the `ip route` command:

```
ip route
```

You should see the following output:

```
default via 10.0.2.2 dev enp0s3
10.0.2.0/24 dev enp0s3  proto kernel
scope link src 10.0.2.15
192.168.56.0/24 dev enp0s8  proto kernel  scope link
src 192.168.56.104
```

9. Now access the Nginx home page using `http://<IP Address>:80`. You should see something similar to the following screenshot:

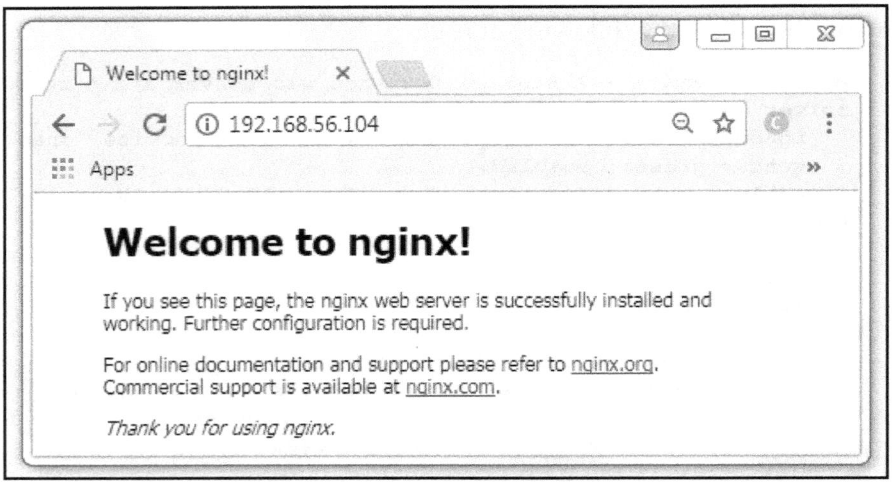

The Nginx index page

Starting, stopping, and restarting the Nginx server

Now that we have your Nginx server up, let's see some commands we can use to manage Nginx. Just like Jenkins, we will use the `systemctl` command to manage Nginx:

1. To stop Nginx, use the following command:

```
sudo systemctl stop nginx
```

2. To start Nginx when it is stopped, use the following command:

```
sudo systemctl start nginx
```

3. To restart Nginx, use the following command:

```
sudo systemctl restart nginx
```

4. To reload Nginx after making configuration changes, use the following command:

```
sudo systemctl reload nginx
```

Securing Nginx using OpenSSL

In this section, we will learn to set up a self-signed SSL certificate for use with our Nginx server.

Creating an SSL certificate

Run the following command to create a self-signed key and a certificate pair using OpenSSL:

```
sudo openssl req -x509 -nodes -days 365 -newkey rsa:2048 \
-keyout /etc/ssl/private/nginx-selfsigned.key -out \
/etc/ssl/certs/nginx-selfsigned.crt
```

The following table explains the arguments used in the previous command:

Parameters	**Description**
`req`	This argument indicates that we want to use X.509 **Certificate Signing Request** (**CSR**) management.
`-x509`	This argument allows us to create a self-signed certificate instead of generating a certificate signing request.
`-nodes`	This argument allows OpenSSL to skip the option to authenticate our certificate with a passphrase.
`-days`	This argument sets the duration for which the certificate is valid.
`-newkey rsa: 2048`	This argument tells OpenSSL to generate a new certificate and a new key at the same time. The `rsa:2048` option makes the RSA key `2048` bits long.
`-keyout`	This argument allows you to store the generated private key file in the location of your choice.
`-out`	This argument allows you to store the generated certificates in the location of your choice.

The moment you issue the following command to generate a private key and new certificate, you will be prompted to provide information. The prompts will look something as shown here:

```
Country Name (2 letter code) [AU]:DK
State or Province Name (full name) [Some-State]:Midtjylland
Locality Name (eg, city) []:Brande
Organization Name (eg, company) [Internet Widgits Pty Ltd]: Deviced.Inc
Organizational Unit Name (eg, section) []:DevOps
Common Name (e.g. server FQDN or YOUR name) []:<IP address of Nginx>
Email Address []:admin@organisation.com
```

The **Common Name** (**CN**) field, also known as the **Fully Qualified Domain Name** (**FQDN**) is very important. You need to provide the IP address or the domain name of your Nginx server.

The `/etc/ssl/private/` will now contain your `nginx-selfsigned.key` file and the `/etc/ssl/certs/` will contain your `nginx-selfsigned.crt` file.

Next, we will create a strong Diffie-Hellman group, which is used in negotiating **Perfect Forward Secrecy** (**PFS**) with clients. We will do this by using `openssl`, as shown in the following command:

```
sudo openssl dhparam -out /etc/ssl/certs/dhparam.pem 2048
```

This will take quite some time, but once it's done it will generate a `dhparam.pem` file inside `/etc/ssl/certs/`.

Creating strong encryption settings

In the following section, we will set up a strong SSL cipher suite to secure our Nginx server:

1. Create a configuration file named `ssl-params.conf` in `/etc/nginx/snippets/` as shown here:

   ```
   sudo nano /etc/nginx/snippets/ssl-params.conf
   ```

2. Copy the following code inside the file:

```
# from https://cipherli.st/
# and https://raymii.org/s/tutorials/
  Strong_SSL_Security_On_nginx.html

ssl_protocols TLSv1 TLSv1.1 TLSv1.2;
ssl_prefer_server_ciphers on;
ssl_ciphers "EECDH+AESGCM:EDH+AESGCM:AES256+EECDH:AES256+EDH";
ssl_ecdh_curve secp384r1;
ssl_session_cache shared:SSL:10m;
ssl_session_tickets off;
ssl_stapling on;
ssl_stapling_verify on;
resolver 8.8.8.8 8.8.4.4 valid=300s;
resolver_timeout 5s;
# disable HSTS header for now
#add_header Strict-Transport-Security "max-age=63072000;
 includeSubDomains; preload";
add_header X-Frame-Options DENY;
add_header X-Content-Type-Options nosniff;

ssl_dhparam /etc/ssl/certs/dhparam.pem;
```

3. Type *Ctrl* + *X* and choose *Y* to save and close the file.

We have used the recommendations by Remy van Elst that are available at `https://cipherli.st/`.

Modifying the Nginx configuration

Next, we will modify our Nginx configuration to enable SSL. Follow these steps:

1. First and foremost, take a backup of your existing Nginx configuration file named `default` that is in `/etc/nginx/sites-available/`:

```
sudo cp /etc/nginx/sites-available/default \
/etc/nginx/sites-available/default.backup
```

2. Now, open the file for editing using the following command:

```
sudo nano /etc/nginx/sites-available/default
```

3. You will find a lot of commented lines inside the file. If you ignore them for a while, you will probably see the following:

```
server {
    listen 80 default_server;
    listen [::]:80 default_server;

    # SSL configuration

    # listen 443 ssl default_server;
    # listen [::]:443 ssl default_server;

    . . .

    root /var/www/html;

    . . .

    index index.html index.htm index.nginx-debian.html;
    server_name _;

    . . .
```

4. We will modify the configuration so that the unencrypted HTTP requests are automatically redirected to encrypted HTTPS. We will do this by adding the following three lines, as highlighted in the following code:

```
server {
    listen 80 default_server;
    listen [::]:80 default_server;
    server_name <nginx_server_ip or nginx domain name>;
    return 301 https://$server_name$request_uri;
}

    # SSL configuration

    # listen 443 ssl default_server;
    # listen [::]:443 ssl default_server;

    . . .
```

5. From the previous code, you can see that we have closed the server block.
6. Next, we will start a new server block, uncomment the two `listen` directives that use port `443`, and add `http2` to these lines in order to enable HTTP/2, as shown in the following code block:

```
server {
    listen 80 default_server;
    listen [::]:80 default_server;
    server_name <nginx_server_ip or nginx domain name>;
    return 301 https://$server_name$request_uri;
}

server {

    # SSL configuration

    listen 443 ssl http2 default_server;
    listen [::]:443 ssl http2 default_server;

    . . .
```

7. Next, we will add the location of our self-signed certificate and key. We just need to include the two snippet files we set up:

```
server {
    listen 80 default_server;
    listen [::]:80 default_server;
    server_name <nginx_server_ip or nginx domain name>;
    return 301 https://$server_name$request_uri;
}
server {

    # SSL configuration

    listen 443 ssl http2 default_server;
    listen [::]:443 ssl http2 default_server;
    ssl_certificate /etc/ssl/certs/nginx-selfsigned.crt;
    ssl_certificate_key /etc/ssl/private/nginx-selfsigned.key;
    include snippets/ssl-params.conf;

    . . .
```

8. Next, we will set the `server_name` value to our Nginx IP or domain name inside our SSL server block. By default, the `server_name` may be set to an *underscore* (_), as shown in the following code block:

```
server {
    # SSL configuration

    . . .

    server_name <nginx_server_ip or nginx domain name>;

    . . .
}
```

9. Type *Ctrl* + *X* and choose *Y* to save and close the file.

Enabling the changes and testing our Nginx setup

We will now restart Nginx to implement our new changes:

1. First, check whether there are any syntax errors in our files. Do this by typing the following command:

```
sudo nginx -t
```

2. If everything is successful, you should see something similar to the following command output:

```
nginx: [warn] "ssl_stapling" ignored, issuer certificate not found
nginx: the configuration file /etc/nginx/nginx.conf syntax is ok
nginx: configuration file /etc/nginx/nginx.conf test is successful
```

3. Restart Nginx using the following command:

```
sudo systemctl restart nginx
```

4. Next, access your Nginx server using `http://<Nginx_IP_Address>:80`. You should notice that you have been automatically redirected to `https://<Nginx_IP_Address>:80`.

5. You will see a warning that looks similar to the following screenshot:

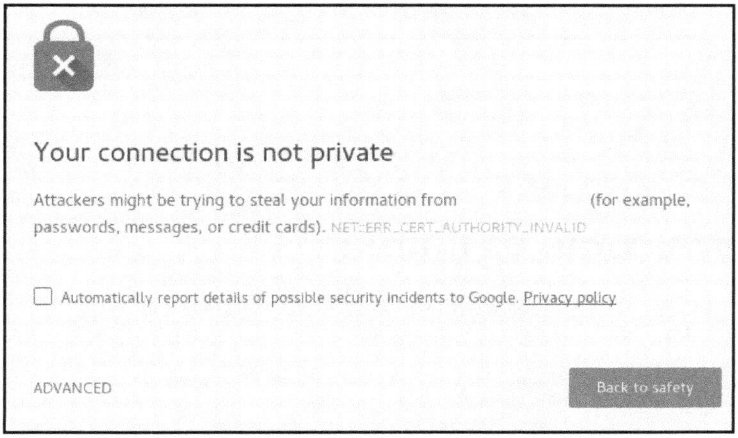

SSL warning

6. This is expected, as the certificate that we created isn't signed by one of your browser's trusted certificate authorities.
7. Click on the **Advanced...** button and then click on **Proceed to 192.168.56.104 (unsafe)**:

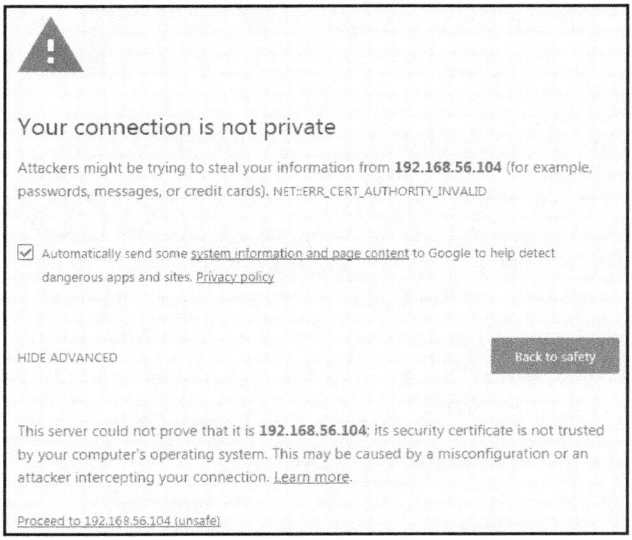

Proceeding as unsafe

8. You should now be able to see the Nginx default page, as shown in the following screenshot:

The Nginx index page with SSL encryption

Configuring the Jenkins server

In this section, we will perform some configurations on our Jenkins server. To set up a Jenkins server in the first place, see the *Installing a standalone Jenkins server on Ubuntu* section.

Once you have a Jenkins server up and running, follow these steps:

1. To make Jenkins work with Nginx, we need to update the Jenkins configuration so that the Jenkins server listens only on the Jenkins IP address or the Jenkins domain name interface rather than all interfaces (`0.0.0.0`). If Jenkins listens on all interfaces, then it's potentially accessible on its original, unencrypted port (`8080`).
2. To achieve this, modify the `/etc/default/jenkins` configuration file, as shown in the following command:

```
sudo nano /etc/default/jenkins
```

3. Inside the file, scroll all the way down to the last line or just look for the `JENKINS_ARGS` line.
4. Append the following argument to the existing value of `JENKINS_ARGS`:

```
-httpListenAddress=<IP Address of your Jenkins>
```

5. The final `JENKINS_ARGS` line should look something like this (single line):

```
JENKINS_ARGS="--webroot=/var/cache/$NAME/war
--httpPort=$HTTP_PORT
--httpListenAddress=192.168.56.105"
```

6. Type *Ctrl* + *X* and choose *Y* to save and close the file.
7. To make the new configuration effective, restart the Jenkins server:

```
sudo systemctl restart jenkins
```

8. To check whether Jenkins is running properly, execute the following command:

```
sudo systemctl status jenkins
```

You should see the following screenshot:

```
● jenkins.service - LSB: Start Jenkins at boot time
  Loaded: loaded (/etc/init.d/jenkins; bad;
  vendor preset: enabled)
  Active: active (exited) since Sat 2017-07-22 23:30:36 UTC;
  18h ago
    Docs: man:systemd-sysv-generator(8)
```

Adding reverse proxy settings to the Nginx configuration

The following steps will help you to add reverse proxy settings to the Nginx configuration:

1. Open the Nginx configuration file for editing:

```
sudo nano /etc/nginx/sites-available/default
```

2. As we're sending all requests to our Jenkins server, comment out the default `try_files` line, as shown in the following code block:

```
location / {
  # First attempt to serve request as file, then
  # as directory, then fall back to displaying a 404.
  # try_files $uri $uri/ =404;
}
```

3. Next, add the proxy settings as shown here:

```
location / {
  # First attempt to serve request as file, then
  # as directory, then fall back to displaying a 404.
  #try_files $uri $uri/ =404;
  include /etc/nginx/proxy_params;
  proxy_pass http://<ip address of jenkins>:8080;
  proxy_read_timeout  90s;
  # Fix potential "It appears that your reverse proxy set up
  is broken" error.
  proxy_redirect http://<ip address of jenkins>:8080
  https://your.ssl.domain.name;
}
```

4. Type *Ctrl* + *X* and choose *Y* to save and close the file.
5. Run the following command to check for any syntax errors in the Nginx configuration file:

```
sudo nginx -t
```

You should see the following output:

```
nginx: [warn] "ssl_stapling" ignored, issuer certificate not found
nginx: the configuration file /etc/nginx/nginx.conf syntax is ok
nginx: configuration file /etc/nginx/nginx.conf test is successful
```

6. If the output is error free, restart Nginx to make the new configuration effective. Use the following command:

```
sudo systemctl restart nginx
```

7. Next, access your Nginx server using `https://<nginx_ip_address>:80`:

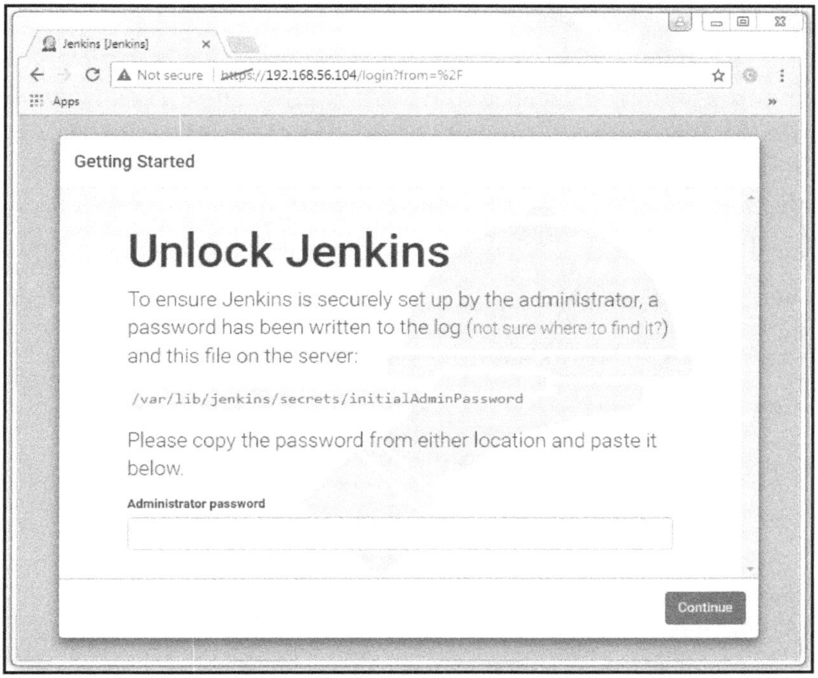

Jenkins getting started page

Running Nginx and Jenkins on the same machine

If you want to run Jenkins behind a reverse proxy server (Nginx) with the Jenkins server and the Nginx server running on the same machine, then perform the following sections in sequence:

1. Set up a machine with at least 4 GB of RAM and a Multi-core processor.
2. Depending on how you manage the infrastructure in your team, the machine could be an instance on a cloud platform (such as AWS, DigitalOcean, or any other cloud platform), or a bare metal machine, or it could be a VM (on VMware vSphere or any other server virtualization software).

3. The machines should have Ubuntu 16.04 or greater installed on it.
4. Check for admin privileges; the installation might ask for an admin username and password.
5. Install Nginx; refer to the *Installing and configuring Nginx* section.
6. Configure the firewall; refer to the *Configuring the firewall on Nginx server* section.
7. Secure the Nginx server using OpenSSL; refer to the *Securing Nginx using OpenSSL* section.
8. Configure the firewall to allow traffic on port `8080` using the following command:

```
sudo ufw allow 8080
```

9. Next, check the firewall status using the following command:

```
sudo ufw status
```

You should see the following output:

```
Status: active
To                          Action      From
--                          ------      ----
OpenSSH                     ALLOW       Anywhere
Nginx Full                  ALLOW       Anywhere
8080                        ALLOW       Anywhere
OpenSSH (v6)                ALLOW       Anywhere (v6)
Nginx Full (v6)             ALLOW       Anywhere (v6)
8080 (v6)                   ALLOW       Anywhere (v6)
```

10. Install Jenkins, refer to the *Installing a standalone Jenkins server on Ubuntu* section.
11. Configure the Jenkins server; refer to the *Configuring the Jenkins server* section. While performing the steps mentioned in this section, make sure to put `127.0.0.1` in place of `<IP Address of your Jenkins>`.
12. Add the reverse proxy settings in Nginx; refer to the *Adding reverse proxy settings to Nginx configuration* section. While performing the steps mentioned in this section, you will be asked to enter the Jenkins server IP at various places inside the Nginx configuration file. Since our Jenkins server is now running on the same machine as Nginx, the value for `<IP Address of your Jenkins>` should be `localhost`.

Running Jenkins on Docker

The true advantage of having Jenkins on Docker is when you have to quickly create multiple development and staging instances of your production Jenkins server. It's also very useful in redirecting the traffic to a secondary Jenkins server while you perform maintenance activities on the primary Jenkins server. While we will see these use cases later, let's first try to run Jenkins on Docker.

Prerequisites

Before we begin, make sure you have the following things ready:

- We need a machine with at least 4 GB of RAM (the more the better) and a Multi-core processor.
- Depending on how you manage the infrastructure in your team, the machine could be an instance on a cloud platform (such as AWS, DigitalOcean, or any other cloud platform), a bare metal machine, or it could be a VM (on VMware vSphere or any other server virtualization software).
- The machines should have Ubuntu 16.04 or greater installed on it.
- Check for admin privileges; the installation might ask for an admin username and password.

Setting up a Docker host

In this section, we will learn how to install Docker using the repository method and using the Debian package. Follow the steps in the following sections to set up a Docker host.

Setting up the repository

Follow these steps to set up a repository:

1. Execute the following command to let `apt` use a repository:

   ```
   sudo apt-get install apt-transport-https ca-certificates
   ```

2. Add Docker's official GPG key using the following command:

   ```
   curl -fsSL https://yum.dockerproject.org/gpg | sudo apt-key add -
   ```

3. Verify that the key ID is exactly `58118E89F3A912897C070ADBF76221572C52609D` using the following command:

```
apt-key fingerprint 58118E89F3A912897C070ADBF76221572C52609D
```

   You should see the following output:

```
pub   4096R/2C52609D 2015-07-14
Key fingerprint = 5811 8E89 F3A9 1289 7C07  0ADB F762 2157 2C52
 609D
uid   Docker Release Tool (releasedocker) docker@docker.com
```

4. Use the following command to set up the stable repository to download Docker:

```
sudo add-apt-repository \
"deb https://apt.dockerproject.org/repo/ubuntu-$(lsb_release \
-cs) main"
```

It's recommended to always use the stable version of repository.

Installing Docker

After setting up the repository, perform the following steps to install Docker:

1. Update the `apt` package index using the following command:

```
sudo apt-get update
```

2. To install the latest version of Docker, run the following command:

```
sudo apt-get -y install docker-engine
```

3. To install a specific version of Docker, list the available versions using the following command:

```
apt-cache madison docker-engine
```

You should see the following output:

```
docker-engine | 1.16.0-0~trusty |
https://apt.dockerproject.org/repo ubuntu-trusty/main amd64
Packages docker-engine | 1.13.3-0~trusty |
https://apt.dockerproject.org/repo ubuntu-trusty/main amd64
Packages
...
```

The output of the previous command depends on the type of repository configured in the previous section (*Setting up the repository*).

4. Next, execute the following command to install the specific version of Docker:

```
sudo apt-get -y install docker-engine=<VERSION_STRING>
sudo apt-get -y install docker-engine=1.16.0-0~trusty
```

5. The Docker service starts automatically. To verify if Docker is installed and running, execute the following command:

```
sudo docker run hello-world
```

6. The previous command should run without any errors, and you should see a `Hello from Docker!` message:

```
Unable to find image 'hello-world:latest' locally
latest: Pulling from library/hello-world
b04784fba78d: Pull complete
Digest: sha256:
  f3b3b28a45160805bb16542c9531888519430e9e6d6ffc09d72261b0d26ff74f
Status: Downloaded newer image for hello-world:latest

Hello from Docker!
This message shows that your installation appears to be working
correctly.
...
```

Installing from a package

Follow these steps to install Docker using the `.deb` package:

1. Download the `.deb` package of your choice from `https://apt.dockerproject.org/repo/pool/main/d/docker-engine/`.
2. To install the downloaded package, execute the following command:

```
sudo dpkg -i /<path to package>/<docker package>.deb
```

3. Verify your Docker installation by running the following command:

```
sudo docker run hello-world
```

You should see the following output:

```
Hello from Docker!
This message shows that your installation appears to be working
correctly.
```

Running the Jenkins container

Now that we have our Docker host ready, let's run Jenkins:

1. Run the following command to start a Jenkins container. This might take some time, as Docker will try to download the Jenkins Docker image (`jenkins/jenkins:lts`) from Docker Hub:

```
docker run -d --name jenkins_dev -p 8080:8080 \
-p 50000:50000 jenkins/jenkins:lts
```

You should see the following output:

```
...
...
...
d52829d9da9e0a1789a3117badc862039a0084677be6a771a959d8467b9cc267
```

2. The following table explains the Docker command that we used in the previous command:

Parameters	Description
`docker`	Used to invoke the Docker utility.
`run`	A Docker command to run a container.
`-d`	This option runs the container in the backend.
`--name`	This option allows you to give your container a name.
`-p`	This option is used to map a container's port with the host.
`jenkins/jenkins:lts`	The name of the Docker image and its version used to create a container. `jenkins/jenkins` is the Jenkins Docker image, and `lts` is a particular version of that image.

3. To see the list of running containers, execute the following command:

```
sudo docker ps --format "{{.ID}}: {{.Image}} {{.Names}}"
```

You should see the following output:

```
d52829d9da9e: jenkins/jenkins:lts jenkins_dev
```

To use the latest LTS release of Jenkins, use the `jenkins/jenkins:lts` Jenkins Docker image.

To use the latest weekly release of Jenkins, use the `jenkins/jenkins` Jenkins Docker image.

4. Make a note of your Docker host IP using the following command:

```
sudo ip route
```

You should see the following output:

```
default via 10.0.2.2 dev enp0s3
10.0.2.0/24 dev enp0s3  proto kernel  scope link  src 10.0.2.15
172.17.0.0/16 dev docker0  proto kernel  scope link  src 172.17.0.1
192.168.56.0/24 dev enp0s8  proto kernel  scope link
src 192.168.56.107
```

5. Your Jenkins server is now available on http:<IP Address of Docker host>:8080. You should now be able to see the Jenkins **Getting Started** page.
6. To proceed with the Jenkins setup, you might need the initialAdminPassword key. This file is inside /var/jenkins_home/secrets/. There are two ways you can get the data inside the initialAdminPassword file. You can use the docker exec command, as illustrated here:

```
sudo docker exec -it jenkins_dev \
cat /var/jenkins_home/secrets/initialAdminPassword
```

   Or, by logging inside the running Jenkins container, using the same docker exec command, as shown here:

```
sudo docker exec -it jenkins_dev bash
```

7. Once you are inside the container, execute the following Linux command to get the contents of the file:

```
cat /var/jenkins_home/secrets/initialAdminPassword \
```

   Both the commands will print the content of the initialAdminPassword file, similar to the one shown as follows:

```
1538ededb4e94230aca12d10dd461e52
```

   Here, the -i option allows you to interact with your Docker container and the -t option allocates a pseudo -tty.

8. While you are still inside the Jenkins container, notice that the jenkins_home directory is present inside the /var/ directory and the jenkins.war file is located inside /usr/share/jenkins.

> The jenkins_home is a very important directory where all your Jenkins jobs, builds, metadata, configurations, users, and everything, are stored.

Running a Jenkins container using a data volume

In the previous sections, we created a Jenkins container without a mechanism to make the data inside the `jenkins_home` directory persistent. In simple words, if for some reason you delete the Jenkins container, you delete your `jenkins_home` directory.

Luckily, there is still a better way to run Jenkins with Docker, and that is by using data volumes. Data volumes are special directories that make the data persistent and independent of the container's life cycle. If a container writes data to a data volume, deleting the container will still make the data available because the container and its associated data volume are two different entities.

Let's create a Jenkins container using a data volume:

1. Run a Jenkins container using the following command:

```
sudo docker run -d --name jenkins_prod -p 8080:8080\
-p 50000:50000 -v jenkins-home-prod:/var/jenkins_home \
jenkins/jenkins:lts
```

2. The `-v jenkins-home-prod:/var/jenkins_home` option will create a data volume named `jenkins-home-prod` and will map it to the `/var/jenkins_home` directory inside the container.
3. Execute the following command to see the contents of the `/var/jenkins_home` directory inside the `jenkins_prod` Jenkins container:

```
sudo docker exec -it jenkins_prod ls -lrt /var/jenkins_home
```

You should see the following output:

```
total 72
drwxr-xr-x  2 jenkins jenkins 4096 Jul 26 20:41 init.groovy.d
-rw-r--r--  1 jenkins jenkins  102 Jul 26 20:41
 copy_reference_file.log
drwxr-xr-x 10 jenkins jenkins 4096 Jul 26 20:41 war
-rw-r--r--  1 jenkins jenkins    0 Jul 26 20:41
 secret.key.not-so-secret
-rw-r--r--  1 jenkins jenkins   64 Jul 26 20:41 secret.key
drwxr-xr-x  2 jenkins jenkins 4096 Jul 26 20:41 plugins
drwxr-xr-x  2 jenkins jenkins 4096 Jul 26 20:41 jobs
drwxr-xr-x  2 jenkins jenkins 4096 Jul 26 20:41 nodes
-rw-r--r--  1 jenkins jenkins  159 Jul 26 20:41
  hudson.model.UpdateCenter.xml
-rw-------  1 jenkins jenkins 1712 Jul 26 20:41 identity.key.enc
drwxr-xr-x  2 jenkins jenkins 4096 Jul 26 20:41 userContent
```

```
-rw-r--r--  1 jenkins jenkins  907 Jul 26 20:41 nodeMonitors.xml
drwxr-xr-x  3 jenkins jenkins 4096 Jul 26 20:41 logs
-rw-r--r--  1 jenkins jenkins    6 Jul 26 20:41
  jenkins.install.UpgradeWizard.state
drwxr-xr-x  3 jenkins jenkins 4096 Jul 26 20:41 users
drwx------  4 jenkins jenkins 4096 Jul 26 20:41 secrets
-rw-r--r--  1 jenkins jenkins   94 Jul 26 20:41 jenkins.CLI.xml
-rw-r--r--  1 jenkins jenkins 1592 Jul 26 20:41 config.xml
drwxr-xr-x  2 jenkins jenkins 4096 Jul 26 20:41 updates
```

4. To list your Docker volume, execute the following command:

```
sudo docker volume ls
```

You should see the following output:

```
DRIVER              VOLUME NAME

local               jenkins-home-prod
```

5. Now you have a Jenkins container with a persistent `jenkins_home` directory.

Testing the data volume

We will test our data volume by performing the following steps:

1. We will make some changes on our Jenkins server; this will modify the content inside the `/var/jenkins_home` directory.
2. We will delete the Jenkins container.
3. We will create a new Jenkins container that will use the same data volume.
4. Check for the active Jenkins container using the following command:

```
sudo docker ps --format "{{.ID}}: {{.Image}} {{.Names}}"
```

You should see the following output:

```
5d612225f533: jenkins/jenkins:lts jenkins_prod
```

5. Access the Jenkins server using `http://<ip address of docker host>:8080`.

6. Get the contents of the `initialAdminPassword` file using the following command:

```
sudo docker exec -it jenkins_prod \
cat /var/jenkins_home/secrets/initialAdminPassword
```

You should see the following output:

```
7834556856f04925857723cc0d0523d7
```

7. Paste the `initialAdminPassword` under the **Administrator password** field on the Jenkins page and proceed with the Jenkins setup.
8. Create a new user at the **Create First Admin User** step, as shown in the following screenshot:

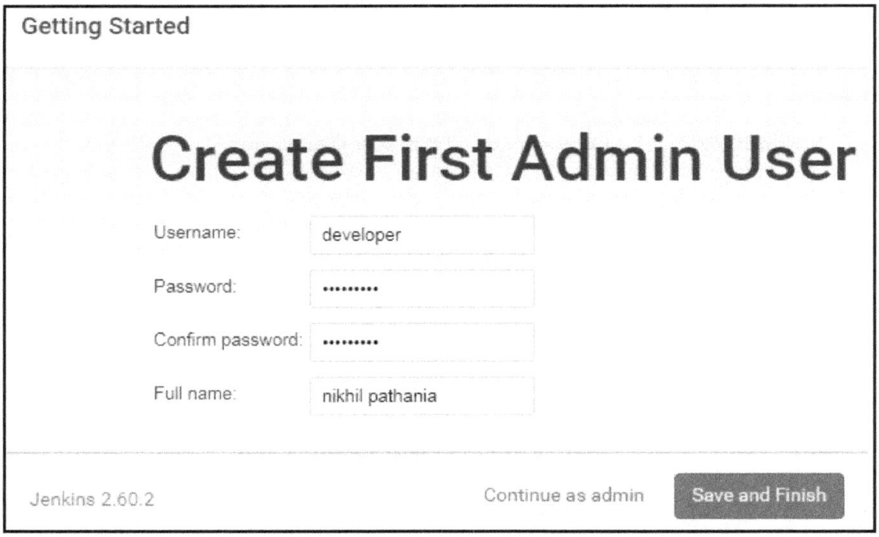

Creating the first admin user on Jenkins

9. Proceed with the remaining steps.
10. Execute the following command to list the content of the `/var/jenkins_home/users` directory. This the is location where you have all the user accounts:

```
sudo docker exec -it jenkins_prod ls -lrt /var/jenkins_home/users
```

Output should be as follows:

```
total 4
drwxr-xr-x 2 jenkins jenkins 4096 Jul 26 21:38 developer
```

11. Notice our newly created user developer is listed under the `users` directory.
12. Now let's delete the `jenkins_prod` Jenkins container using the following commands:

```
sudo docker kill jenkins_prod
sudo docker rm jenkins_prod
```

13. List the existing Docker containers (running/stopped) using the following command:

```
sudo docker ps -a --format "{{.ID}}: {{.Image}} {{.Names}}"
```

You should see the following output. However, you shouldn't see `jenkins_prod` in the list:

```
3511cd609b1b: hello-world eloquent_lalande
```

14. List the volumes using the following command:

```
sudo docker volume ls
```

You should see something similar. You can see that deleting the container did not delete its associated data volume:

```
DRIVER              VOLUME NAME

local               jenkins-home-prod
```

15. Now let's create a new Jenkins container named `jenkins_prod` that uses the existing `jenkins-home-prod` volume:

```
sudo docker run -d --name jenkins_prod -p 8080:8080 \
-p 50000:50000 -v jenkins-home-prod:/var/jenkins_home \
jenkins/jenkins:lts
```

16. Try to access the Jenkins dashboard using http://<IP Address of Docker host>:8080. You will not see the Jenkins setup page; instead, you should see the login page.
17. Log in to Jenkins using the user that we created earlier. You should be able to log in. This proves that our entire Jenkins configuration is intact.

Creating development and staging instances of Jenkins

Many times you are in need of a development or a staging instance of your Jenkins production server to test something new. Docker makes it easy and safe to create multiple instances of your Jenkins servers.

Here is how to do it. In this section, we will create a development and a staging instance of Jenkins using our Jenkins production instance.

Prerequisites

Before we begin, make sure you have the following things ready:

- We need a Docker host running a Jenkins instance (production), utilizing data volumes
- Refer to the *Running a Jenkins container using a data volume* section

Creating an empty data volume

We will create a data volume named `jenkins-home-staging` and `jenkins-home-development` for our staging and development instances of Jenkins, respectively:

1. To create an empty `jenkins-home-staging` data volume, run the following command:

   ```
   sudo docker volume create --name jenkins-home-staging
   ```

2. To create an empty `jenkins-home-development` data volume, run the following command:

   ```
   sudo docker volume create --name jenkins-home-development
   ```

3. List the newly create data volumes using the `docker volume` command:

   ```
   sudo docker volume ls
   ```

You should see the following output:

```
DRIVER              VOLUME NAME

local               jenkins-home-prod
local               jenkins-home-development
local               jenkins-home-staging
```

4. From the previous list, you can see the newly created data volumes named `jenkins-home-staging` and `jenkins-home-development`.

> If you have followed the previous section, you should also see the data volume `jenkins-home-prod` that is being used by our Jenkins production instance `jenkins_prod`.

Copying data between data volumes

We now have our newly created empty data volumes. Let's copy the content of `jenkins-home-prod` to each of them:

1. Copy the content of `jenkins-home-prod` to `jenkins-home-staging` using the following command:

```
sudo docker run --rm -it --user root \
-v jenkins-home-prod:/var/jenkins_home \
-v jenkins-home-staging:/var/jenkins_home_staging \
jenkins/jenkins:lts bash -c "cd /var/jenkins_home_staging \
&& cp -a /var/jenkins_home/* ."
```

2. The previous command will do the following:
    - It will first create an interactive container using the Docker image for Jenkins `jenkins/jenkins:lts` (the container is temporary).
    - All actions performed on this temporary container will be using the `root` user. Notice the `--user root` option in the previous command.
    - It will mount the content of the `jenkins-home-prod` data volume onto the `/var/jenkins_home` directory present inside the container. Notice the `-v jenkins-home-prod:/var/jenkins_home` option.

- Similarly, it will mount the non-existing content of the `jenkins-home-staging` data volume onto the non-existing `/var/jenkins_home_staging` directory inside the container. Notice the `-v jenkins-home-staging:/var/jenkins_home_staging` option.
- It will then, copy the content of `/var/jenkins_home` to `/var/jenkins_home_staging`. Notice the `bash -c "cd /var/jenkins_home_staging && cp -a /var/jenkins_home/*"` option.

3. Now, copy the content of `jenkins-home-prod` to `jenkins-home-development` using the following command:

```
sudo docker run --rm -it --user root \
-v jenkins-home-prod:/var/jenkins_home \
-v jenkins-home-development:/var/jenkins_home_development \
jenkins/jenkins:lts bash -c "cd /var/jenkins_home_development \
&& cp -a /var/jenkins_home/* ."
```

4. Now we have the same data on all the three data volumes: `jenkins-home-prod`, `jenkins-home-staging`, and `jenkins-home-development`.

Creating the development and staging instances

Now that we have data volumes for development and staging, let's spawn the containers using them:

1. To create a Jenkins staging instance named `jenkins_staging` using the `jenkins-home-staging` data volume, run the following command:

```
sudo docker run -d --name jenkins_staging \
-v jenkins-home-staging:/var/jenkins_home -p 8081:8080 \
-p 50001:50000 jenkins/jenkins:lts
```

The previous command will create a Jenkins instance running on port 8080 and mapped to port 8081 of the Docker host. We choose a different port on Docker host because we already have our Jenkins production instance, jenkins_prod, running on port 8080, which is mapped to port 8080 of the Docker host.

The same reason applies to mapping port 50000 on the Jenkins instance to port 50001 on the Docker host.

2. Try to access your Jenkins staging instance using http:<IP Address of Docker host>:8081.
3. Similarly, to create a Jenkins development instance named jenkins_development using the jenkins-home-development data volume, run the following command:

```
sudo docker run -d --name jenkins_development \
-v jenkins-home-development:/var/jenkins_home -p 8082:8080 \
-p 50002:50000 jenkins/jenkins:lts
```

The previous command will create a Jenkins instance running on port 8080 and mapped to port 8082 of the Docker host. We choose a different port on the Docker host because port 8080 and 8081 are already in use on the Docker host.

The same reason applies to mapping port 50000 on the Jenkins instance to port 50002 on the Docker host.

4. Try to access your Jenkins development instance using http:<IP Address of Docker host>:8082.

Summary

In this chapter, we learned how to install Jenkins on an Apache Tomcat server and as a standalone application on various operating systems. We also learned how to set up a reverse proxy server (Nginx) in front of our Jenkins server and secured the connection using SSL.

Above all, we learned how to run Jenkins on Docker. We also saw the advantages of using data volumes on Docker and learned how to leverage them to create on-demand instances (development or staging) of our Jenkins server.

The main objective of the current chapter was to show the readers how diverse Jenkins is in many ways when it comes to the installation process and the variety of operating systems that it supports. The Jenkins administration will be discussed in `Chapter 4`, *Configuring Jenkins*.

In the next chapter, we will have a quick overview of what's new in Jenkins 2.x.

3
The New Jenkins

In this chapter, we will look at some of the new features that are now part of the Jenkins 2.x release. After completing this chapter, you will have an understanding of the following:

- The new Jenkins setup wizard
- Jenkins pipeline as a code (Jenkins pipeline job)
- Jenkins Stage view
- Jenkins Declarative Pipeline syntax
- Jenkins Multibranch pipeline
- Jenkins pipeline syntax utility (Snippet Generator)
- Jenkins credentials
- Jenkinsfile
- Jenkins Blue Ocean
- Creating a pipeline in Jenkins Blue Ocean

The Jenkins setup wizard

When you access Jenkins for the first time, you are presented with the **Getting Started** wizard. We have already been through this exercise in the previous chapter; nevertheless, in the following section, we will take a deeper look at some of its important sections.

Prerequisites

Before we begin, make sure you have the following things ready:

- A Jenkins server running on any of the platforms discussed in the previous chapter (Docker, standalone, cloud, VM, servlet container, and so on).
- Make sure your Jenkins server has access to the internet. This is necessary to download and install plugins.

Unlocking Jenkins

When you access Jenkins for the first time, you are asked to unlock it using a secret initial admin password. This password is stored inside the file `initialAdminPassword`, which is located inside your `jenkins_home` directory. The file, along with its full path, is displayed on the Jenkins page, as shown in the following screenshot:

- **On Windows**: You can find the file under `C:\Program Files (x86)\Jenkins\secrets`. If you have chosen to install Jenkins somewhere else, then look for the file under `<Jenkins installation directory>\secrets`.
- **On Linux**: You can find the file under `/var/jenkins_home/secrets`:

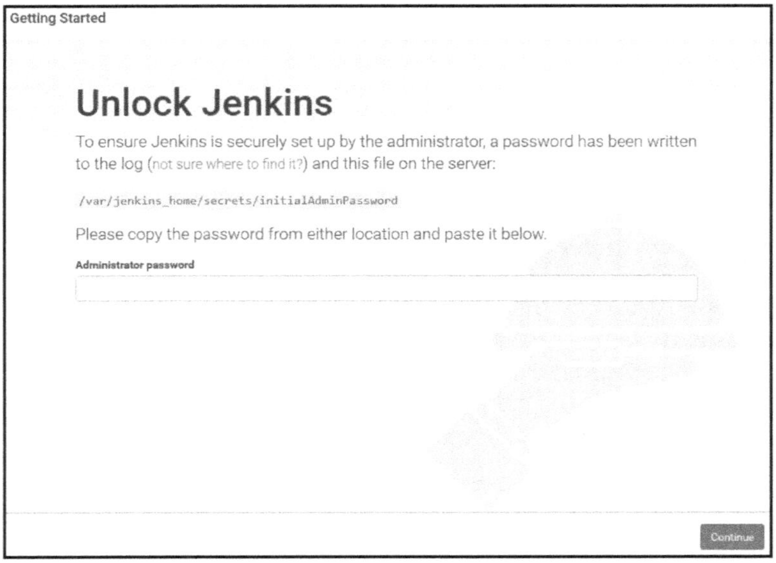

Unlocking Jenkins

Get the password from the `initialAdminPassword` file, paste it under the **Administrator password** field, and click on **Continue**.

> You can always log in to Jenkins using the password from the `intialAdminPassword` file and the username `admin`.

Customizing Jenkins

Next, you are presented with two options to install the Jenkins plugins, as shown in the following screenshot:

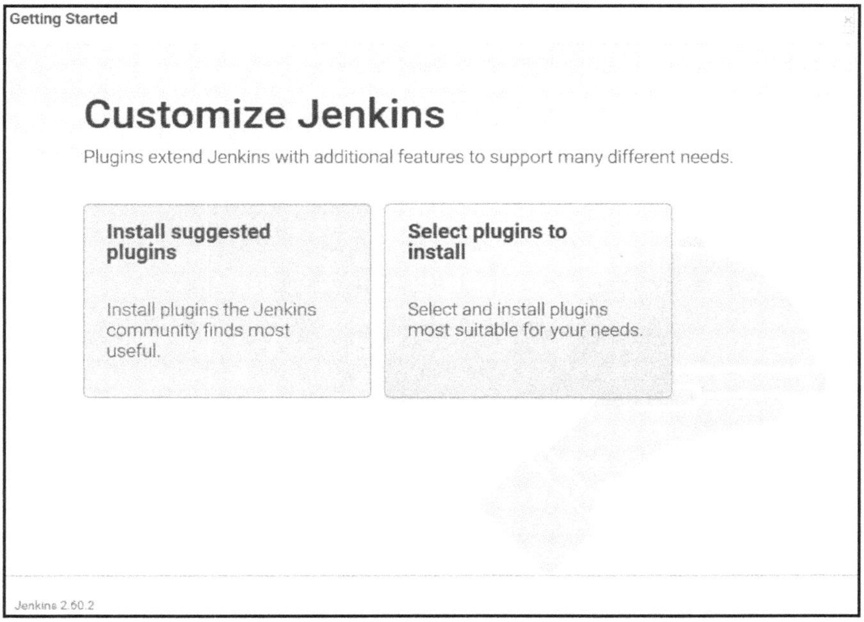

Customizing Jenkins

Choosing **Install suggested plugins** will install all the generic plugins for Jenkins, like Git, Pipeline as Code, and so on (as suggested by the Jenkins community).

Choosing **Select plugins to install** will let you install the plugins of your choice.

In the following section, we will go ahead and choose the option **Select plugins to install**. When you do, you should see the screen shown in the following screenshot. The following page will list some of the most popular plugins, although it's not a complete list of Jenkins plugins. You will notice that the suggested plugin is already selected (ticked) by default:

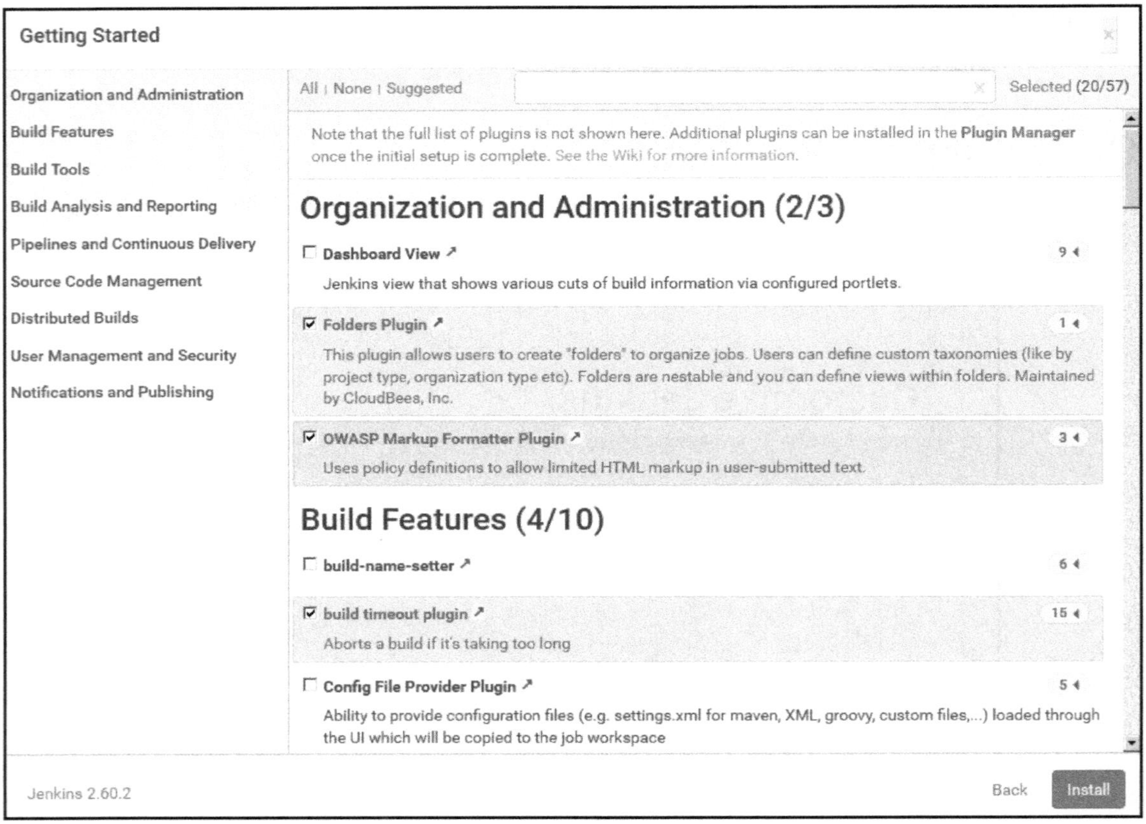

Choosing plugins to install

You can choose **All**, **None**, or the **Suggested** plugins.

Once you are done choosing plugins, click **Install** at the bottom of the page. The following screenshot shows the Jenkins plugin installation:

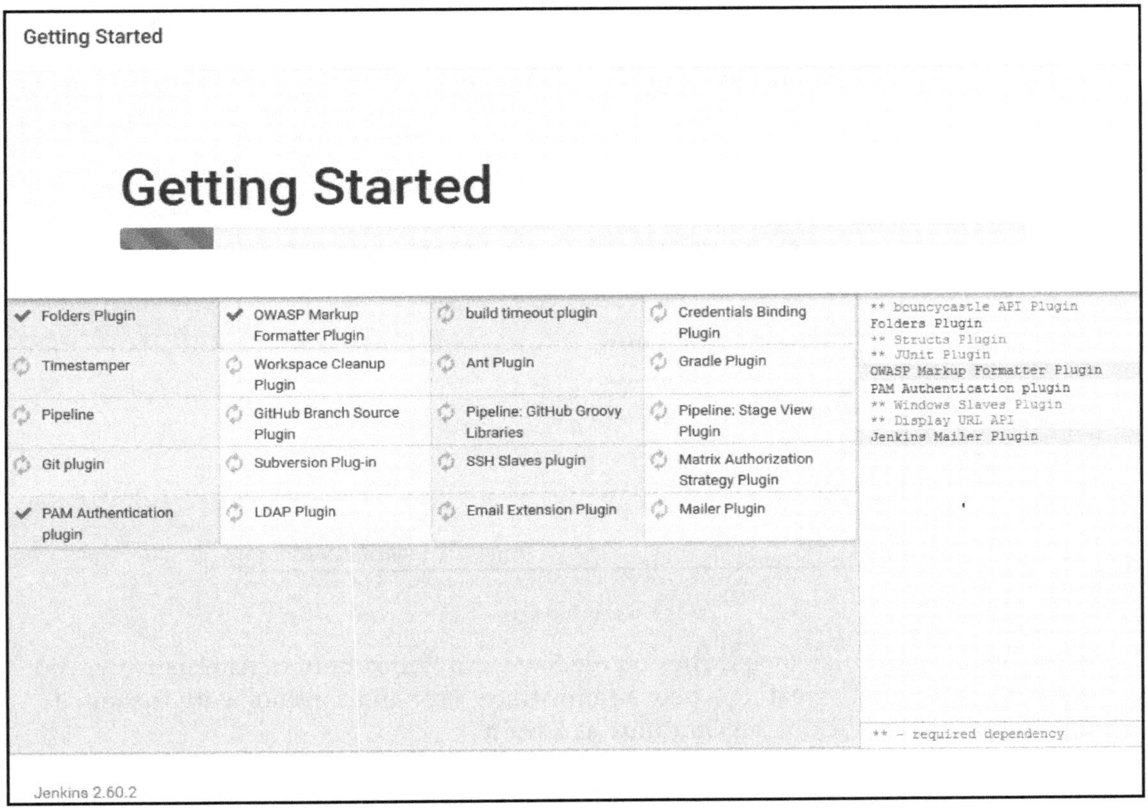

Installing Jenkins plugins

Creating the first admin user

Once the plugins are installed, you will be asked to create an administrator user account, as shown in the following screenshot. The following administrator account is different from the temporary administrator user account that was used at the beginning of the setup wizard (the initial admin account):

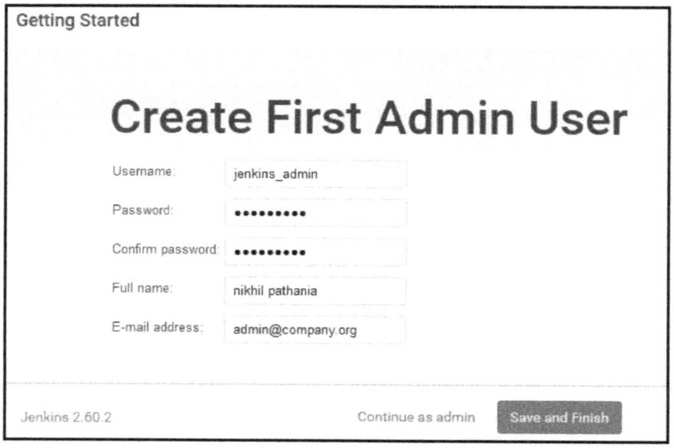

Creating your first Jenkins user

Fill in the fields appropriately and click on the **Save and Finish** button. Alternatively, you can also choose to ignore creating a new administrator user and continue with the initial administrator user by clicking on **Continue as admin**.

Next, on the following page, you will be greeted with a message saying, **Jenkins is ready! Your Jenkins setup is complete**. Click on **Start using Jenkins** to proceed to the Jenkins dashboard.

The new Jenkins pipeline job

Those who are already familiar with Jenkins are well aware of the freestyle Jenkins job. The classic way of creating a pipeline in Jenkins is by using the *freestyle job*, wherein each CI stage is represented using a Jenkins job (freestyle).

The Jenkins freestyle job is a web-based, GUI-propelled configuration. Any modification to the CI pipeline requires you to log in to Jenkins and reconfigure each of the Jenkins freestyle jobs.

The concept of **Pipeline as Code** rethinks the way we create a CI pipeline. The idea is to write the whole CI/CD pipeline as a code that offers some level of programming and that can be version controlled.

The following are some of the advantages of taking the Pipeline as Code route:

- It's programmable
- All of your CI/CD pipeline configurations can be described using just a single file (Jenkinsfile)
- It's version controllable, just like any other code
- It comes with an option to define your pipeline using the Declarative Pipeline syntax, which is an easy and elegant way of coding your pipeline

Let's take a look at the Jenkins pipeline job. We will try to look and get the feel of it by creating a simple CI pipeline.

Prerequisite

Before we begin, make sure you have the following things ready:

- A Jenkins server running on any of the platforms discussed in the previous chapter (Docker, standalone, cloud, VM, servlet container, and so on).
- Make sure your Jenkins server has access to the internet. This is necessary to download and install plugins.
- Make sure your Jenkins server has all the suggested plugins installed. See the *Customizing Jenkins* section.

Creating a Jenkins pipeline job

Follow the given steps to create a Jenkins pipeline job:

1. From the Jenkins dashboard, click on the **New Item** link.
2. On the resultant page, you will be presented with various types of Jenkins jobs to choose from.
3. Choose **Pipeline**, and give a name to your pipeline using the **Enter an item name** field.

4. Once you are done, click on the **OK** button at the bottom of the page.
5. All kinds of Jenkins jobs (freestyle, pipeline, multibranch, and so on) now come with a featured tab, as shown in the following screenshot:

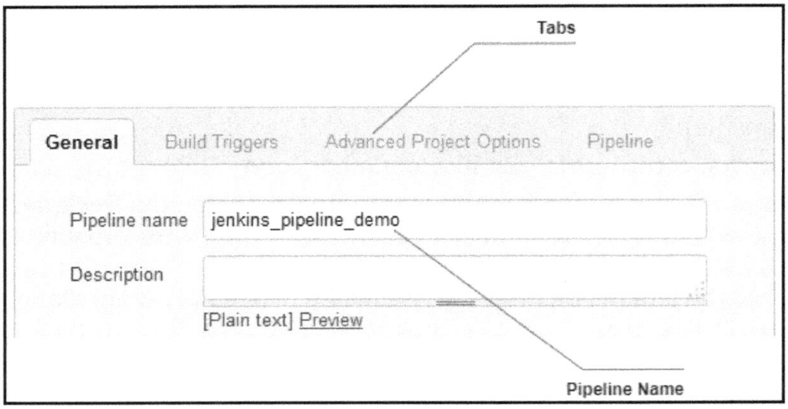

The new tab feature in Jenkins jobs

6. We will quickly navigate to the pipeline section by clicking on the **Pipeline** tab.
7. The following screenshot depicts the pipeline section. Let us see this section in detail:
    - The **Definition** field gives you two options to choose from—**Pipeline script** and **Pipeline script from SCM**. If you choose the option **Pipeline script**, then you define your pipeline code inside the **Script** field. But, if you choose the option **Pipeline script from SCM** (not shown in the screenshot), then your pipeline script (Jenkinsfile) is automatically fetched from the Version Control System (We will explore this option in the upcoming section).
    - To get a short description about any of the options, you can click on the question mark icon.
    - The **Pipeline Syntax** is a utility that helps you to convert GUI configurations into code. (We will explore this option in the upcoming section).

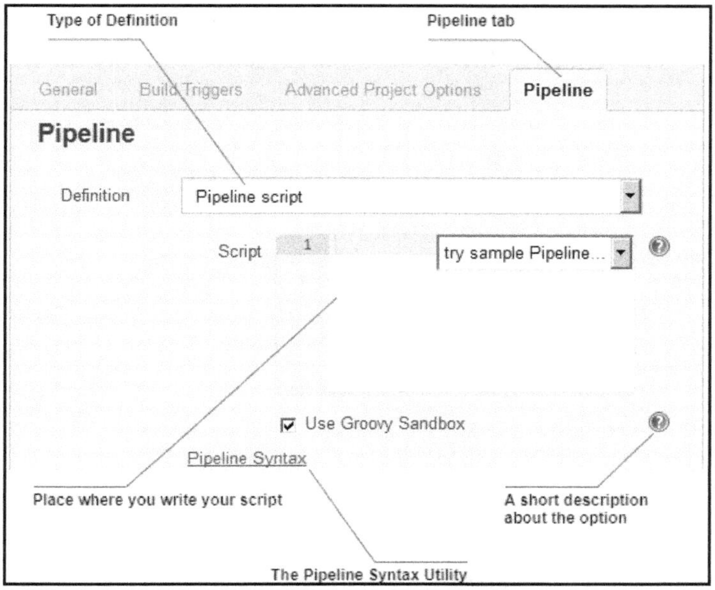

The pipeline section

8. Now let us write some code inside the **Script** field to see how the pipeline works. We will try some of the example code provided by Jenkins.
9. To do so, click on the **try sample Pipeline...** field and choose the **GitHub + Maven** option, as shown in the following screenshot:

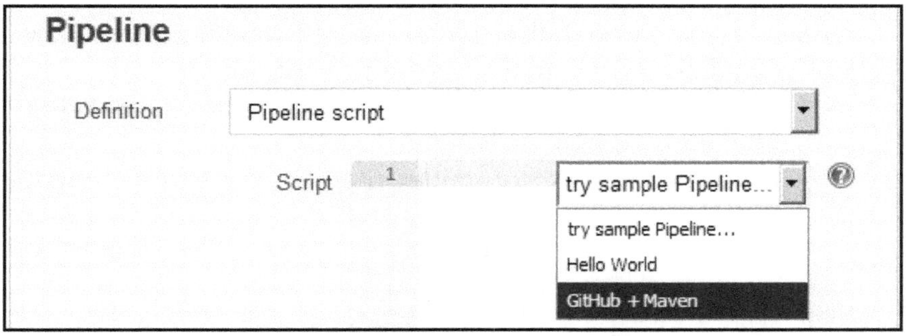

Choosing a sample pipeline script

10. This will fill the **Script** field with a sample code.
11. The code is shown as follows. It's in the Declarative Pipeline syntax form:

```
node {
  def mvnHome
  stage('Preparation') { // for display purposes
    // Get some code from a GitHub repository
    git 'https://github.com/jglick/
    simple-maven-project-with-tests.git'
    // Get the Maven tool.
    // ** NOTE: This 'M3' Maven tool must be configured
    // **       in the global configuration.
    mvnHome = tool 'M3'
  }
  stage('Build') {
    // Run the maven build
    if (isUnix()) {
      sh "'${mvnHome}/bin/mvn'
      -Dmaven.test.failure.ignore clean package"
    } else {
      bat(/"${mvnHome}\bin\mvn"
      -Dmaven.test.failure.ignore clean package/)
    }
  }
  stage('Results') {
    junit '**/target/surefire-reports/TEST-*.xml'
    archive 'target/*.jar'
  }
}
```

12. Let us quickly scan through the pipeline script (we will explore more about Declarative Pipeline syntax in the upcoming section):
    - The `node {}` is the main container which tells Jenkins to run the whole pipeline script on the Jenkins master.
    - Inside the `node {}` container, there are three more containers, shown as follows:

```
stage('Preparation') {...}
stage('Build') {...}
stage('Results') {...}
```

- The `Preparation` stage will download the Maven source code from a GitHub repository and will tell Jenkins to use the M3 Maven tool that is defined in the global configuration (we need to do this before we run our pipeline).
- The `Build` stage will build the Maven project.
- The `Results` stage will archive the build artifacts along with the JUnit testing results.

13. Save the changes made to the pipeline job by clicking on the **Save** button at the bottom of the page.

The Global Tool Configuration page

Before we run the pipeline, it is important that we take a look at the **Global Tool Configuration** page in Jenkins. This is the place where you configure tools that you think will be used globally across all your pipelines: for example, Java, Maven, Git, and so on.

Let's say you have multiple build agents (Jenkins slave agents) that build your Java code, and your build pipeline requires Java JDK, Maven, and Git. All you need to do is configure these tools inside the **Global Tool Configuration**, and Jenkins will automatically summon them while building your code on the build agents (Jenkins slave agents). There is no need for you to install these tools on any of the build agents.

Let us configure the Maven tool inside **Global Tool Configuration** to make our pipeline work. Follow the given steps:

1. To access the **Global Tool Configuration** page, do any one of the following:
    1. From the Jenkins dashboard, click on **Manage Jenkins** | **Global Tool Configuration**.
    2. Or paste the URL `http://<IP Address of your Jenkins server>:8080/configureTools/` in your browser.
2. Scroll all the way down to the **Maven** section and click on the **Add Maven** button. You will be presented with a list of options, as shown in the following screenshot. Fill the information in as follows:
    1. Provide a unique name for your Maven installation by filling the **Name** field. (Make it `M3` for our example pipeline to work.)

2. The **Install from Apache** option will appear by default. This will make Jenkins download the Maven application from Apache:

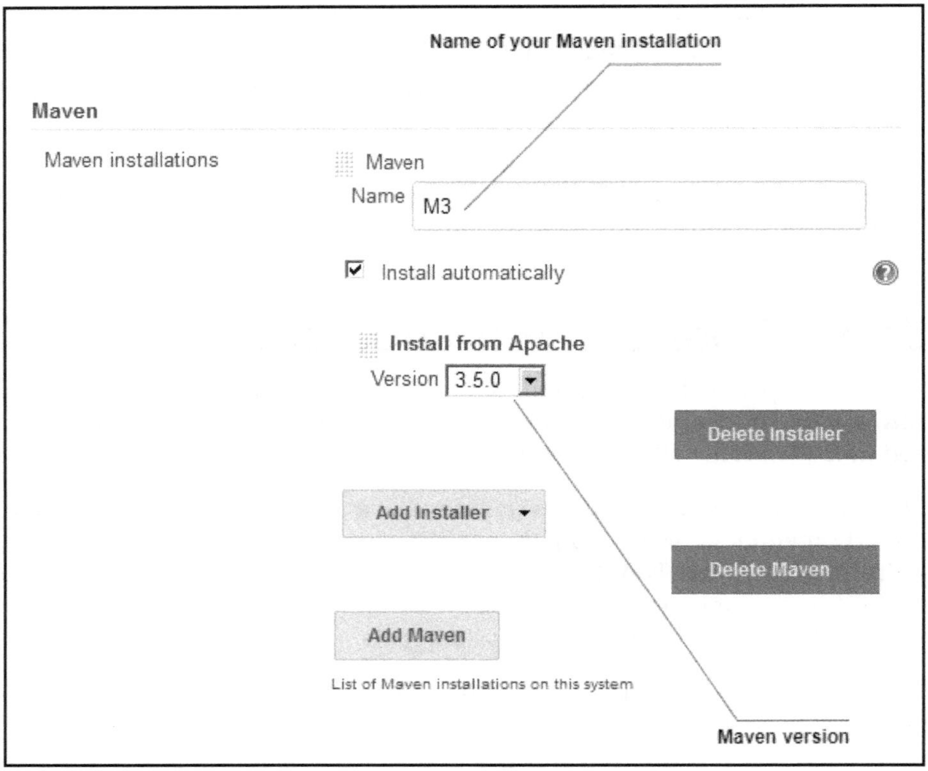

Configuring Maven inside the Global Tool Configuration

3. Choose the latest Maven version using the **Version** field; I have chosen to use Maven **3.5.0**, as shown in the previous screenshot.

To choose a different installer first, delete the existing installer by clicking on the **Delete Installer** button. Next, click on the **Add Installer** drop-down menu and choose a different installer. The other options, apart from **Install from Apache** are, **Run Batch Command**, **Run Shell Command**, and **Extract *.zip/*.tar.gz** (not shown in the screenshot).

3. The Java tool is also needed to build the Maven project, but since we are building our code on Jenkins master (which already has Java JDK), we can skip installing the Java tool for now.
4. Once you are done with configuring Maven, scroll down to the bottom of the page and click on the **Save** button.

Jenkins pipeline Stage View

Jenkins *Stage View* is a new feature that comes as a part of release 2.x. It works only with Jenkins Pipeline and Jenkins Multibranch pipeline jobs.

Jenkins Stage View lets you visualize the progress of various stages of your pipeline in real time. Let us see that in action by running our example pipeline:

1. On the Jenkins dashboard, under the **All** view tab, you will see your pipeline.
2. Click on the build trigger icon to run the pipeline, as shown in the following screenshot:

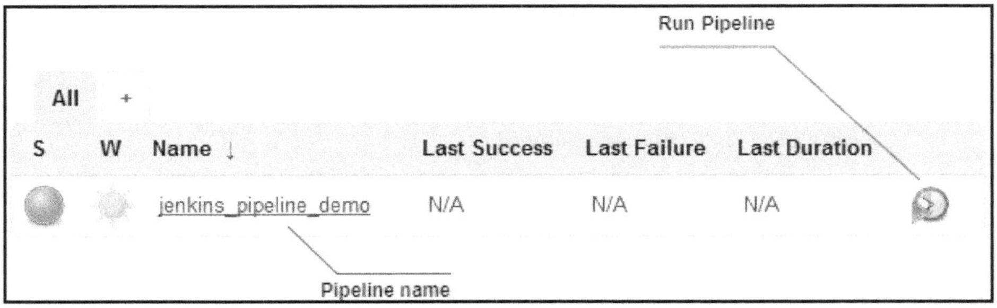

Viewing pipeline on the Jenkins dashboard

3. To get to the Stage View, click on your pipeline name (which also happens to be a link to your pipeline project page).

4. Alternatively, you can mouse over your pipeline name to get a drop-down menu with a list of action items and links, as shown in the following screenshot:

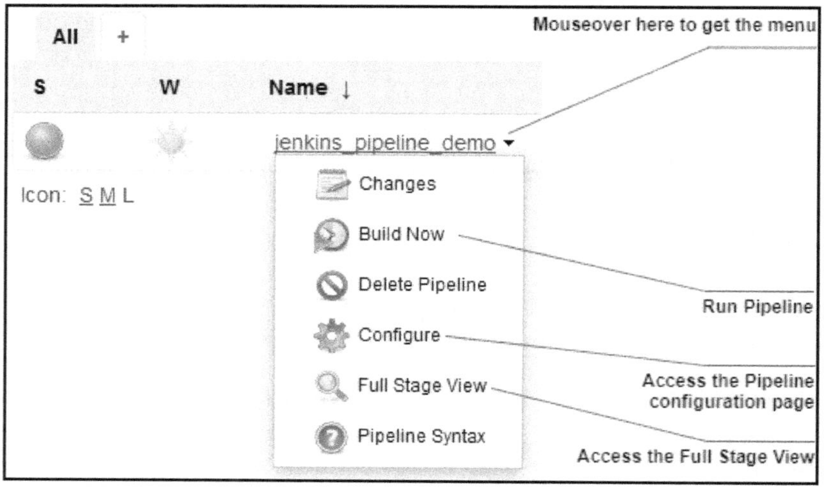

A view of the pipeline menu

5. The **Stage View** page will look something like the following screenshot:

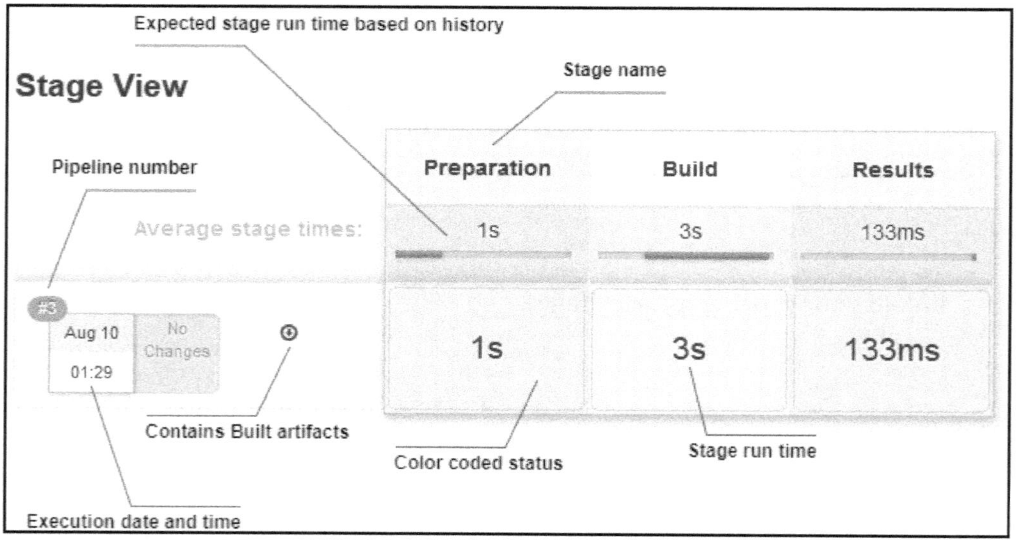

The Stage View

6. To view the build logs of a particular stage, mouse over the color-coded status box, and you should see an option to view the logs. Clicking it will open up a small pop-up window displaying the logs, as shown in the following screenshot:

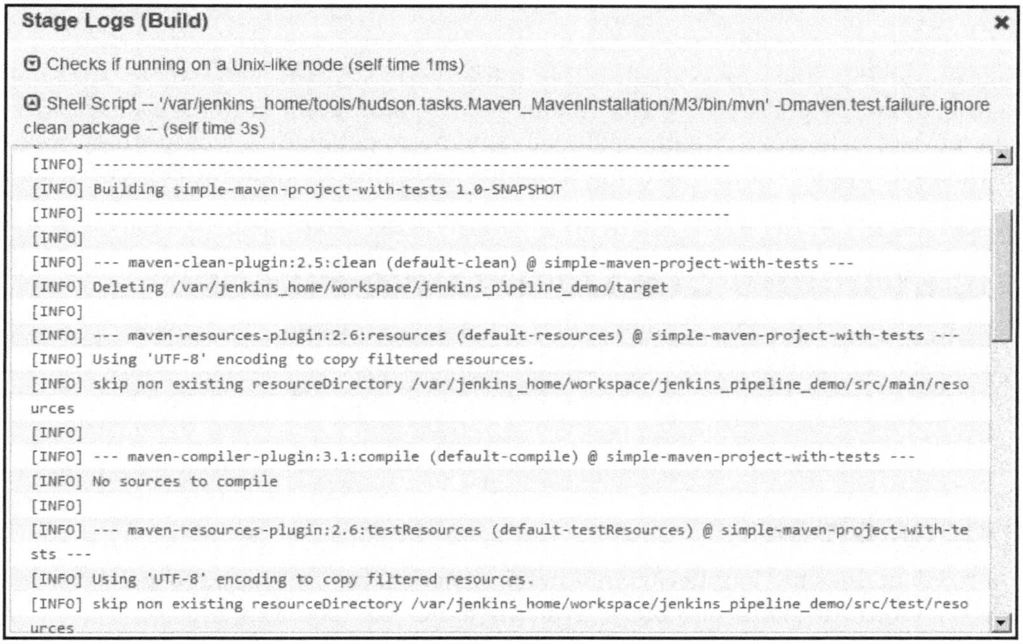

Jenkins individual stage logs

7. To view the complete build log, look for the **Build History** on the left-hand side. The **Build History** tab will list all the builds that have been run. Right-click on the desired build number and click **Console Output**:

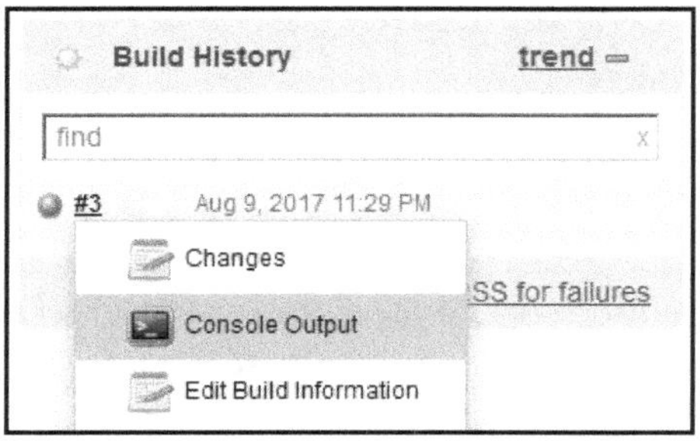

Accessing the console output

Declarative Pipeline syntax

In the previous section, we created a Jenkins pipeline to get a look at and feel for its various components. We utilized the pipeline script that followed a declarative syntax to define our pipeline.

The Declarative Pipeline syntax is a more simplified and structured version of the Groovy syntax, the latter being more powerful due to its programmability. In this section, we will learn about the Declarative Pipeline syntax in a bit more detail. This is important because in the upcoming chapters we will be using the same to define our CI and CD pipelines.

Basic structure of a Declarative Pipeline

In simple terms, a Declarative Pipeline is a collection of multiple `node` blocks (nodes), `stage` blocks (stages), directives, and steps. A single `node` block can have multiple `stage` blocks, and vice versa. We can also run multiple stages in parallel. Let's see each of them in detail.

The node block

A `node` block defines the Jenkins agent wherein its constituents (stage blocks, directives, and steps) should run. The `node` block structure looks like the following:

```
node ('<parameter>') {<constituents>}
```

The following gives more information about the `node` block:

- **Defines**: The node where the `stage`, directives, or steps should run
- **Constituents**: Multiple `stage` blocks, directives, or steps
- **Required**: Yes
- **Parameters**: Any, label

The stage block

A `stage` block is a collection of closely related steps and directives that have a common objective. The `stage` block structure looks like the following:

```
stage ('<parameter>') {<constituents>}
```

The following gives more information about the `stage` block:

- **Defines**: A collection of steps and directives
- **Constituents**: Multiple `node` blocks, directives, or steps
- **Required**: Yes
- **Parameters**: A string that is the name of the stage (mandatory)

Directives

The main purpose of directives is to assist the `node` block, `stage` block, and steps by providing them with any of the following elements: environments, options, parameters, triggers, tools.

The following gives more information about the `stage` block:

- **Defines**: The node where the stage should run
- **Constituents**: Environments, options, parameters, triggers, tools
- **Required**: No, but every CI/CD pipeline has it
- **Parameters**: None

Steps

Steps are the fundamental elements that make up the Declarative Pipeline. A step could be a batch script or a shell script, or any other command that's executable. Steps have various purposes, such as cloning a repository, building code, running tests, uploading artifacts to the repository server, performing static code analysis, and so on. In the upcoming section, we will see how to generate steps using the Jenkins pipeline syntax utility.

The following gives more information about the `stage` block:

- **Defines**: It tells Jenkins what to do
- **Constituents**: Commands, scripts, and so on. It's the fundamental block of a pipeline
- **Required**: No. But every CI/CD pipeline has it
- **Parameters**: None

The following is the pipeline code that we used earlier. The `node` block, the `stage` blocks, the directives, and the steps are highlighted using comments (`//`). As you can see, there are three `stage` blocks inside the `node` block. A `node` block can have multiple `stage` blocks. In addition to that, each `stage` block contains multiple steps, and one of them also contains a directive:

```
// Node block
node ('master') {
  // Directive 1
  def mvnHome

  // Stage block 1
  stage('Preparation') {
    // Step 1
    git 'https://github.com/jglick/simple-maven-project-with-tests.git'
    // Directive 2
    mvnHome = tool 'M3'
   }

   // Stage block 2
   stage('Build') {
     // Step 2
     sh "'${mvnHome}/bin/mvn' clean install"
   }

   // Stage block 3
   stage('Results') {
     // Step 3
     junit '**/target/surefire-reports/TEST-*.xml'
     // Step 4
     archive 'target/*.jar'
   }

}
```

In the preceding code, note the line: `node ('master') {`. Here, the string `master` is a parameter (`label`) that tells Jenkins to use the Jenkins master for running the contents of the `node` block.

If you choose the parameter value as any, then all the stage nodes and their respective steps and directives will be executed on any one of the available Jenkins slave agents.

We will learn more about the Declarative Pipeline in the upcoming chapters, wherein we will try to write a CI/CD pipeline using it.

> For more information about Declarative Pipeline syntax, refer to `https://jenkins.io/doc/book/pipeline/syntax/#declarative-sections`.
> To get a list of all the available steps that are compatible with the Declarative Pipeline, refer to `https://jenkins.io/doc/pipeline/steps/`.

Jenkins pipeline syntax utility

The Jenkins pipeline syntax utility is a quick and easy way to create pipeline code. The pipeline syntax utility is available inside the Jenkins pipeline job; see the screenshot: *The pipeline section* in the *Creating a Jenkins pipeline job* section.

In this section, we will recreate the pipeline that we created in the previous section, but this time using the pipeline syntax utility.

Prerequisite

Before we begin, make sure you have the following things ready:

- The Maven tool configured inside the **Global Tool Configuration** page (refer to the *The Global Tool Configuration page* section)
- Install **Pipeline Maven Integration Plugin**
- The Java tool is also needed to build the Maven project, but since we are building our code on Jenkins master (which already has Java JDK), we can skip installing the Java tool

Installing the Pipeline Maven Integration Plugin

Follow the given steps to install the **Pipeline Maven Integration Plugin**. The following plugin will allow us to use the Maven tool inside our pipeline code:

1. From the Jenkins dashboard, click on **Manage Jenkins** | **Manage Plugins** | **Available** tab.
2. Type `Pipeline Maven Integration` inside the **Filter** field to search the respective plugin, as shown in the following screenshot:

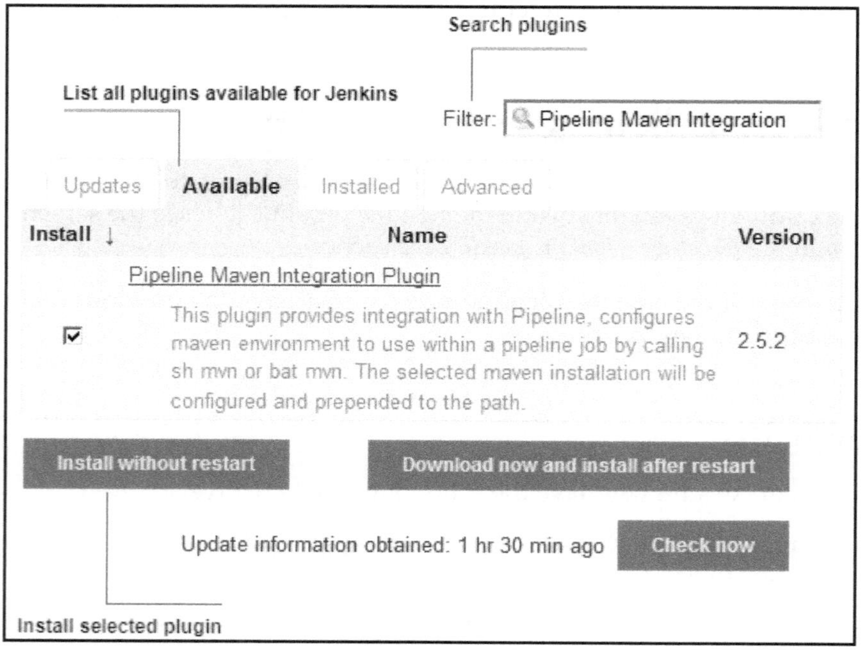

The Plugin Manager page

3. Click on the checkbox to select the respective plugin, and then click on the **Install without restart** button to install it.
4. Once you click on the **Install without restart** button, you will see the plugin getting installed, as shown in the following screenshot. Jenkins will first check for the network connection, after which it will install the dependencies, and lastly, it will install the plugin.

5. Some plugins might need a restart before they can be used. To do so, check the option, **Restart Jenkins when installation is complete and no jobs are running**:

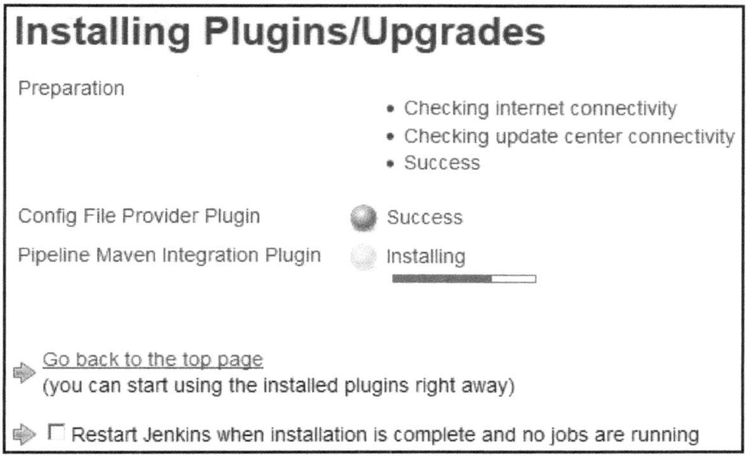

Plugin installation in progress

Creating a Jenkins pipeline using the pipeline syntax utility

Follow the given steps to create a new Jenkins pipeline job:

1. From the Jenkins dashboard, click on the **New Item** link.
2. On the resultant page, you will be presented with various types of Jenkins jobs to choose from.
3. Choose **Pipeline**, and give a name to your pipeline using the **Enter an item** name field.
4. Once you are done, click on the **OK** button at the bottom of the page.
5. We will quickly navigate to the pipeline section by clicking on the **Pipeline** tab.

6. Under the **Pipeline** tab, click on the link named **Pipeline Syntax**. This will open up a new tab, as shown in the following screenshot:

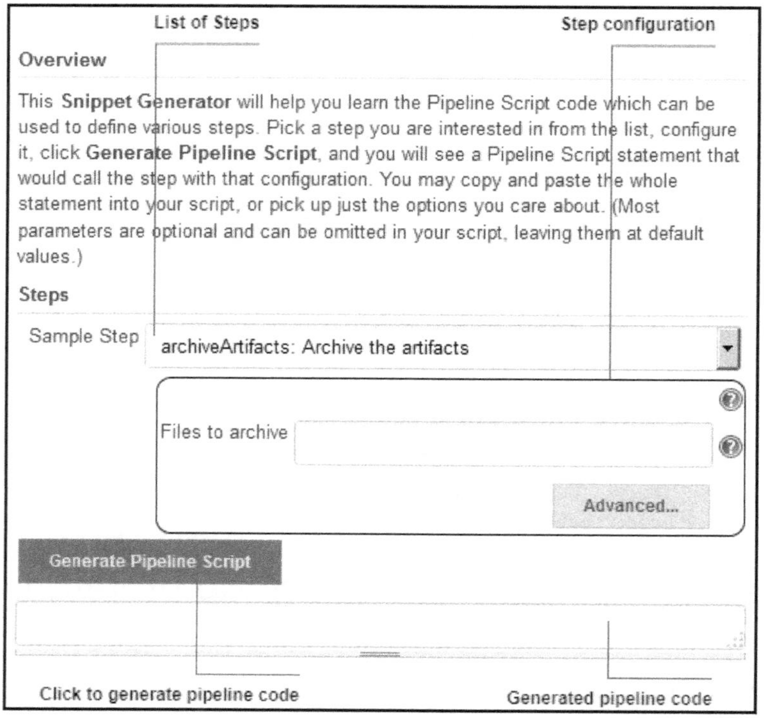

The Pipeline Syntax page

7. We will be using the following **Snippet Generator** to create pipeline code for various blocks and steps.
8. Let us first generate a code for a `node` block:
    1. On the **Pipeline Syntax** page, under the **Steps** section, choose **node: Allocate node** using the **Sample Step** field, as shown in the following screenshot.
    2. In the **Label** field, add a string `master`. By doing so we tell Jenkins to use the Jenkins master as the node of choice to execute our pipeline.
    3. Click on the **Generate Pipeline Script** button to generate the code.
    4. Copy the generated code and keep it aside on a text editor:

Generating code for the node block

9. Now, let us create two `stage` blocks named `Preparation` and `Build`:
    1. On the **Pipeline Syntax** page, under the **Steps** section, choose **stage: Stage** using the **Sample Step** field, as shown in the following screenshot.
    2. In the **Stage Name** field, add a string `Preparation`.
    3. Click on the **Generate Pipeline Script** button to generate the code.
    4. Copy the generated code and paste it inside the `node` block that we generated earlier:

Generating code for the stage block

10. Similarly, repeat *step 9* to create a `stage` block named `Build`. Paste the generated code inside the `node` block and after the `Preparation` (the `stage` block).
11. Our pipeline code, so far, should look something like the following (without the `// some block` lines):

```
node('master') {

  stage('Preparation') {
  }

  stage('Build') {
  }

}
```

12. Let us now create a step to download the source code from GitHub:
    1. On the **Pipeline Syntax** page, under the **Steps** section, choose **git: Git** using the **Sample Step** field, as shown in the following screenshot.
    2. In the **Repository URL** field, add the link to the example GitHub repository: `https://github.com/jglick/simple-maven-project-with-tests.git`.
    3. Leave the rest of the options as is.
    4. Click on the **Generate Pipeline Script** button to generate the code.
    5. Copy the generated code, and paste it into the `Preparation` (the `stage` block) that we generated earlier:

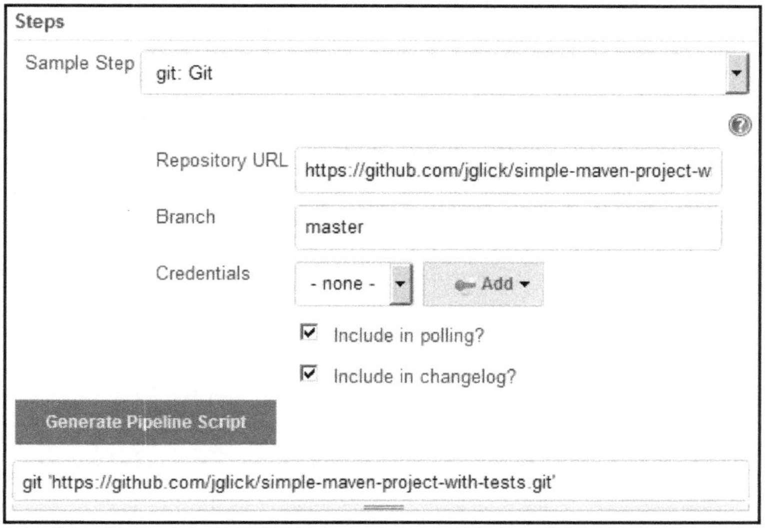

Generating code for the Git step

13. Next, let us generate a directive that will tell Jenkins to use the M3 Maven tool that we have configured inside the **Global Tool Configuration**:
    1. On the **Pipeline Syntax** page, under the **Steps** section, choose **withMaven: Provide Maven environment** using the **Sample Step** field, as shown in the following screenshot.
    2. In the **Maven** field, choose `M3`, which is the Maven tool that we have configured inside the **Global Tool Configuration**.
    3. Leave the rest of the options as is.
    4. Click on the **Generate Pipeline Script** button to generate the code.

5. Copy the generated code and paste it into the `Build` (the `stage` block) that we generated earlier:

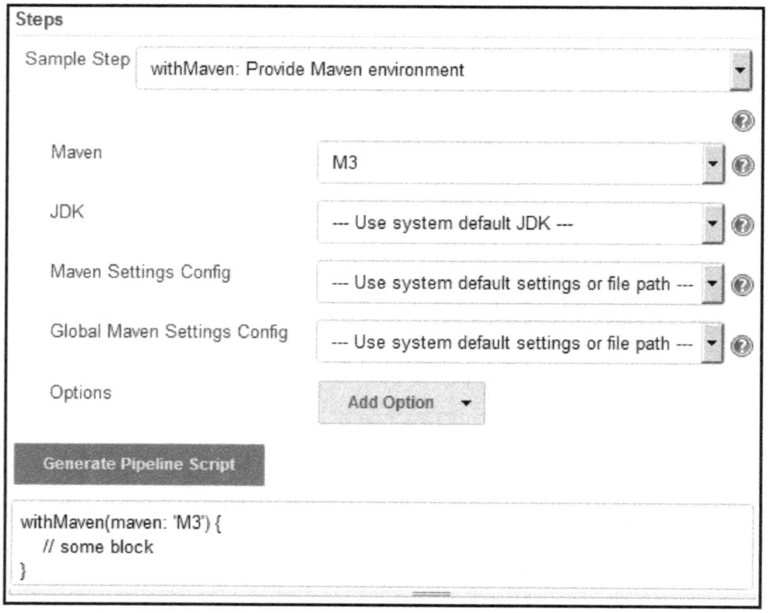

Generating code for the withMaven directive

14. Lastly, generate a pipeline code for our Maven build command:
    1. On the **Pipeline Syntax** page, under the **Steps** section, choose **sh: Shell Script** using the **Sample Step** field, as shown in the following screenshot. This is a step to create a shell script.
    2. In the **Shell Script** field, type `mvn -Dmaven.test.failure.ignore clean package`, which is the Maven command to build, test, and package the code. This will be the content of our shell script.
    3. Click on the **Generate Pipeline Script** button to generate the code.
    4. Copy the generated code and paste it into the `withMaven` (directive) that we generated earlier:

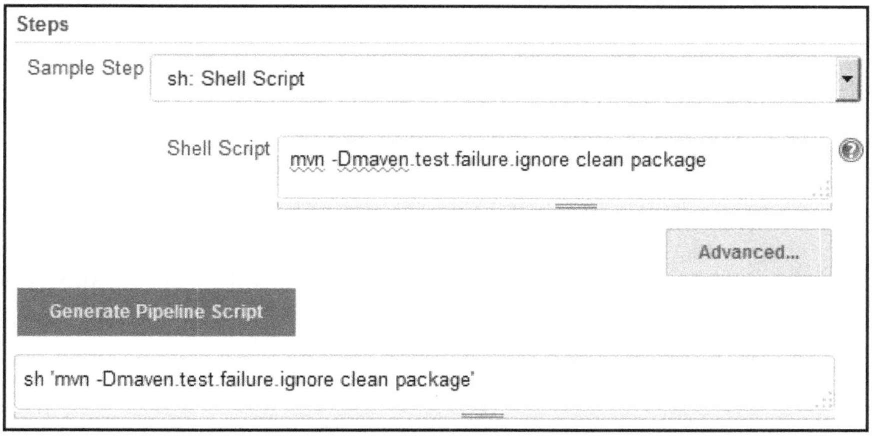

Generating code for the maven build

15. Our final pipeline script should look something like the following (without the `// some block` lines):

```
node('master') {

  stage('Preparation') {
    git 'https://github.com/jglick/
    simple-maven-project-with-tests.git'
  }

  stage('Build') {
    withMaven(maven: 'M3') {
      sh 'mvn -Dmaven.test.failure.ignore clean
      package'
    }
  }

}
```

16. Now switch to the pipeline job configuration page.
17. Scroll to the **Pipeline** section and paste the preceding pipeline code inside the **Script** field.
18. Click on the **Save** button at the bottom of the page.

We will see more examples in the upcoming chapters when we try to create a CI/CD pipeline using the Declarative Pipeline syntax, utilizing the pipeline syntax utility.

Multibranch pipeline

In this section, we will learn about the multibranch pipeline job in Jenkins. This is one of the new features added to Jenkins release 2.x.

The Multibranch pipeline allows you to automatically create a pipeline for each branch on your source control repository. This is depicted in the following screenshot. A Multibranch pipeline works using a **Jenkinsfile** that is stored along with your source code inside a version control repository. A **Jenkinsfile** is nothing but a pipeline script that defines your CI pipeline:

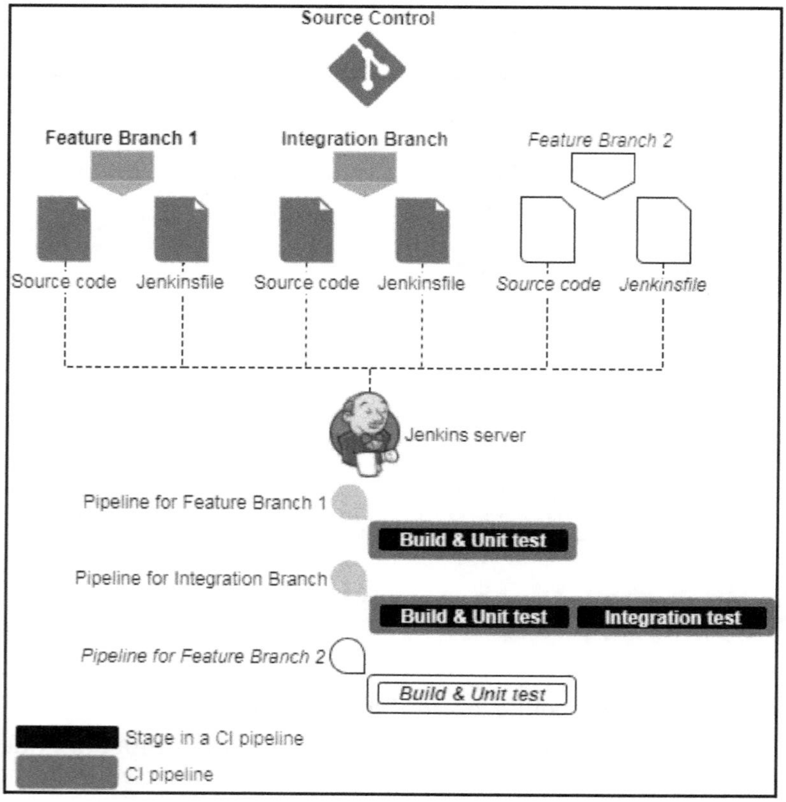

Auto-generated pipeline for a new branch

In addition to that, the Multibranch pipeline is designed to trigger a build whenever there is a new code change on any of the branches on your Git/GitHub repository. This is depicted in the following screenshot:

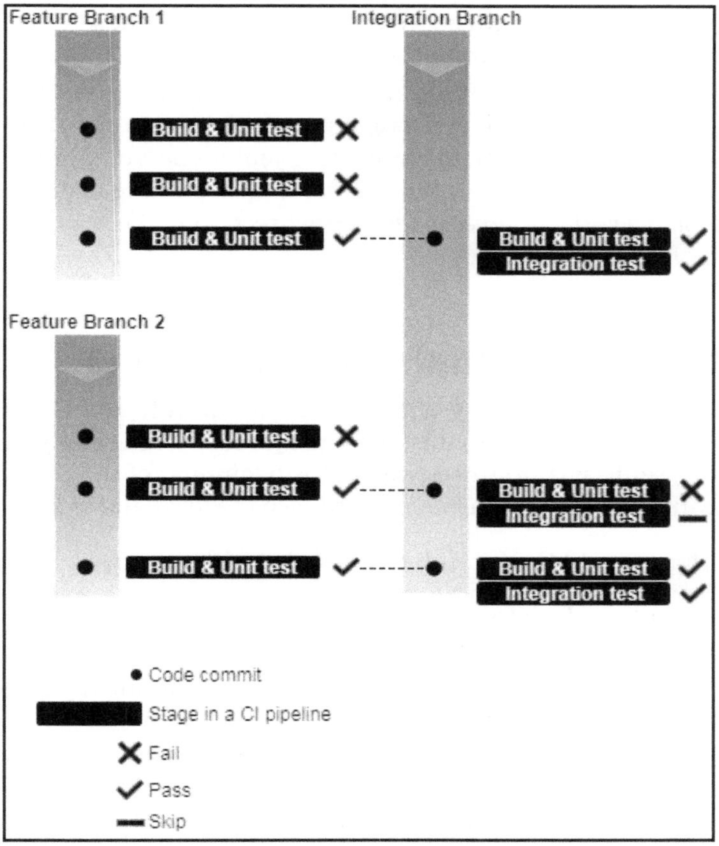

Usage of multibranch pipeline for continuous integration

Prerequisite

Before we begin, make sure you have the following things ready:

- The Maven tool configured inside the **Global Tool Configuration** page (refer to the section: *The Global Tool Configuration page*).
- Install **Pipeline Maven Integration Plugin**.
- The Java tool is also needed to build the Maven project, but since we are building our code on Jenkins master (which already has Java JDK), we can skip installing the Java tool.

- Install **GitHub plugin** (already installed if you have chosen to install the recommended plugins during the Jenkins setup wizard).
- Make sure your Jenkins URL is accessible from the internet. If you are using a staging or a development environment to perform this exercise, and your Jenkins server doesn't have a domain name, your Jenkins server might not be accessible from the internet. To make your Jenkins URL accessible over the internet, refer to the *Exposing your local server to the internet* section in the `Appendix`, *Supporting Tools and Installation Guide.*

Adding GitHub credentials inside Jenkins

In order to make Jenkins communicate with GitHub, we need to add GitHub account credentials inside Jenkins. We will do this using the Jenkins **Credentials Plugin**. If you have followed the Jenkins setup wizard (discussed at the beginning of the chapter), you will find the **Credentials** feature on the Jenkins dashboard (see the left-hand side menu).

Follow the given steps to add the GitHub credentials inside Jenkins:

1. From the Jenkins dashboard, click on **Credentials** | **System** | **Global credentials (unrestricted)**.
2. On the **Global credentials (unrestricted)** page, from the left-hand side menu, click on the **Add Credentials** link.
3. You will be presented with a bunch of fields to configure (see the following screenshot):
    1. Choose **Username with password** for the **Kind** field.
    2. Choose **Global (Jenkins, nodes, items, all child items, etc)** for the **Scope** field.
    3. Add your GitHub username to the **Username** field.
    4. Add your GitHub password to the **Password** field.
    5. Give a unique ID to your credentials by typing a string in the **ID** field.
    6. Add some meaningful description to the **Description** field.
    7. Click on the **Save** button once done:

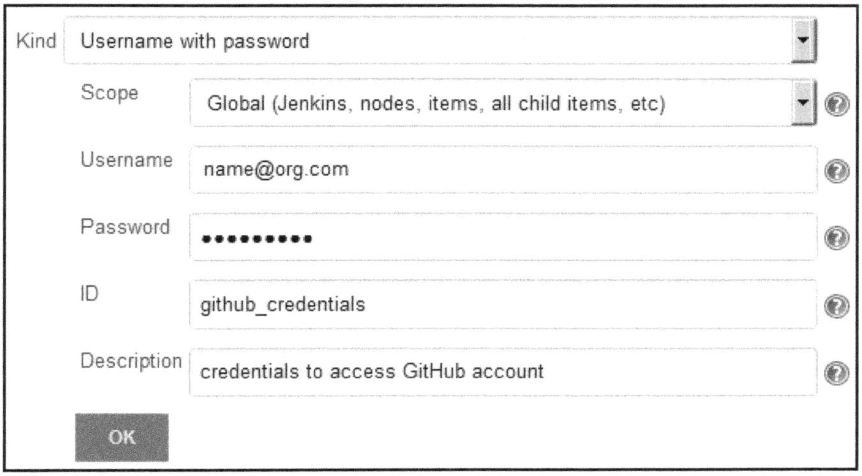

Adding GitHub credentials inside Jenkins

4. And that's how you save credentials inside Jenkins. We will use these GitHub credentials shortly.

Configuring Webhooks on GitHub from Jenkins

Now that we have saved GitHub account credentials inside Jenkins, let's configure Jenkins to talk to GitHub. We will do this by configuring the GitHub settings inside the Jenkins configuration.

Carefully follow the given steps to configure GitHub settings inside Jenkins:

1. From the Jenkins dashboard, click on **Manage Jenkins** | **Configure System**.
2. On the resultant Jenkins configuration page, scroll all the way down to the **GitHub** section.
3. Under the **GitHub** section, click on the **Add GitHub Server** button and choose **GitHub Servers** from the available drop-down list. Doing so will display a bunch of options for you to configure.
4. Let us configure them one by one, as follows:
    1. Give your GitHub server a name by adding a string to the **Name** field.
    2. Under the **API URL** field, add `https://api.github.com` (default value) if you are using a public GitHub account. Otherwise, if you are using GitHub Enterprise, then specify its respective API endpoint.

3. Make sure the **Manage hooks** option is checked:

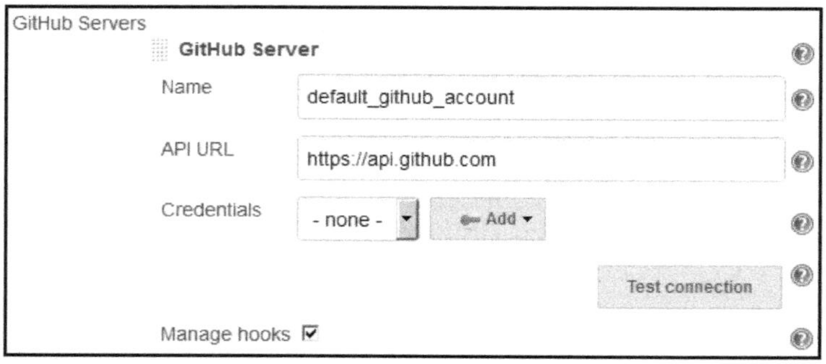

Configuring the GitHub server

4. Click on the **Advanced...** button (you will see two of them; click on the second one). Doing so will display a few more fields to configure.
5. Under the **Additional actions** field, click on **Manage additional GitHub actions** and choose **Convert login and password to token** from the available list (you will see only one option to choose).
6. This will further disclose new fields to configure.
7. Select the **From credentials** option (active by default). Using the **Credentials** field, choose the GitHub credentials that we created in the previous section (`ID: github_credentials`).
8. Next, click on the **Create token credentials** button. This will generate a new personal access token on your GitHub account:

Converting GitHub credentials to a token

   9. To view your personal access token on GitHub, log in to your GitHub account and navigate to **Settings** | **Developer settings** | **Personal access tokens**:

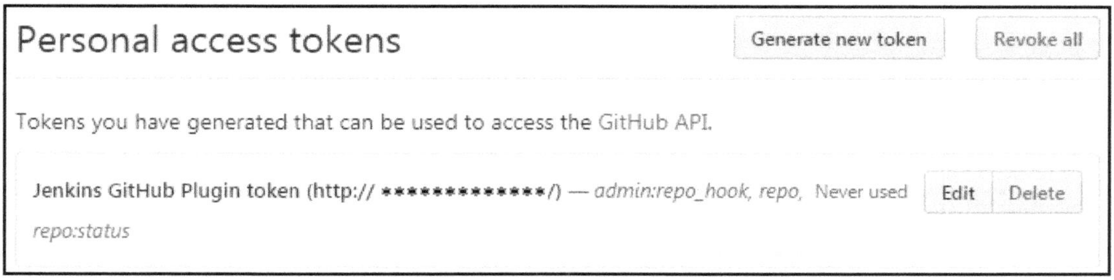

Personal access token on GitHub

   10. Once done, click on the **Save** button at the bottom of the Jenkins configuration page.
   11. An entry of the respective personal access token will also be added inside the Jenkins credentials. To view it, navigate to **Jenkins dashboard** | **Credentials** | **System** | `api.github.com`, and you should see a credential entry of the **Kind** secret text.

5. We are not yet done with our GitHub configuration inside Jenkins. Follow the remaining steps as follows:
   1. From the Jenkins dashboard, click on **Manage Jenkins** | **Configure System**.
   2. Scroll all the way down to the **GitHub** section.
   3. Using the **Credentials** field, choose the newly generated credentials of the **Kind** secret text (the personal access token entry inside Jenkins).
   4. Now, click on the **Test connection** button to test our connection between Jenkins and GitHub.

5. Once done, click on the **Save** button at the bottom of your Jenkins configuration page:

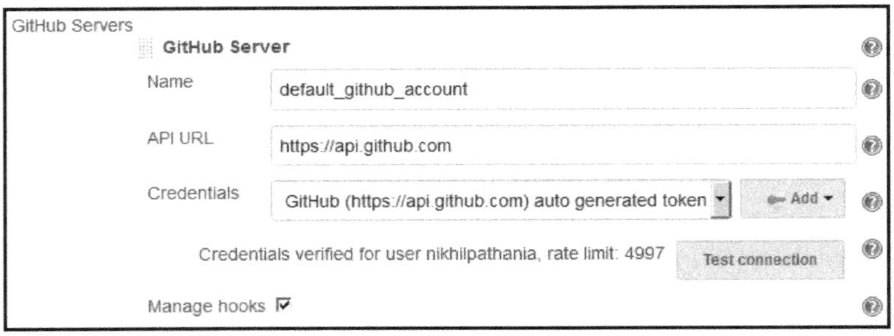

Testing the connection between Jenkins and GitHub

6. We are now done with configuring GitHub settings inside Jenkins.

Create a new repository on GitHub

In this section, we will create a new repository on GitHub. Make sure you have Git installed on the machine that you will use to perform the steps mentioned in the following section (refer to the *Installing Git on Windows/Linux* section in the `Appendix`, *Supporting Tools and Installation Guide*).

Follow the given steps to create a repository on GitHub:

1. Log in to your GitHub account.
2. To keep things simple, we will reuse the source code from the repository at `https://github.com/jglick/simple-maven-project-with-tests.git`. This is the repository that we have been using to create a Jenkins pipeline.
3. The easiest way to reuse a GitHub repository is to fork it. To do so, just access the above repository from your internet browser and click on the **Fork** button, as shown in the following screenshot:

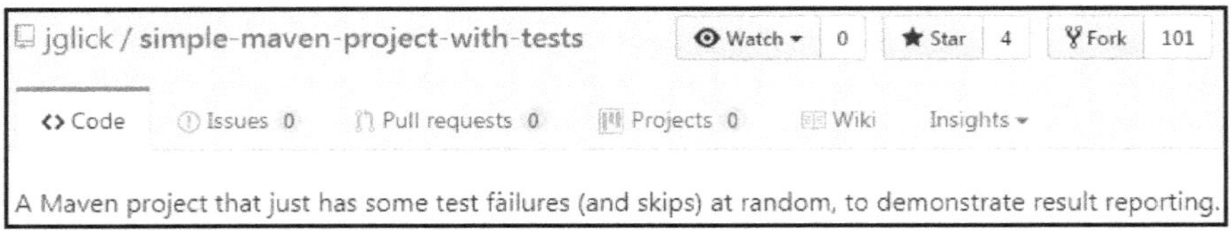

Forking a GitHub project

4. Once done, a replica of the preceding repository will be visible on your GitHub account.

Using a Jenkinsfile

Jenkins multibranch pipeline utilizes Jenkinsfile. In the following section, we will learn how to create a Jenkinsfile. We will reuse the example pipeline script that we created in the previous section to create our Jenkinsfile. Follow the given steps:

1. Log in to your GitHub account.
2. Navigate to the forked repository `simple-maven-project-with-tests`.
3. Once on the repository page, click on the **Create new file** button to create a new empty file that will be our Jenkinsfile, as shown in the following screenshot:

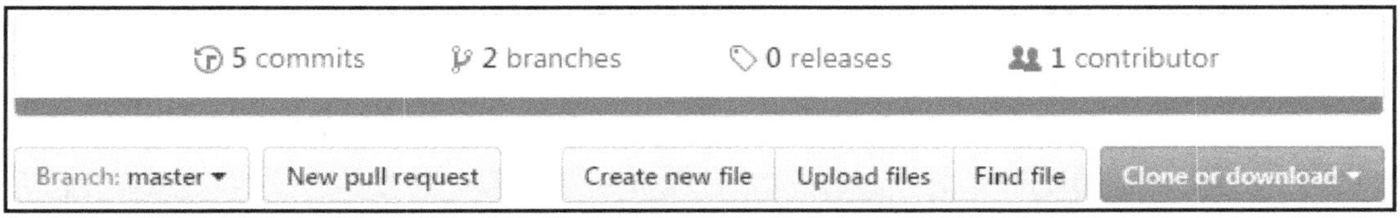

Creating a new file on GitHub

4. Name your new file `Jenkinsfile` by filling the empty text box, as shown in the following screenshot:

Naming your new file on GitHub

5. Add the following code to your `Jenkinsfile`:

```
node ('master') {
  checkout scm
  stage('Build') {
    withMaven(maven: 'M3') {
```

```
      if (isUnix()) {
        sh 'mvn -Dmaven.test.failure.ignore clean package'
      }
      else {
        bat 'mvn -Dmaven.test.failure.ignore clean package'
      }
    }
  }
  stage('Results') {
    junit '**/target/surefire-reports/TEST-*.xml'
    archive 'target/*.jar'
  }
}
```

6. Once done, commit the new file by adding a meaningful comment, as shown in the following screenshot:

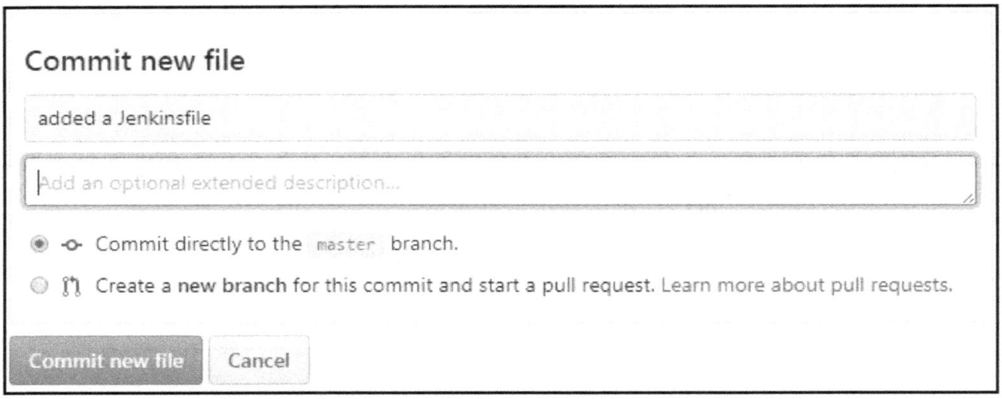

Committing your new file on GitHub

Creating a Multibranch pipeline in Jenkins

Follow the given steps to create a new Jenkins pipeline job:

1. From the Jenkins dashboard, click on the **New Item** link.
2. On the resultant page, you will be presented with various types of Jenkins jobs to choose from.
3. Choose **Multibranch Pipeline**, and give a name to your pipeline using the **Enter an item name** field.

4. Once you are done, click on the **OK** button at the bottom of the page.
5. Scroll to the section **Branch Sources**. This is the place where we configure the GitHub repository that we want to use.
6. Click on the **Add Source** button and choose **GitHub**. You will be presented with a list of fields to configure. Let us see them one by one (see the following screenshot):
    1. For the **Credentials** field, choose the GitHub account credentials (**Kind** as **Username with Password**) that we created in the previous section.
    2. Under the **Owner** field, specify the name of your GitHub organization or GitHub user account.
    3. The moment you do so, the **Repository** field will list all the repositories that are on your GitHub account.
    4. Choose `simple-maven-project-with-tests` under the **Repository** field.
    5. Leave the rest of the options at their default values:

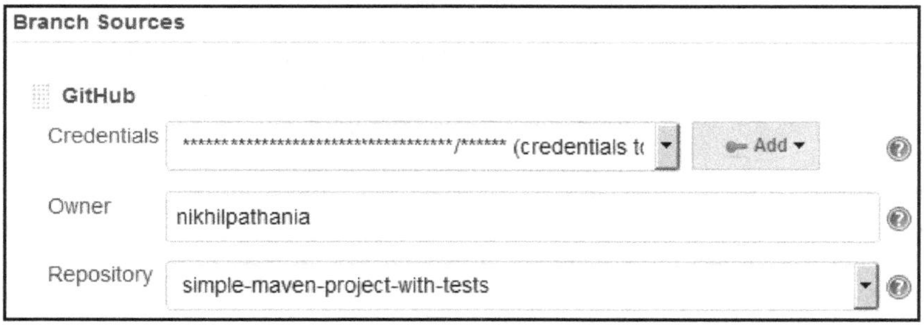

Configuring the multibranch pipeline

7. Scroll all the way down and click on the **Save** button.

Re-register the Webhooks

Before we proceed, let us re-register the Webhooks for all our Jenkins pipelines:

1. To do so, from the Jenkins dashboard, click on **Manage Jenkins** | **Configure System**.
2. On the Jenkins configuration page, scroll all the way down to the **GitHub** section.
3. Under the **GitHub** section, click on the **Advanced...** button (you will see two of them; click on the second one).

4. This will display a few more fields and options. Click on the **Re-register hooks for all jobs** button.
5. The preceding action will create new Webhooks for our multibranch pipeline on the respective repository inside your GitHub account. Do the following to view the Webhooks on GitHub:
    1. Log in to your GitHub account.
    2. Go to your GitHub repository, `simple-maven-project-with-tests` in our case.
    3. Click on the repository **Settings**, as shown in the following screenshot:

Repository Settings

    4. On the Repository **Settings** page, click on **Webhooks** from the left-hand side menu. You should see the Webhooks for your Jenkins server, as shown in the following screenshot:

Webhooks on GitHub repository

Jenkins Multibranch pipeline in action

Follow the given steps:

1. From the Jenkins dashboard, click on your Multibranch pipeline.
2. On your Jenkins Multibranch pipeline page, from the left-hand side menu, click on the **Scan Repository Now** link. This will scan the repository for branches with Jenkinsfile, and will immediately run a pipeline for every branch that has got a Jenkinsfile, as shown in the following screenshot:

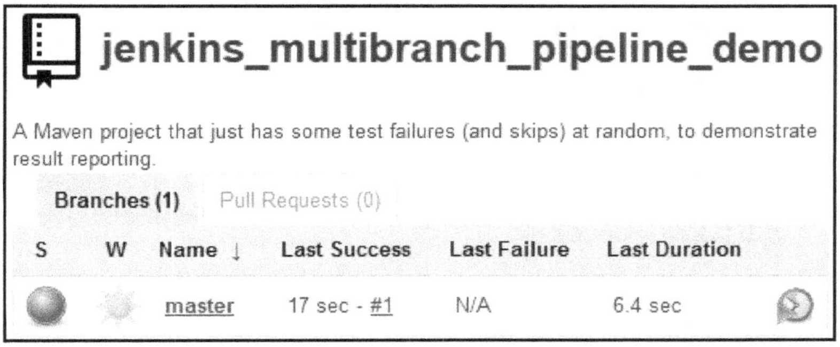

Pipeline for the master branch

3. On your Multibranch pipeline page, from the left-hand side menu, click on **Scan Repository Log**. You will see something like that which is shown as follows. Notice the highlighted code. You can see that the `master` branch met the criteria, as it had a Jenkinsfile and a pipeline was secluded for it. There was no pipeline scheduled for the testing branch since there was no Jenkinsfile on it:

```
Started by user nikhil pathania
[Mon Aug 14 22:00:57 UTC 2017] Starting branch indexing...
22:00:58 Connecting to https://api.github.com using
******/****** (credentials to access GitHub account)
22:00:58 Connecting to https://api.github.com using
******/****** (credentials to access GitHub account)
Examining nikhilpathania/simple-maven-project-with-tests

  Checking branches...

  Getting remote branches...

    Checking branch master

  Getting remote pull requests...
```

```
        'Jenkinsfile' found
      Met criteria
Scheduled build for branch: master

      Checking branch testing
        'Jenkinsfile' not found
      Does not meet criteria

    2 branches were processed

    Checking pull-requests...

    0 pull requests were processed

Finished examining nikhilpathania/simple-maven-project-with-
tests

[Mon Aug 14 22:01:00 UTC 2017] Finished branch indexing.
Indexing took 2.3 sec
Finished: SUCCESS
```

4. You need not always scan the repository. The GitHub Webhooks is configured to trigger a pipeline automatically whenever there is a push or a new branch on your GitHub repository. Remember, a Jenkinsfile should also be present on the respective branch to tell Jenkins what it needs to do when it finds a change in the repository.

Creating a new feature branch to test the multibranch pipeline

Let us now create a feature branch out of the master branch and see if Jenkins can run a pipeline for it:

1. To do so, log in to your GitHub account.
2. Go to your respective GitHub repository; in our case it's `simple-maven-project-with-tests`.

3. Click on the **Branch: master** button and type a name for your new branch in the empty text box. Next, click on the **Create branch: feature** option to create a new branch named feature, as shown in the following screenshot:

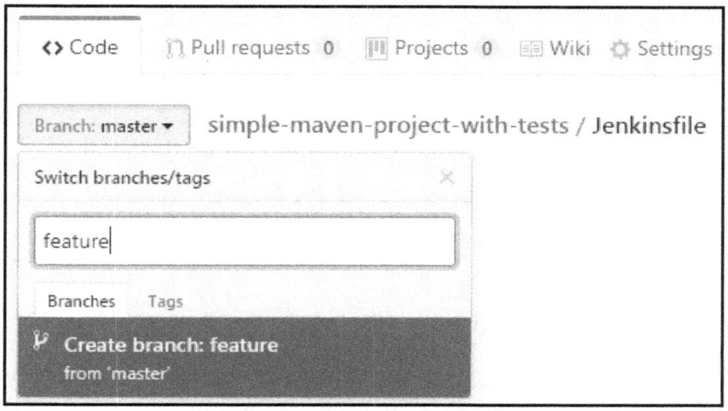

Creating a feature branch

4. This should immediately trigger a pipeline inside Jenkins for our new feature branch:

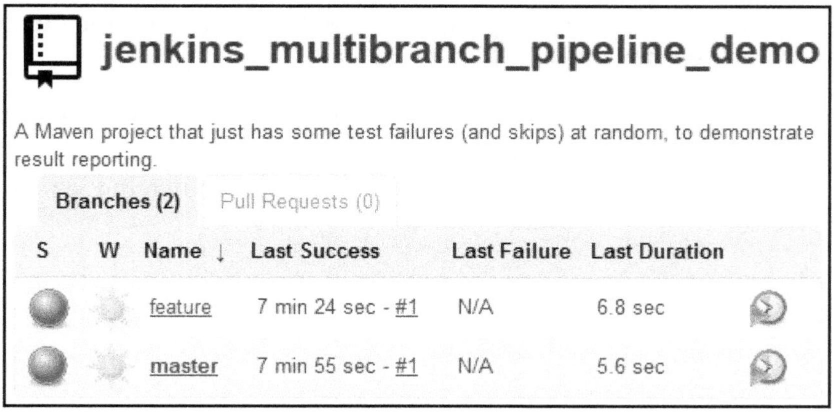

Pipeline for the new feature branch

Jenkins Blue Ocean

The Jenkins Blue Ocean is a completely new way of interacting with Jenkins. It's more of a UI sidekick to the main Jenkins application. The following are some the features of Jenkins Blue Ocean:

- Improved visualizations
- Pipeline editor
- Personalization
- Quick and easy pipeline setup wizard for Git and GitHub

The pipelines that you create using your classic Jenkins interface can be visualized in the new Jenkins Blue Ocean, and vice versa. As I said earlier, Jenkins Blue Ocean is a UI sidekick to the main Jenkins application.

In the following section, we will visualize the Jenkins pipelines that we created in the previous section in Blue Ocean. We will also create a new pipeline, just to get a look at and feel for the new Jenkins Blue Ocean interface.

Installing the Jenkins Blue Ocean plugin

In order to use the Jenkins **Blue Ocean** plugin, we need to install the **Blue Ocean** plugin for Jenkins. Follow the given steps:

1. From the Jenkins dashboard, click on **Manage Jenkins** | **Manage Plugins**.
2. On the **Plugin Manager** page, click on the **Available** tab.
3. Using the **Filter** option, search for `Blue Ocean`, as shown in the following screenshot:

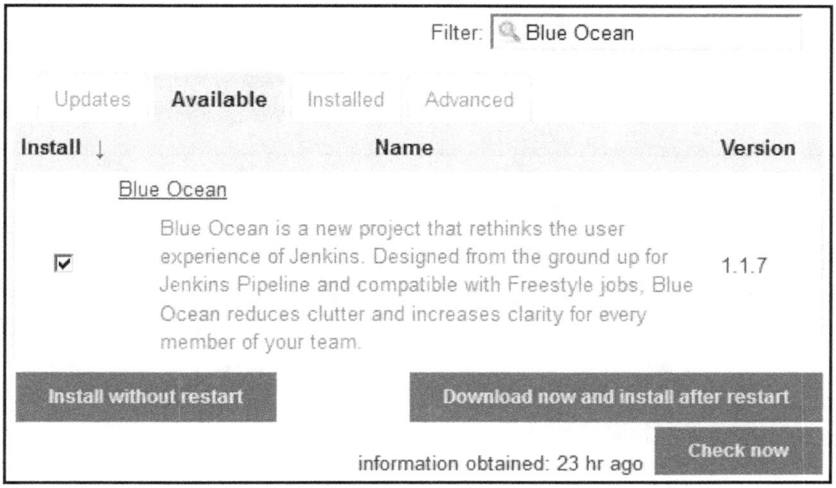

Installing the Jenkins Blue Ocean plugin

4. From the list of items, choose **Blue Ocean** and click on **Install without restart**. You only need Blue Ocean and nothing else.
5. The dependency list for Blue Ocean is big, so you will see a lot of stuff getting installed along with the **Blue Ocean** plugin on the **Installing Plugins/Upgrades** page.

View your regular Jenkins pipeline in Blue Ocean

In this section, we will try to visualize our existing Jenkins pipelines that we have created in the previous sections:

1. On the Jenkins dashboard, you should now see a new link on the left-hand side menu with the name **Open Blue Ocean**.
2. Click on the **Open Blue Ocean** link to go to the Jenkins Blue Ocean dashboard. The following is what you should see (refer to the following screenshot):
    1. The **Administration** link will take you to the **Manage Jenkins** page.
    2. The **Pipelines** link will take you to the Jenkins Blue Ocean dashboard that you are seeing now.
    3. The icon (arrow within a square) will take you to the classic Jenkins dashboard.

4. The **New Pipeline** button will open up the pipeline creation wizard for Git- and GitHub-based projects.
5. A list of pipelines (highlighted as **e**):

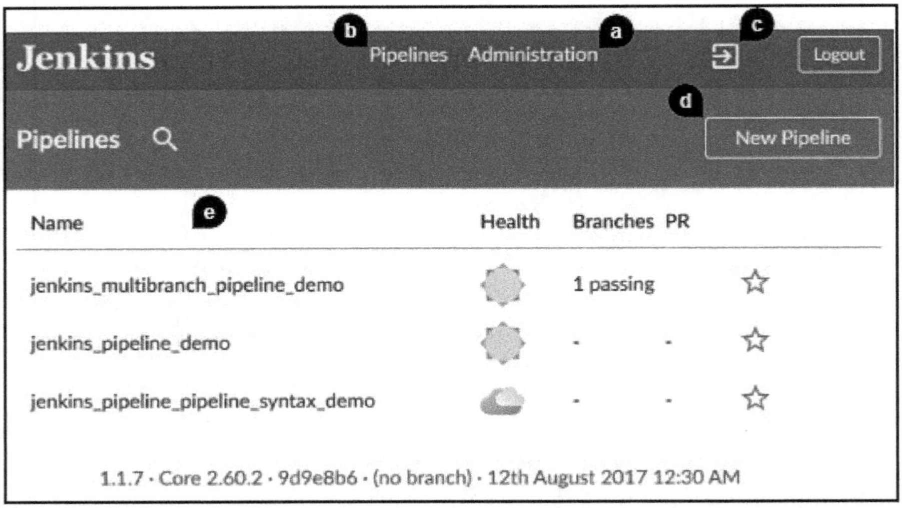

The Jenkins Blue Ocean dashboard

3. Let us have a look at our multibranch pipeline. Click on your multibranch pipeline from the Jenkins Blue Ocean dashboard. Doing so will open up the respective multibranch pipeline page, as shown in the following screenshot:
    1. The button (highlighted as **a**) will take you to the pipeline configuration page.
    2. The **Activity** tab will list all the current and past pipelines.
    3. The **Branches** tab will show you an aggregate view of the pipelines for each branch.
    4. The **Pull Requests** tab will list all the open pull requests on your branches.

5. The button (highlighted as **e**) is used to rerun the pipeline:

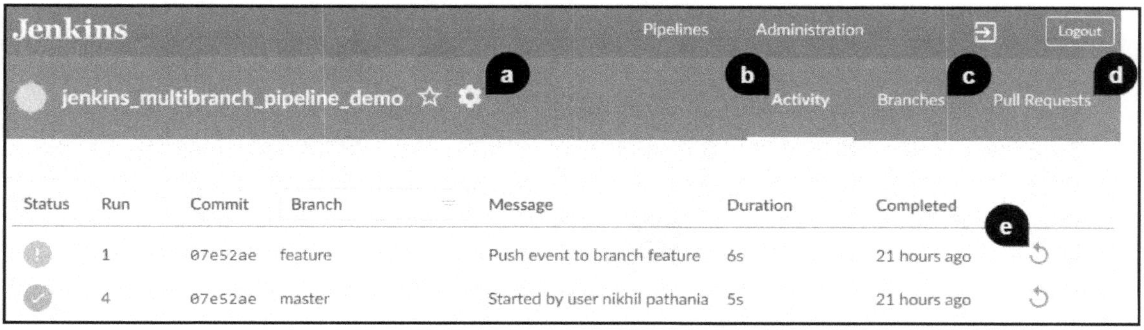

Multibranch pipeline in Blue Ocean

4. Now let us see the individual build page. To do so, from the Jenkins pipeline page (see the preceding screenshot), click on any of the builds, and you will be taken to the build page of the respective pipeline, as shown in the following screenshot:
    1. The **Changes** tab will list the code changes that triggered the build.
    2. The **Artifacts** tab will list all the artifacts that are generated by the build.
    3. The button (highlighted as **c**) will rerun your build.
    4. The section (highlighted as **d**) displays some metrics about your build.
    5. This Stage View (highlighted as **e**) will list all the sequential and parallel stages.
    6. The **Steps Results** section will show you all the steps of a particular stage that you have selected (in the following screenshot, I have selected the stage **Results**).

7. Each listed step (highlighted as **g**) can be expanded and its log can be viewed:

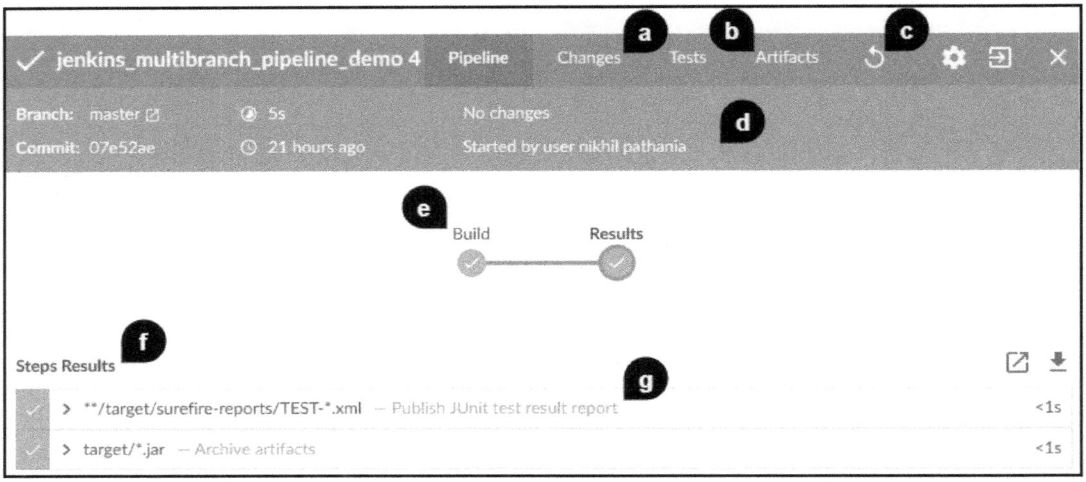

Build page in Blue Ocean

This was a short overview of how your Jenkins pipeline (the one that you created using the classic Jenkins UI) should look in Blue Ocean. It has demonstrated pretty much everything. However, I encourage readers to keep exploring.

Creating a pipeline in Blue Ocean

In this section, we will see how to create a new pipeline from the Jenkins Blue Ocean dashboard. We will look at the new pipeline creation wizard in Blue Ocean. Before you begin make the following things ready:

- Fork the following repository: `https://github.com/nikhilpathania/hello-world-example.git` into your GitHub account. We will be using it in the example described in the following section
- Install the JUnit plugin (`https://plugins.jenkins.io/junit`) for Jenkins

Follow the given steps:

1. From the Jenkins Blue Ocean dashboard, click on the **New Pipeline** button. Jenkins will ask you to choose between **Git** and **GitHub**. For our current exercise, we will choose **GitHub**:

Choosing between Git and GitHub repositories

2. Next, Jenkins will ask you to provide the GitHub access token for your GitHub account. Click on the **Create an access key here** link to create a new one:

GitHub access token field

3. In a new tab, you will be asked to log in to your GitHub account.
4. Once you log in, you will be taken directly to the GitHub settings page to create a **New personal access token**.
5. Type a small description for the **Token description** field to identify your token. Leave the options under the **Select scopes** section at their default values:

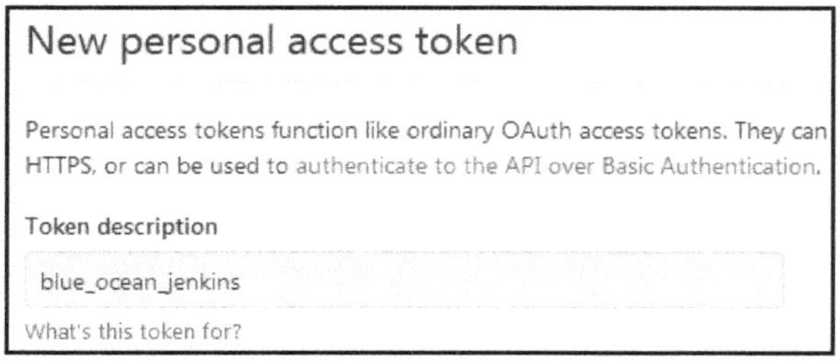

Creating a GitHub personal access token

6. Click on the **Generate new token** button at the bottom of the page to generate a new **Personal access token**:

GitHub personal access token

7. Copy the newly created personal access token and paste it inside your GitHub access token field, then click on the **Connect** button (see the following screenshot).
8. Next, click on the listed organization:

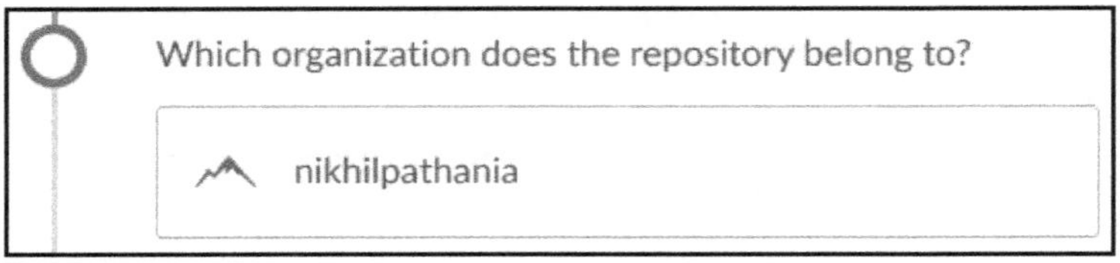

Choosing the GitHub account

9. You can choose between **New Pipeline** and **Auto-discover Jenkinsfiles**. In the following example, we will choose the **New Pipeline** option:

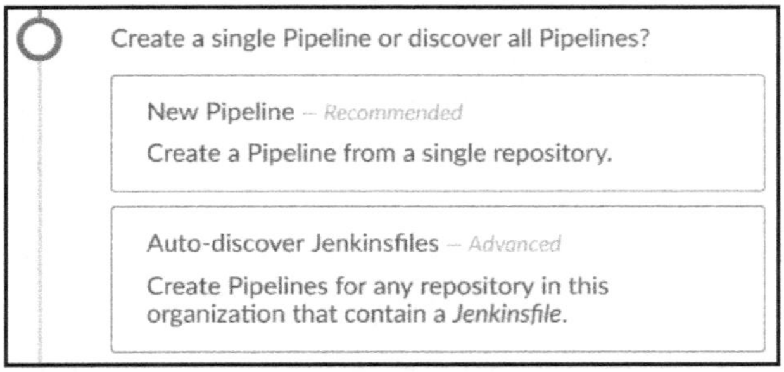

Choosing between creating and discovering pipelines

10. Next, you will be asked to choose a repository from the list of available repositories on your GitHub account. You can utilize the **Search...** option to look for the desired repository in case it's not listed. In our current example, we will choose the `hello-world-example` repo:

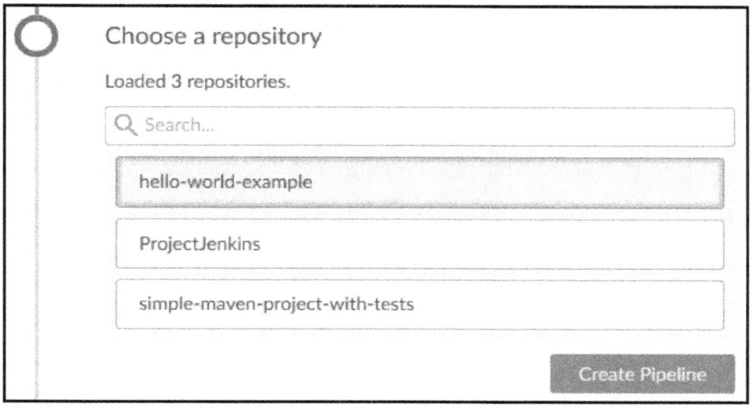

Choosing a repository

11. The next thing Jenkins will ask you to do is create a pipeline. Since there is no Jenkinsfile found on the respective repository, click on the **Create Pipeline** button to create a Jenkinsfile:

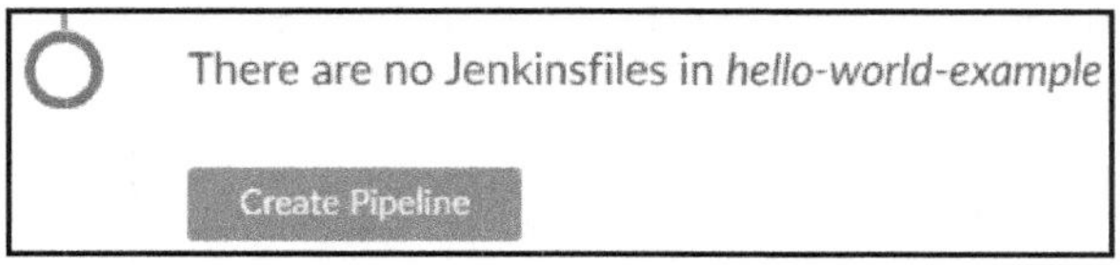

Creating a new pipeline

12. The page to create a pipeline will look like that which follows. On the left-hand side, you will find a visualization of your pipeline, and on the right-hand side, you will find the utility to choose the blocks, stages, and steps (similar to the pipeline syntax utility that we saw in the previous section):

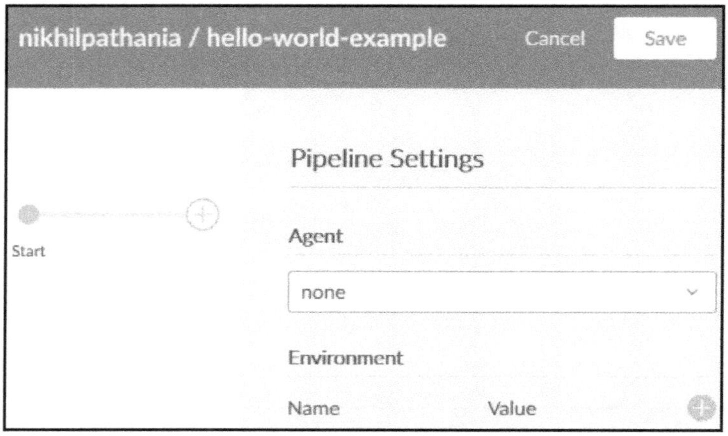

Blue Ocean pipeline editor

13. Let us first choose an **Agent** to run our pipeline. To do so, from the **Pipeline Settings**, using the **Agent** field, choose the option **label**. Then type `master` under the **Label** field, as shown in the following screenshot. In this way, we are telling Jenkins to run our pipeline on the Jenkins master:

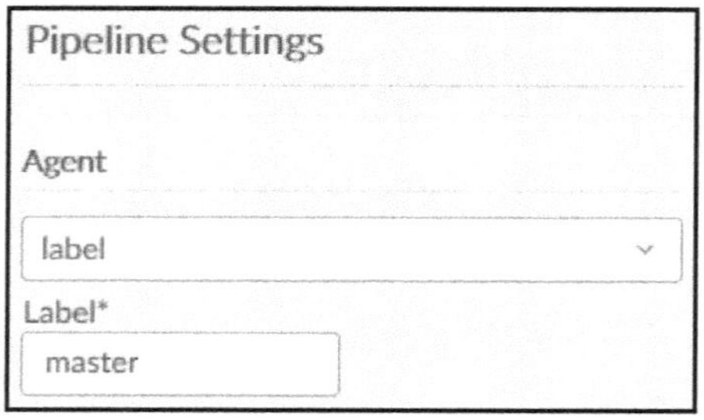

Creating a node block

14. Next, let us create a stage named `Build` that will build our source code. To do so, click on the **+** button, available on the pipeline visualization.

15. You will be asked to name your new stage. Do so by typing `Build` under the **Name your stage** field, as shown in the following screenshot:

Creating a build stage

16. Next, we will add a step to build our Maven code. To do so, click on the **+ Add step** button.
17. You will be asked to choose from a list of available steps, as shown in the following screenshot:

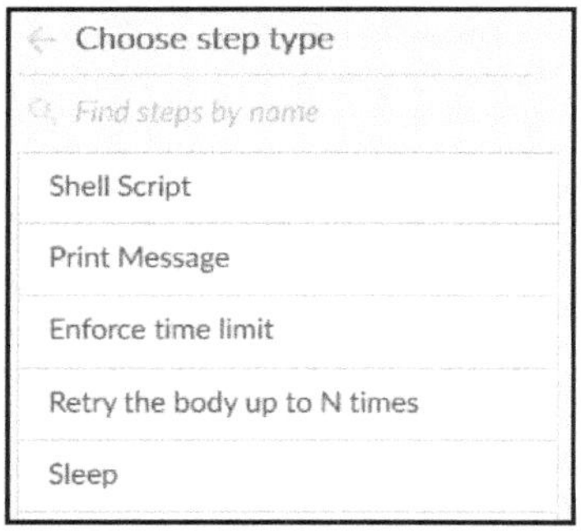

The step menu

18. Ours is a Maven project. Therefore, we might need to set up the Maven environment first, to tell Jenkins which Java and Maven tool it can use.
19. To do so, search for `Provide Maven environment` using the search box (find steps by name):

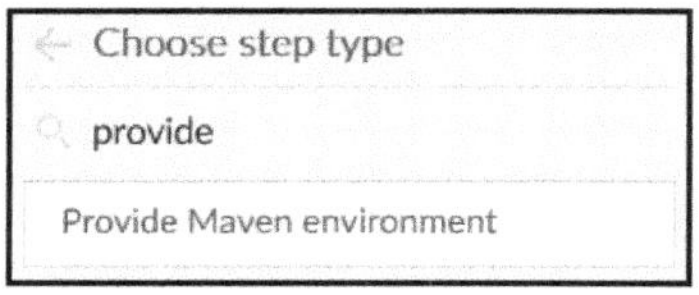

Choosing the provide Maven environment step

Not all Jenkins plugins are compatible with Jenkins Blue Ocean. The list is still small. However, it's expected to grow over time.

20. When you click on the **Provide Maven environment** step, you will be presented with a list of fields to configure, as shown in the following screenshot. Type `M3` under the **Maven** field and leave rest of the options as is:

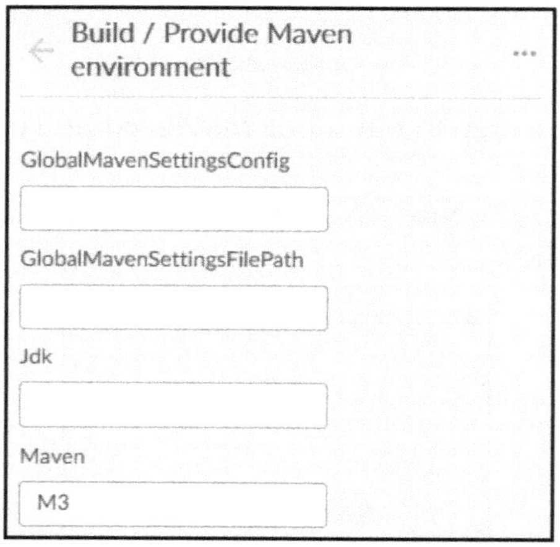

Configuring the provide maven environment step

21. At the bottom of the configuration page, click on the **+ Add step** button to create a new child step that will build our Maven code.
22. Choose **Shell Script** from the list of available steps, if your Jenkins master is a Linux machine. Choose **Windows Batch Script**, if it's a Windows machine.
23. Type the following code inside the textbox for **Shell Script/Windows Batch Script**:

```
mvn clean install
```

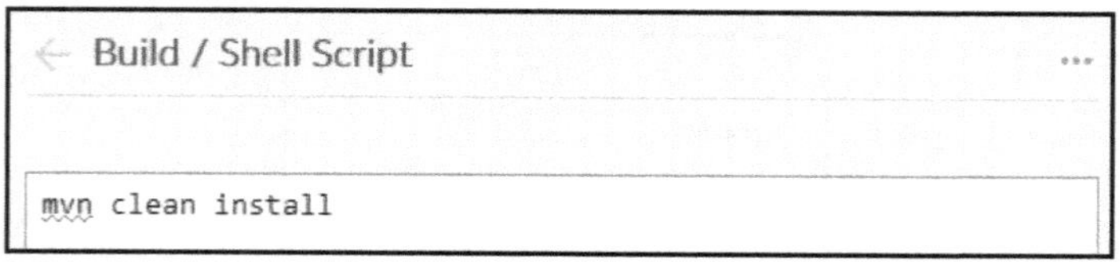

Configuring the shell script child step

24. Click on the back arrow to go back to the previous menu. You should now see your new step, **Shell Script**, listed under the **Child steps** section, as shown in the following screenshot:

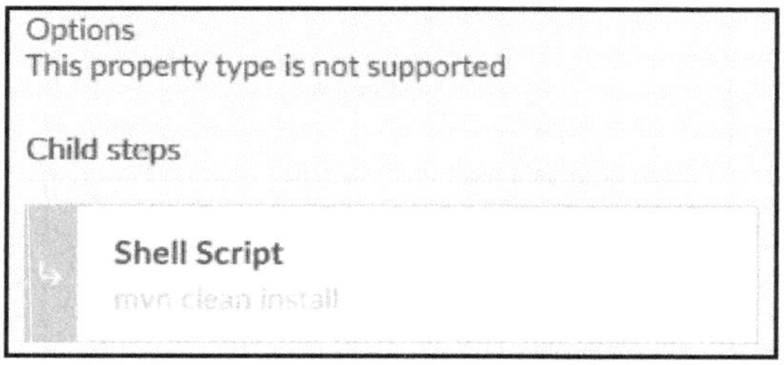

Shell script as one of the child steps

25. Click on the back arrow to go back to the previous menu.
26. Next, let us create a stage named **Results**, wherein we will archive our built artifacts and the XML result reports. To do so, click on the **+** button available on the pipeline visualization.
27. You will be asked to name your new stage. Do so by typing `Results` under the **Name your stage** field, as shown in the following screenshot:

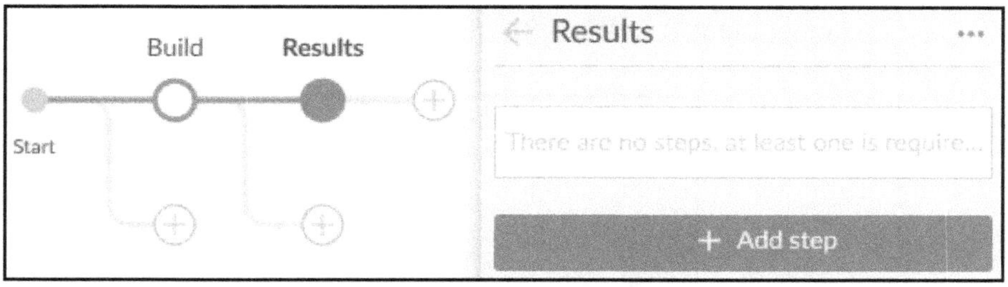

Creating a results stage

28. Next, we will add a few steps on our new stage. The first one will be a step to publish our test results report. To do so, click on the **+ Add step** button.
29. Choose **Publish JUnit test result report** from the list of available steps. You will be presented with a list of options to configure:
    1. Add `**/target/surefire-reports/TEST-*.xml` under the **TestResults** field.

    2. Leave the rest of the options as is:

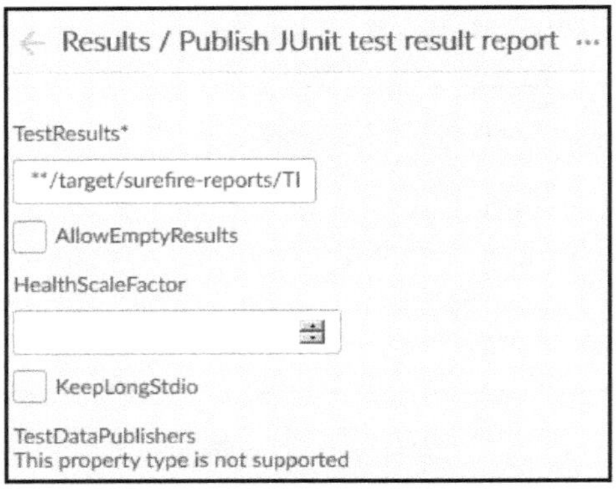

Configuring the publish JUnit test result report step

30. Click on the back arrow to go back to the previous menu.
31. Click on the **+ Add step** button again to add a new step.
32. Choose **Archive the artifacts** from the list of available steps. You will be presented with a list of options to configure:
    1. Add `target/*.jar` under the **Artifacts** field.
    2. Leave the rest of the options as is:

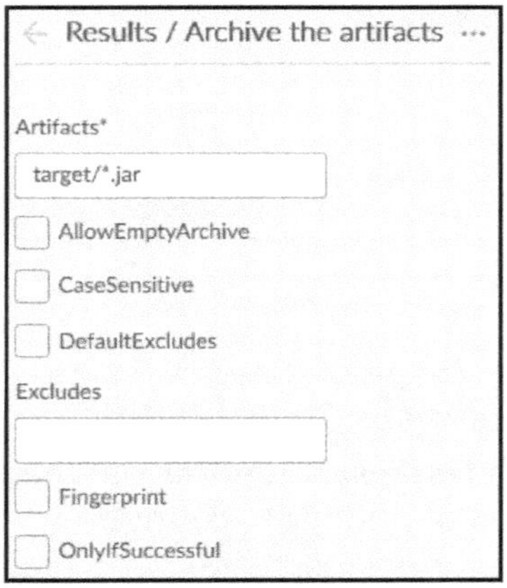

Configuring the Archive the artifacts step

33. Click on the back arrow to go back to the previous menu.
34. Finally, click on the **Save** button at the top-right corner of the page to save your pipeline configuration.
35. A pop-up window will ask you to add some **Description** and choose the branch on which to commit the pipeline configuration.
36. Once done, click on the **Save & run** button:

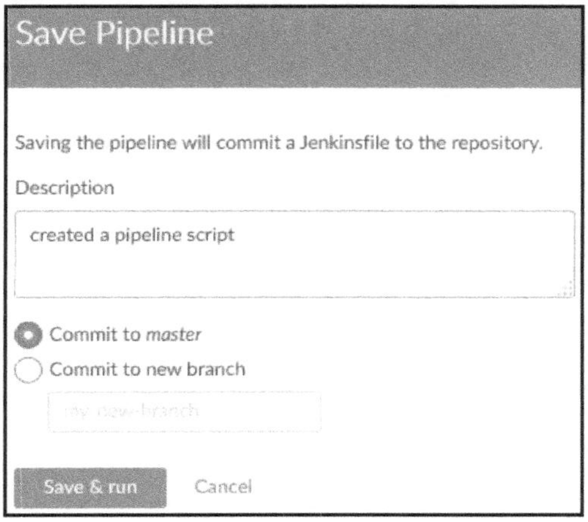

Saving the pipeline

37. This will immediately run a pipeline on the respective branch, as shown in the following screenshot:

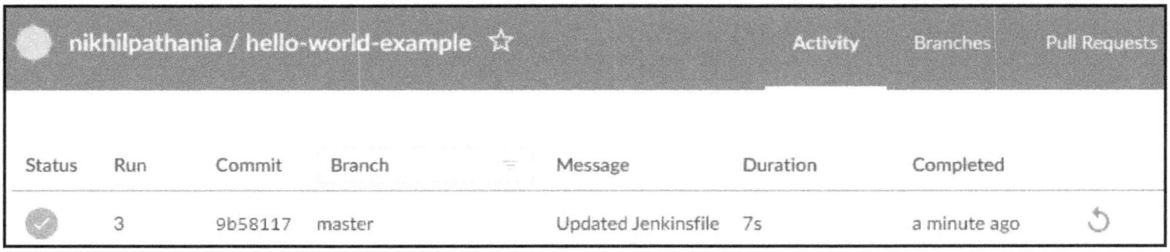

A successful build on the master branch

38. You will notice that a new file has been created inside your repository under the master branch:

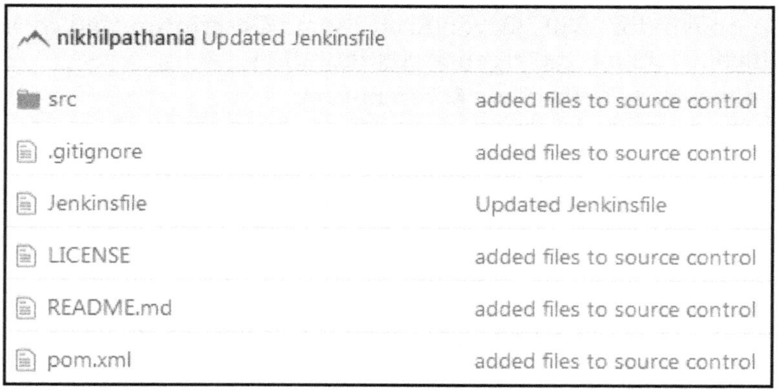

Jenkinsfile listed inside the source code

39. The following should be the content of the file:

```
pipeline {
  agent {
    node {
      label 'master'
    }
  }
  stages {
    stage('Build') {
      steps {
        withMaven(maven: 'M3') {
          sh 'mvn clean install'
        }
      }
    }
    stage('Results') {
      steps {
        junit '**/target/surefire-reports/TEST-*.xml'
        archiveArtifacts 'target/*.jar'
      }
    }
  }
}
```

Summary

In the preceding chapter, we got hands-on experience of almost all of the new features in Jenkins. We chose modest examples to keep our pipelines simple. Nevertheless, in the upcoming chapters, we will learn to create a full-fledged CI/CD pipeline using all of the new features in Jenkins.

In the next chapter, we will take a look at some of the administrative tasks in Jenkins.

4
Configuring Jenkins

In this chapter, we will learn how to perform some basic Jenkins administration tasks, as follows:

- Updating/installing/uninstalling/downgrading Jenkins plugins
- Installing Jenkins plugins manually
- Performing Jenkins backup and restore
- Upgrading Jenkins on various platforms (Windows/Linux/servlet)
- Upgrading Jenkins running inside a Docker container
- Creating and managing users in Jenkins
- Learning various authentication methods in Jenkins
- Configuring various authorization methods in Jenkins

Jenkins comes with a pile of items to configure. The more plugins you install, the more there is to configure. In this chapter, we will cover only the basic administrative tasks in Jenkins. We will learn more about the Jenkins configuration in the upcoming chapters, wherein we will try to add up more plugins to Jenkins in order to achieve **Continuous Integration** (**CI**) and **Continuous Delivery** (**CD**).

The Jenkins Plugin Manager

Jenkins derives most of its power from plugins. Jenkins plugins are pieces of software that upon installation enhance the Jenkins functionality. A plugin that is installed inside Jenkins manifests itself as a parameter or a configurable item inside a Jenkins job or inside the Jenkins system configuration, or event as a step under the **Snippet Generator** (in case it's compatible with the *Declarative Pipeline syntax*).

The following screenshot shows the Jenkins system configuration. It's a setting to configure the **SonarQube** tool (a static code analysis tool). The respective configuration is available only after installing the Jenkins plugin for SonarQube:

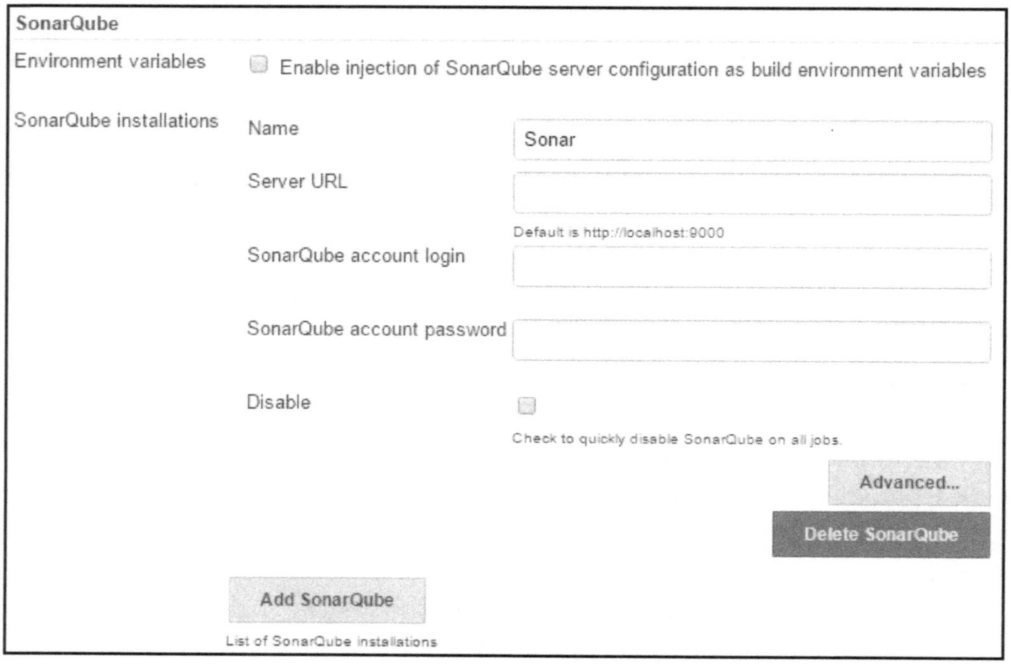

SonarQube settings inside Jenkins system configuration

There is a special section inside Jenkins to manage plugins. In this section, we will learn how to manage plugins using the Jenkins **Plugin Manager**:

1. From the Jenkins dashboard click on **Manage Jenkins**.
2. Once on the **Manage Jenkins** page, click on **Manage Plugins**. You can also access the same Jenkins **Plugin Manager** page using the `<Jenkins URL>/pluginManager` link.
3. You will see the following four tabs: **Updates**, **Available**, **Installed**, and **Advanced**.

Updating Jenkins plugins

The **Updates** tab lists out all of the plugins that need an update, as shown in the following screenshot:

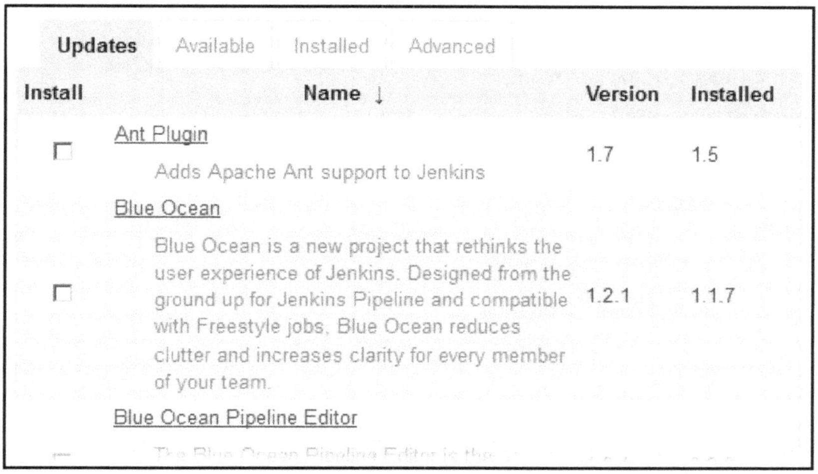

Updates
Available
Installed
Advanced
Install
Name ↓
Version
Installed
Ant Plugin
Adds Apache Ant support to Jenkins
1.7
1.5
Blue Ocean
Blue Ocean is a new project that rethinks the user experience of Jenkins. Designed from the ground up for Jenkins Pipeline and compatible with Freestyle jobs, Blue Ocean reduces clutter and increases clarity for every member of your team.
1.2.1
1.1.7
Blue Ocean Pipeline Editor

Updating Jenkins plugins

To update a plugin, select it by clicking on its respective checkbox and click on the **Download now and install after restart** button.

To update all plugins listed under the **Update** tab, click on **All** (available at the bottom of the page). This will select all the plugins. Then, click on the **Download now and install after restart** button to install the updates.

On the **Updates** tab, at the bottom of the page, you will see a button named **Check now**. Click on it to refresh the list of plugins that are displayed under the **Updates** tab. This will check for plugin updates.

Installing a new Jenkins plugin

The **Available** tab lists all plugins available for Jenkins. Plugins that are installed on your Jenkins instance will not be listed here.

The following screenshot shows a list of available plugins for Jenkins:

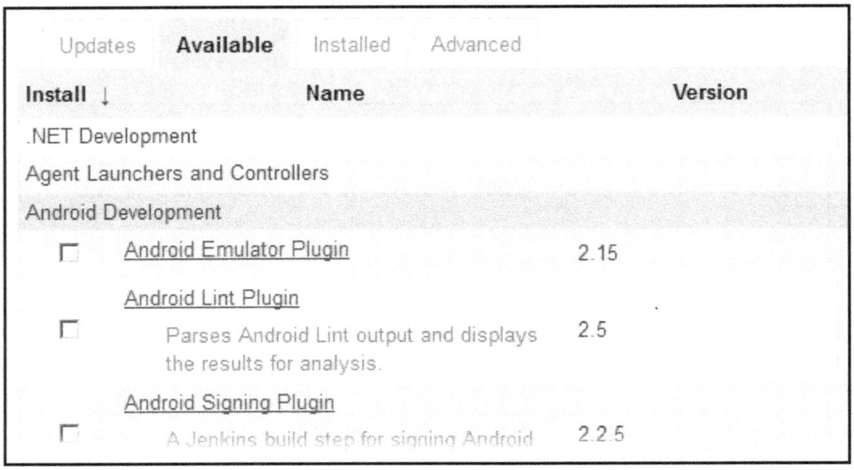

The plugins are grouped based on their functionality

To install a plugin, select it by clicking on its respective checkbox. Then, at the bottom of the page click on either the **Install without restart** button (to install the plugin immediately) or on the **Download now and install after restart** button (the name is self-explanatory).

Just like the **Updates** tab, here too you will see a button named **Check now**. Clicking on it will refresh the list of plugins under the **Available** tab.

Uninstalling or downgrading a Jenkins plugin

The **Installed** tab lists all the plugins currently installed on your Jenkins instance. As shown in the following screenshot, you can see there is an option to uninstall a plugin as well as downgrade it.

You can always choose to downgrade a plugin, in the event your Jenkins instance becomes unstable or your CI/CD pipeline does not do well, after a plugin update:

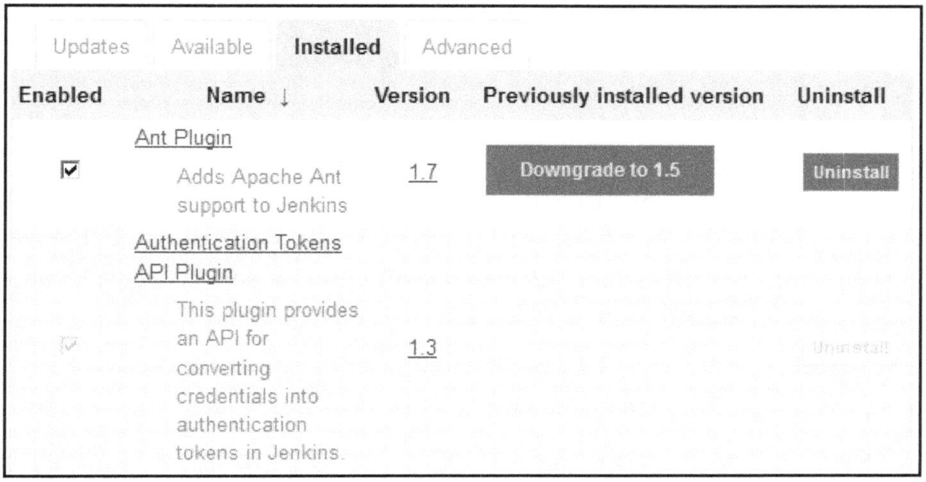

Updates
Available
Installed
Advanced
Enabled
Name ↓
Version
Previously installed version
Uninstall
Ant Plugin
Adds Apache Ant support to Jenkins
1.7
Downgrade to 1.5
Uninstall
Authentication Tokens API Plugin
This plugin provides an API for converting credentials into authentication tokens in Jenkins.
1.3
Uninstall

List of installed Jenkins plugin

Configuring proxy settings in Jenkins

Under the **Advanced** tab, you will see a section named **HTTP Proxy Configuration**. This is the place where you configure your proxy settings to allow Jenkins to fetch updates from the internet:

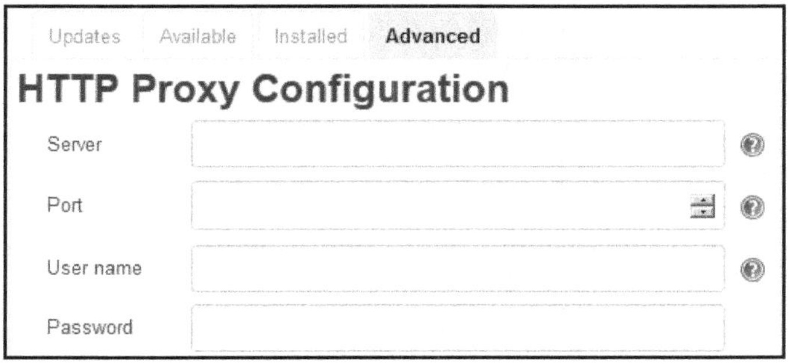

HTTP Proxy Configuration settings

Leave these fields empty if your Jenkins server is not behind any firewall and has direct access to the internet.

Jenkins uses the **HTTP Proxy Configuration** details when you try to install or upgrade a Jenkins plugin. It also uses this information to update the list of Jenkins plugins available on the **Update** tab and the **Available** tab.

To test your proxy settings, do the following:

1. Under the **HTTP Proxy Configuration** section, click on the **Advanced...** button.
2. Add a URL to the **Test URL** field and click on the **Validate Proxy** button.
3. You should see a message: **Success**, as shown in the following screenshot.
4. Click on the **Submit** button to save the settings:

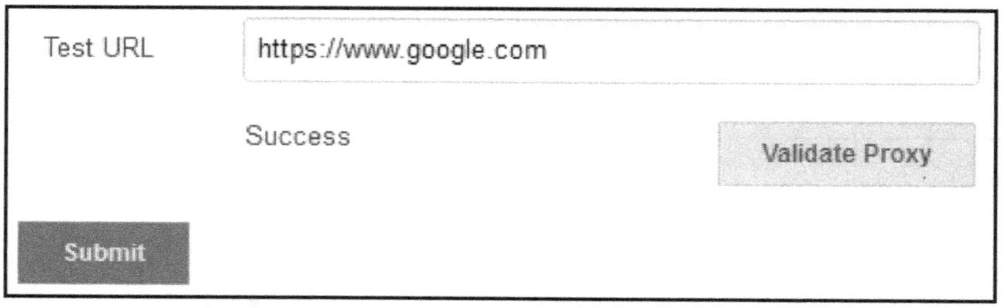

Checking the proxy settings

Manually installing a Jenkins plugin

Under the **Advanced** tab, just after the **HTTP Proxy Configuration** section, you will see another section named **Upload Plugin**. It provides you with the facility to install or upgrade a Jenkins plugin.

This feature is helpful when your Jenkins instance does not have internet access and you are in need of a new plugin or you need to upgrade an existing plugin. Imagine a situation where you have a Jenkins instance running inside a local area network, but with no access to the internet, or shall we say the Jenkins online plugin repository. In such cases, you will first download the required Jenkins plugin from the online Jenkins repository, and then you will transport it to the Jenkins master server using a removable media. And finally, you will use the **Upload Plugin** section to install the required Jenkins plugin.

Let us try to install a plugin manually by following the given steps:

1. From a machine that has access to the internet, open the website: `https://updates.jenkins-ci.org/download/plugins/`.

2. The preceding site contains the list of all plugins available for Jenkins, as shown in the following screenshot:

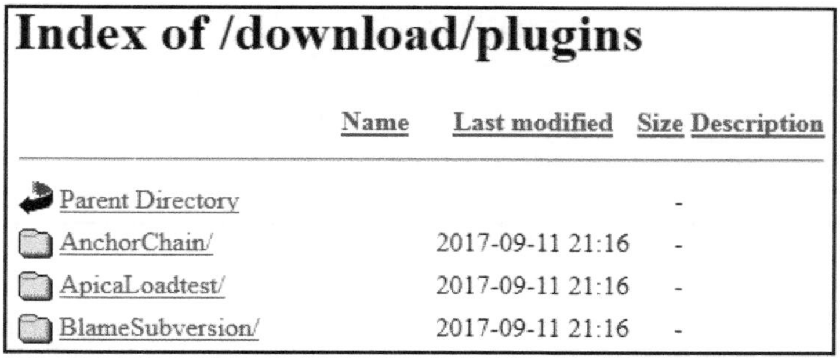

Index of /download/plugins
Name
Last modified
Size
Description
Parent Directory
-
AnchorChain/
2017-09-11 21:16
-
ApicaLoadtest/
2017-09-11 21:16
-
BlameSubversion/
2017-09-11 21:16
-

Jenkins plugin index

3. In the following example, we will install a plugin named `logstash`.
4. On the index page, search for `logstash` and click on it.
5. You will see all available versions of the respective plugin. Click on the one that you need (I choose to install the latest):

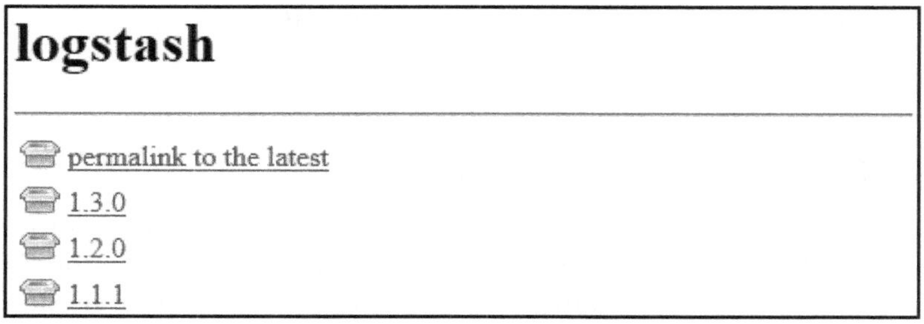

List of versions available for a plugin

6. This will download a `.hpi` file on your system.
7. When you download a plugin, it is also important that you download its dependencies (other Jenkins plugins).
8. All the dependencies (Jenkins plugins) must be installed before installing the desired plugin.
9. Copy this `.hpi` file (`logstash.hpi`) to your Jenkins server or to any machine that has access to your Jenkins dashboard.

10. Now, log in to your Jenkins server. From the Jenkins dashboard, navigate to **Manage Jenkins** | **Manage Plugins** | **Advanced**.
11. On the **Advanced** tab, under the **Upload Plugin** section, do the following (as shown in the following screenshot):
12. Click on the **Browse...** button under the **File** field.
13. From the resultant window, upload the downloaded `.hpi` file.
14. Once done, click on the **Upload** button:

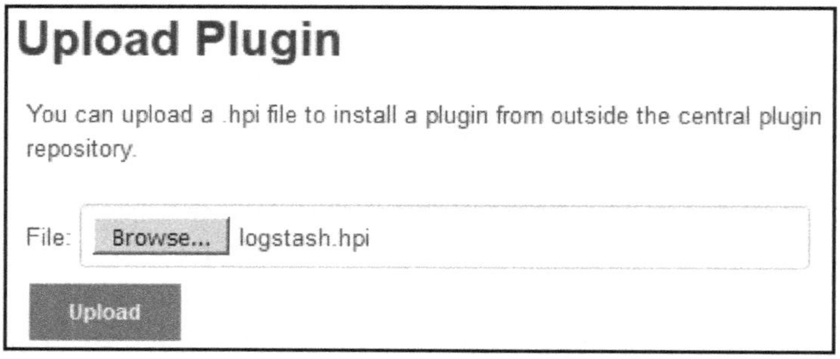

Manually uploading a Jenkins plugin

15. Jenkins will now proceed with the plugin installation.

Jenkins backup and restore

What happens if someone accidentally deletes important Jenkins configurations? Although this can be avoided using stringent user permissions that we will see in the *User Administration* section, imagine a situation where someone working on the Jenkins configuration wants to restore to a previous stable Jenkins configuration.

From what we have learned so far, we know that the entire Jenkins configuration is stored under the Jenkins home directory. It is `C:\jenkins` (Windows), `/var/jenkins_home` (Apache Tomcat), `/var/lib/jenkins` (Linux). In the following section, we will learn how to back up and restore the Jenkins configuration using a plugin, the **Periodic Backup** plugin.

Installing the Periodic Backup plugin

Follow the given steps to install the **Periodic Backup** plugin:

1. From the Jenkins dashboard, click on **Manage Jenkins** | **Manage Plugins**.
2. On the **Plugin Manager** page, click on the **Available** tab.
3. Using the **Filter** option, search for `Periodic Backup`, as shown in the following screenshot:

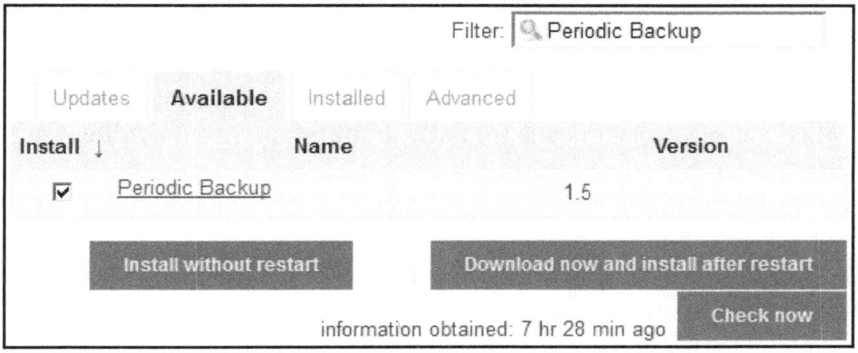

Installing the Periodic Backup plugin

4. From the list of items choose **Periodic Backup** and click on **Install without restart**. You only need **Blue Ocean** and nothing else.

Configuring the Periodic Backup plugin

We need to tell the **Periodic Backup** plugin what to back up, where to back up, and how frequent to back up before we even start using it. Follow the given steps:

1. From the Jenkins dashboard go to **Manage Jenkins** | **Periodic Backup Manager**.
2. When you access the **Periodic Backup Manager** for the first time you will see the following notification:

   The Periodic Backup plugin has not been configured yet. Click here to configure it.

3. Click on the **Click here to configure it** link.
4. You will be taken to the **Periodic Backup Manager** page, and you will find quite a few options to configure. Let us see them one by one (as shown in the following screenshot).
5. The **Root Directory,** `<your Jenkins home directory>`, is your Jenkins home directory.
6. The **Temporary Directory** field should be a directory located on your Jenkins server machine. As the name says, this directory is used as a temporary location to perform archive/unarchive operations during the backup/restore process. It can be any directory and should be outside Jenkins home directory.
7. The **Backup schedule (cron)** field is where you define when or how frequent to make a backup. Do not leave this field empty. Note that the field accepts cron syntax. For example, to back up daily at midnight, use the following cron syntax without quotes: `0 0 * * *`.
8. The **Validate cron syntax** button is to validate the cron that you have entered in the **Backup schedule (cron)** field.
9. The **Maximum backups in location** field tells Jenkins not to store backups greater than the number described here.
10. The **Store no older than (days)** field tells Jenkins to delete any backup that is older than this value.
11. Under **File Management Strategy**, you have two options to choose from: **ConfigOnly** and **FullBackup**. If you choose the **ConfigOnly** option, Jenkins will back up all the `.xml` files from the Jenkins home directory and the `config.xml` files of all the jobs. But, if you choose **FullBackup**, then Jenkins will back up the whole Jenkins home directory.
12. Under **Storage Strategy**, you have three options to choose from: **NullStorage**, **TarGzStorage**, and **ZipStorage** (with multi-volume support). You can choose the one that suits your requirement.
13. Under **Backup Location**, you can add multiple backup locations to store your backups. To do so, click on the **Add Location** button and choose **LocalDirectory**. Next, under the **Backup directory path** field, add the location where you want Jenkins to store the backup. Also, do not forget to check the **Enable this location** checkbox. You can choose multiple locations and enable all of them.

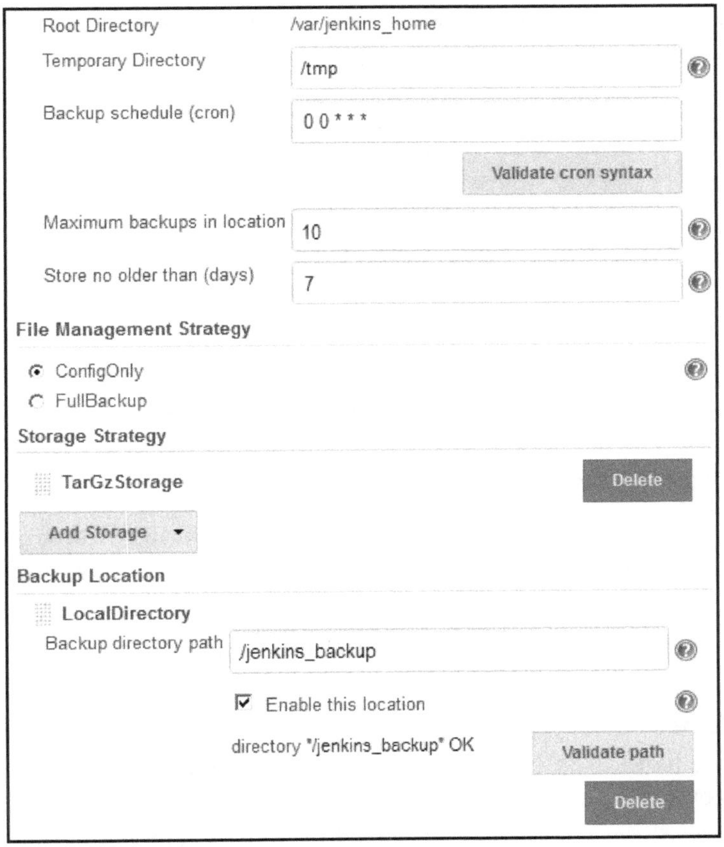

Periodic Backup configurations

Creating a Jenkins backup

Now that we have configured the **Periodic Backup** plugin, let us run a backup to test our settings. To do so, on the **Periodic Backup Manager** page, click on the **Backup Now!** link available on the left-hand side menu.

You will see the notification on the **Periodic Backup Manager** page while the backup is in progress as **Creating backup...**.

Once the backup is complete, you will see it listed on the same page, as shown in the following screenshot:

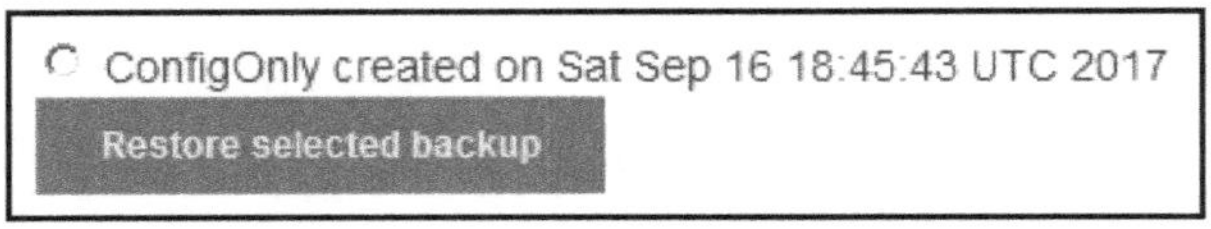

List of backup

Restoring a Jenkins backup

Let us now test restoring a Jenkins backup. But before we do that, let us make some configuration changes to see if the restore operation works. We will do this by making some configuration changes on the **Configure System** page:

1. From the Jenkins dashboard, click on **Manage Jenkins** | **Configure System**.
2. On the **Configure System** page, change the values for the following fields.
3. Change the value of the # **of executors** field from `2` to `5`.
4. Change the value of the **Quiet period** field from `5` to `10`.
5. Click on the **Save** button at the bottom of the page.
6. Now, let us restore Jenkins to a point previous to the above changes.
7. From the Jenkins dashboard, click on **Manage Jenkins** | **Periodic Backup Manager**.
8. On the resultant page, choose the backup that we created in the previous section and click on the **Restore selected backup** button.
9. You will see the following message:

   Restoring backup...

10. Refresh the page, and from the Jenkins dashboard click on **Manage Jenkins** | **Configure System**.
11. You will find the value of the # **of executors** field as two and the **Quiet period** field as five.

Viewing the backup and restore logs

You can see the whole log with respect to Jenkins backup and restore. To view the details logs, perform the following steps:

1. From the Jenkins dashboard, click on **Manage Jenkins** | **System Log**.
2. On the **Logs** page, under the **Log Recorders** section, click on `org.jenkinsci.plugins.periodicbackup`.
3. You will find the complete log of the backup and the restore action performed here, as shown in the following screenshot:

```
Started PeriodicBackup
backup_2017_09_16_23_15_36_131.tar.gz copied to
/jenkins_backup/backup_2017_09_16_23_15_36_131.tar.gz
backup_2017_09_16_23_15_36_131.pbobj copied to /jenkins_backup
/backup_2017_09_16_23_15_36_131.pbobj
Deleting the temporary file
/tmp/backup_2017_09_16_23_15_36_131.pbobj
Checking for redundant and old backups in the location.
Deleting temporary file
/tmp/backup_2017_09_16_23_15_36_131.tar.gz
Backup finished successfully after 18 ms
Finished PeriodicBackup. 19 ms
The final result directory /tmp/finalResult is not empty,
deleting...
/tmp/finalResult does not exist, making new directory
Copying /jenkins_backup/backup_2017_09_16_23_11_31_835.tar.gz
to /tmp/backup_2017_09_16_23_11_31_835.tar.gz
Archive /jenkins_backup/backup_2017_09_16_23_11_31_835.tar.gz
copied to /tmp/backup_2017_09_16_23_11_31_835.tar.gz
Extracting files from
/tmp/backup_2017_09_16_23_11_31_835.tar.gz to /tmp/finalResult
Deleting /tmp/backup_2017_09_16_23_11_31_835.tar.gz
Restoring of files finished
Reloading configuration...
Restoration finished after 592 ms
```

Jenkins Periodic Backup log

Upgrading Jenkins

There are two kinds of Jenkins releases: *LTS Release* and *Weekly Release*. The *Jenkins Weekly Release* contains new features and bug fixes, whereas the *LTS (Long Term Support) Release* are special releases that are considered stable over a period of 12 weeks. It's recommended that you always choose an *LTS Release* for your Jenkins server:

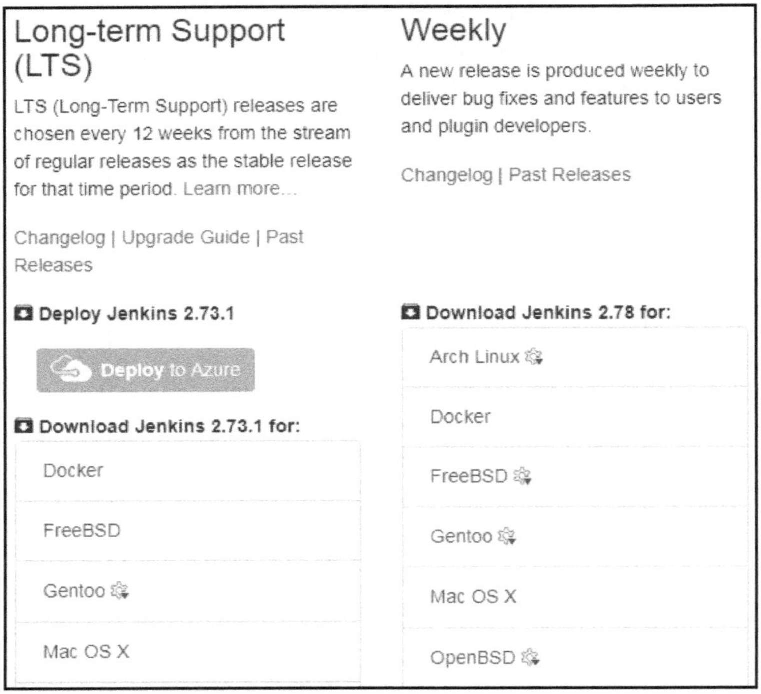

Jenkins download page

Jenkins by itself notifies you when there is a newer version available (provided your Jenkins server has access to the internet), as shown in the following screenshot:

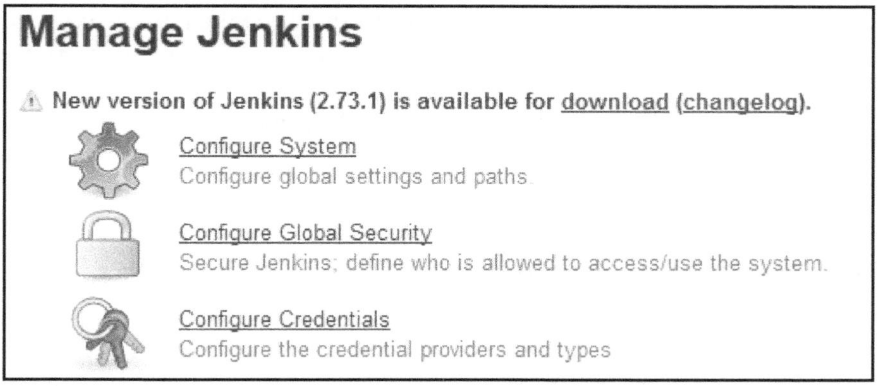
Manage Jenkins
New version of Jenkins (2.73.1) is available for download (changelog).
Configure System
Configure global settings and paths.
Configure Global Security
Secure Jenkins; define who is allowed to access/use the system.
Configure Credentials
Configure the credential providers and types

Jenkins notification about the availability of a new version

Upgrading Jenkins running on Tomcat Server

In the following section, we will learn to update Jenkins running inside a servlet (Apache Tomcat). Follow the given steps:

1. Log in to your Apache Tomcat server machine as the root user.
2. Download the latest (LTS) version of `jenkins.war` under the `/tmp` directory using the following command:

```
cd /tmp

wget http://mirrors.jenkins.io/war-stable/latest/jenkins.war
```

To download a specific version of Jenkins (LTS), go to the following link: `http://mirrors.jenkins.io/war-stable/` and choose the desired version of Jenkins (for example, `http://mirrors.jenkins.io/war-stable/2.73.1/jenkins.war`).

To download a specific version of Jenkins (Weekly), go to the following link: `http://mirrors.jenkins.io/war/` and choose the desired version of Jenkins (for example, `http://mirrors.jenkins.io/war/2.78/jenkins.war`).

3. Before we upgrade Jenkins, it is important that we take a backup of our `jenkins_home` directory. Refer to the *Creating a Jenkins backup* section.

> Always run a backup of Jenkins before upgrading Jenkins.

4. Now, stop the `tomcat` service using the following command:

```
systemctl stop tomcat
```

5. Next, go to the location where the current `jenkins.war` file is present. In our case, it is `/opt/tomcat/webapps`:

```
cd /opt/tomcat/webapps/
```

> If you have chosen to use Tomcat Server solely to run Jenkins, you may find `ROOT.war` instead of `jenkins.war` under the `webapps` directory. Refer to the *Installing Jenkins alone on Apache Tomcat Server* section, from `Chapter 2`, *Installing Jenkins.*

6. Take a backup of your existing `jenkins.war` or `ROOT.war` and place it somewhere outside the `webapps` directory (for example, the `/tmp` directory):

```
cp jenkins.war /tmp/jenkins.war.last.stable.version
```

Or:

```
cp ROOT.war /tmp/ROOT.war.last.stable.version
```

7. Now, delete the current `jenkins.war` or `ROOT.war` file inside the webapps directory:

```
rm -r jenkins.war
```

Or:

```
rm -r ROOT.war
```

8. Next, move the new `jenkins.war` that you have downloaded from the `/tmp` directory to the `webapps` directory. If you are using Apache Tomcat Server solely for running Jenkins, then rename the `destination.war` file as `ROOT.war`:

   ```
   mv /tmp/jenkins.war /opt/tomcat/webapps/jenkins.war
   ```

   Or:

   ```
   mv /tmp/jenkins.war /opt/tomcat/webapps/ROOT.war
   ```

9. Now, start the Tomcat service using the following command:

   ```
   systemctl start tomcat
   ```

10. Log in to your Jenkins instance. To confirm the Jenkins version, look at the bottom-right corner of your Jenkins dashboard, where you will find a new Jenkins version number.

Upgrading standalone Jenkins running on Windows

Upgrading a standalone Jenkins server on Windows is a simple task. Follow the given steps:

1. Download the latest `jenkins.war` from `https://jenkins.io/download/`. Or, if you are looking for a particular Jenkins version that you want to upgrade to, then download it from the following link: `http://mirrors.jenkins.io/war-stable/`.
2. Before we upgrade Jenkins it is important that we take a backup of our `jenkins_home` directory. Refer to the *Creating a Jenkins backup* section under the *Jenkins backup and restore* section.

> Always run a backup of Jenkins before upgrading Jenkins.
>
> On a Jenkins standalone instance (running on a Windows machine), the `jenkins.war` file is present inside the `jenkins_home` directory. Hence, backing up the `jenkins_home` directory is enough.

3. Next, stop the Jenkins service. To do that, execute `services.msc` from Windows **Run**. This will open the Windows services page.
4. Search for the Jenkins service (usually named **Jenkins**). Stop the Jenkins service, as shown in the following screenshot:

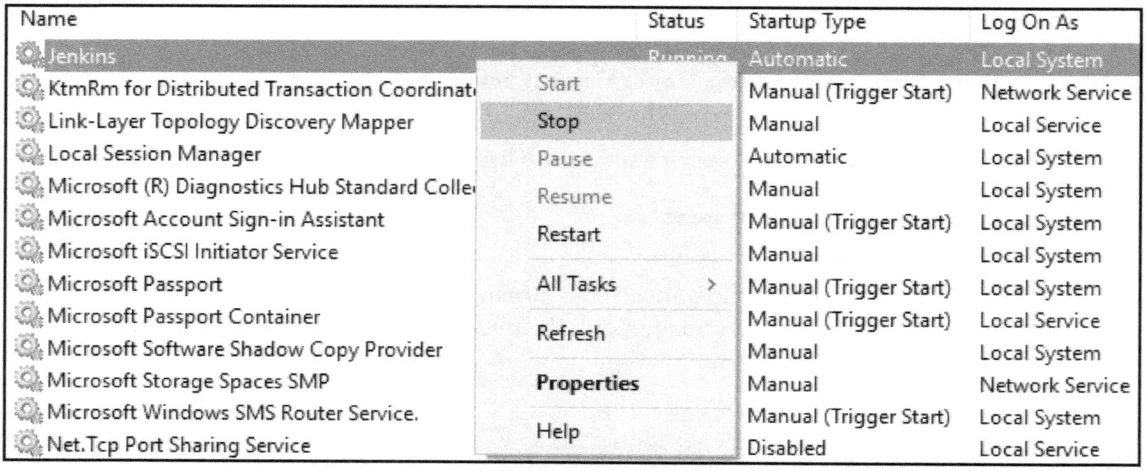

Stopping a Jenkins service

5. Or, you can also stop the Jenkins service from the Windows Command Prompt (**Run as administrator**), using the following command:

```
net stop Jenkins
```

The output is as follows:

```
The Jenkins service is stopping.
The Jenkins service was stopped successfully.
```

6. Next, replace the `jenkins.war` file, present under `C:\Program Files (x86)\Jenkins\`, with the newly downloaded `jenkins.war` file.
7. After replacing the `jenkins.war` file, start the Jenkins service from the services window, as shown in the following screenshot:

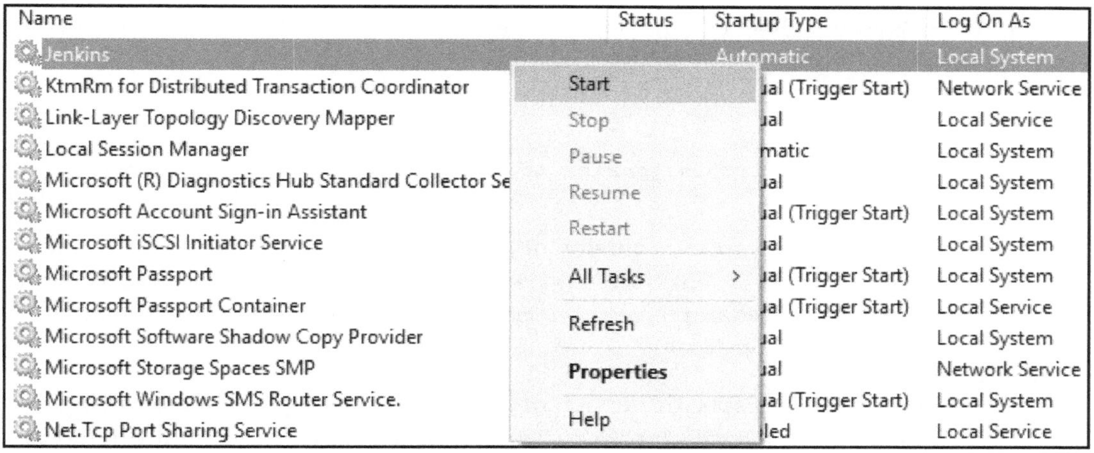

Starting a Jenkins service

8. Or, you can also start the Jenkins service from the Windows Command Prompt (**Run as administrator**), using the following command:

```
net start Jenkins
```

The output is as follows:

```
The Jenkins service is starting.
The Jenkins service was started successfully.
```

9. Log in to your Jenkins instance. To confirm the Jenkins version, look at the bottom-right corner of your Jenkins dashboard, where you should see a new Jenkins version number.

Upgrading standalone Jenkins running on Ubuntu

In the following section, we will learn how to update Jenkins running on Ubuntu. Follow the given steps:

1. Log in to your Jenkins server machine as a root user.

2. Download the latest (LTS) version of `jenkins.war` under the `/tmp` directory, using the following command:

```
cd /tmp

wget http://mirrors.jenkins.io/war-stable/latest/jenkins.war
```

> To download a specific version of Jenkins (LTS), go to the following link: `http://mirrors.jenkins.io/war-stable/` and choose the desired version of Jenkins (for example, `http://mirrors.jenkins.io/war-stable/2.73.1/jenkins.war`).
>
> To download a specific version of Jenkins (Weekly), go to the following link: `http://mirrors.jenkins.io/war/` and choose the desired version of Jenkins (for example, `http://mirrors.jenkins.io/war/2.78/jenkins.war`).

3. Before we upgrade Jenkins, it is important that we take a backup of our `jenkins_home` directory. Refer to the *Creating a Jenkins Backup* section under the *Jenkins backup and restore* section.

> Always run a backup of Jenkins before upgrading Jenkins.

4. Now, stop the `jenkins` service, using the following command:

```
systemctl stop jenkins
```

5. Next, go to the location where the current `jenkins.war` file is present. In our case, it is `/usr/share/jenkins/`:

```
cd /usr/share/jenkins/
```

6. Take a backup of your existing `jenkins.war` and place it somewhere outside the `jenkins` directory (for example, the `/tmp` directory):

```
cp jenkins.war /tmp/jenkins.war.last.stable.version
```

7. Now, delete the current `jenkins.war` file inside the `jenkins` directory:

```
rm -r jenkins.war
```

8. Next, move the new `jenkins.war` file that you have downloaded from the `/tmp` directory to the `jenkins` directory:

```
mv /tmp/jenkins.war /usr/share/jenkins/jenkins.war
```

9. Now, start the `jenkins` service using the following command:

```
systemctl start jenkins
```

10. Log in to your Jenkins instance. To confirm the Jenkins version, look at the bottom-right corner of your Jenkins dashboard, where you will find a new Jenkins version number.

Upgrading Jenkins running on a Docker container

In the following section, we will learn how to update a Jenkins instance running inside a Docker container:

> The following section is applicable only if you are running your Jenkins instance using a data volume for your `jenkins_home` directory. See the *Running Jenkins on Docker, Running a Jenkins container using a data volume* sections from the `Chapter 2`, *Installing Jenkins*.

1. Log in to your Docker host machine.
2. Look for the running Jenkins container, using the following command:

```
sudo docker ps --format "{{.ID}}: {{.Image}} {{.Names}}"
```

The output is as follows:

```
d52829d9da9e: jenkins/jenkins:lts jenkins_prod
```

3. You should get an output similar to the previous snippet. Note the Jenkins container name, in my example it is `jenkins_prod`.
4. We will stop and then delete the running Jenkins container using the following Docker commands. But, before you stop and delete your Jenkins instance, make sure that there is no job running on your Jenkins server:

```
sudo docker stop <your jenkins container name>
sudo docker rm <your jenkins container name>
```

5. List the available Docker images on your Docker host, using the following command. You can see we have a Jenkins Docker image: `jenkins/jenkins:lts`. However, that is no longer the latest:

```
sudo docker images
```

The output is as follows:

```
REPOSITORY        TAG       IMAGE ID       CREATED         SIZE
jenkins/jenkins   lts       6376a2961aa6   7 weeks ago     810MB
hello-world       latest    1815c82652c0   3 months ago    1.84kB
```

6. Download the latest Jenkins Docker image, using the following command:

```
sudo docker image pull jenkins/jenkins:2.73.1
```

The aforementioned command may take a while to download the Jenkins Docker image.

At the time of writing this chapter, 2.73.1 was the latest Jenkins release (LTS). Choose the desired version of Jenkins by modifying the command.

7. Once the download is completed, execute the `sudo docker images` command again, as shown in the following segment. Note the new Jenkins Docker image. In my example, it is `jenkins/jenkins:2.73.1`:

```
sudo docker images
```

The output is as follows:

```
REPOSITORY          TAG       IMAGE ID       CREATED          SIZE
jenkins/jenkins     2.73.1    c8a24e6775ea   24 hours ago     814MB
jenkins/jenkins     lts       6376a2961aa6   7 weeks ago      810MB
hello-world         latest    1815c82652c0   3 months ago     1.84kB
```

8. Now let us start a new Jenkins container using the newly downloaded Jenkins Docker image (we will reuse the old Jenkins container name):

```
sudo docker run -d --name jenkins_prod \
-p 8080:8080 -p 50000:50000 \
-v jenkins-home-prod:/var/jenkins_home \
jenkins/jenkins:2.73.1
```

9. The following table explains the Docker commands that we used before:

`docker`	Used to invoke Docker utility.
`run`	It's a Docker command to run a container.
`-d`	This option runs the container on the backend.
`--name`	This option gives a name to your container.
`-p`	This option is used to map a container's port with the host.
`jenkins/jenkins:2.73.1`	The name of the Docker image and its version used to create a container. `jenkins/jenkins` is the Jenkins Docker image and `2.73.1` is a particular version of that image.

10. Log in to your Jenkins instance. You should see all your jobs/settings intact. To confirm the Jenkins version, look at the bottom-right corner of your Jenkins dashboard, where you will find a new Jenkins version number.

User administration

Let's see what Jenkins has to offer in the area of user administration. From the Jenkins dashboard, click on **Manage Jenkins** | **Configure Global Security** to access the **Configure Global Security** page.

You can also access the **Configure Global Security** page by using the `<Jenkins URL>/configureSecurity/` link.

In the following section, we will stick to the options that are related to user authentication and permissions. We will look at the other security options in the upcoming chapters.

Enabling/disabling global security on Jenkins

Once on the **Configure Global Security** page, you will see that the **Enable security** option is already enabled. The **Enable security** option should always be on; disabling it will make Jenkins accessible to anyone who has the Jenkins URL, with no restrictions of any kind.

Enabling/disabling computers to remember user credentials

When users try to access Jenkins, they are offered an option to be remembered on their respective computers, as shown in the following screenshot:

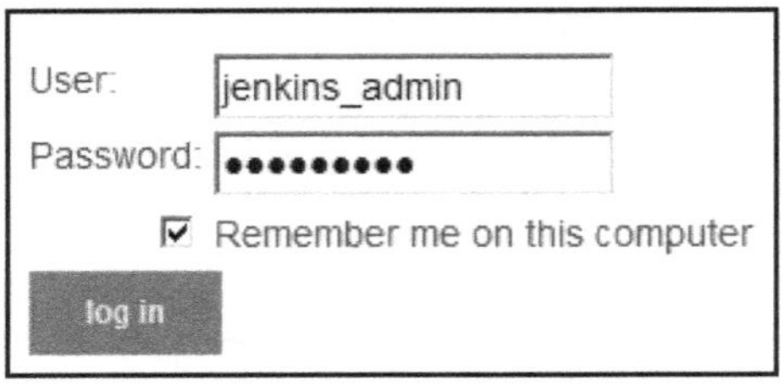

Remember me on this computer option

This behavior is enabled by default. To disable this feature, tick the **Disable remember me** option available under the **Configure Global Security** page.

Authentication methods

Jenkins offers a variety of authentication methods to choose from. The following is a list of available options:

- Delegate to servlet container
- Jenkins' own user database
- LDAP
- Unix user/group database

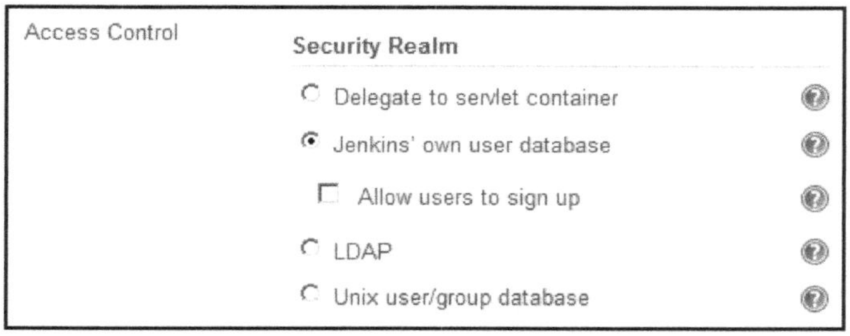

Jenkins' authentication methods

The **Jenkins' own user database** option is enabled by default. The initial users that we created during the Jenkins setup wizard are all stored under the **Jenkins' own user database**. There is no actual database of any kind, and all user information is saved as XML files. Let us take a quick look at each of the authentication methods.

Delegating to a servlet container

This option can be used only when you are running your Jenkins server from a servlet container, such as Apache Tomcat and so on. Enabling this option will allow Jenkins to authenticate users using the servlet containers' realm.

For example, in the *Configure the Apache Tomcat Server* sub-section under the *Running Jenkins inside a servlet container* section from the `Chapter 2`, *Installing Jenkins*, we modified the `tomcat-user.xml` file to create users and access. That is an example of the `UserDatabaseRealm`.

That means, if your Jenkins server is running on Apache Tomcat server and you have configured the `UserDatabaseRealm`, then all users defined in the `tomcat-user.xml` file will be able to access Jenkins.

Refer to the following website to see all types of realms supported by Apache Tomcat: `http://tomcat.apache.org/tomcat-8.0-doc/realm-howto.html#Standard_Realm_Implementations`.

Jenkins' own user database

This option is enabled by default. Under this scheme, Jenkins stores all the user information inside XML files. This option is good for small organizations or if you are exploring Jenkins and are yet to make it a part of your organization.

There is also an option to allow users to sign up at the login page. To enable it, tick the **Allow users to sign up** option available under **Jenkins' own user database**.

This will enable a link named **Create an account** at the Jenkins login page, as shown in the following screenshot:

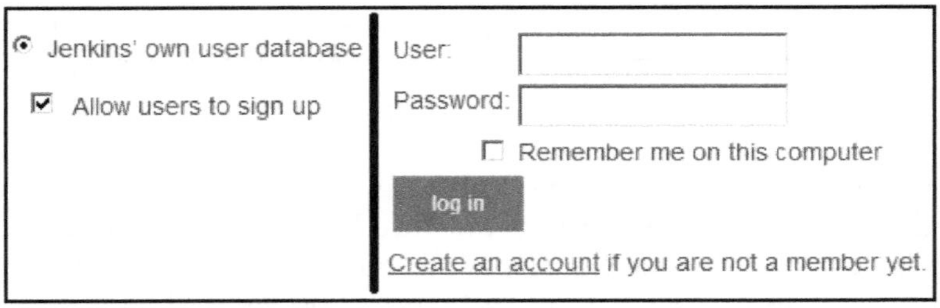

Allow user to sign up option

As a new user, when you click on the **Create an account** link you will be asked to fill in some basic details about yourself, such as username, password, email, full name, and so on. Once you are done filling in the necessary information you will be allowed to access Jenkins.

What you as a new user are allowed to see/do on Jenkins depends on the **Authorization** settings inside Jenkins. We will learn about the **Authorization** settings later in the current chapter.

LDAP

This is one of the most widely used authentication methods in most organizations. If you do not see the **LDAP** option listed under the **Access Control** | **Security Realm** section, then check for the **LDAP plugin**.

The following option, as shown in the following screenshot allows Jenkins to authenticate users using an LDAP server. Contact the IT administration team in your organization to provide the LDAP server details (if your organization uses LDAP).

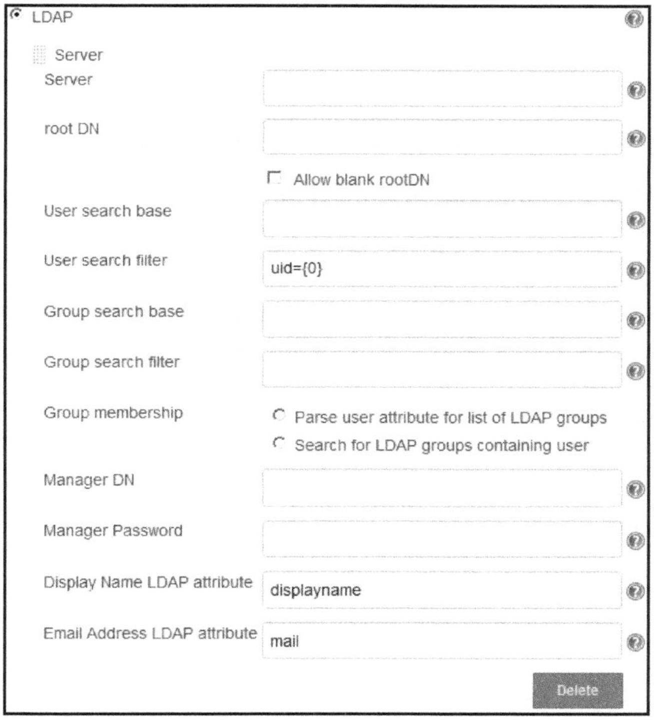

For more information about the LDAP configuration, refer to the LDAP plugin page: `https://wiki.jenkins.io/display/JENKINS/LDAP+Plugin`.

Unix user/group database

The following option works if Jenkins is installed on a Unix/Linux machine. When enabled, Jenkins delegates the authentication to the underlying OS. In other words, all users/groups that are configured on the underlying OS get access to Jenkins.

You need not configure anything inside Jenkins to make this option work. However, all users on the underlying OS should have access to the `/etc/shadow` file.

Use the following command to make the `/etc/shadow` file accessible to all users:

```
sudo chmod g+r /etc/shadow
```

Creating new users inside Jenkins

The following section is only applicable if you are using **Jenkins' own user database** as the **Authentication** method. Perform the following steps to manually add users to your Jenkins server.

1. From the Jenkins dashboard, click on **Manage Jenkins** | **Manage Users**.
2. On the **Manage Users** page, from the left-hand side menu, click on **Create User**.
3. On the resultant page, you will be asked to provide some basic information about the user, as shown in the following screenshot:

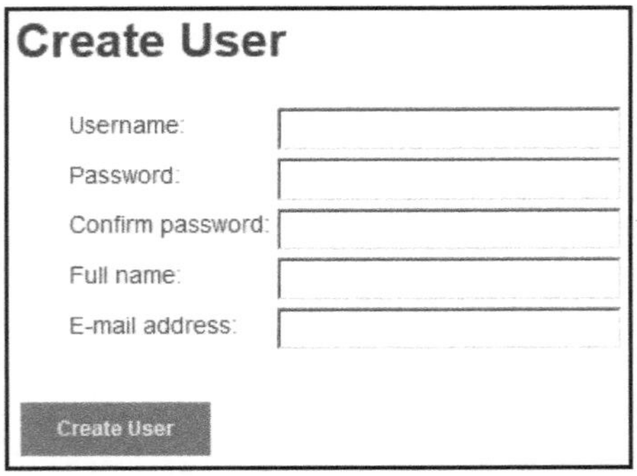

Creating a user in Jenkins

4. Fill the fields with appropriate values and click on the **Create User** button.

The **Manage Users** link is only available if you are using **Jenkins' own user database** as the **Authentication** method.

People page

The **People** page displays all users that have access to the Jenkins server, as shown in the following screenshot:

User Id
Name
Last Commit Activity ↑
On
nikhilpathania
nikhilpathania
1 mo 1 day
nikhilpathania » hello-world-example » temp
jenkins_admin
nikhil pathania
N/A

The Jenkins People page

User information and settings in Jenkins

Click on any particular user ID or name (see the following screenshot) to get information about the respective user. You will be taken to the users' **Status** page, as seen in the following screenshot:

The users' Status page

On the users' **Status** page you will see the following options on the left-hand side menu: **Status, Builds, Configure, My Views** and **Credentials**. Let us explore some of them in detail:

- The **Builds** page will display information about all the Jenkins builds that were run by the current user.
- The **My Views** page will take you to the views that are accessible by the current user. If no views are configured for the current user, then the **My Views** page will show the default **All** view (Jenkins dashboard).
- The **Credentials** link will take you to the **Credentials** page. However, the **Credentials** page will display additional information with respect to the current user, as shown in the following screenshot:

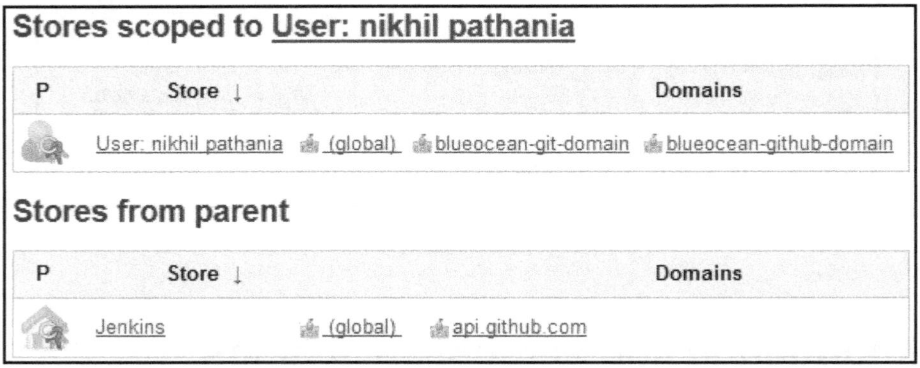

Jenkins credentials scoped to a user

Authorization methods

Jenkins offers a variety of authorization methods to choose from. The following is a list of available options:

- Anyone can do anything
- Legacy mode
- Logged-in users can do anything
- Matrix-based
- Project-based Matrix Authorization Strategy

The **Logged-in users can do anything** option is enabled by default. Let us take a quick look at each of the authorization methods.

To access the Jenkins **Authorization** settings, from the Jenkins dashboard navigate to **Manage Jenkins | Configure Global Security | Access Control**.

Anyone can do anything

When you choose this option, Jenkins does not perform any authorization. Anyone who has access to Jenkins gets full control, including anonymous users. This option is not recommended.

Legacy mode

When you choose this option, Jenkins behaves the way it used to be before release 1.164. In simple terms, Jenkins will look for a user named `Admin` (irrespective of the **Authentication** method you use). This `Admin` user will be provided administrative privilege, and the rest of the users will be treated as anonymous users. This option is again not recommended.

Logged-in users can do anything

This is the default authentication setting that Jenkins comes with when you install and set up a new Jenkins server. The name is self-explanatory, that is, logged-in users are administrators by default. Again, this option is not recommended.

Under the **Logged-in users can do anything** field, there is an option named **Allow anonymous read access** (disabled by default). When this option is ticked (enabled), anyone who has access to the Jenkins URL will be straight away taken to the Jenkins dashboard with read-only access to all Jenkins jobs. However, you are required to log in in order to edit a Jenkins job or view Jenkins' configuration.

Matrix-based security

This is one of the most widely used **Authorization** methods in Jenkins. Let us explore it in detail by performing the following steps:

1. Enable the **Matrix-based security** authorization method by selecting it. You will be presented with the following matrix:

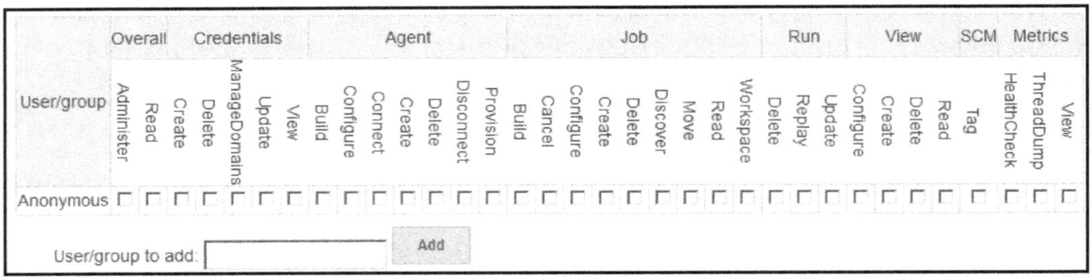

Matrix-based security configurations

2. From the previous screenshot, you can see the columns represent various items in Jenkins and the rows represent various users. At the bottom of the matrix there is an option to add users.
3. Let us add some users and provide them some permissions.
4. To add a user, enter the exact username of the user in the **User/group to add** field, and click on the **Add** button.
5. You can see from the following screenshot that I have added four users (refer to the *People page* section to see the list of users that you can add in here). If you are using **Jenkins' own user database** then create a few users (refer to the *Creating new users inside Jenkins* section):

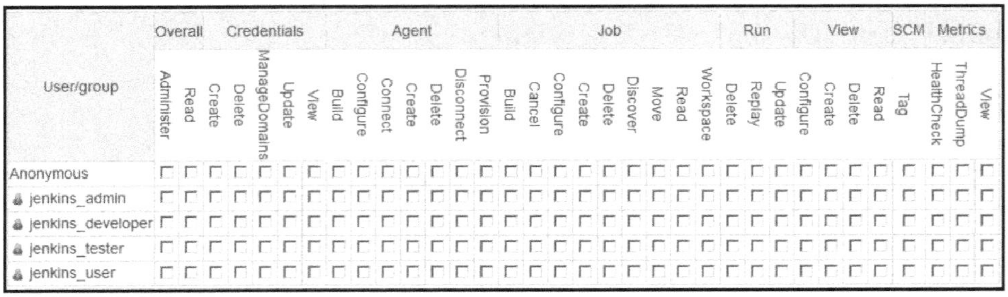

Adding users to the matrix

6. Now, let us give them some permissions by selecting the appropriate checkbox. You can see from the following screenshot that I have given full access to the user `jenkins_admin`. The users `jenkins_developer` and `jenkins_tester` have been given access to read and execute Jenkins jobs, and the `jenkins_user` user has been given only read access:

User/group	Overall		Credentials					Agent							Job									Run			View				SCM	Metrics		
	Administer	Read	Create	Delete	ManageDomains	Update	View	Build	Configure	Connect	Create	Delete	Disconnect	Provision	Build	Cancel	Configure	Create	Delete	Discover	Move	Read	Workspace	Delete	Replay	Update	Configure	Create	Delete	Read	Tag	HealthCheck	ThreadDump	View
jenkins_admin	☑	☑	☑	☑	☑	☑	☑	☑	☑	☑	☑	☑	☑	☑	☑	☑	☑	☑	☑	☑	☑	☑	☑	☑	☑	☑	☑	☑	☑	☑	☑	☑	☑	☑
jenkins_developer	☐	☑	☐	☐	☐	☐	☐	☐	☐	☐	☐	☐	☐	☐	☑	☑	☑	☐	☐	☐	☐	☑	☐	☐	☑	☐	☑	☑	☐	☑	☑	☑	☑	☑
jenkins_tester	☐	☑	☐	☐	☐	☐	☐	☐	☐	☐	☐	☐	☐	☐	☑	☑	☑	☐	☐	☐	☐	☑	☐	☐	☑	☐	☑	☑	☐	☑	☑	☑	☑	☑
jenkins_user	☐	☑	☐	☐	☐	☐	☐	☐	☐	☐	☐	☐	☐	☐	☐	☐	☐	☐	☐	☐	☐	☐	☐	☐	☐	☐	☐	☐	☐	☑	☑	☑	☑	☑
Anonymous	☐	☑	☐	☐	☐	☐	☐	☐	☐	☐	☐	☐	☐	☐	☐	☐	☐	☐	☐	☐	☐	☐	☐	☐	☐	☐	☐	☐	☐	☐	☐	☐	☐	☐

Providing permissions using the Matrix

7. Leave the rest of the settings as they are and click on the **Save** button at the bottom of the page.
8. To check the configuration, log in as each user and confirm what you see on the Jenkins dashboard.

Project-based Matrix Authorization Strategy

In the previous section, we saw the matrix-based security authorization feature, which gave us a good amount of control over the users and permissions.

However, imagine a situation where your Jenkins server has grown to a point where it contains hundreds of Jenkins jobs and many users, and you want to control user permissions at the job level (project level).

In such a case, we need the **Project-based Matrix Authorization Strategy**:

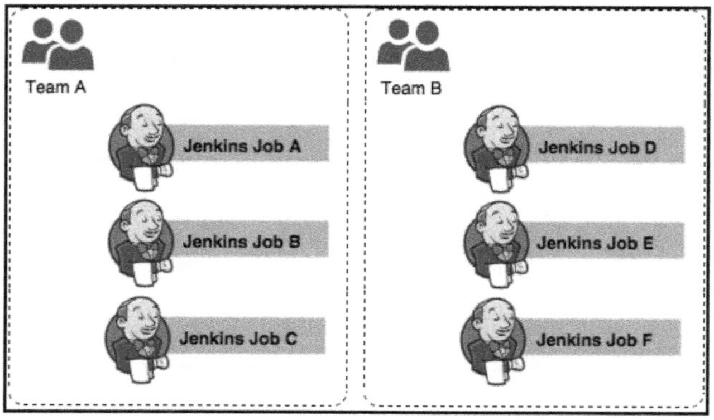

User permission at job level

Let us learn how to configure the **Project-based Matrix Authorization Strategy**. Perform the following steps:

1. To access the Jenkins **Authorization** settings, from the Jenkins dashboard navigate to **Manage Jenkins | Configure Global Security | Access Control**.
2. Select the **Project-based Matrix Authorization Strategy** option. You will be presented with the following matrix:

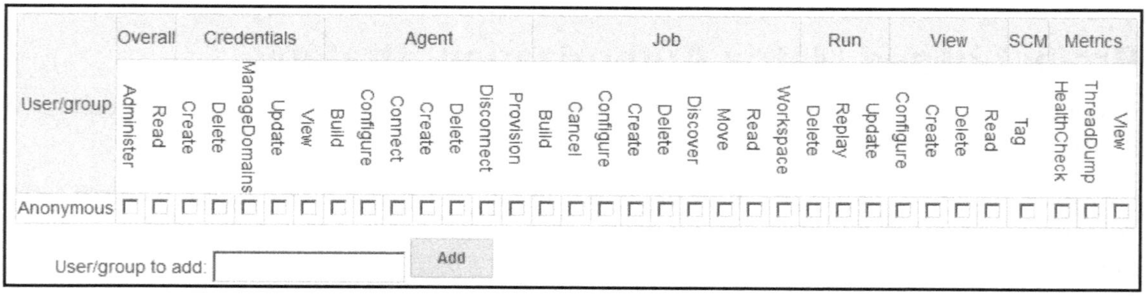

Project-based Matrix Authorization Strategy configurations

3. For now, add a user and give it full permissions. To add a user, type the exact username of the user in the **User/group to add** field, and click on the **Add** button.

4. You can see from the following screenshot that I have added the user `jenkins_admin` with full permissions:

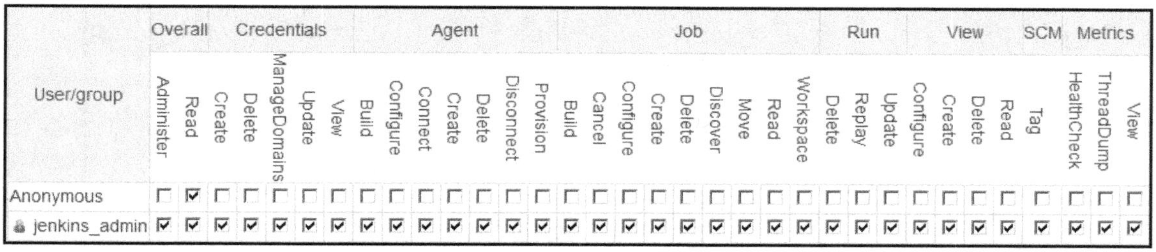

Adding users to the matrix

5. Leave the rest of the settings as they are and click on the **Save** button at the bottom of the page.
6. Next, from the Jenkins dashboard right-click on any of the Jenkins jobs and select **Configure**.
7. Once on the Jobs Configuration page, scroll all the way down to the **Enable project-based security** option and enable it.
8. The moment you enable the project-based security, a matrix table will appear, as shown in the following screenshot:

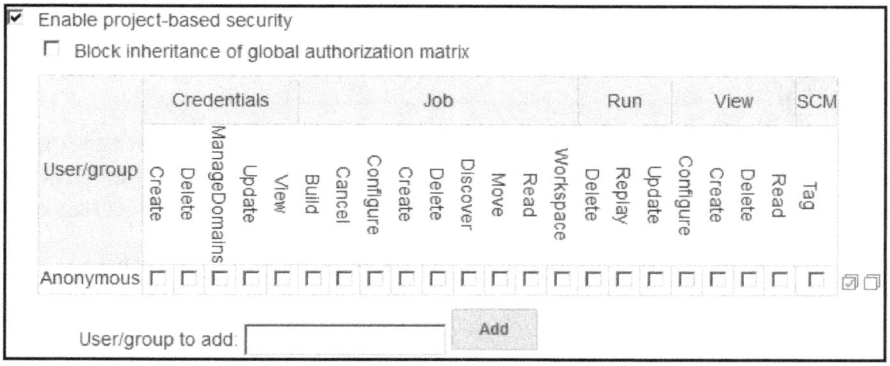

Project-based security configurations inside Jenkins job

9. Let us add some users and provide them some permissions.
10. To add a user, enter the exact username of the user in the **User/group to add** field, and click on the **Add** button.

11. You can see from the following screenshot that I have added the user `jenkins_developer` with some permissions:

User/group	Credentials					Job									Run			View				SCM
	Create	Delete	ManageDomains	Update	View	Build	Cancel	Configure	Create	Delete	Discover	Move	Read	Workspace	Delete	Replay	Update	Configure	Create	Delete	Read	Tag
Anonymous	☐	☐	☐	☐	☐	☐	☐	☐	☐	☐	☐	☐	☐	☐	☐	☐	☐	☐	☐	☐	☐	☐
jenkins_developer	☐	☐	☐	☐	☐	☑	☑	☐	☐	☐	☐	☐	☑	☐	☐	☑	☐	☑	☑	☑	☑	☑

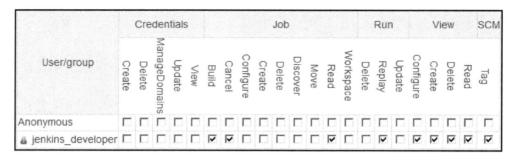

Providing permissions using the Matrix

12. Once done, click on the **Save** button at the bottom of the page.
13. Now log in as the user that you have just given permissions to for the respective Jenkins job (in our example it is `jenkins_developer`).
14. You will find that the user can only see the Jenkins job that it has permission to access.
15. Similarly, you can configure user permissions on each and every job that you create in Jenkins.

Summary

In this chapter, we saw how to configure some of the basic but important elements in Jenkins, all with the help of some practical examples. Jenkins upgrade, Jenkins backup, and Jenkins user management are some of the important things we learned in this chapter.

The next chapter is all about the Jenkins master-slave architecture and the Jenkins *Distributed Build System*.

5 Distributed Builds

Jenkins' master-slave architecture makes it easy to distribute work across multiple slave machines. This chapter is all about configuring Jenkins slaves across various platforms. The following are the topics that we will cover:

- An overview of the Jenkins node manager
- Installing a Jenkins slave on a standalone Linux machine
- Installing a Jenkins slave on a standalone Windows machine
- Installing and configuring the Docker plugin for creating on-demand Jenkins slaves

Distributed build and test

In the following section let us learn a little bit about the distributed build and testing. Imagine you have a really fat unit test or integration test suite. If you can divide them in small parts then you can run them in parallel. To run them in parallel you need multiple clones of your build/test machines. If you have them in place either using Docker or using some other mechanism, then the remaining thing to do is to make them a Jenkins slave agent.

The following illustration shows how a Jenkins pipeline to build, unit test and integration test utilizes the distributed build/test farm in Jenkins. You can see, we have two categories of Jenkins slave agents: Standalone Jenkins slave for build and unit test, and standalone Jenkins slave for integration test.

The unit testing is distributed across three Jenkins slave agents for build and unit test (category 1), and the integration testing is distributed across two Jenkins slave agents for integration testing (category 2).

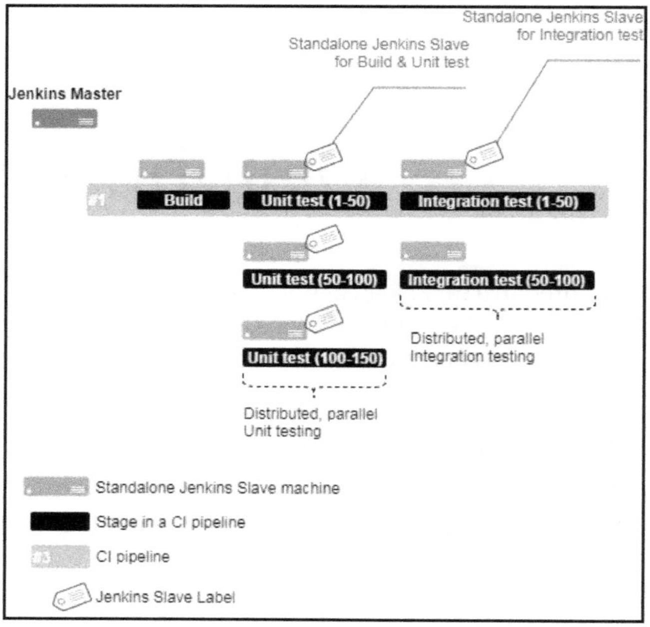

Distributed build and testing farm using Jenkins standalone slave agents

The Jenkins slave agents are categorized using **labels**. We will learn more about labels in the up-coming sections.

It is also much better and easy to spawn on demand Jenkins slaves using Docker. Shown as follows is the Docker version of the same concept that we discussed previously. Here the Jenkins slave are created on demand using the Docker images.

You can see in the following illustration, we have two types of Docker images: Docker image for build and unit test, and Docker image for integration test. The Docker slave agents are created using these Docker images. The unit testing is distributed across three Docker slave agents for build and unit test (category 1), and the integration testing is distributed across two Docker slave agents for integration testing (category 2).

Again here the Docker slave agents are categorized using labels. We will learn more about labels in the up-coming sections:

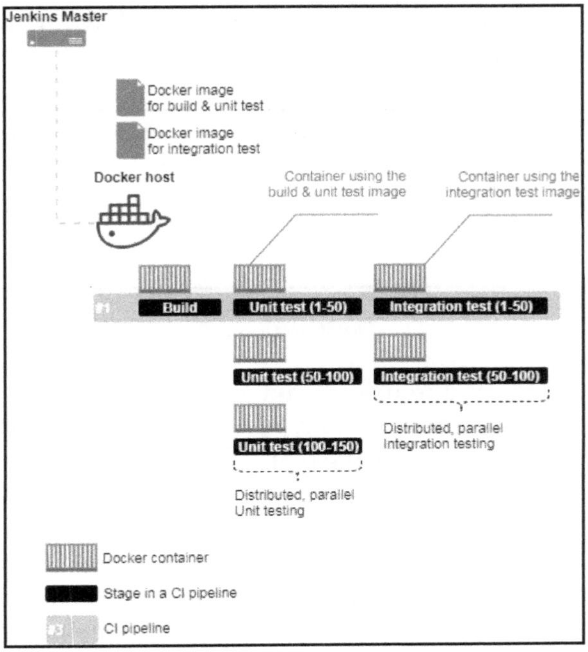

Distributed build and testing farm using Jenkins and Docker slave agents

The Jenkins Manage Nodes page

In the following section, we will take a look at the Jenkins **Manage Nodes** page:

1. From the Jenkins dashboard, click on **Manage Jenkins** | **Manage Nodes**.
2. On the left-hand side, you will see a menu; the options are as explained in the following screenshot:

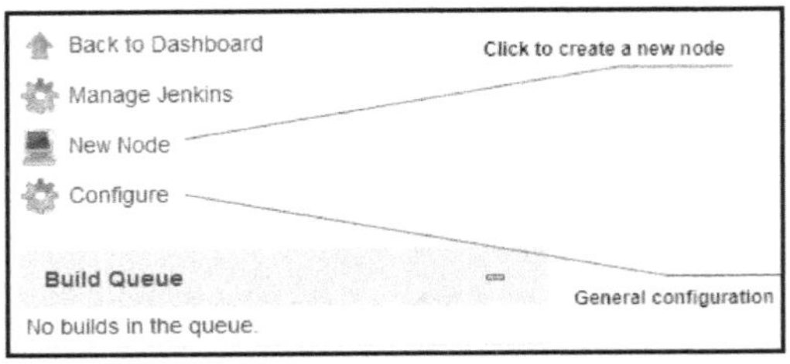

Jenkins Manage Nodes page

3. On the right-hand side, you will also see a table showing the list of available Jenkins slaves, as shown in the following screenshot:

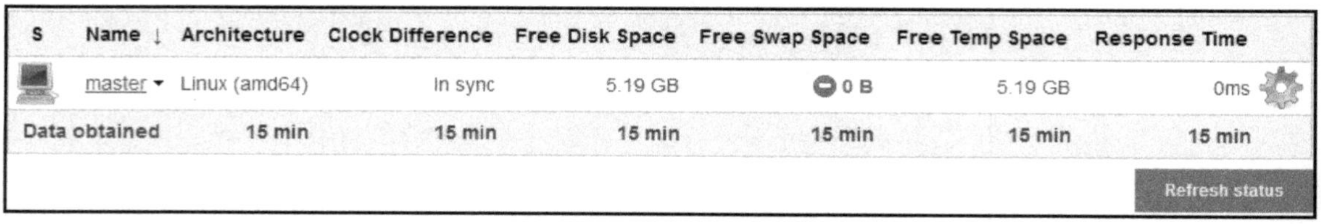
S
Name ↓
Architecture
Clock Difference
Free Disk Space
Free Swap Space
Free Temp Space
Response Time
master
Linux (amd64)
In sync
5.19 GB
0 B
5.19 GB
0ms
Data obtained
15 min
15 min
15 min
15 min
15 min
15 min
Refresh status

List of available nodes

4. Since we haven't configured any Jenkins slaves yet, the list (as shown in the preceding screenshot) contains only one entry: that is, **master**.
5. Along with the node's **Name**, the table also displays other useful information about the node, such as its **Architecture**, the amount of **Free Disk Space**, and the **Response Time**.
6. To enable/disable the amount of information being displayed about each node, click on the **Configure** link (see the *Jenkins Manage Nodes page* screenshot). This will take you to the next page, as shown in the following screenshot:

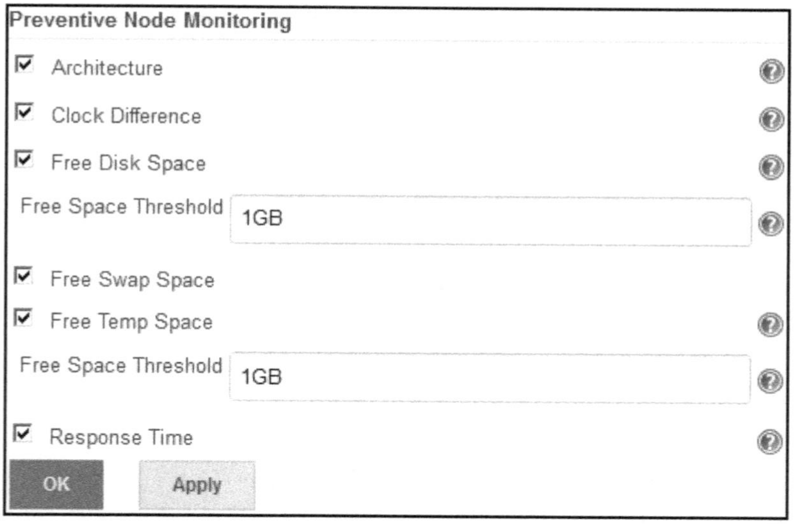

Preventive Node Monitoring options

7. Uncheck/Check the relevant options to disable/enable them. The **Free Space Threshold** option is important. If the amount of **Free Disk Space** and **Free Temp Space** goes below the specified value (by default it's set to `1GB`), then the nodes go offline. This prevents the Jenkins pipeline from running on slaves that have run out of disk space and eventually failing.

Adding Jenkins slaves – standalone Linux machine/VMs

In the following section, we will try to add a standalone Linux machine as a Jenkins slave. Make sure you have Java installed on your soon-to-be Jenkins slave machine. Follow the given steps:

1. From the Jenkins dashboard, click on **Manage Jenkins** | **Manage Nodes**.
2. From the left-hand side menu, click on **New Node**. On the resultant page you will be asked to provide a name for your node and choose the type, as shown in the following screenshot:

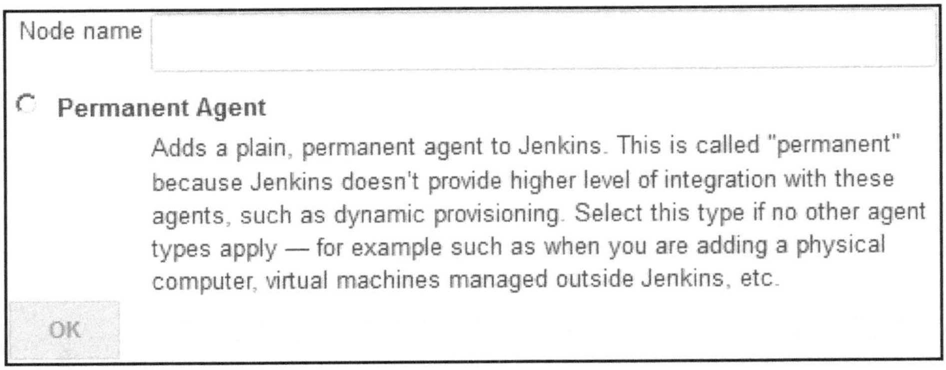

Adding a name and choosing the agent type (type of slave)

3. Add a meaningful name under the **Node name** field and choose the agent type. For now, there is only one type of agent to choose from: that is, **Permanent Agent**. These are the types of agents that are mainly physical machines and VMs.
4. Click on the **OK** button to proceed.

5. On the resultant page, you will see the following options to configure, as shown in the following screenshot:

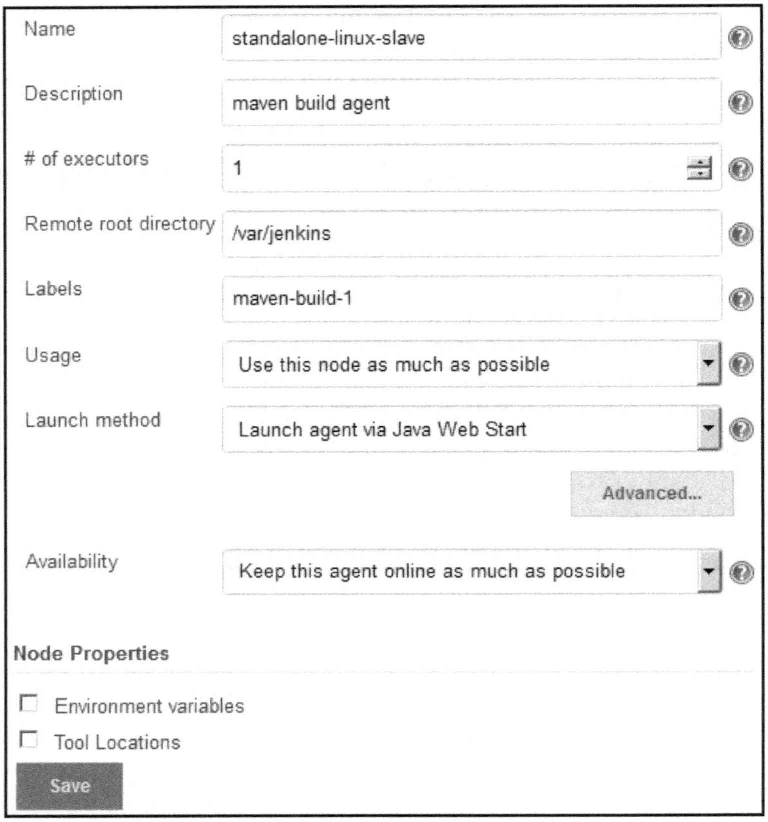

Jenkins slave configuration

Let's see them one by one:

1. We already used the **Name** field to give a name to our Jenkins slave.
2. Use the **Description** field to add some notes about the Jenkins slave: for example, purpose, type, what it can build or test, and tools installed.
3. The **# of executors** field is used to describe the number of parallel builds a Jenkins slave (agent) is allowed to run. Choosing a value greater than `1`, say `3`, will allow the Jenkins slave to run three builds in parallel. This could also result in each build taking more time than usual. Choose wisely.

4. The **Remote root directory** field is used to define a directory path on the Jenkins slave that will serve as a dedicated workspace for Jenkins to perform build activities.
5. The **Labels** field is the most important. You can add multiple labels (separated by a space) to your Jenkins slave. In order to run a pipeline on a particular slave you will use its label, as shown in the preceding screenshot. We have added a `maven-build-1` label, which says it's a Jenkins slave to build a Maven project.
6. The **Usage** field is used to define how Jenkins schedules build on this node. It contains two options, as follows:
    - **Use this node as much as possible**: This is the default option. This mode makes the current Jenkins slave open to all the pipelines that haven't been configured to run on a specific Jenkins slave.
    - **Only build jobs with label expressions matching this node**: In this mode, Jenkins will only build a project on this node when that project is restricted to certain nodes using a label expression, and that expression matches this node's name and/or labels.
7. The **Launch method** field describes how Jenkins starts this Jenkins slave. It contains four options, shown as follows. In the following example, we will use the SSH method to launch our Jenkins slave. See the *Launching a Jenkins slave via SSH* section:
    - **Launch agent via Java Web Start**: This allows an agent to be launched using Java Web Start. In this case, a **Java Network Launch Protocol** (**JNLP**) file must be opened on the agent machine, which will establish a TCP connection to the Jenkins master. If you have enabled security via the **Configure Global Security** page, you can customize the port on which the Jenkins master will listen for incoming JNLP agent connections.
    - **Launch agent via execution of command on the master**: This starts an agent by having Jenkins execute a command from the master. Use this when the master is capable of remotely executing a process on another machine, for example, via SSH or **remote shell** (**RSH**).
    - **Launch slave agents via SSH**: This starts a slave by sending commands over a secure SSH connection. The slave needs to be reachable from the master, and you will have to supply an account that can log in on the target machine. No root privileges are required.
    - **Let Jenkins control this Windows slave as a Windows service**: This starts a Windows slave by a remote management facility built into Windows. It is suitable for managing Windows slaves. Slaves need to be IP reachable from the master.

8. The **Availability** field defines how Jenkins starts, stops, and uses the Jenkins slaves. It has three options, as follows:
    - **Keep this agent online as much as possible**: In this mode, Jenkins will keep this agent online as much as possible. If the agent goes offline, for example, due to a temporary network failure, Jenkins will periodically attempt to restart it.
    - **Take this agent online and offline at specific times**: In this mode, Jenkins will bring this agent online at the scheduled time(s), remaining online for a specified amount of time. If the agent goes offline while it is scheduled to be online, Jenkins will periodically attempt to restart it. After this agent has been online for the number of minutes specified in the **Scheduled Uptime** field, it will be taken offline. If **Keep online while builds are running** is checked, and the agent is scheduled to be taken offline, Jenkins will wait for any builds that may be in progress to be completed.
    - **Take this agent online when in demand, and offline when idle**: In this mode, Jenkins will bring this agent online if there is demand, that is, if there are queued builds that meet the following criteria: They have been in the queue for at least the specified **In demand delay** time period
    - They can be executed by this agent (for example, have a matching label expression)

      This agent will be taken offline if:

        - There are no active builds running on this agent
        - This agent has been idle for at least the specified **Idle delay** time period

Passing environment variables to Jenkins slaves

Follow the given steps to pass the environment variables:

1. You will see a section named **Node Properties**. Using these options, you can pass predefined environment variables to the Jenkins slaves and tools locations.
2. As shown in the following screenshot, you can pass environment variables to the Jenkins slaves. It is possible to pass multiple environment variables (by clicking on the **Add** button). These environment variables are available to the Jenkins pipeline during its execution:

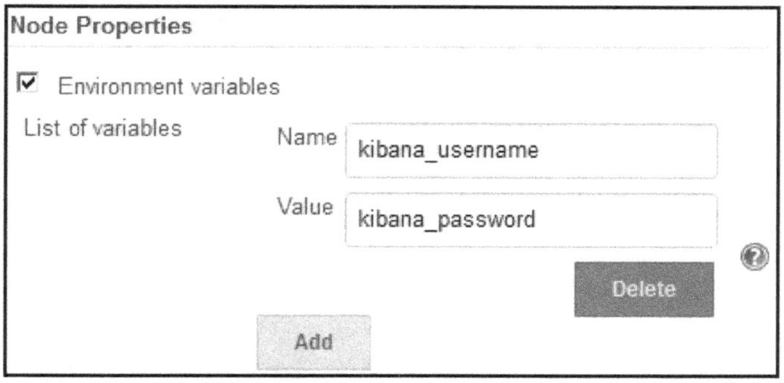

Passing environment variables to the Jenkins slaves

With the advent of *Pipeline as Code* feature in Jenkins, it is possible to define and use environment variables right within the Jenkins pipeline code (pipeline script/Jenkinsfile). Therefore, the option of defining environment variables (as demonstrated in the preceding screenshot) become less significant.

Passing tools' locations to Jenkins slaves

As shown in the following screenshot, you can specify the location of certain tools on the Jenkins slave, overriding the global configuration:

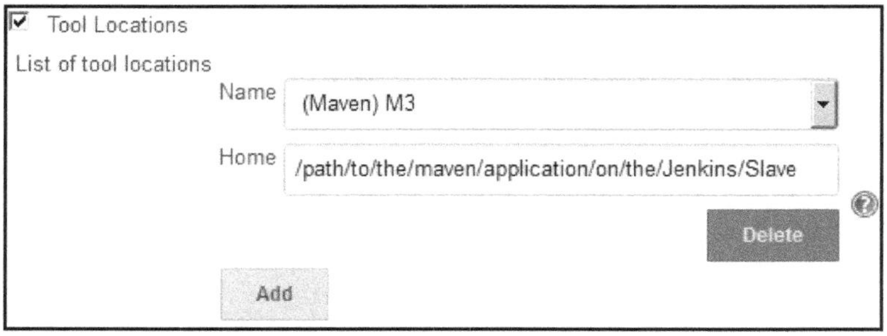

Passing tools' locations to the Jenkins slaves

Launching a Jenkins slave via SSH

To launch the slave via SSH, follow these steps:

1. When you choose the **Launch slave agents via SSH** option, you are presented with options, as shown in the following screenshot.
2. The **Host** field is where you can define the IP address or the hostname of the Jenkins slave machine.
3. The **Credentials** field allows you to choose the relevant credentials saved inside Jenkins to authenticate the Jenkins slave. To create a new credential, click on the **Add** button beside the **Credentials** field (create a credential of the **Kind**: **Username with password**):

Configure Launch slave agent via SSH properties

The user that you use to authenticate the Jenkins slave should have read/write permissions for the directory path defined under the **Remote root directory** field.

4. The last option, **Host Key Verification Strategy**, defines how Jenkins verifies the SSH key presented by the remote host while connecting. This option is valid only when using credentials of the **Kind**: **SSH username with private key**. There are four options available, as follows:
    - **Known hosts file Verification Strategy**: This checks the `known_hosts` file (`~/.ssh/known_hosts`) for the user Jenkins is executing under, to see if an entry exists that matches the current connection. This method does not make any updates to the `known_hosts` file, instead it uses the file as a read-only source and expects someone with suitable access to the appropriate user account on the Jenkins master to update the file as required, potentially using the `ssh hostname` command to initiate a connection and update the file appropriately.
    - **Manually provide key Verification Strategy**: This checks that the key provided by the remote host matches the key set by the user who configured this connection.
    - **Known trusted key Verification Strategy**: This checks that the remote key matches the key currently marked as trusted for this host. Depending on the configuration, the key will be automatically trusted for the first connection, or an authorized user will be asked to approve the key. An authorized user will be required to approve any new key that gets presented by the remote host.
    - **Non verifying Verification Strategy**: This does not perform any verification of the SSH key presented by the remote host, allowing all connections regardless of the key they present.
5. Once you are done configuring all the options, click on the **Save** button.

More about the active Jenkins slave

In the following section, we will take a look at the various other configurable options available to us for the Jenkins slave agent that we have just added. Jenkins also provides a lot of general information about its slaves that we will see here. Follow these steps:

1. From the Jenkins dashboard, click on **Manage Jenkins** | **Manage Nodes**.
2. On the right-hand side you will also see a table showing the list of available Jenkins slaves. New to the list will be our newly added Jenkins slave.
3. Click on the Jenkins slave name to access its configurations and metadata.

4. On the resultant page (Jenkins slave **Status** page), on the left-hand side menu you will see a few options, as shown in the following screenshot:

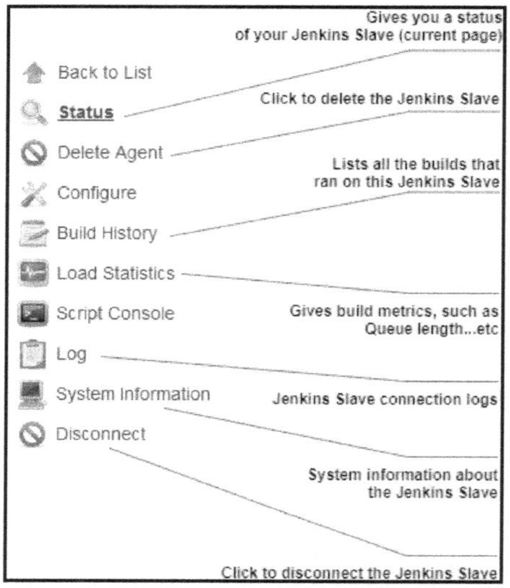

Jenkins slave page

5. Most of the preceding links (from the preceding screenshot) are self-explanatory. However, let's look at some of them in detail.
6. The **Log** link is where you will find all the logs with respect to the Jenkins slave. After adding a Jenkins slave, if it does not come online, the **Log** is where you need to look. Authentication issues, permission issues, and everything else while connecting to the Jenkins slaves gets listed here. See the following screenshot:

```
[SSH] Starting slave process: cd "/var/jenkins" && java  -jar slave.jar
<===[JENKINS REMOTING CAPACITY]===>channel started
Slave.jar version: 3.7
This is a Unix agent
Evacuated stdout
Agent successfully connected and online
```

Jenkins slave logs

7. The **System Information** link will show you most of the system information about the respective Jenkins slave, such as **System Properties**, and **Environment Variables**. See the preceding screenshot. You won't be visiting here frequently. Nevertheless, it's useful when debugging build errors caused due to system tools, environment variables, and so on:

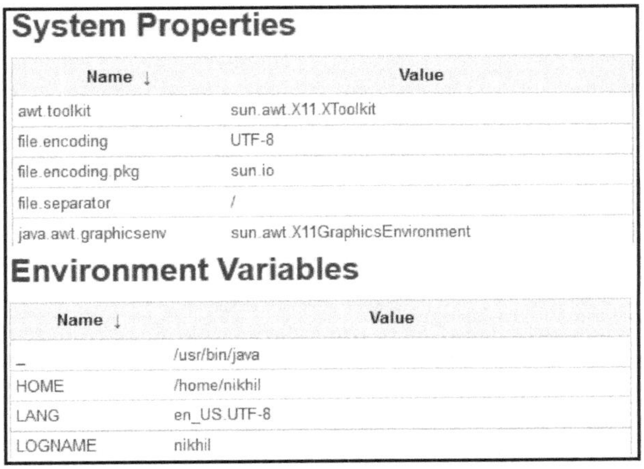
System Properties

Name ↓	Value
awt.toolkit	sun.awt.X11.XToolkit
file.encoding	UTF-8
file.encoding.pkg	sun.io
file.separator	/
java.awt.graphicsenv	sun.awt.X11GraphicsEnvironment

Environment Variables

Name ↓	Value
_	/usr/bin/java
HOME	/home/nikhil
LANG	en_US.UTF-8
LOGNAME	nikhil

Jenkins slave System Information

8. The **Build History** link will show you a timeline of all the builds that were performed on the respective Jenkins slave.
9. On the Jenkins slave **Status** page, you will see the labels that are attached to the respective Jenkins slave and, also, information about the projects that are associated with the following Jenkins slave. See the following screenshot:

Jenkins slave Status page

10. There is an option to make the Jenkins slave temporarily offline by clicking on the **Mark this node temporarily offline** button. When you click on the button, you will be asked to add a note (optional) before taking the Jenkins slave offline:

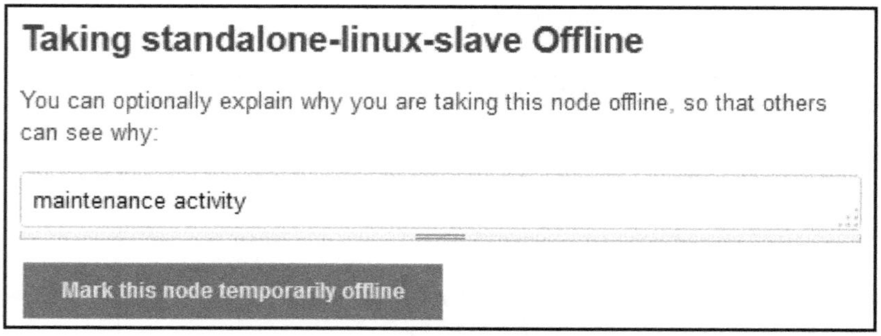

Making a Jenkins slave offline

11. To bring the offline node back online, from the Jenkins **Status** page, click on the **Bring this node back online** button:

Bringing a Jenkins slave online

Adding Jenkins slaves – standalone Windows machine/VMs

In the following section, we will try to add a standalone Windows machine as a Jenkins slave. Make sure you have Java installed on your soon-to-be Jenkins slave machine. Follow the given steps:

1. From the left-hand side menu, click on **New Node**. On the resultant page, you will be asked to provide a name for your node and choose the type, as shown in the following screenshot:
2. From the Jenkins dashboard, click on **Manage Jenkins** | **Manage Nodes**.

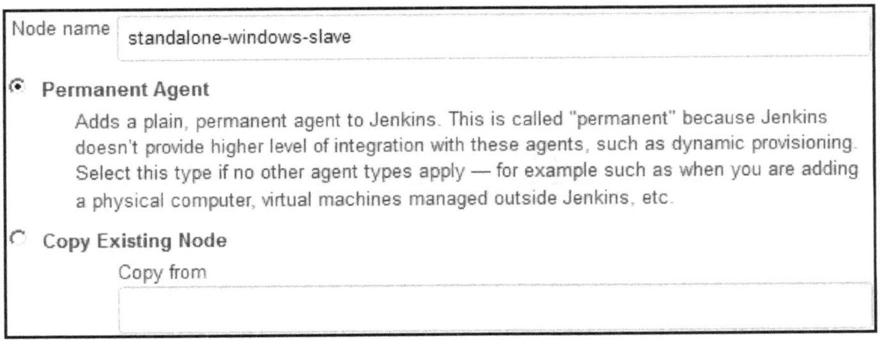

Adding a name and choosing the agent type (type of slave)

3. Add a meaningful name under the **Node name** field and choose the agent type as **Permanent Agent**. These are the types of agents that are mainly physical machines and VMs. Also, there is an option to clone an existing Jenkins slave. To do so, choose the **Copy Existing Node** option and under the **Copy from** field, enter the name of the Jenkins slave source.
4. In the following example however, we will choose the **Permanent Agent** option.
5. Click on the **OK** button to proceed.

6. On the resultant page, you will see the following options to configure, as shown in the following screenshot. We have already seen them before:

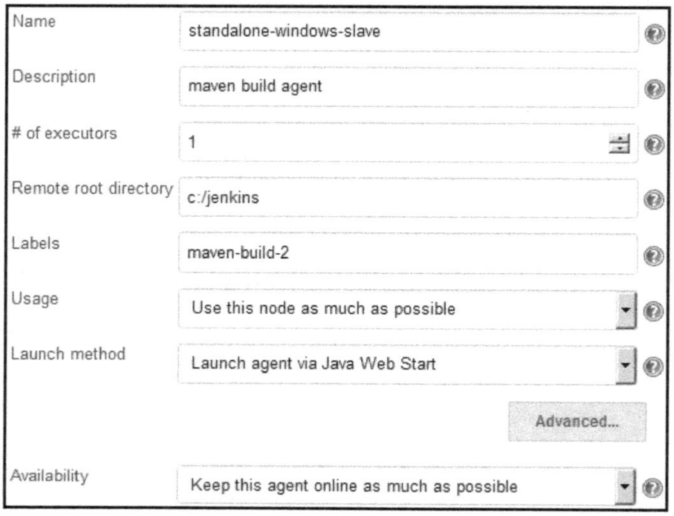

Jenkins slave configurations

7. Since this is a Windows build agent, there are two ways we can launch the Jenkins slave, as shown here:
    - **Launch agent via Java Web Start**: This allows an agent to be launched using Java Web Start. In this case, a JNLP file must be opened on the agent machine, which will establish a TCP connection to the Jenkins master. If you have enabled security via the **Configure Global Security** page, you can customize the port on which the Jenkins master will listen for incoming JNLP agent connections.
    - **Let Jenkins control this Windows slave as a Windows service**: This starts a Windows slave by a remote management facility built into Windows. It is suitable for managing Windows slaves. Slaves need to be IP reachable from the master.

Launching a Jenkins slave via Java Web Start

In the following section, we will learn how to launch a Jenkins slave on Windows using the Java Web Start method.

1. For the **Launch method** field, choose **Launch agent via Java Web Start**.
2. Click on the **Save** button.
3. From the Jenkins **Manage Nodes** page, click on the Jenkins slave name. In our example it's `standalone-windows-slave`.
4. On the resultant page (Jenkin slave **Status** page), you will see the following options, as shown here:

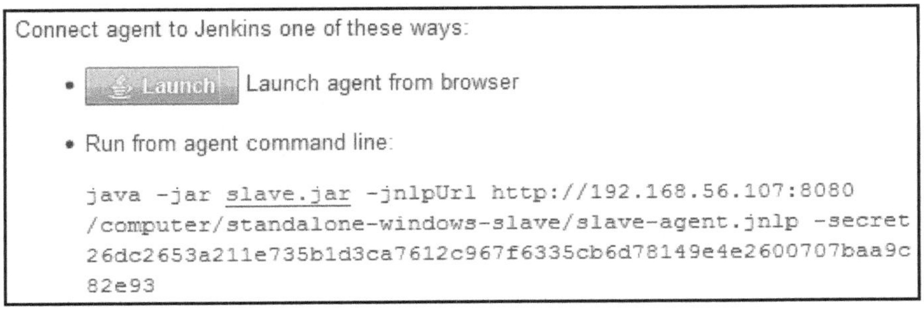
Connect agent to Jenkins one of these ways:
Launch
Launch agent from browser
Run from agent command line:
java -jar slave.jar -jnlpUrl http://192.168.56.107:8080
/computer/standalone-windows-slave/slave-agent.jnlp -secret
26dc2653a211e735b1d3ca7612c967f6335cb6d78149e4e2600707baa9c
82e93

Jenkins slave connection method (Java Web Start)

5. Do nothing on the Jenkins server.
6. Now, log in to your prospective Jenkins slave machine (Windows) and open the Jenkins dashboard.
7. From the Jenkins dashboard, click on **Manage Jenkins** | **Manage Nodes**.
8. From the Jenkins **Manage Nodes** page, click on the Jenkins slave name. In our example it's `standalone-windows-slave`.
9. Now, either run the command, as shown in the following screenshot, or click on the **Launch** button.

10. If you choose to click on the **Launch** button, you will see the following pop-up window, as shown in the following screenshot:

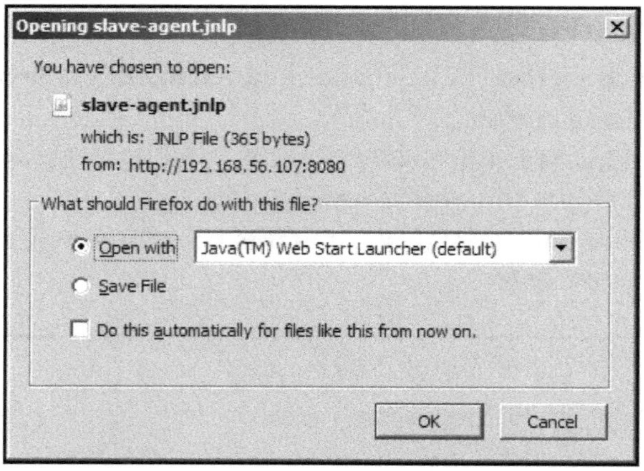

Opening the slave-agent.jnlp file

11. Choose as the **Open with** option the **Java(TM) Web Start Launcher (default)** option, and click on the **OK** button.
12. You will get another pop-up window, asking you to confirm that you would like to run this application. Click on **Run**, as shown in the following screenshot:

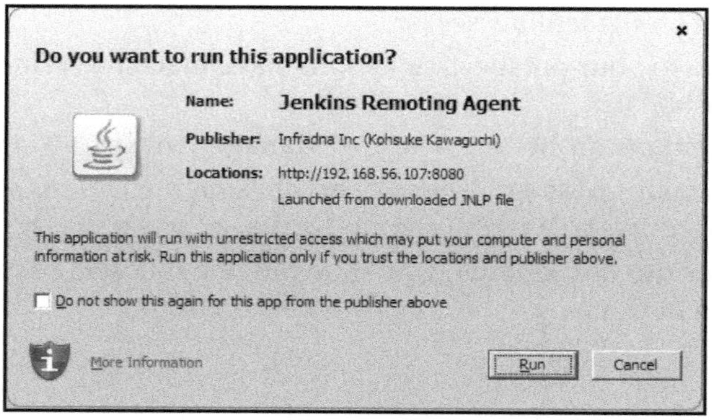

Running the Jenkins Remoting Agent

13. Finally, you will see a small window showing the Jenkins slave connection status as **Connected**, as shown in the following screenshot:

Jenkins slave agent window

14. Your Jenkins slave (Windows) is now connected. To make it a Windows service, click on **File** (previous screenshot), and choose **Install as a service**.
15. Open the **Run** utility and give the command `services.msc` to open the Windows **Services** utility. In the list of services, you will find the Jenkins slave agent service, as shown in the following screenshot:

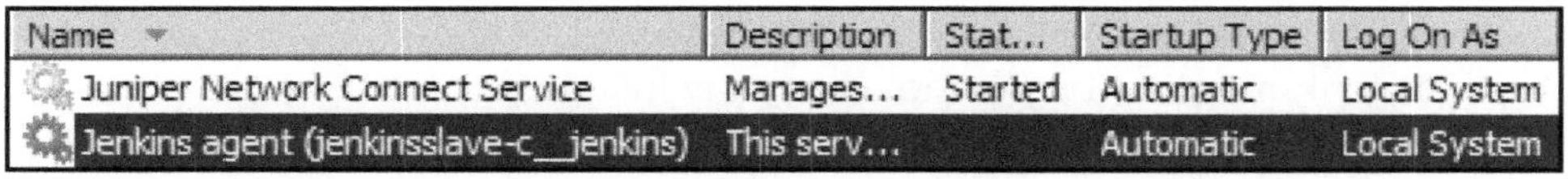

Jenkins slave listed as a Windows service

16. Right-click on the Jenkins slave Windows service and choose **Properties**.

17. In the **Properties** window, go to the **Log On** tab. Under the **Log on as** section, choose the **This account** option, and provide the administrator account details (a user with admin privileges on the Jenkins slave machine), as shown in the following screenshot:

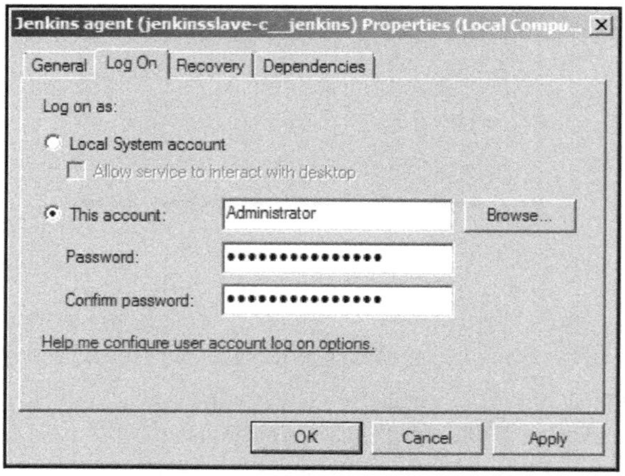

Jenkins slave service properties

18. Your Jenkins slave (on Windows) is now installed.

Adding Jenkins slaves – Docker containers

In the following section, we will learn how to install and configure the Docker plugin that will allow us to spawn on-demand Jenkins slaves (Docker containers) from a CI pipeline. The Docker containers are started by the CI pipeline, and once the build is done, they are destroyed. In the following section, we will only see the configuration part. It is in the next chapter that we will see this process in action.

Prerequisites

Before we begin, make sure you have the following things ready:

- A Jenkins server running on any of the following platforms: Docker, standalone, cloud, VM, servlet container, and so on. (refer to `Chapter 2`, *Installing Jenkins*).

- Your Jenkins server should have access to the internet. This is necessary to download and install plugins.
- Your Jenkins server can talk to GitHub using the **GitHub plugin**. (Refer to the *Add GitHub credentials inside Jenkins* and *Configure Webhooks on GitHub from Jenkins* sections from `Chapter 3`, *The New Jenkins*).
- You might also need Java, Git, and Maven configured on your Jenkins server. (Refer to the *The new Jenkins pipeline job* subsection under the *The Global Tool Configuration page* section of `Chapter 3`, *The New Jenkins*).
- A Docker server.

Setting up a Docker server

To install Docker, you need a machine with any one of the following Ubuntu OSes (64-bit): Yakkety Yak 16.10, Xenial Xerus 16.04, or Trusty Tahr 14.04. Make sure `curl` is also installed. Follow the steps given to set up a Docker server.

Setting up the repository

Follow the given steps to set up a repository:

1. Execute the following command to let `apt` use a repository:

```
sudo apt-get install apt-transport-https ca-certificates
```

2. Add the Docker's official GPG key using the following command:

```
curl -fsSL https://yum.dockerproject.org/gpg | sudo apt-key add -
```

3. Verify that the key ID is exactly `58118E89F3A912897C070ADBF76221572C52609D`, using the following command:

```
apt-key fingerprint 58118E89F3A912897C070ADBF76221572C52609D
```

4. You should see a similar output:

```
pub 4096R/2C52609D 2015-07-14
Key fingerprint = 5811 8E89 F3A9 1289 7C07 0ADB F762 2157 2C52 609D
Uid Docker Release Tool (releasedocker) docker@docker.com
```

5. Use the following command to set up a stable repository to download Docker:

```
sudo add-apt-repository \
"deb https://apt.dockerproject.org/repo/ubuntu-$(lsb_release -cs) \
main"
```

It's recommended to always use the stable version of the repository.

Installing Docker using apt-get

Now that you have set up the repository, perform the following steps to install Docker:

1. Update the `apt` package index using the following command:

```
sudo apt-get update
```

2. To install the latest version of Docker, execute the following command:

```
sudo apt-get -y install docker-engine
```

3. However, if you wish to install a specific version of Docker, execute the following command:

```
apt-cache madison docker-engine
```

4. This will give you a list of available versions:

```
docker-engine | 1.16.0-0~trusty |
https://apt.dockerproject.org/repo
ubuntu-trusty/main amd64 Packages
docker-engine | 1.13.3-0~trusty |
https://apt.dockerproject.org/repo
ubuntu-trusty/main amd64 Packages
```

The output of the preceding command depends on the type of repository configured in the previous section, *Setting up the repository*.

5. Next, execute the following command to install the specific version of Docker:

```
sudo apt-get -y install docker-engine=<VERSION_STRING>
```

Example: `sudo apt-get -y install docker-engine=1.16.0-0~trusty`

6. The `docker` service starts automatically. To verify whether Docker is installed and running, run the following command:

```
sudo docker run hello-world
```

7. If the preceding command runs without any errors, and you see a `hello world` message, it means Docker is installed and running.

```
Hello from Docker!
This message shows that your installation appears to be
working correctly.
```

Installing Docker using a .deb package

For some reason, if you are unable to install Docker using the preceding repository method, you can download the `.deb` package.

1. Download the `.deb` package of your choice from `https://apt.dockerproject.org/repo/pool/main/d/docker-engine/`.
2. To install the downloaded package, type the following:

```
sudo dpkg -i /<path to package>/<docker package>.deb
```

3. Verify your Docker installation by running the following command:

```
sudo docker run hello-world
```

4. If the preceding command runs without any errors, and you see a `hello world` message, it means Docker is installed and running.

```
Hello from Docker!
This message shows that your installation appears to be
working correctly.
```

Enabling Docker remote API

Jenkins (through the Docker plugin) uses the *Docker remote API* to communicate with a Docker server. The Docker remote API allows external applications to communicate with the Docker server using REST APIs. Docker remote APIs can also be used to get information about all the running containers inside the Docker server.

To enable the Docker remote API, we need to modify Docker's configuration file. Depending on your OS version and the way you have installed Docker on your machine, you might need to choose the right configuration file to modify. Shown, as follows, are two methods that work on Ubuntu.

Modifying the docker.conf file

Follow these steps to modify the `docker.conf` file. These configurations are important to allow Jenkins to communicate with the Docker host:

1. Log in to your Docker server, make sure you have `sudo` privileges.
2. Execute the following command to edit the `docker.conf` file:

```
sudo nano /etc/init/docker.conf
```

3. Inside the `docker.conf` file, go to the line containing `DOCKER_OPTS=`.

> You will find the `DOCKER_OPTS=` variable at two places inside the `docker.conf` file. First, in the pre-start script section, and next in the post-start script section. Use the `DOCKER_OPTS=` variable under the pre-start script section.

4. Set the value of `DOCKER_OPTS` to the following:

```
DOCKER_OPTS='-H tcp://0.0.0.0:4243 -H unix:///var/run/docker.sock'
```

5. The preceding setting will bind the Docker server to the Unix socket, as well as on TCP port `4243`. `0.0.0.0`, which makes the Docker engine accept connections from anywhere.

> If you want your Docker server to accept connections from only your Jenkins server, then replace `0.0.0.0` with your Jenkins server IP.

6. Restart the Docker server using the following command:

```
sudo service docker restart
```

7. To check if the configuration has worked, type the following:

```
curl -X GET http://<Docker server IP>:4243/images/json
```

The preceding command will list all the images present on your Docker server, if any.

Modifying the docker.service file

Follow the given steps to modify the `docker.service` file:

1. Execute the following command to edit the `docker.service` file:

```
sudo nano /lib/systemd/system/docker.service
```

2. Inside the `docker.service` file, go to the line containing `ExecStart=`.
3. Set the value of `ExecStart=` as shown:

```
ExecStart=/usr/bin/docker daemon -H fd:// -H tcp://0.0.0.0:4243
```

4. The preceding setting will bind the Docker server to the Unix socket. Furthermore, on TCP port `4243`. `0.0.0.0`, it makes the Docker engine accept connections from anywhere.

If you want your Docker server to accept connections from only your Jenkins server, replace `0.0.0.0` with your Jenkins server IP.

5. Execute the following command to make the Docker daemon notice the modified configuration:

```
systemctl daemon-reload
```

6. Restart the Docker server using the following command:

```
sudo service docker restart
```

7. To check whether the configuration has worked, type the following:

```
curl -X GET http://<Docker server IP>:4243/images/json
```

The preceding command will list all the images present on your Docker server, if any.

Installing the Docker plugin

To create Docker containers (build agents) on the fly, we need to install the **Docker plugin** for Jenkins. To achieve this, follow the given steps:

1. From the Jenkins dashboard, click on **Manage Jenkins** | **Manage Plugins** | **Available** tab. You will be taken to the Jenkins **Manage Plugins** page.
2. Enter `Docker Plugin` in the **Filter** field, as shown in the following screenshot:

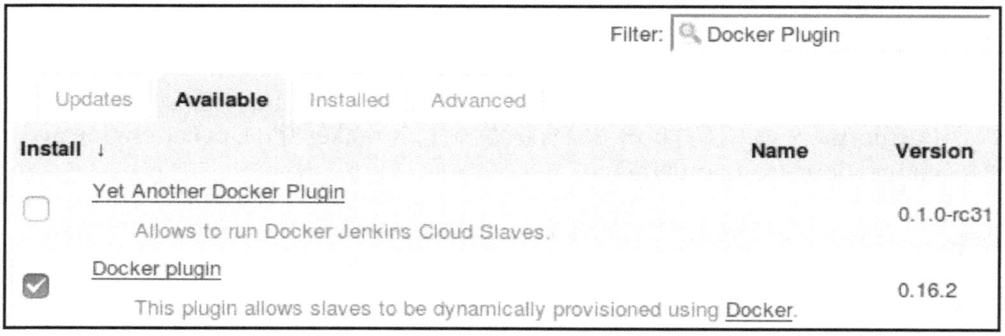

Installing the Docker plugin

3. Select the **Docker Plugin** from the list and click on the **Install without restart** button.
4. Restart Jenkins if needed.

Configuring the Docker plugin

Now that we have our **Docker plugin** installed, let's configure it:

1. From the Jenkins dashboard, click **Manage Jenkins** | **Configure System**.
2. Once on the **Configure System** page, scroll all the way down to the **Cloud** section (see the following screenshot).

3. Click on the **Add a new cloud** button and choose **Docker** from the available options.
4. On the resultant page, you will find a good number of settings to configure.
5. Give your Docker server a name using the **Name** field.
6. Add your Docker server URL under the **Docker URL** field.
7. Click on the **Test Connection** button to check whether Jenkins can communicate with Docker server:

Configuring the Docker plugin to talk to the Docker server

8. At the end of the page, click on the **Apply** and **Save** buttons. We will come back here later to make further configurations.

Creating a Docker image – Jenkins slave

Enabling the Docker remote API made the communication between Jenkins and the Docker server possible. Now we need a Docker image on the Docker server. This Docker image will be used by Jenkins to create Docker containers (Jenkins slaves) on the fly. To achieve this, follow the steps as shown:

1. Log in to your Docker server. Give the following command to check the available Docker images:

```
sudo docker images
```

2. From the following screenshot, you can see we have two `docker images` (`ubuntu` and `hello-world`) already on our Docker server:

ubuntu@node4:~$ sudo docker images
REPOSITORY TAG IMAGE ID CREATED SIZE
ubuntu latest f49eec89601e 3 weeks ago 129 MB
hello-world latest 48b5124b2768 4 weeks ago 1.84 kB
ubuntu@node4:~$

List the Docker images

3. If your Docker server is a freshly backed-up machine, then you will see no images at this point.
4. We will build a Docker image for our use from the `ubuntu` Docker image. To do so, download the Docker image for `ubuntu` using the following command:

```
docker pull ubuntu
```

> You can find more Docker images for various OSes at `https://hub.docker.com/`.

5. Once the pull gets completed, give the `sudo docker images` command again. Now you should see a Docker image for Ubuntu, as shown in the preceding screenshot.

6. We will now upgrade our Ubuntu Docker image with all the necessary applications that we need to run our build. They are as follows:
    - Java JDK (latest)
    - Git
    - Maven
    - A user account to log in to the Docker container
    - `sshd` (to accept an SSH connection)

7. Execute the following command to run a Docker container using the Ubuntu Docker image. This will create a container, and open up its bash shell:

```
sudo docker run -i -t ubuntu /bin/bash
```

8. Now, install all the required applications as you would do on any normal Ubuntu machine. Let's begin by creating a `jenkins` user:
    1. Execute the following command and follow the user creation steps, as shown in the following screenshot:

```
adduser jenkins
```

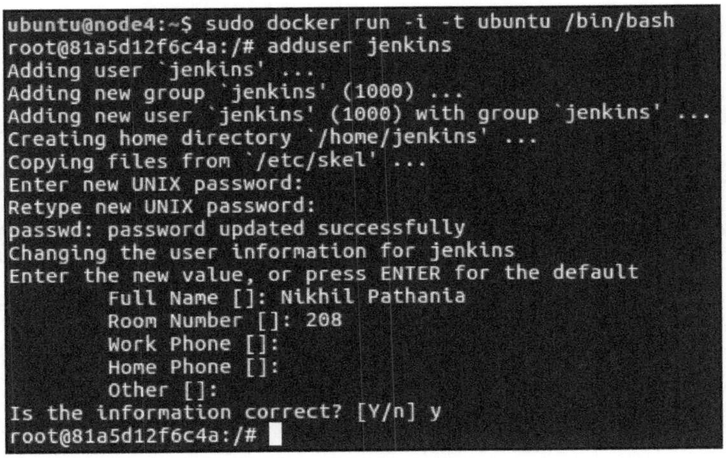

ubuntu@node4:~$ sudo docker run -i -t ubuntu /bin/bash
root@81a5d12f6c4a:/# adduser jenkins
Adding user `jenkins' ...
Adding new group `jenkins' (1000) ...
Adding new user `jenkins' (1000) with group `jenkins' ...
Creating home directory `/home/jenkins' ...
Copying files from `/etc/skel' ...
Enter new UNIX password:
Retype new UNIX password:
passwd: password updated successfully
Changing the user information for jenkins
Enter the new value, or press ENTER for the default
Full Name []: Nikhil Pathania
Room Number []: 208
Work Phone []:
Home Phone []:
Other []:
Is the information correct? [Y/n] y
root@81a5d12f6c4a:/#

Creating a user

    2. Check the new user using the switch user command:

```
su jenkins
```

9. Switch back to the root user by typing `exit`.
10. Next, we will install the SSH server. Execute the following commands in sequence:

```
apt-get update
apt-get install openssh-server
mkdir /var/run/sshd
```

11. Next, we will install Git using the following command:

```
apt-get install git
```

12. Install Java JDK using the following command:

```
apt-get install openjdk-8-jdk
```

13. Install Maven using the following command:

```
apt-get install maven
```

14. Next, exit the container by typing `exit`.
15. We need to save (`commit`) all the changes that we made to our Docker container.
16. Get the `CONTAINER ID` of the container that we worked on recently by listing all the inactive containers, as shown in the following screenshot:

```
sudo docker ps -a
```

List of inactive containers

17. Note the `CONTAINER ID`, and execute the `commit` command to commit the changes that we made to our container, shown as follows:

```
sudo docker commit <CONTAINER ID> <new name for the container>
```

18. We have named the container `maven-build-slave-0.1`, as shown in the following screenshot:

ubuntu@node4:~$ sudo docker commit 81a5d12f6c4a maven-build-slave-0.1
sha256:317fb6ec990f235fc2f2f42beab6f73e44fb4bd2d0bba0479858386c569a7c7d
ubuntu@node4:~$

Docker commit command

19. Once you have committed the changes, a new Docker image gets created.
20. Execute the following Docker command to list the images:

```
sudo docker images
```

ubuntu@node4:~$ sudo docker images
REPOSITORY TAG IMAGE ID CREATED SIZE
maven-build-slave-0.1 latest 317fb6ec990f About a minute ago 298 MB
ubuntu latest f49eec89601e 3 weeks ago 129 MB
hello-world latest 48b5124b2768 4 weeks ago 1.84 kB
ubuntu@node4:~$

List the Docker images

21. You can see our new Docker image, with the name `maven-build-slave-0.1`. We will now configure our Jenkins server to use the Docker image to create Jenkins slaves (build agents).

Adding Docker container credentials in Jenkins

Follow the given steps to add credentials inside Jenkins to allow it to talk to Docker:

1. From the Jenkins dashboard, navigate to **Credentials** | **System** | **Global credentials (unrestricted)**.
2. Click on the **Add Credentials** link on the left-hand side menu to create a new credential (see the following screenshot).
3. Choose a **Kind** as **Username with Password**.
4. Leave the **Scope** field to its default value.
5. Add a username for your Docker image (`jenkins`, as per our example) under the **Username** field.
6. Under the **Password** field, add the password.
7. Add an ID under the **ID** field, and some description under the **Description** field.

8. Once done, click on the **OK** button:

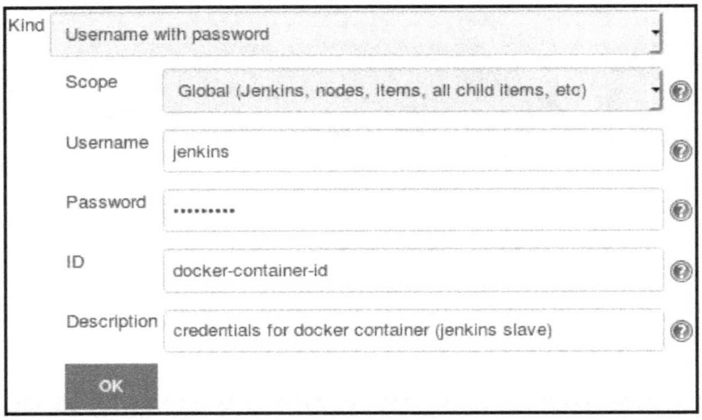

Create credentials inside Jenkins

Updating the Docker settings inside Jenkins

Follow the given steps to update the Docker settings inside Jenkins:

1. From the Jenkins dashboard, click on **Manage Jenkins** | **Configure System**.
2. Scroll all the way down to the **Cloud** section (see the following screenshot).
3. Under the **Cloud** section, click on the **Add Docker Template** button and choose **Docker Template**.
4. You will be presented with lots of settings to configure. However, to keep this demo simple, let's stick to the important settings:
    1. Under the **Docker Image** field, enter the name of the Docker image that we created earlier. In our case, it's `maven-build-slave-0.1`.
    2. Under the **Labels** field, add a label. The Docker container will be recognized using this label by your Jenkins pipeline. Add a `docker` label.
    3. The **Launch Method** should be **Docker SSH computer launcher**.
    4. Under the **Credentials** field, choose the credentials that we created to access the Docker container.
    5. Make sure the **Pull strategy** option is set to **Never pull**.
    6. Leave the rest of the other options to their default values.
    7. Once done, click on **Apply** and then **Save**:

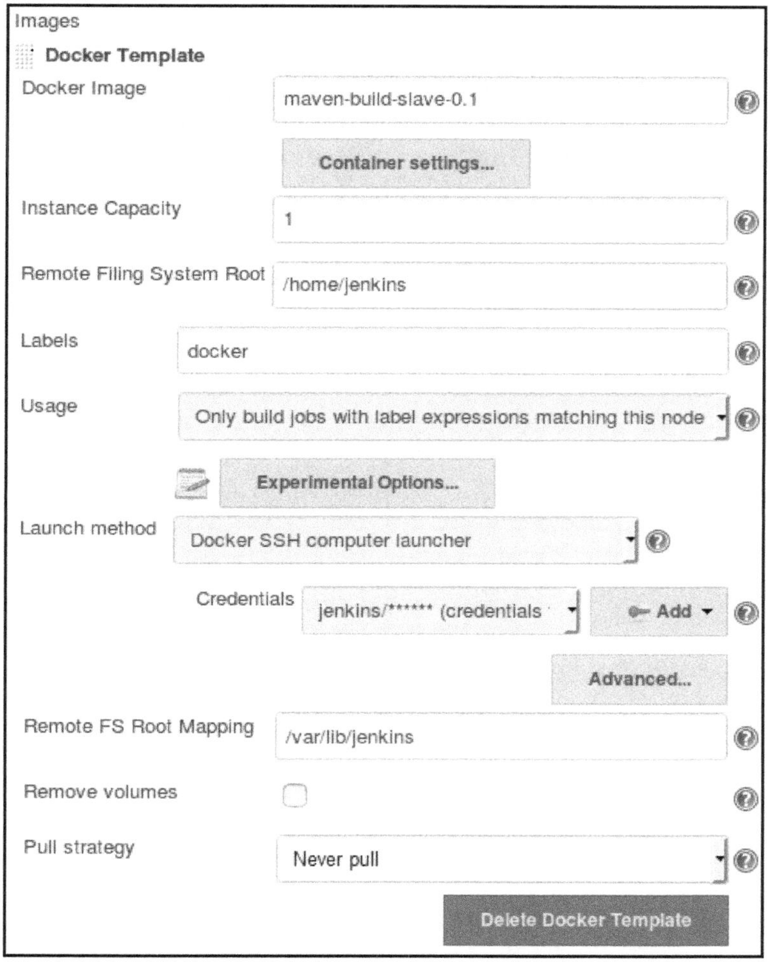

Configuring the Docker plugin settings

5. Now your Jenkins server is all set to create Jenkins slaves on demand using Docker.

Summary

In this chapter, we learned how to add and configure Jenkins slaves on standalone Windows and Linux machines (physical/VMs), using two widely used methods: **Launching Jenkins slave via SSH** and **Launching Jenkins Slave via Java Web Start**. We also learned how to install and configure the **Docker plugin** for Jenkins that allows us to create on-demand Docker containers (Jenkins slaves) for our CI.

In the next chapter, we will learn how to implement continuous integration using Jenkins, and we will utilize the distributed build farm using Jenkins Docker containers (Jenkins slaves) to perform our CI.

6
Installing SonarQube and Artifactory

In this chapter, we will learn about SonarQube, which is a popular open source tool for static code analysis. We will also learn about Artifactory, which is another popular open source tool for version controlling binary files. In this chapter, you will learn about the following topics:

- Installing a standalone SonarQube server
- Creating a project inside SonarQube
- Installing the build breaker plugin for SonarQube
- Creating a quality gate and a quality profile
- Installing and configuring the SonarQube plugin in Jenkins
- Installing a standalone Artifactory server
- Creating a repository inside Artifactory
- Installing and configuring the Artifactory plugin in Jenkins

Installing and configuring SonarQube

Apart from integrating code in a continuous way, CI pipelines nowadays also include tasks that perform continuous inspection—inspecting code for its quality in a continuous approach.

Continuous inspection deals with inspecting and avoiding code that is of poor quality. Tools such as SonarQube help us in achieving this. Every time a code gets checked-in (committed), a code analysis is performed on the code.

This analysis is based on some rules defined by the code analysis tool. If the code passes the error threshold, it's allowed to move to the next step in its life cycle. But, if it crosses the error threshold, it's dropped.

Some organizations prefer checking the code for its quality, right at the moment when the developer tries to check-in the code. If the analysis is good, the code is allowed to be checked-in, or else the check-in is cancelled and the developer needs to work on the code again.

SonarQube is a code quality management tool that allows teams to manage, track, and improve the quality of their source code. It is a web-based application that contains rules, alerts, and thresholds, all of which can be configured. It covers the seven types of code quality parameters, which are architecture and design, duplications, unit tests, complexity, potential bugs, coding rules, and comments.

SonarQube is an open source tool that supports almost all popular programming languages with the help of plugins. SonarQube can also be integrated with a CI tool such as Jenkins to perform continuous inspection, which we will see shortly.

So, first let's learn how to install SonarQube. In the following section, we will learn how to install SonarQube on Ubuntu 16.04.

Installing Java

Follow these steps to install Java:

1. Update the package index:

   ```
   sudo apt-get update
   ```

2. Next, install Java. The following command will install the JRE:

   ```
   sudo apt-get install default-jre
   ```

3. To set the `JAVA_HOME` environment variable, first get the Java installation location. Do this by executing the following command:

   ```
   update-java-alternatives -l
   ```

4. You should get a similar output:

   ```
   java-1.8.0-openjdk-amd64 1081 /usr/lib/jvm/java-1.8.0-openjdk-amd64
   ```

5. The path in the preceding output is the `JAVA_HOME` location. Copy it.
6. Open the `/etc/environment` file for editing:

```
sudo nano /etc/environment
```

7. Add the following line inside the `/etc/environment` file, as shown here:

```
JAVA_HOME="/usr/lib/jvm/java-1.8.0-openjdk-amd64"
```

8. Type *Ctrl* + *X* and choose *Y* to save and close the file.
9. Next, reload the file using the following command:

```
sudo source /etc/environment
```

Downloading the SonarQube package

The following steps will help you to download the SonarQube package:

1. Download the latest version of the SonarQube installation package by navigating to `https://www.sonarqube.org/downloads/`.

> It is recommended that you always install the latest LTS* version of SonarQube.

2. Move to the `/tmp` folder:

```
cd /tmp
```

3. Download the SonarQube ZIP package, using `wget`, as shown in the following command. Here, I am downloading SonarQube version 5.6.7 (LTS*):

```
wget https://sonarsource.bintray.com/Distribution/sonarqube/
sonarqube-5.6.7.zip
```

4. Next, unzip the SonarQube ZIP package inside the `/opt` directory, using the following command:

```
unzip sonarqube-5.6.7.zip -d /opt/
```

To use the `unzip` command, make sure you have the zipping tool installed on your Ubuntu machine. To install the ZIP tool, execute the following command:
`sudo apt-get install zip`

You can also download the SonarQube ZIP package on a different machine and then move it to your SonarQube server, using WinSCP.

5. Move to the extracted folder and list its content:

```
cd /opt/sonarqube-5.6.7/

ls -lrt
```

The `bin/` folder contains all the scripts to install and start SonarQube, and the `logs/` folder contains the SonarQube logs.

Running the SonarQube application

Follow these steps to start the SonarQube server:

1. Move to `/opt/sonarqube-5.6.6/bin/linux-x86-64/`. In our current example, we are starting SonarQube on a 64-bit Linux OS:

```
cd /opt/sonarqube-5.6.6/bin/linux-x86-64/
```

2. Run the `sonar.sh` script to start SonarQube, as shown in the following command:

```
./sonar.sh start
```

3. You should see a similar output:

```
Starting SonarQube...
Started SonarQube.
```

4. To access SonarQube, use the following link in your favorite web browser: `http://localhost:9000/` or `http://<IP-Address>:9000`.

Right now there are no user accounts configured in SonarQube. However, by default there is an admin account with the username as `admin` and the password as `admin`.
Make sure you have at least 4 GB of memory to run the 64-bit version of SonarQube.

Resetting the default credentials and generating a token

Follow these steps to reset the credentials and generate a token:

1. Open the SonarQube link in your favorite browser and switch to admin user.
2. From the SonarQube dashboard, click on **Administrator** | **My Account** | **Security** (tab).
3. On the resultant page, under the **Change password** section, do the following:
    1. Add your old password (`admin`) under the **Old Password** field.
    2. Add a new password under the **New Password** field.
    3. Reconfirm your new password by adding it again in the **Confirm Password** field.
    4. Once done, click on the **Change Password** button.
4. On the same page under the **Tokens** section, there is an option to generate a token. Jenkins can use this token to access SonarQube. Perform the following steps to generate a new token:
    1. Under the **Tokens** section, add a name for your new token, using the **Generate Tokens** field by clicking on the **Generate** button.
    2. A new token will get generated, as shown in the following screenshot.

3. Copy and save this token, has we will need it later:

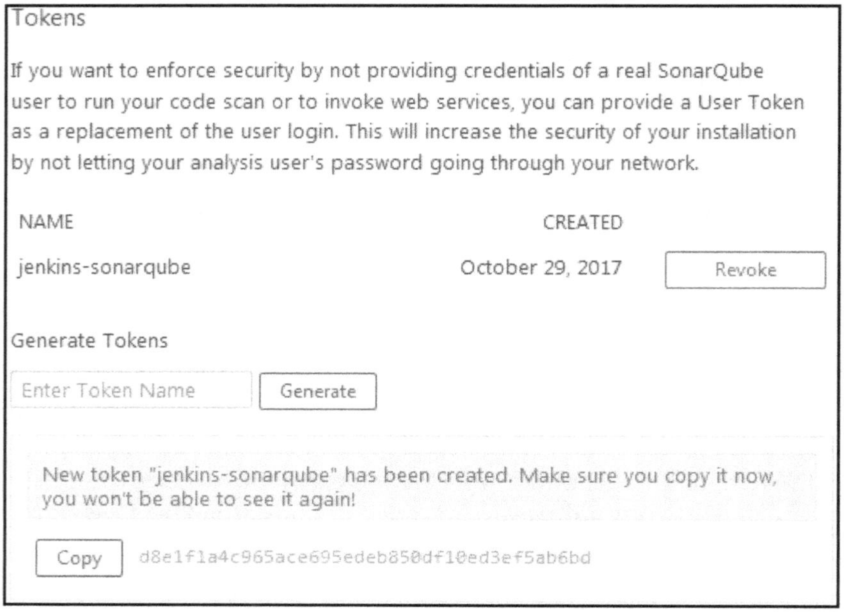

Creating a token inside SonarQube

Creating a project inside SonarQube

In the following section, we will create a project inside SonarQube. The project will be used to display the static code analysis:

1. From the SonarQube dashboard, click on **Administration** | **Projects** (tab) | **Management**.
2. On the resultant page, click on the **Create Project** button.

3. On the resultant window, fill in the respective details, as illustrated in the following steps:
    1. Add a name under the **Name** field.
    2. Add a key under the **Key** field.
    3. Click on the **Create** button to create the project:

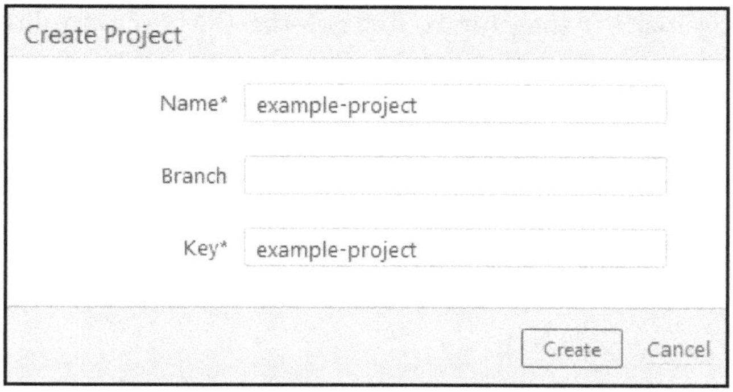

Creating a project inside SonarQube

4. You can see your newly created project on the **Project Management** page, as shown in the following screenshot:

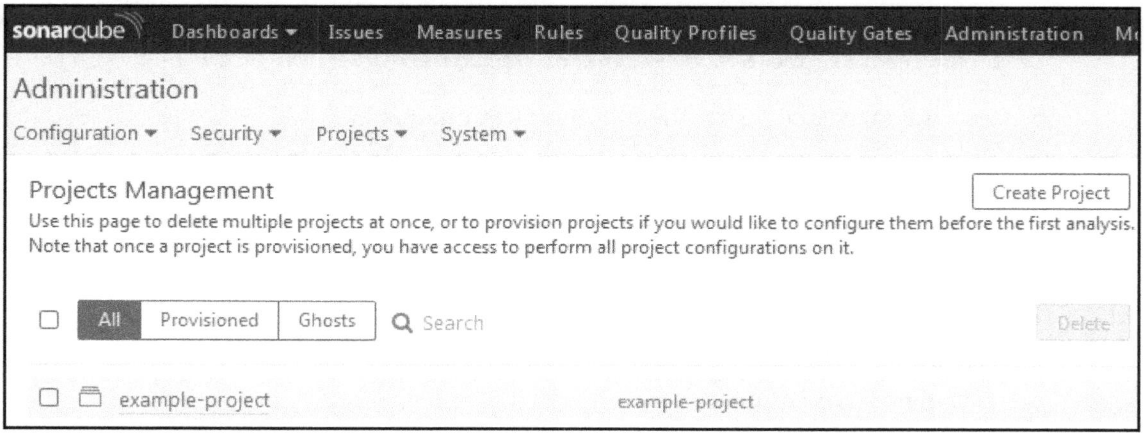

Newly created project inside SonarQube

Installing the build breaker plugin for SonarQube

The build breaker plugin is available for SonarQube. It's exclusively a SonarQube plugin and not a Jenkins plugin. This plugin allows the CI system (Jenkins) to forcefully fail a Jenkins build if a quality gate condition is not satisfied. To install the build breaker plugin, perform the following steps:

1. Before downloading the plugin, first refer to the compatibility table. This will help us in downloading the right plugin version. The compatibility table is available at `https://github.com/SonarQubeCommunity/sonar-build-breaker`.
2. Download the build breaker plugin from `https://github.com/SonarQubeCommunity/sonar-build-breaker/releases`.
3. Move to the `/tmp` directory and download the build breaker plugin, using the following command:

```
cd /tmp

wget https://github.com/SonarQubeCommunity/
sonar-build-breaker/releases/download/2.2/
sonar-build-breaker-plugin-2.2.jar
```

4. Move the downloaded `.jar` file to the location `opt/sonarqube-5.6.7/extensions/plugins/`:

```
cp sonar-build-breaker-plugin-2.2.jar \
/opt/sonarqube-5.6.7/extensions/plugins/
```

5. Restart SonarQube, using the following commands:

```
cd /opt/sonarqube-5.6.7/bin/linux-x86-64

sudo ./sonar.sh restart
```

6. You should see a similar output:

```
Stopping SonarQube...
Waiting for SonarQube to exit...
Stopped SonarQube.
Starting SonarQube...
Started SonarQube.
```

7. After a successful restart, go to the SonarQube dashboard and log in as administrator.

8. Click on the **Administration** link from the menu bar.
9. On the **Administration** page, you will see the **Build Breaker** option under the **CATEGORY** sidebar, as shown in the following screenshot; do nothing:

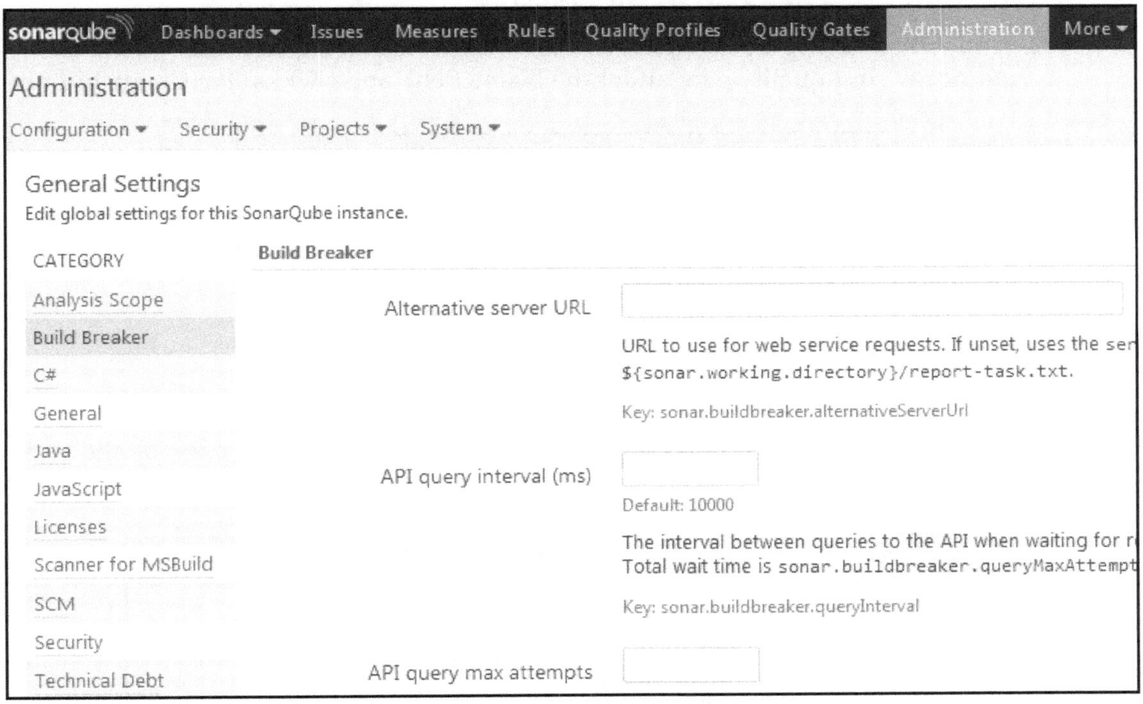

The build breaker plugin settings inside SonarQube

10. The build breaker plugin has been installed successfully.

Creating quality gates

For the build breaker plugin to work, we need to create a *quality gate*; it's nothing but a rule with some conditions. When a Jenkins pipeline runs, it will execute the *quality profiles* and the quality gate. If the quality gate check passes successfully then the Jenkins pipeline continues, but if it fails then the Jenkins pipeline is aborted. Nevertheless, the analysis still happens.

Follow these steps to create a quality gate in SonarQube:

1. From the SonarQube dashboard, click on the **Quality Gates** link from the menu bar.
2. On the resultant page, click on the **Create** button at the top-left corner.
3. You will get a pop-up window, as shown in the following screenshot. Add a name for your quality gate under the **Name** field, and click on the **Create** button:

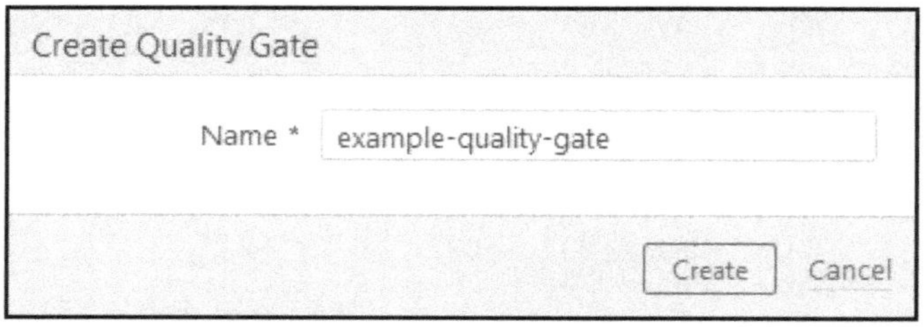

Creating a new quality gate

4. You will see your new quality gate listed on the **Quality Gates** page, as shown in the following screenshot:

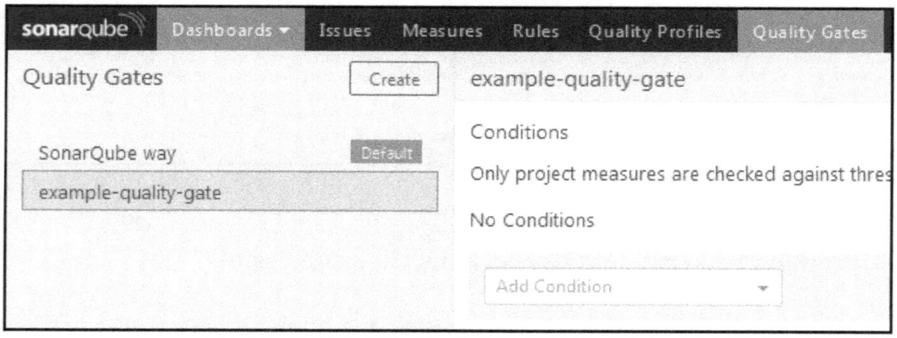

The new quality gate

5. Let us now add a condition to our quality gate by choosing one from the **Add Condition** menu:

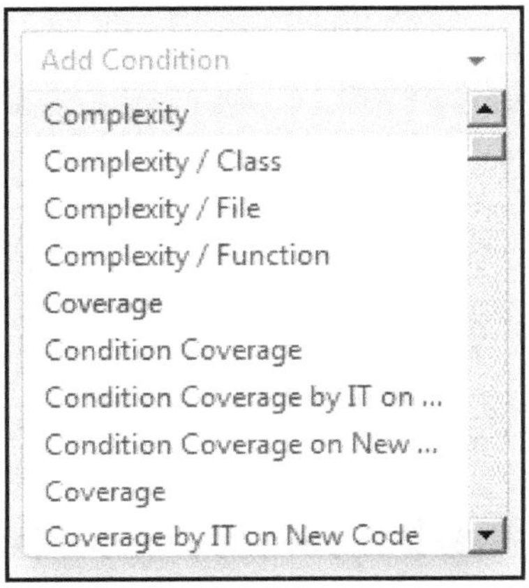

Condition menu

6. The following screenshot shows a condition named **Major Issues**. If it's greater than `1` but less than `50` it's a **WARNING**, and if it's greater than `50`, it's an **ERROR**, as shown in the following screenshot. This is just an example; you can configure any number of conditions you like:

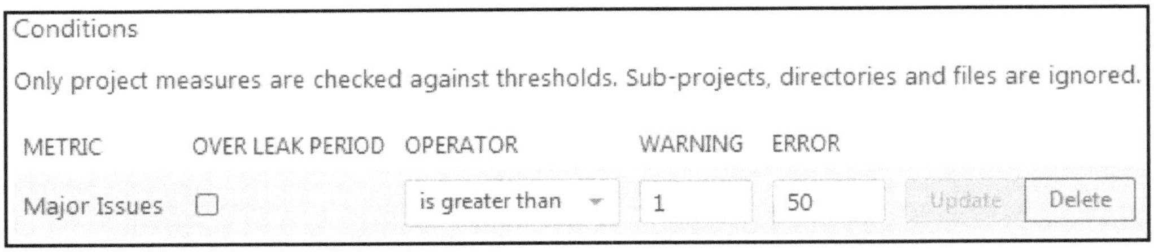

Configuring the quality gate

7. Next, let us make sure that the example project that we created earlier in SonarQube uses our newly created quality gate. To do so, from the SonarQube dashboard click on **Administration** | **Projects** (tab) | **Management**.
8. On the resultant page, you will see the example project that we created earlier in SonarQube. Click on it.
9. On the resultant page, click on **Administration** (tab) | **Quality Gate**.

10. Under the **Quality Gate** section, you will see an option to choose the quality gate from the list of available quality gates in SonarQube. Choose the one that we created recently and click on the **Update** button:

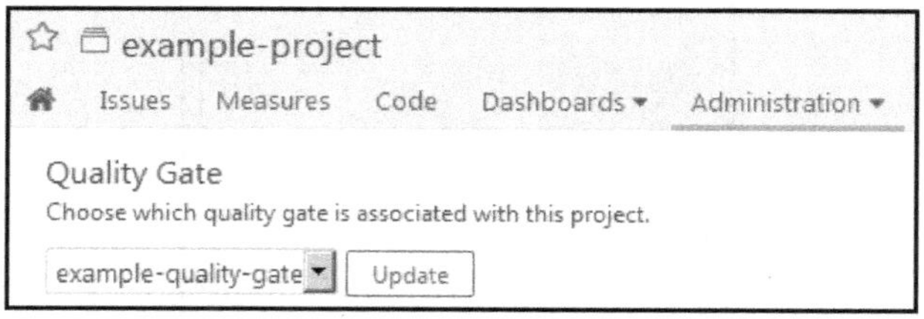

Associating a quality gate to a project

Updating the default quality profile

In the following section, we will modify the default quality profile for Java (Sonar way), which we intend to use for our static code analysis. Follow these steps:

1. From the SonarQube dashboard, click on the **Quality Profiles** link from the menu bar. On the resultant page, you will see all the quality profiles that exist on SonarQube, as shown in the following screenshot:

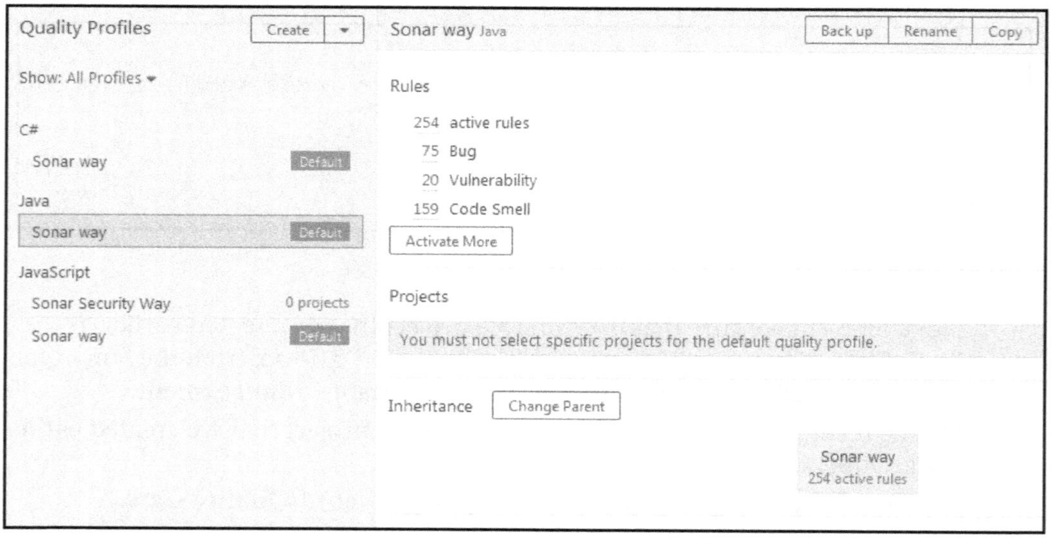

List of quality profiles in SonarQube

2. From the previous screenshot, you can see that the default quality profile for **Java**: **Sonar way** contains **254 active rules**. Let us try to add more rules.
3. Click on the **Activate More** button.
4. On the resultant page, you will see something, as shown in the following screenshot:

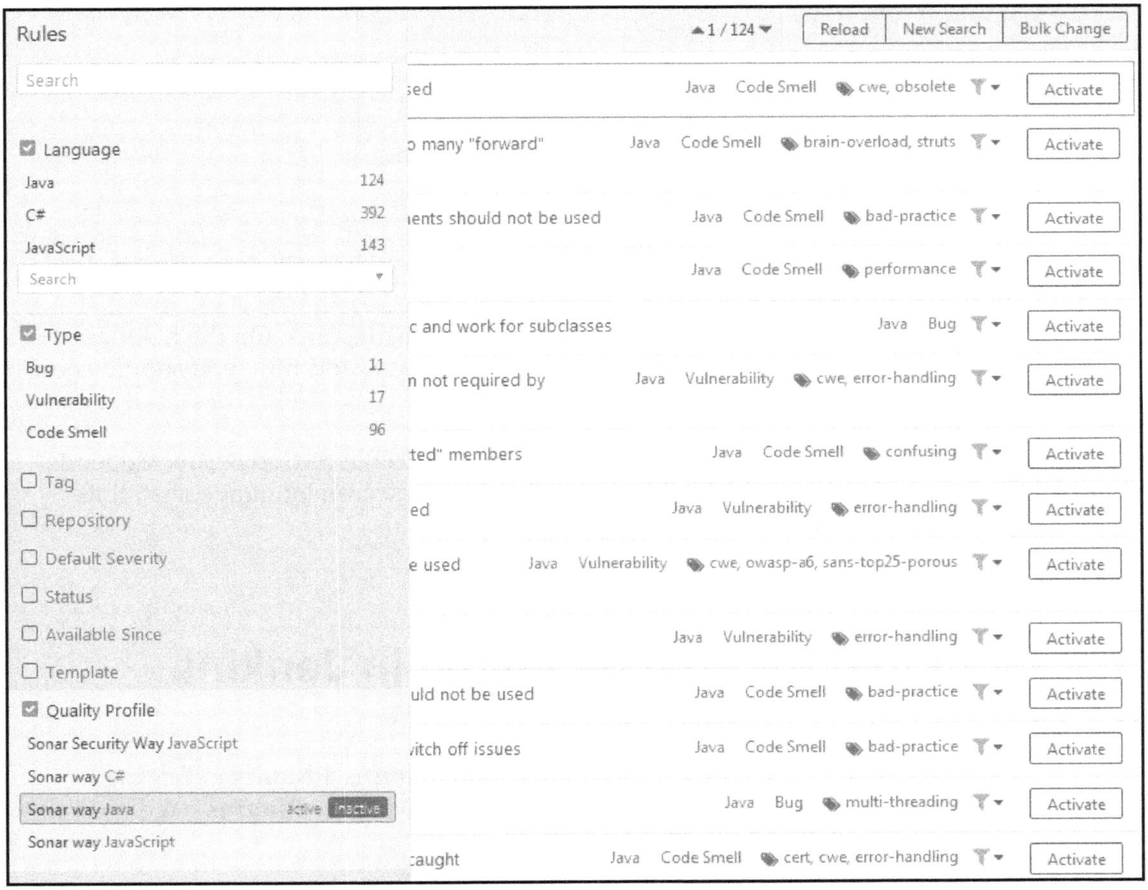

List of inactive rules

5. This is the place where you can add and remove rules from your quality profile. Let us activate all the inactive rules for Java.

6. To do this, from the top-right corner of the page, click on **Bulk Change** | **Activate In Sonar way**, as shown in the following screenshot:

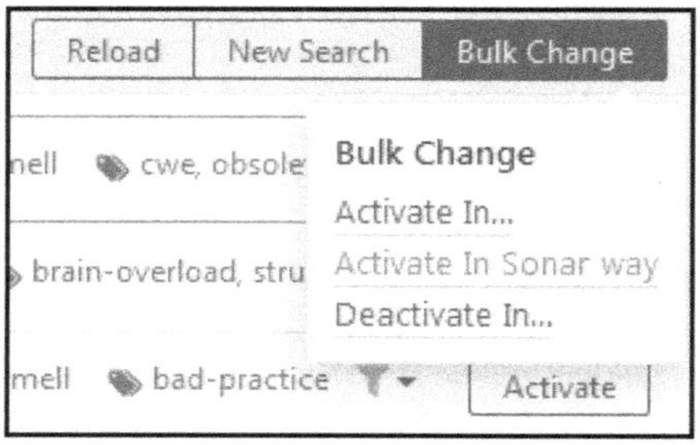

Activating rules in bulk

7. You will see a popup asking you to confirm the changes. Click on the **Apply** button and proceed.
8. Next, from the menu bar, click on the **Quality Profiles** link. On the resultant page, click on the **Sonar way** quality profile for **Java**, and now you should see a greater number of rules than before.

The list of rules and default quality profiles visible on SonarQube depends on the installed plugin. To get rules for your desired language, install its respective SonarQube plugin.

Installing the SonarQube plugin in Jenkins

Follow these steps to install the SonarQube plugin for Jenkins:

1. From the Jenkins dashboard, click on **Manage Jenkins** | **Manage Plugins** | **Available** (tab). You will be taken to the Jenkins **Manage Plugins** page.

2. Enter `SonarQube` in the **Filter** field, as shown in the following screenshot:

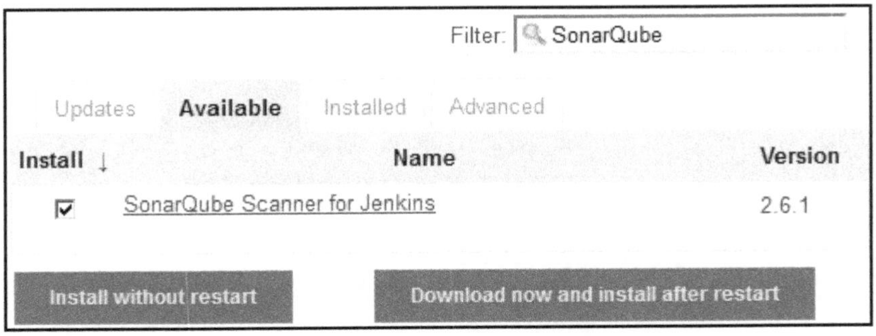

Installing the SonarQube plugin

3. Select **SonarQube Scanner for Jenkins** from the list and click on the **Install without restart** button.
4. Restart Jenkins if needed.

Configuring the SonarQube plugin in Jenkins

Now that we have our SonarQube plugin installed, let us configure it:

1. From the Jenkins dashboard, click **Manage Jenkins** | **Configure System**.
2. Once on the **Configure System** page, scroll down all the way to the **SonarQube servers** section.
3. Under the **SonarQube servers** section, click on the **Add SonarQube** button. You will be presented with settings to configure, as shown in the following screenshot. Let us see them one by one.
4. Give your SonarQube server a name using the **Name** field.
5. Enter the SonarQube server URL under the **Server URL** field.
6. Add Artifactory credentials under the **Default Deployer Credentials**.
7. Add the token that we created inside SonarQube under the **Server authentication token** field.

8. Click on the **Test Connection** button to test the Jenkins connection with Artifactory:

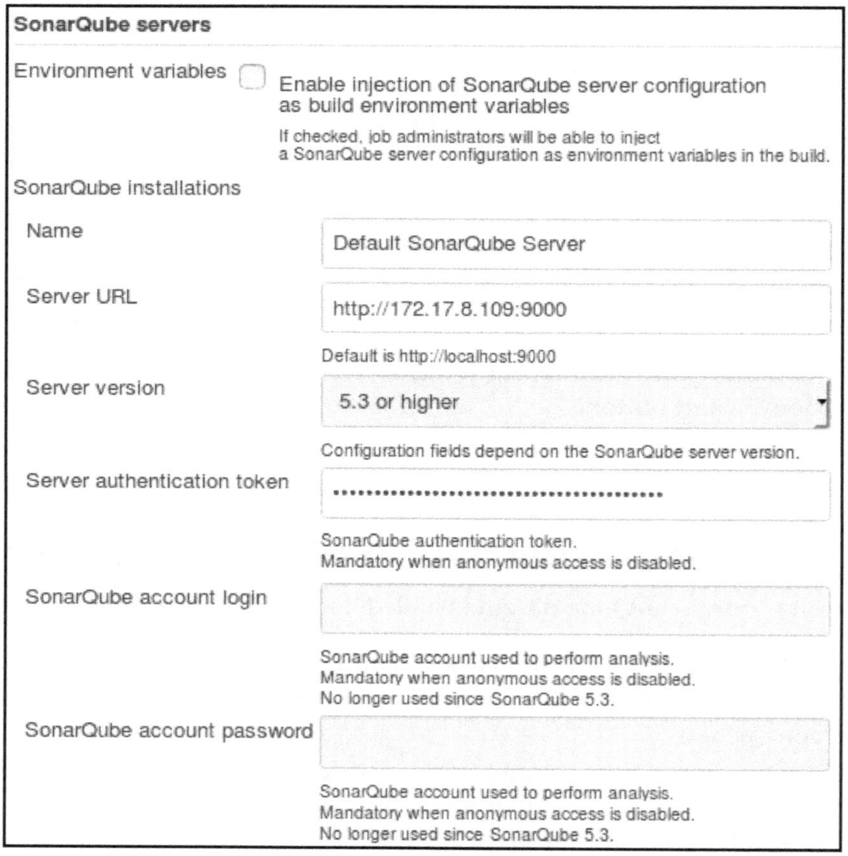

SonarQube servers
Environment variables
Enable injection of SonarQube server configuration as build environment variables
If checked, job administrators will be able to inject a SonarQube server configuration as environment variables in the build.
SonarQube installations
Name
Default SonarQube Server
Server URL
http://172.17.8.109:9000
Default is http://localhost:9000
Server version
5.3 or higher
Configuration fields depend on the SonarQube server version.
Server authentication token
SonarQube authentication token.
Mandatory when anonymous access is disabled.
SonarQube account login
SonarQube account used to perform analysis.
Mandatory when anonymous access is disabled.
No longer used since SonarQube 5.3.
SonarQube account password
SonarQube account used to perform analysis.
Mandatory when anonymous access is disabled.
No longer used since SonarQube 5.3.

Configuring the SonarQube plugin

9. Once done, click on the **Save** button at the end of the page to save the settings.

Installing and configuring Artifactory

Continuous integration results in frequent builds and packages. Hence, there is a need for a mechanism to store all this binary code (builds, packages, third-party plugins, and so on) in a system akin to a version control system.

Since version control systems such as Git, TFS, and SVN store code and not binary files, we need a binary repository tool. A binary repository tool such as Artifactory or Nexus tightly integrated with Jenkins provides the following advantages:

- Tracking builds (who triggers? What code was built?)
- Dependencies
- Deployment history

The following diagram depicts how a binary repository tool such as Artifactory works with Jenkins to store build artifacts. In the coming topics, we will learn how to achieve this by creating a Jenkins job to upload code to Artifactory:

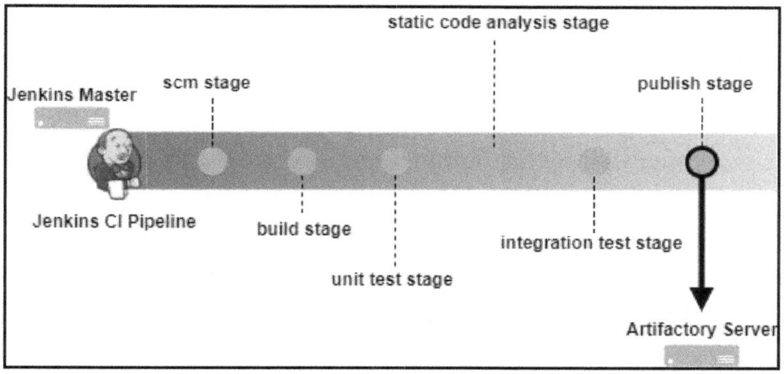

Jenkins pipeline pushing built artifacts to Artifactory

In the current book, we will be dealing with Artifactory to store our builds. Artifactory is a tool used to version control binaries. The binaries can be anything from built code, packages, executables, Maven plugins, and so on.

In the following section, we will set up Artifactory on Ubuntu 16.04.

Installing Java

Follow these steps to install Java:

1. Update the package index:

```
sudo apt-get update
```

2. Next, install Java. The following command will install the JRE:

   ```
   sudo apt-get install default-jre
   ```

3. To set the `JAVA_HOME` environment variable, first get the Java installation location. Do this by executing the following command:

   ```
   update-java-alternatives -l
   ```

4. You should get a similar output:

   ```
   java-1.8.0-openjdk-amd64 1081 /usr/lib/jvm/java-1.8.0-openjdk-amd64
   ```

5. The path in the preceding output is the `JAVA_HOME` location. Copy it.
6. Open the `/etc/environment` file for editing:

   ```
   sudo nano /etc/environment
   ```

7. Add the following line inside the `/etc/environment` file, as shown here:

   ```
   JAVA_HOME="/usr/lib/jvm/java-1.8.0-openjdk-amd64"
   ```

8. Type *Ctrl* + *X* and choose *Y* to save and close the file.
9. Next, reload the file using the following command:

   ```
   sudo source /etc/environment
   ```

Downloading the Artifactory package

Follow the given steps to download the Artifactory package:

1. Download the latest version of Artifactory (open source) from `https://www.jfrog.com/open-source/` or `https://bintray.com/jfrog/artifactory/jfrog-artifactory-oss-zip`.
2. To download Artifactory Pro, visit `https://bintray.com/jfrog/artifactory-pro/` or `https://bintray.com/jfrog/artifactory-pro/jfrog-artifactory-pro-zip`.

It is recommended that you always install the latest LTS version of Artifactory.

In the following chapter, we will use Artifactory Pro to demonstrate code promotion using properties in the upcoming chapter.

Refer to `https://www.jfrog.com/confluence/display/RTF/Artifactory+Pro#ArtifactoryPro-ActivatingArtifactoryPro` to learn the process of activating Artifactory Pro.

3. Move to the `/tmp` folder:

```
cd /tmp
```

4. Download the Artifactory Pro ZIP package, using `wget`, as shown in the following code. Here, I am downloading Artifactory version 5.5.2 (LTS*):

```
wget
https://jfrog.bintray.com/artifactory-pro/org/artifactory/pro/jfrog
-artifactory-pro/5.5.2/jfrog-artifactory-pro-5.5.2.zip
```

You can download the Artifactory ZIP package on a different machine (from a browser) and then move it to your to-be Artifactory server, using WinSCP.

5. Next, unzip the SonarQube ZIP package inside the `/opt` directory, as shown in the following code:

```
sudo unzip jfrog-artifactory-pro-5.5.2.zip -d /opt/
```

Or, if the downloaded ZIP package has a strange name:

```
sudo unzip \
download_file\?file_path\=jfrog-artifactory-pro-5.5.2.zip \
-d /opt/
```

To use the `unzip` command, make sure you have the zipping tool installed on your Ubuntu machine. To install the ZIP tool, execute the following command:
`sudo apt-get install zip`

6. Move to the extracted folder and list its content:

```
cd /opt/artifactory-pro-5.5.2/

ls -lrt
```

The `bin/` folder contains all the scripts to install and start Artifactory, and the `logs/` folder contains the Artifactory logs.

Running the Artifactory application

Follow the given steps to start the Artifactory server:

1. Move to the `/opt/artifactory-pro-5.5.2/bin/` directory and run the `installService.sh` script:

```
sudo ./installService.sh
```

2. You should see a similar output:

```
Installing artifactory as a Unix service that will run as user
artifactory
Installing artifactory with home /opt/artifactory-pro-5.5.2
Creating user artifactory...creating... DONE

Checking configuration link and files in
/etc/opt/jfrog/artifactory...
Moving configuration dir /opt/artifactory-pro-5.5.2/etc
/opt/artifactory-pro-5.5.2/etc.original...creating the link and
updating dir... DONE
Creating environment file
/etc/opt/jfrog/artifactory/default...creating... DONE
** INFO: Please edit the files in /etc/opt/jfrog/artifactory to set
the correct environment
Especially /etc/opt/jfrog/artifactory/default that defines
ARTIFACTORY_HOME, JAVA_HOME and JAVA_OPTIONS
Initializing artifactory.service service with systemctl... DONE

Setting file permissions... DONE

************ SUCCESS ****************
Installation of Artifactory completed

Please check /etc/opt/jfrog/artifactory, /opt/artifactory-
pro-5.5.2/tomcat and /opt/artifactory-pro-5.5.2 folders
```

```
You can activate artifactory with:
> systemctl start artifactory.service
```

3. Start the Artifactory service, using any of the following commands:

```
sudo service artifactory start
```

Or:

```
sudo /etc/init.d/artifactory start
```

Or:

```
sudo systemctl start artifactory
```

4. You can check the Artifactory installation by executing any of the following commands:

```
service artifactory check
```

Or:

```
/etc/init.d/artifactory check
```

Or:

```
sudo ./artifactoryctl check
```

5. Access the Artifactory dashboard by navigating to `http://<Server IP Address>:8081/`.

> Right now there are no user accounts configured in Artifactory. However, by default there is an admin account with the username as `admin` and the password as `password`.
>
> Make sure you have at least 4 GB of memory to run the 64-bit version of Artifactory.

Resetting the default credentials and generating an API key

Follow the given steps to reset the Artifactory credentials:

1. Access the Artifactory dashboard using the following link: `http://<Server IP Address>:8081/`.
2. Log in as admin using the initial default credentials for admin.
3. From the Artifactory dashboard, click on **Welcome, admin** | **Edit Profile**.
4. Enter your current password in the **Current Password** field and press the **Unlock** button.
5. On the resultant page, under **Personal Settings**, add your email ID.
6. Under the **Change Password** section, add a new password to reset the default credentials for the admin user.
7. Next, under the **Authentication Settings** section, click on **Generate key** (gear logo) to generate a new API key.
8. Copy the generated API key by clicking on the copy button (see the following screenshot).
9. We might need this API key later for authentication:

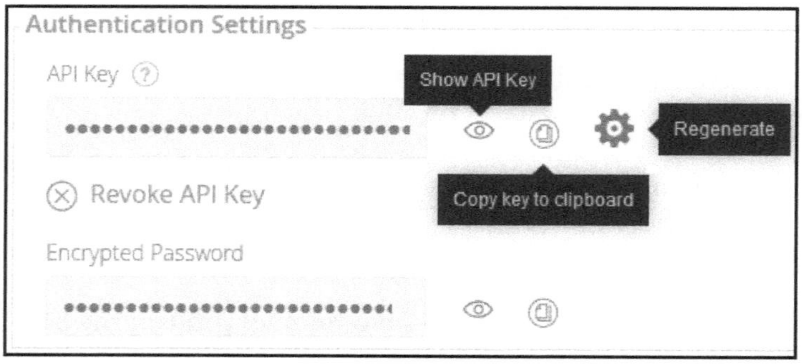

Artifactory API key

10. Once done, click on the **Save** button.

Creating a repository in Artifactory

In the following section, we will create a genetic repository inside Artifactory. The repository will be used to store the build artifacts:

1. From the Artifactory dashboard, on the left-hand side menu, click on **Admin** | **Repositories** | **Local**, as shown in the following screenshot:

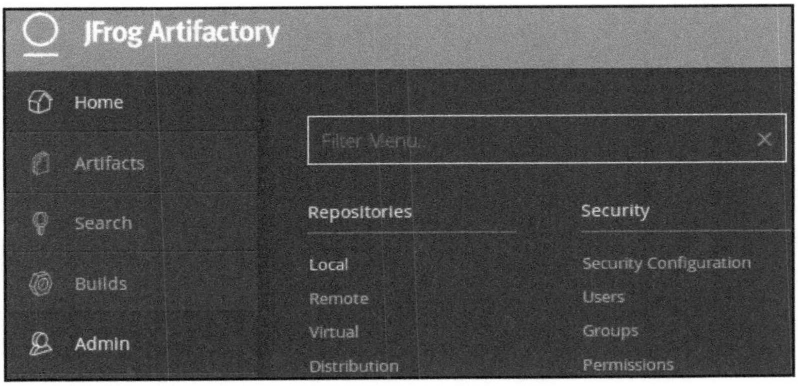

Creating a local repository in Artifactory

2. The resultant page will show you all the **Local Repositories** currently available, as shown in the following screenshot:

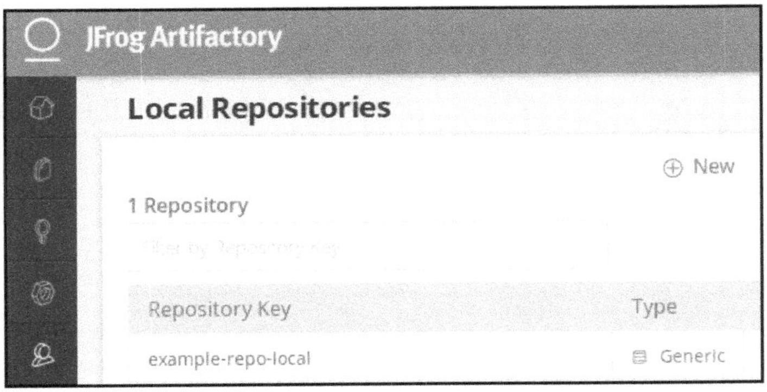

List of all the Local Repositories

3. Click on the **New** button at the top-right corner to create a new local repository (see the following screenshot).
4. You will be presented with a pop-up window with a list of various types of repositories to choose from, shown as follows. Choose the **Generic** type (see the following screenshot):

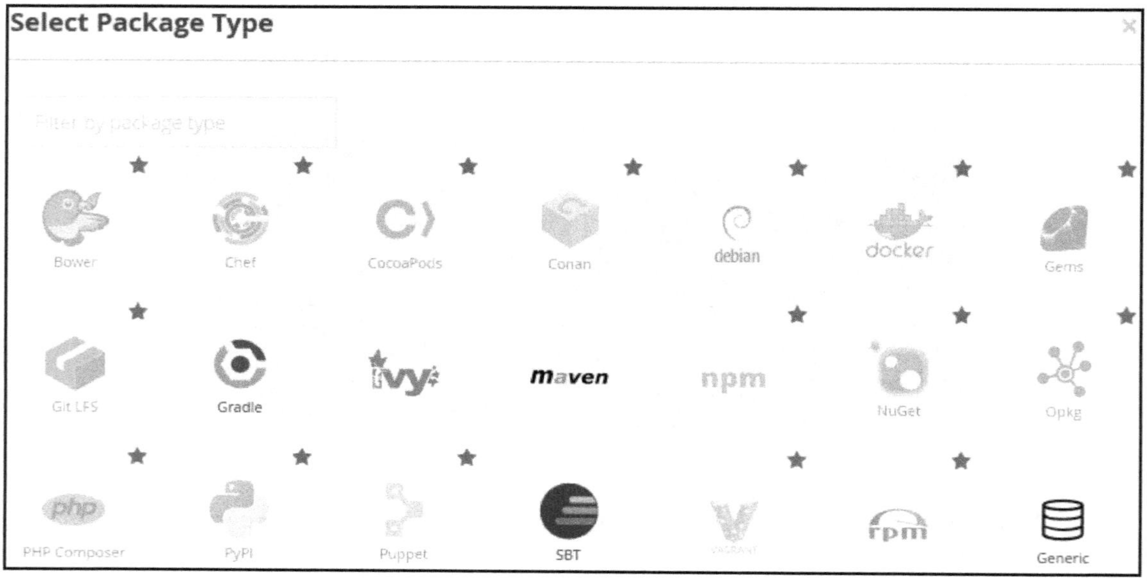

Option to choose various types of repositories

5. Give your repository a name by adding a value under the **Repository Key** field, as shown in the following screenshot. Leave the rest of the settings to their default values:

Naming our new local repository

6. Once done, click on the **Save & Finish** button.
7. Now we have our new local repository, as shown in the following screenshot:

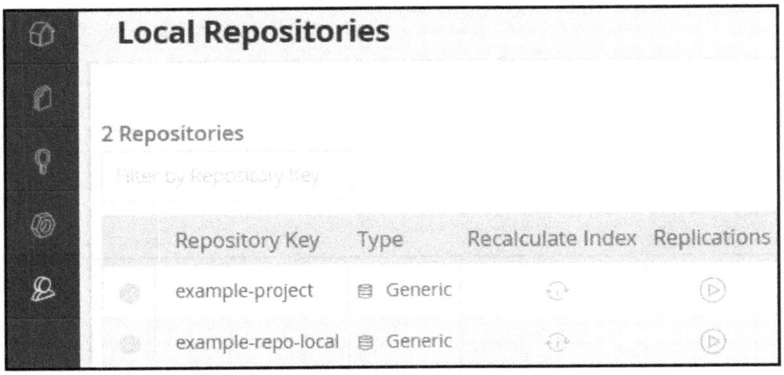

Our newly created local repository

Adding Artifactory credentials inside Jenkins

Follow the given steps to create credentials inside Jenkins to talk to Artifactory:

1. From the Jenkins dashboard, click on **Credentials** | **System** | **Global credentials (unrestricted)**.
2. Click on the **Add Credentials** link on the left-hand side menu to create a new credential (see the following screenshot).
3. Choose **Kind** as **Username with Password**.
4. Leave the **Scope** field to its default value.
5. Add the Artifactory username under the **Username** field.
6. Under the **Password** field, add the password.
7. Add an ID under the **ID** field and a description under the **Description** field.
8. Once done, click on the **OK** button:

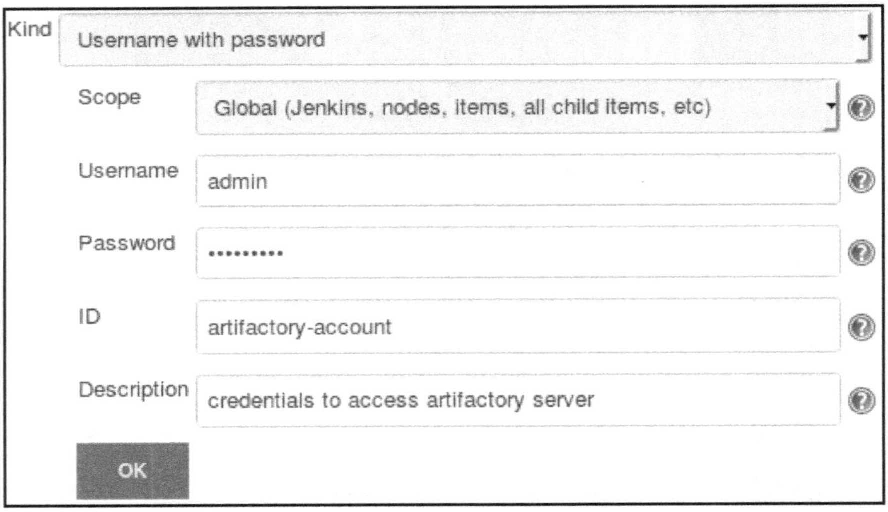

Adding Artifactory credentials inside Jenkins

Installing the Artifactory plugin in Jenkins

Follow the given steps to install the Artifactory plugin for Jenkins:

1. From the Jenkins dashboard, click on **Manage Jenkins** | **Manage Plugins** | **Available** (tab). You will be taken to the Jenkins **Manage Plugins** page.
2. Enter `Artifactory` in the **Filter** field, as shown in the following screenshot:

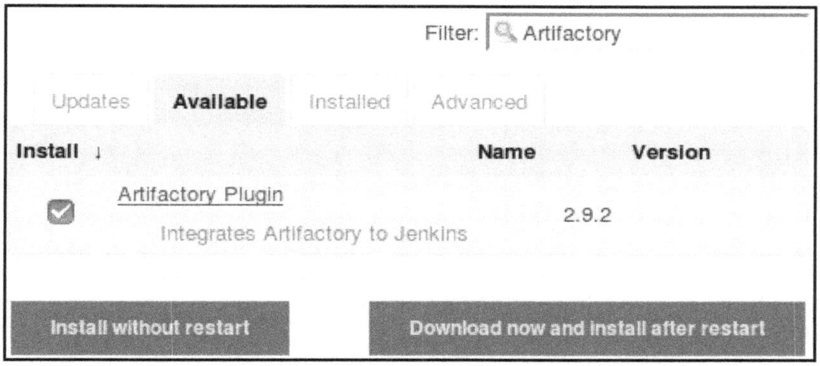

Installing the Artifactory Plugin

3. Select the **Artifactory Plugin** from the list and click on **Install without restart** button.
4. Restart Jenkins if needed.

Configuring the Artifactory Plugin

Now that we have our **Artifactory Plugin** installed, let us configure it:

1. From the Jenkins dashboard, click **Manage Jenkins** | **Configure System**.
2. Once on the **Configure System** page, scroll down all the way to the **Artifactory** section.
3. Under the **Artifactory** section, click on the **Add** button. You will be presented with the following settings to configure, as shown in the following screenshot. Let us look at them one by one.

4. Give your Artifactory server a name, using the **Server ID** field.
5. Enter the Artifactory server URL under the **URL** field.
6. Add Artifactory credentials under the **Default Deployer Credentials**, as shown in the following screenshot.
7. Click on the **Test Connection** button to test the Jenkins connection with Artifactory:

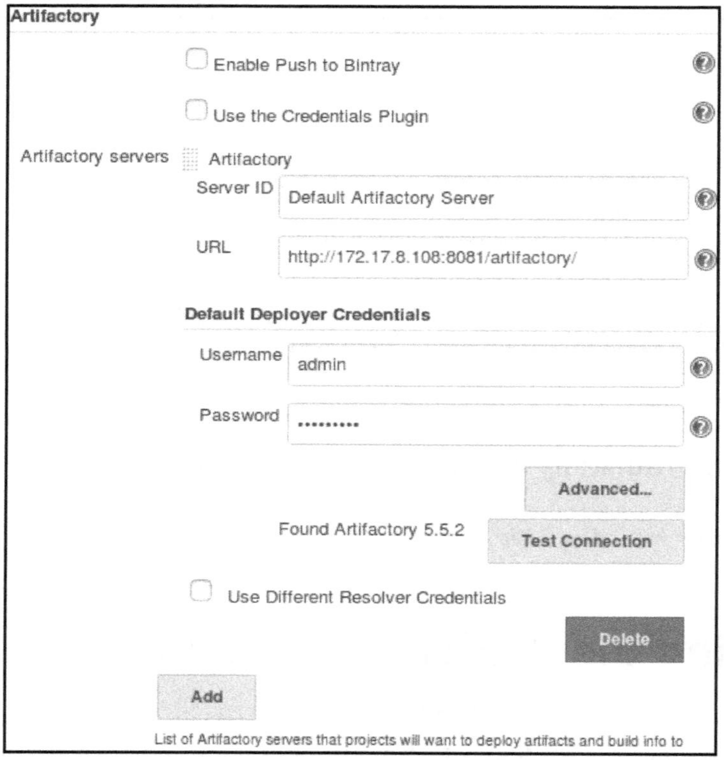

Configuring the Artifactory Plugin

8. Once done, click on the **Save** button at the end of the page to save the settings.

Summary

In this chapter, we learned how to install and configure SonarQube and Artifactory. In today's world, static code analysis forms an important part of the CI pipeline (although it is not necessary). Similarly, Artifactory is a popular tool used to store all the build artifacts that are generated by the CI pipeline. Once the CI pipeline is complete, Artifactory take the center stage. It is from Artifactory that all the built artifacts are deployed to various testing environments, and it is with Artifactory that we perform code promotion.

We will learn more about these tools in the next chapter, which is about implementing continuous integration using Jenkins.

7
Continuous Integration Using Jenkins

We will begin this chapter with a **Continuous Integration** (**CI**) design that covers the following areas:

- A branching strategy
- A list of tools for CI
- A Jenkins pipeline structure

The CI design will serve as a blueprint that will guide the readers in answering the how, why, and where of CI being implemented. The design will cover all the necessary steps involved in implementing an end-to-end CI pipeline.

The CI design discussed in this chapter should be considered as a template for implementing CI, and not a full and final model. The branching strategy and the tools used can all be modified and replaced to suit the purpose.

Jenkins CI design

Almost every organization creates one before they even begin to explore the CI and DevOps tools. In this section, we will go through a very general CI design.

Continuous Integration includes not only Jenkins or any other similar CI tool for that matter, but it also deals with how you version control your code, the branching strategy you follow, and so on.

Various organizations may follow different kinds of strategies to achieve CI, since it all depends on the requirement and type of the project.

Branching strategy

It's always good to have a branching strategy. Branching helps you organize your code. It is a way to isolate your working code from the code that is under development. In our CI design, we will start with three types of branches:

- The master branch
- The integration branch
- The feature branch

This branching strategy is a slimmer version of the GitFlow workflow branching model.

The master branch

One can also call it a **production branch**. It holds the working copy of the code that has been delivered. The code on this branch has passed all the testing. No development happens on this branch.

The integration branch

The integration branch is also known as the **mainline branch**. This is where all the features are integrated, built, and tested for integration issues. Again, no development happens here. However, developers can create feature branches out of the integration branch and work on them.

The feature branch

Lastly, we have the feature branch. This is where the actual development takes place. We can have multiple feature branches spanning out of the integration branch.

The following illustration shows a typical branching strategy that we will be using as part of our CI design. We will be creating two feature branches spanning out from the **Integration/Mainline Branch**, which itself spans out from the master branch:

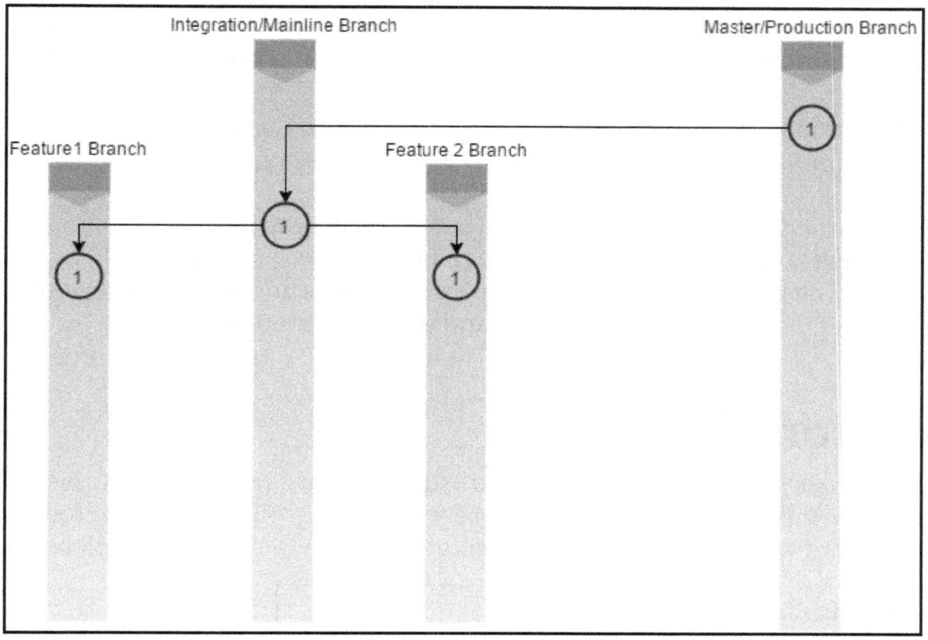

Branching strategy

A commit on the feature branch or the integration branch (a merge will create a commit) will go through a build, static code analysis, and integration test phase. If the code passes these phases successfully, the resultant package is uploaded to Artifactory (binary repository).

The CI pipeline

We are now at the heart of the CI design. We will be creating a Multibranch Pipeline in Jenkins that will have the following stages:

1. Fetch the code from the **version control system** (**VCS**) on a push event (initialization of the CI pipeline).
2. Build and unit test the code, and publish a unit test report on Jenkins.

3. Perform static code analysis on the code and upload the result to SonarQube. Fail the pipeline if the number of bugs crosses the threshold defined in the quality gate.
4. Perform integration testing and publish a unit test report on Jenkins.
5. Upload the built artifacts to Artifactory along with some meaningful properties.

The purpose of the previous CI pipeline is to automate the process of continuously building, testing (unit test and integration test), performing static code analysis, and uploading the built artifacts to the binary repository. Reporting for failures/success happens at every step. Let us discuss these pipelines and their constituents in detail.

Toolset for CI

The example project for which we are implementing CI is a simple Maven project. In this chapter, we will see Jenkins working closely with many other tools. The following table contains the list of tools and technologies involved in everything that we will be seeing:

Technology	Characteristic
Java	Primary programming language used for coding
Maven	Build tool
JUnit	Unit testing and integration testing tools
Jenkins	Continuous Integration tool
GitHub	Version control system
SonarQube	Static code analysis tool
Artifactory	Binary repository manager

Creating the CI pipeline

In this section, we will learn how to create the CI pipeline discussed in the previous section. We will perform the following steps:

- We will create a source code repository in GitHub
- We will create a Jenkinsfile to describe the way we build, unit test, perform static code analysis, integration test, and publish built artifacts to Artifactory

- We will utilize Docker to spawn build agents to run our CI pipeline
- We will create a Multibranch Pipeline in Jenkins

It is important that you have configured the *Configuring Webhooks on GitHub from Jenkins* section from `Chapter 3`, *The New Jenkins*.

Creating a new repository on GitHub

Let us create a new repository on GitHub. Make sure you have Git installed on the machine that you will use to perform the steps mentioned in the following section:

1. Log in to your GitHub account.
2. In this chapter, we will use the source code from `https://github.com/nikhilpathania/hello-world-greeting.git` as an example.
3. Try to fork the repository mentioned in the previous link. To do so, just access the repository from your internet browser and click on the **Fork** button, as shown in the following screenshot:

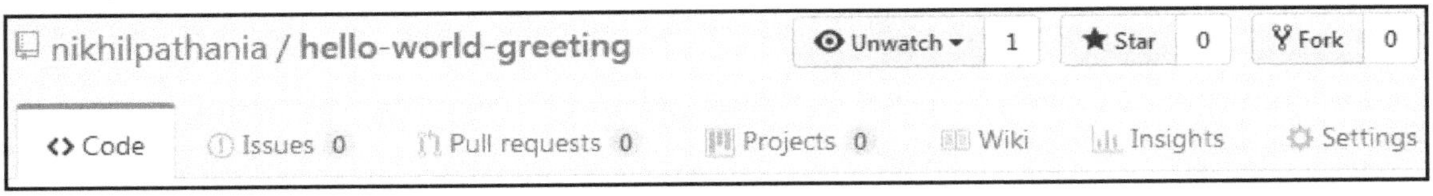

Forking a GitHub project

4. Once done, a replica of the repository will be visible under your GitHub account.

Using the SonarQube scanner for Maven

Ideally, we need the SonarQube scanner to perform static code analysis on a project. However, we will use the SonarQube scanner utility for Maven instead, as the example source code that we are using in the current chapter is a Maven project.

To do so, add the following code to your `.pom` file:

```
<properties>
    <project.build.sourceEncoding>UTF-8</project.build.sourceEncoding>
    <sonar.language>java</sonar.language>
</properties>
```

You need not perform the previous step if you have forked the following repository:
`https://github.com/nikhilpathania/hello-world-greeting.git`.

Writing the Jenkinsfile for CI

In the following section, we will learn how to write pipeline code for our Continuous Integration.

Spawning a Docker container – build agent

First, let us create pipeline code to create a Docker container (Jenkins slave), which will act as our build agent.

If you can recall, in the *Adding Jenkins slaves – Docker containers* section from `Chapter 5`, *Distributed Builds*, we learned to create a Docker image (`maven-build-slave-0.1`) that was meant for creating Docker containers (Jenkins slaves). We will use the same Docker image over here to spawn Jenkins Slave Agents for our CI pipeline.

In our Jenkinsfile, to spawn a Docker container (Jenkins slave) we need to write a code block for `node` with the label as `docker`:

```
node('docker') {
}
```

Where `docker` is a label for the `maven-build-slave-0.1` Docker template.

We would like to perform the following tasks on the `docker` node:

- Perform build
- Perform unit tests and publish the unit test report
- Perform static code analysis and upload the results on SonarQube
- Perform integration testing and publish the integration test report
- Publish artifacts to Artifactory

All the previous tasks are various stages of our CI pipeline. Let's write pipeline code for each one of them.

Downloading the latest source code from VCS

We want our Jenkins pipeline to download the latest change pushed to the master branch on our GitHub repository:

```
scm checkout
```

Wrap the previous step inside a stage called `Poll`:

```
stage('Poll') {
    scm checkout
}
```

Pipeline code to perform the build and unit test

The example project that we are using in the current chapter is a Maven project. Therefore, the pipeline code for the build is a simple shell script that runs the `mvn clean` command:

```
sh 'mvn clean verify -DskipITs=true';
junit '**/target/surefire-reports/TEST-*.xml'
archive 'target/*.jar'
```

Where `-DskipITs=true` is the option to skip the integration test and perform only the build and unit test.

The `junit '**/target/surefire-reports/TEST-*.xml'` command enables Jenkins to publish JUnit unit test reports on the Jenkins pipeline page. `**/target/surefire-reports/TEST-*.xml` is the directory location where the unit test reports are generated.

> Your Maven `.pom` file should have `maven-surefire-plugin` and `maven-failsafe-plugin` for the previous command to work.
> You also need the Jenkins JUnit plugin (installed by default).

Wrap the previous step inside a stage called `Build & Unit test`:

```
stage('Build & Unit test'){
    sh 'mvn clean verify -DskipITs=true';
    junit '**/target/surefire-reports/TEST-*.xml'
    archive 'target/*.jar'
}
```

Pipeline code to perform static code analysis

The pipeline code to perform static code analysis is a simple shell script that will run the Maven commands, as shown in the following command block. This is made possible using the SonarQube scanner utility for Maven. Remember the configuration that we saw in the *Using the SonarQube scanner for Maven* section:

```
sh 'mvn clean verify sonar:sonar -Dsonar.projectName=example-project
-Dsonar.projectKey=example-project -Dsonar.projectVersion=$BUILD_NUMBER';
```

The `-Dsonar.projectName=example-project` option is the option to pass the SonarQube project name. In this way, all our results will be visible under the `projectName=example-project` that we created in the previous chapter.

Similarly, the `-Dsonar.projectKey=example-project` option allows the SonarQube scanner for the Maven utility to confirm the `projectKey=example-project` with SonarQube.

The `-Dsonar.projectVersion=$BUILD_NUMBER` option allows us to attach the Jenkins build number with every analysis that we perform and upload to SonarQube. `$BUILD_NUMBER` is the Jenkins environment variable for the build number.

Wrap the previous step inside a stage called `Static Code Analysis`:

```
stage('Static Code Analysis'){
    sh 'mvn clean verify sonar:sonar -Dsonar.projectName=example-project
    -Dsonar.projectKey=example-project -
Dsonar.projectVersion=$BUILD_NUMBER';
}
```

Pipeline code to perform integration testing

The pipeline code to perform integration testing is a shell script that will run the Maven commands, as shown in the following command block:

```
sh 'mvn clean verify -Dsurefire.skip=true';
junit '**/target/failsafe-reports/TEST-*.xml'
archive 'target/*.jar'
```

Where -Dsurefire.skip=true is the option to skip unit testing and perform only the integration testing.

The junit '**/target/failsafe-reports/TEST-*.xml' command enables Jenkins to publish JUnit unit test reports on the Jenkins pipeline page. **/target/failsafe-reports/TEST-*.xml is the directory location where the integration test reports are generated.

Wrap the previous step inside a stage called Integration Test:

```
stage ('Integration Test'){
    sh 'mvn clean verify -Dsurefire.skip=true';
    junit '**/target/failsafe-reports/TEST-*.xml'
    archive 'target/*.jar'
}
```

Your Maven .pom file should have maven-surefire-plugin and maven-failsafe-plugin for the previous command to work. You also need the Jenkins JUnit plugin (installed by default).

Pipeline code to publish built artifacts to Artifactory

To upload the build artifacts to Artifactory, we will use the *File Specs*. The File Specs code is shown in the following code block:

```
"files": [
    {
      "pattern": "[Mandatory]",
      "target": "[Mandatory]",
      "props": "[Optional]",
      "recursive": "[Optional, Default: 'true']",
      "flat" : "[Optional, Default: 'true']",
      "regexp": "[Optional, Default: 'false']"
    }
  ]
```

The following table states the parameters from the preceding code:

Parameters	Condition	Description
`pattern`	`[Mandatory]`	Specifies the local filesystem path to artifacts that should be uploaded to Artifactory. You can specify multiple artifacts by using wildcards or a regular expression, as designated by the `regexp` property. If you use a `regexp`, you need to escape any reserved characters (such as `.`, `?`, and so on) used in the expression using a backslash `\`. Since version 2.9.0 of the Jenkins Artifactory plugin and version 2.3.1 of the TeamCity Artifactory plugin, the pattern format has been simplified and uses the same file separator `/` for all operating systems, including Windows.
`target`	`[Mandatory]`	Specifies the target path in Artifactory in the following format: `[repository_name]/[repository_path]`. If the pattern ends with a slash, for example, `repo-name/a/b/`, then `b` is assumed to be a folder in Artifactory and the files are uploaded into it. In the case of `repo-name/a/b`, the uploaded file is renamed to `b` in Artifactory. For flexibility in specifying the upload path, you can include placeholders in the form of `{1}, {2}, {3}...` which are replaced by corresponding tokens in the source path that are enclosed in parentheses. For more details, please refer to the *Using Placeholders* article (`https://www.jfrog.com/confluence/display/RTF/Using+File+Specs#UsingFileSpecs-UsingPlaceholders`).
`props`	`[Optional]`	List of `key=value` pairs separated by a semicolon (`;`) to be attached as properties to the uploaded properties. If any key can take several values, then each value is separated by a comma (`,`). For example, `key1=value1;key2=value21,value22;key3=value3`.
`flat`	`[Default: true]`	If `true`, artifacts are uploaded to the exact target path specified and their hierarchy in the source filesystem is ignored. If `false`, artifacts are uploaded to the target path while maintaining their filesystem hierarchy.
`recursive`	`[Default: true]`	If `true`, artifacts are also collected from subdirectories of the source directory for upload. If `false`, only artifacts specifically in the source directory are uploaded.

`regexp`	`[Default: false]`	If `true`, the command will interpret the pattern property, which describes the local filesystem path of artifacts to upload, as a regular expression. If `false`, the command will interpret the pattern property as a wildcard expression.

The following is the File Specs code that we will use in our pipeline:

```
def server = Artifactory.server 'Default Artifactory Server'
def uploadSpec = """{
  "files": [
    {
       "pattern": "target/hello-0.0.1.war",
       "target": "example-project/${BUILD_NUMBER}/",
       "props": "Integration-Tested=Yes;Performance-Tested=No"
    }
  ]
}"""
server.upload(uploadSpec)
```

The following table states the parameters from the preceding code:

Parameters	**Description**
`def server = Artifactory.server 'Default Artifactory Server'`	This line tells Jenkins to use the existing Artifactory server configured in Jenkins. In our example, it is the default Artifactory server.
`Default Artifactory Server`	This is the name of the Artifactory server configured inside Jenkins.
`"pattern": "target/hello-0.0.1.war",`	This line of code will look at a file named `hello-0.0.1.war` inside the directory target, which is again inside the Jenkins workspace directory.
`"target": "example-project/${BUILD_NUMBER}/",`	This line of code will try to upload the build artifacts to the Artifactory repository named `helloworld-greeting-project`. It will place the artifact inside a folder named after the build number inside the Artifactory repository.

`${BUILD_NUMBER}`	The Jenkins environment variable for the build number.
`"props": "Integration-Tested=Yes;Performance-Tested=No"`	This code creates two key-value pairs and assigns them to the uploaded artifacts. These key-value pairs can be used as labels for code promotion in Artifactory.

Wrap the previous step inside a stage called `Publish`:

```
stage ('Publish'){
    def server = Artifactory.server 'Default Artifactory Server'
    def uploadSpec = """{
      "files": [
        {
          "pattern": "target/hello-0.0.1.war",
          "target": "helloworld-greeting-project/${BUILD_NUMBER}/",
          "props": "Integration-Tested=Yes;Performance-Tested=No"
        }
      ]
    }"""
  server.upload(uploadSpec)
}
```

Combined CI pipeline code

The following is the complete combined code that will run inside the `docker` node:

```
node('docker') {
  stage('Poll') {
    checkout scm
  }
  stage('Build & Unit test'){
    sh 'mvn clean verify -DskipITs=true';
    junit '**/target/surefire-reports/TEST-*.xml'
    archive 'target/*.jar'
  }
  stage('Static Code Analysis'){
    sh 'mvn clean verify sonar:sonar -Dsonar.projectName=example-project
    -Dsonar.projectKey=example-project -
Dsonar.projectVersion=$BUILD_NUMBER';
  }
  stage ('Integration Test'){
    sh 'mvn clean verify -Dsurefire.skip=true';
```

```
      junit '**/target/failsafe-reports/TEST-*.xml'
      archive 'target/*.jar'
    }
    stage ('Publish'){
      def server = Artifactory.server 'Default Artifactory Server'
      def uploadSpec = """{
        "files": [
          {
            "pattern": "target/hello-0.0.1.war",
            "target": "example-project/${BUILD_NUMBER}/",
            "props": "Integration-Tested=Yes;Performance-Tested=No"
          }
        ]
      }"""
      server.upload(uploadSpec)
    }
  }
```

Using a Jenkinsfile

Jenkins Multibranch Pipelines utilize Jenkinsfiles. In this section, we will learn how to create a Jenkinsfile. We will use the example pipeline script that we created in the previous section to create our Jenkinsfile. Follow these steps:

1. Log in to your GitHub account.
2. Navigate to the forked repository.
3. Once on the repository page, click on the **Create new file** button to create a new empty file that will be our Jenkinsfile, as shown in the following screenshot:

Creating a new file on GitHub

4. Name your new file `Jenkinsfile` by filling in the empty textbox, as shown in the following screenshot:

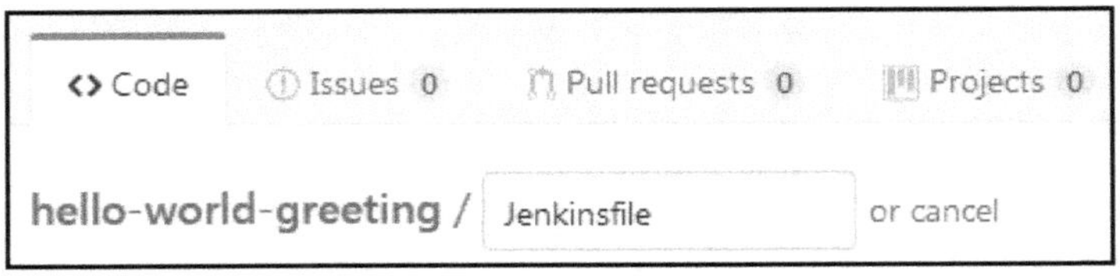

Naming your new file on GitHub

5. Add the following code in your Jenkinsfile:

```
node('docker') {
  stage('Poll') {
    checkout scm
  }
  stage('Build & Unit test'){
    sh 'mvn clean verify -DskipITs=true';
    junit '**/target/surefire-reports/TEST-*.xml'
    archive 'target/*.jar'
  }
  stage('Static Code Analysis'){
    sh 'mvn clean verify sonar:sonar
    -Dsonar.projectName=example-project
    -Dsonar.projectKey=example-project
    -Dsonar.projectVersion=$BUILD_NUMBER';
  }
  stage ('Integration Test'){
    sh 'mvn clean verify -Dsurefire.skip=true';
    junit '**/target/failsafe-reports/TEST-*.xml'
    archive 'target/*.jar'
  }
  stage ('Publish'){
    def server = Artifactory.server 'Default Artifactory
Server'
    def uploadSpec = """{
      "files": [
        {
          "pattern": "target/hello-0.0.1.war",
          "target": "example-project/${BUILD_NUMBER}/",
          "props": "Integration-Tested=Yes;Performance-
Tested=No"
        }
      ]
    }"""
```

```
            server.upload(uploadSpec)
        }
    }
```

6. Once done, commit the new file by adding a meaningful comment, as shown in the following screenshot:

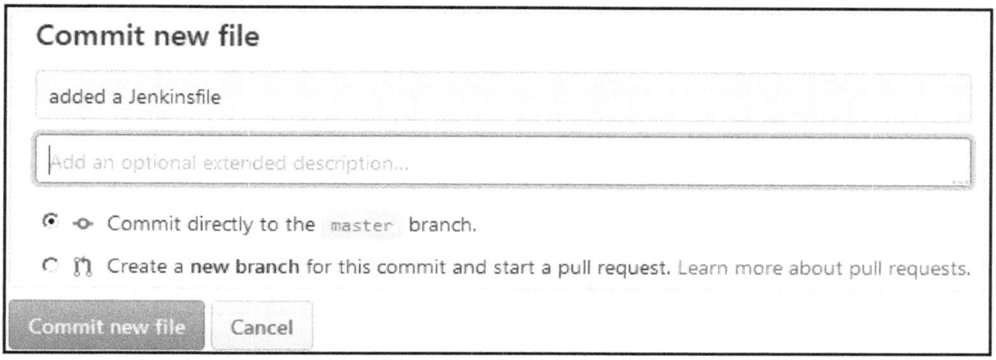

Committing your new file on GitHub

Creating a Multibranch Pipeline in Jenkins

Follow these steps to create a new Jenkins pipeline job:

1. From the Jenkins dashboard, click on the **New Item** link.
2. On the resultant page, you will be presented with various types of Jenkins jobs to choose from.
3. Choose **Multibranch Pipeline**, and give a name to your pipeline using the **Enter an item name** field.
4. Once you are done, click on the **OK** button at the bottom of the page.
5. Scroll to the **Branch Sources** section. This is the place where we configure the GitHub repository that we want to use.
6. Click on the **Add Source** button and choose **GitHub**. You will be presented with a list of fields to configure. Let us see them one by one (see the following screenshot).
7. For the **Credentials** field, choose the GitHub account credentials (**Kind**: **Username with Password**) that we created in the previous section.

8. Under the **Owner** field, specify the name of your GitHub organization or GitHub user account.
9. The moment you do so, the **Repository** field will list all the repositories that are on your GitHub account.
10. Choose **hello-world-greeting** under the **Repository** field.
11. Leave the rest of the options to their default values:

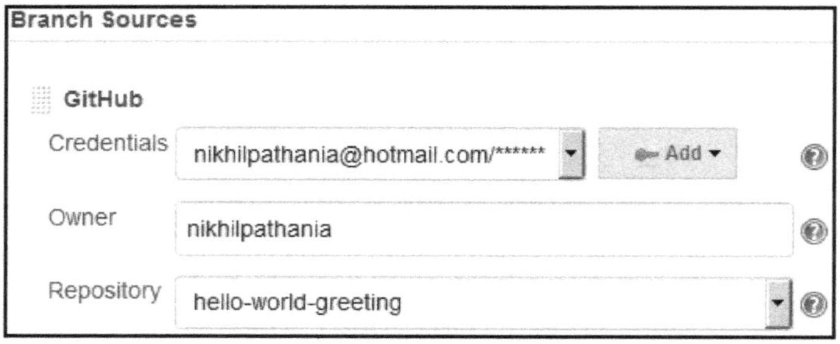

Configuring the Multibranch Pipeline

12. Scroll all the way down to the **Build Configuration** section. Make sure the **Mode** field is set to **by Jenkinsfile** and the **Script Path** field is set to `Jenkinsfile`:

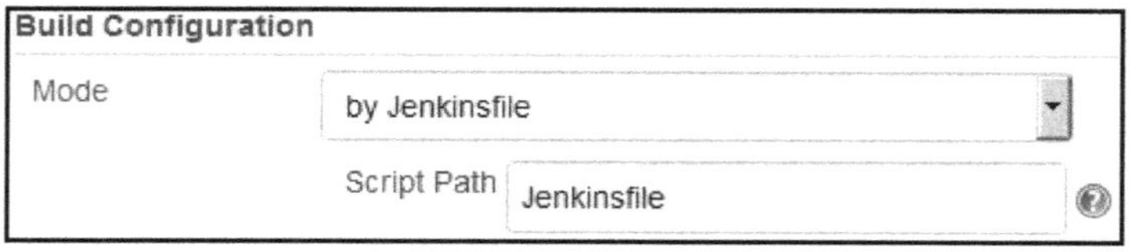

Build configuration

13. Scroll all the way down and click on the **Save** button.

Re-registering the Webhooks

Now, let us re-register the Webhooks for all our Jenkins pipelines. To do so, perform the following steps:

1. On the Jenkins dashboard, click on **Manage Jenkins** | **Configure System**.
2. On the Jenkins configuration page, scroll all the way down to the **GitHub** section.

3. Under the **GitHub** section, click on the **Advanced...** button (you will see two of them; click on the second one).
4. This will display a few more fields and options. Click on the **Re-register hooks for all jobs** button.
5. The previous action will create new Webhooks for our Multibranch Pipeline on the respective repository inside your GitHub account. Do the following to view the Webhooks on GitHub:
    1. Log in to your GitHub account.
    2. Go to your GitHub repository, `hello-world-greeting` in our case.
    3. Click on the repository **Settings** button, as shown in the following screenshot:

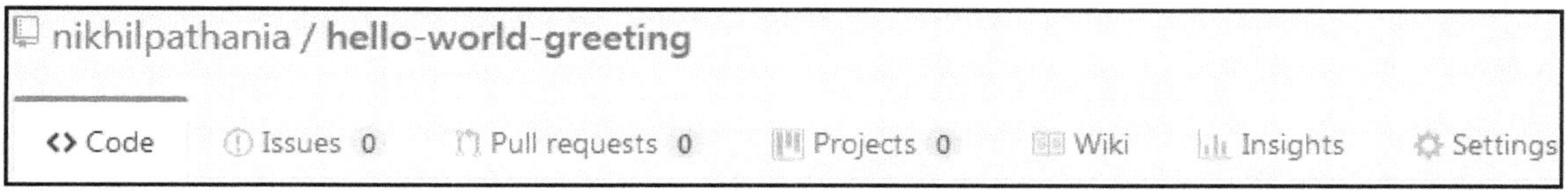

Repository settings

    4. On the repository **Settings** page, click on **Webhooks** from the left-hand side menu. You should see the Webhooks for your Jenkins server, as shown in the following screenshot:

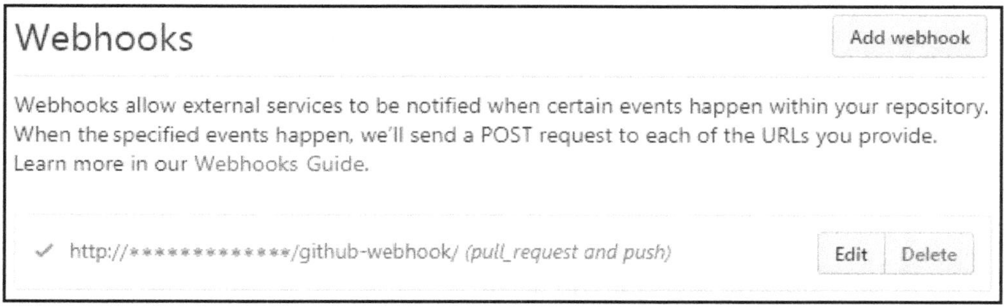

Webhooks on GitHub repository

Continuous Integration in action

Follow the given steps:

1. From the Jenkins dashboard, click on your Multibranch Pipeline.
2. On the Jenkins Multibranch Pipeline page, from the left-hand side menu, click on the **Scan Repository Now** link. This will scan the repository for branches and Jenkinsfiles, and will immediately run a pipeline for every branch that has got a Jenkinsfile, as shown in the following screenshot:

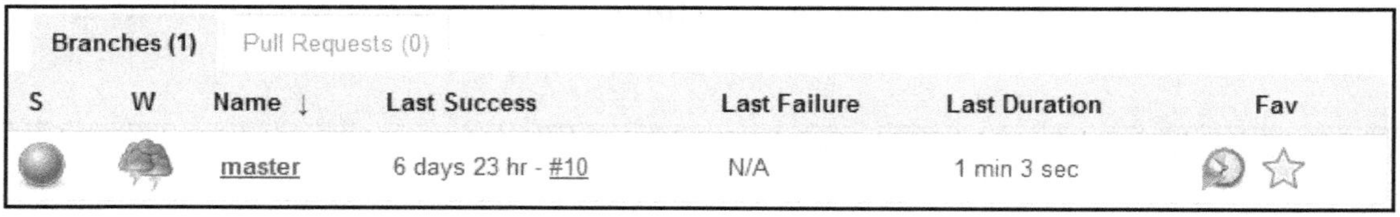

Pipeline for the master branch

3. On the Multibranch Pipeline page, from the left-hand side menu, click on **Scan Repository Log**. You will see something similar to the following output. Notice the highlighted code. You can see the **master** branch met the criteria, as it had a Jenkinsfile and a pipeline was scheduled for it. There was no pipeline scheduled for the testing branch since there was no Jenkinsfile on it:

```
Started by user nikhil pathania
[Sun Nov 05 22:37:19 UTC 2017] Starting branch indexing...
22:37:19 Connecting to https://api.github.com using
nikhilpathania@hotmail.com/****** (credentials to access GitHub
account)
22:37:20 Connecting to https://api.github.com using
nikhilpathania@hotmail.com/****** (credentials to access GitHub
account)
Examining nikhilpathania/hello-world-greeting
  Checking branches...
  Getting remote branches...
    Checking branch master
  Getting remote pull requests...
      'Jenkinsfile' found
    Met criteria
Changes detected: master
(c6837c19c3906b0f056a87b376ca9afdff1b4411
1e5834a140d572f4d6f9665caac94828b779e2cd)Scheduled build for
branch: master
1 branches were processed
```

```
Checking pull-requests...
0 pull requests were processed
Finished examining nikhilpathania/hello-world-greeting
[Sun Nov 05 22:37:21 UTC 2017] Finished branch indexing.
Indexing took 2.1 sec
Finished: SUCCESS
```

> You need not always scan for the repository. The GitHub Webhooks are configured to automatically trigger a pipeline whenever there is a push or a new branch on your GitHub repository. Remember, a Jenkinsfile should also be present on the respective branch to tell Jenkins what it needs to do when it finds a change in the repository.

4. From your Jenkins Multibranch Pipeline page (`<Jenkins URL>/job/<Jenkins Multi-branch pipeline name>/`), click on the respective branch pipeline (see the following screenshot).
5. On the resultant page, you will see the **Stage View** for the master branch pipeline:

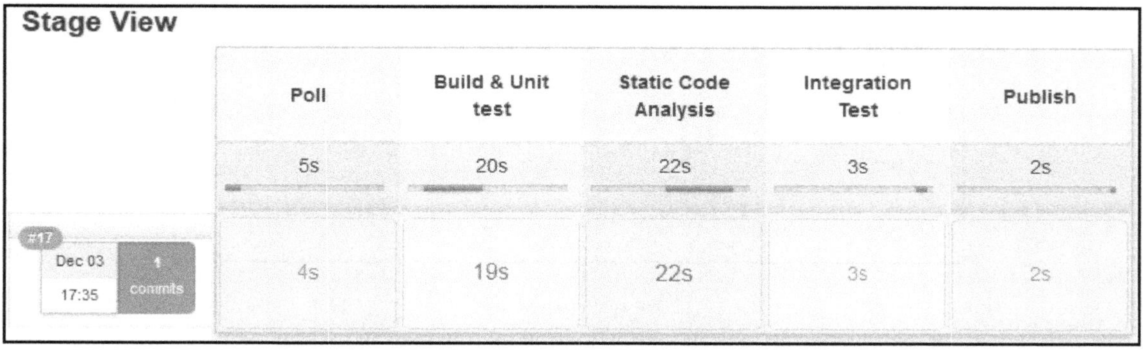

Pipeline Stage View

6. To see the unit test and integration test results, click on **Latest Test Result** link, which is available on the same page below the **Stage View**, as shown in the following screenshot:

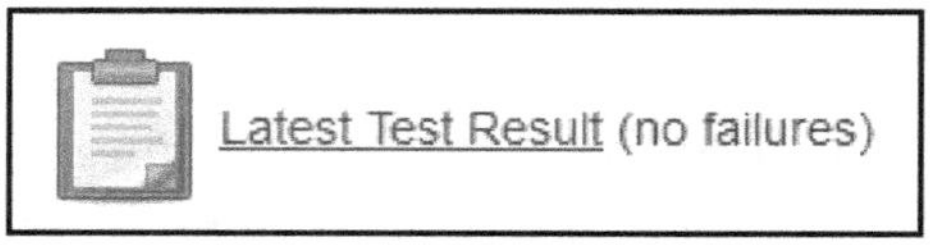

7. On the resultant page, you will see a detailed report about the unit as well as the integration test execution, as shown in the following screenshot:

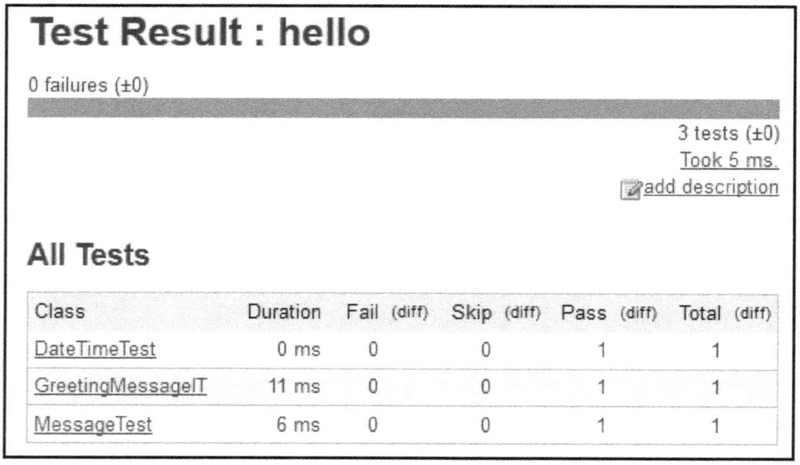

Test report using JUnit plugin

8. You can click on the individual tests to get more details.

9. While on the same page, on the left-hand side menu there is a link named **History**, which gives you a historic graph about the number of metrics related to the test execution over a period of time:

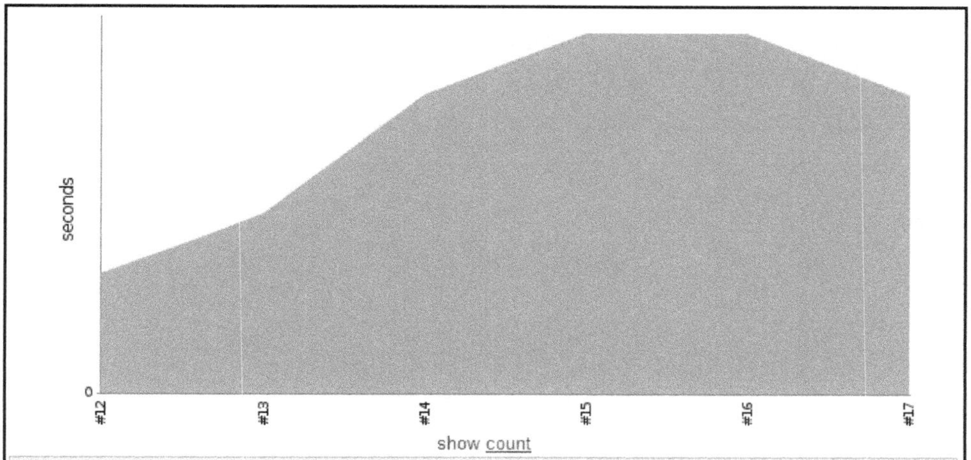

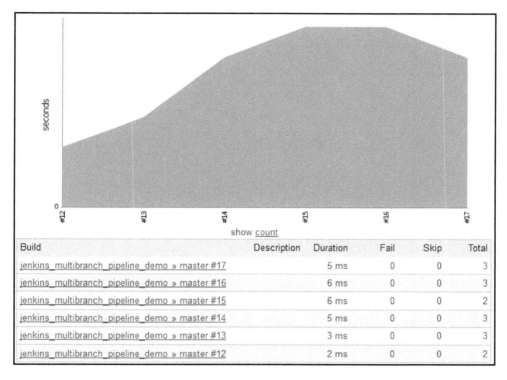

Build	Description	Duration	Fail	Skip	Total
jenkins_multibranch_pipeline_demo » master #17		5 ms	0	0	3
jenkins_multibranch_pipeline_demo » master #16		6 ms	0	0	3
jenkins_multibranch_pipeline_demo » master #15		6 ms	0	0	2
jenkins_multibranch_pipeline_demo » master #14		5 ms	0	0	3
jenkins_multibranch_pipeline_demo » master #13		3 ms	0	0	3
jenkins_multibranch_pipeline_demo » master #12		2 ms	0	0	2

Test execution history

Viewing static code analysis in SonarQube

Let us take a look at the static code analysis report performed as part of our CI pipeline. Follow these steps:

1. Open the SonarQube link, using your favorite browser. You should see something similar to the following screenshot:

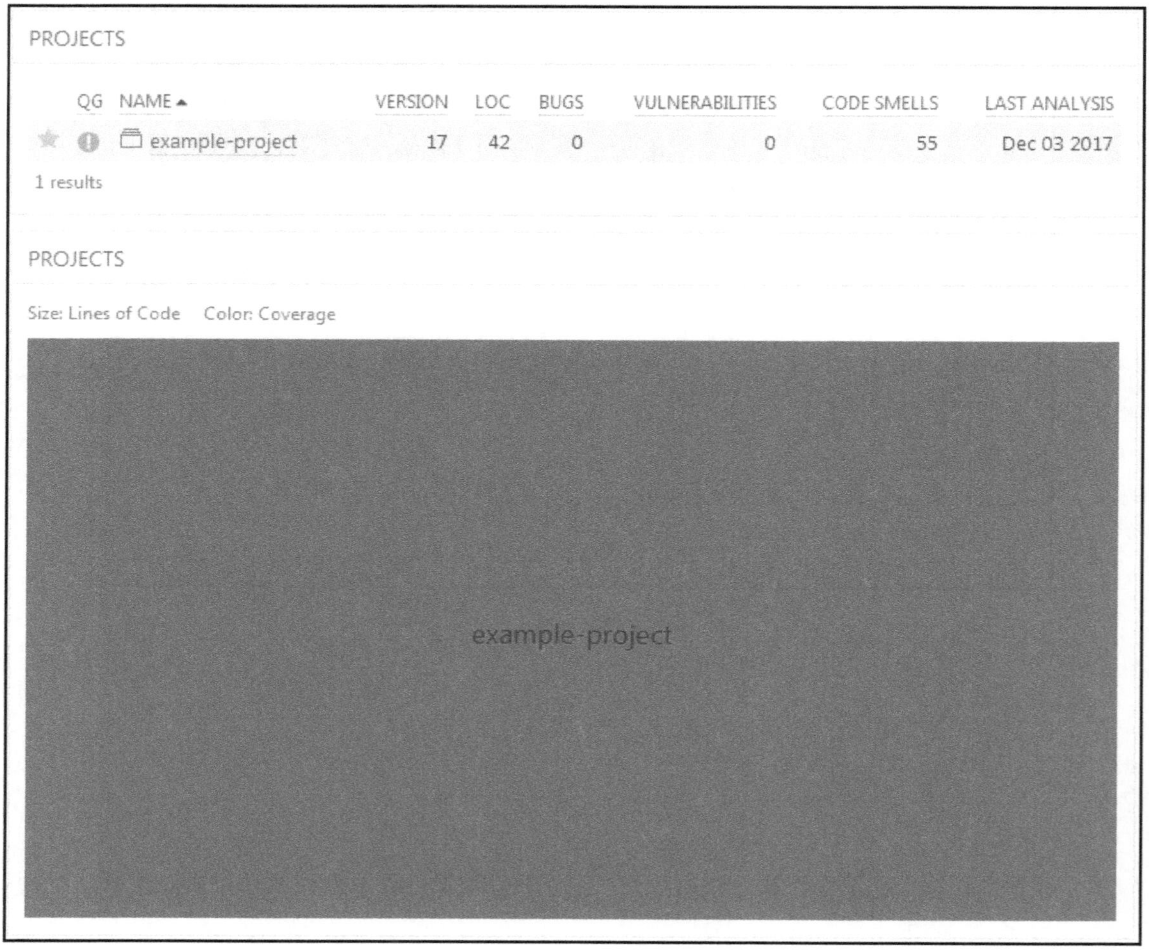

SonarQube homepage

2. From the SonarQube dashboard, using the menu option, click on the **Log in** link.
3. Enter your SonarQube credentials.
4. On the resultant page, under the **PROJECTS** widget, click on the `example-project` project.
5. You will see an overview of the static code analysis of your project (see the following screenshot):

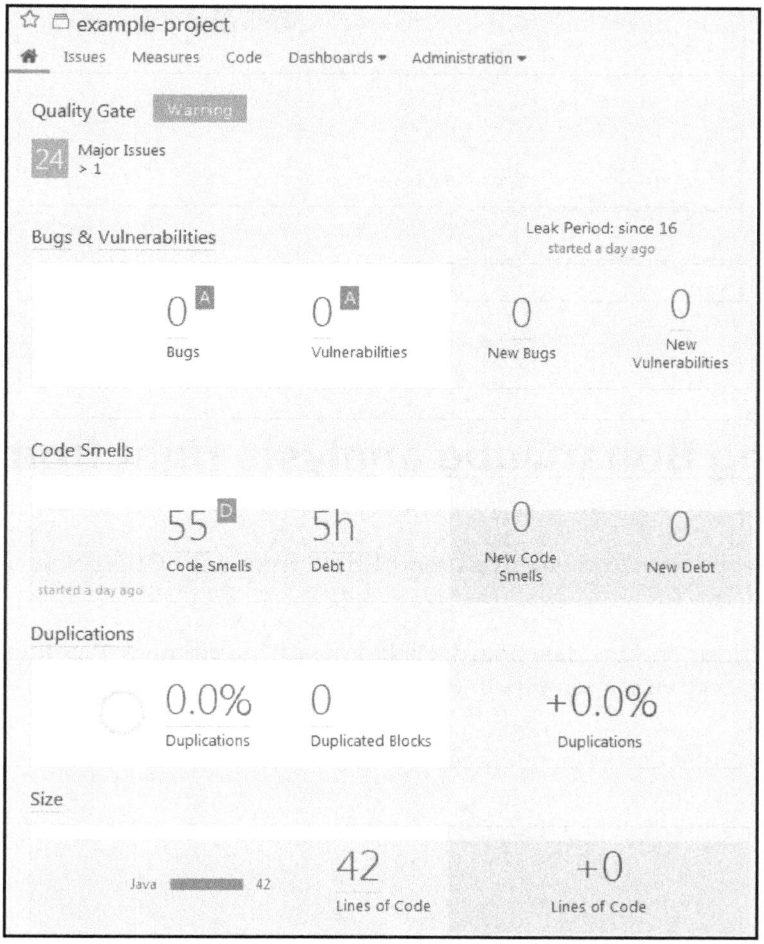

Static code analysis overview

6. Click on **Measures** | **Coverage**. On the resultant page, you will get a nice overview of your code coverage and unit test result report, as shown in the following screenshot:

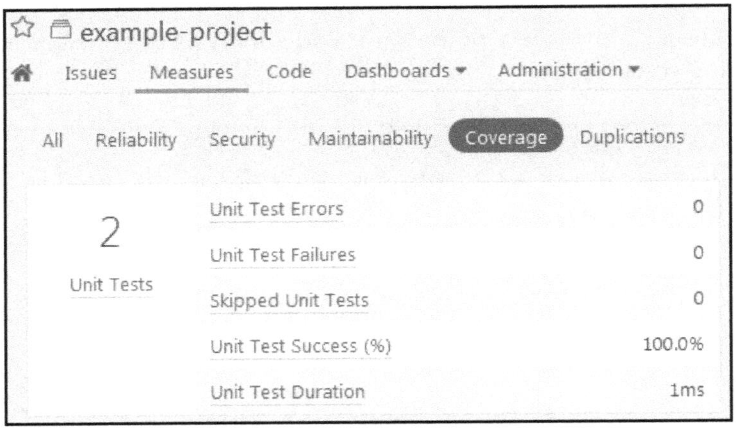

Code coverage report and unit test report

Accessing SonarQube analysis right from Jenkins

You can access your static code analysis report right from your CI pipeline. Follow these steps:

1. From your Jenkins dashboard, click on your Multibranch Pipeline. Next, click on the respective branch pipeline (**master** in our example).

2. Once you are on your branch pipeline, hover your mouse on the **Static Code Analysis** stage and click on **Logs**. See the following screenshot:

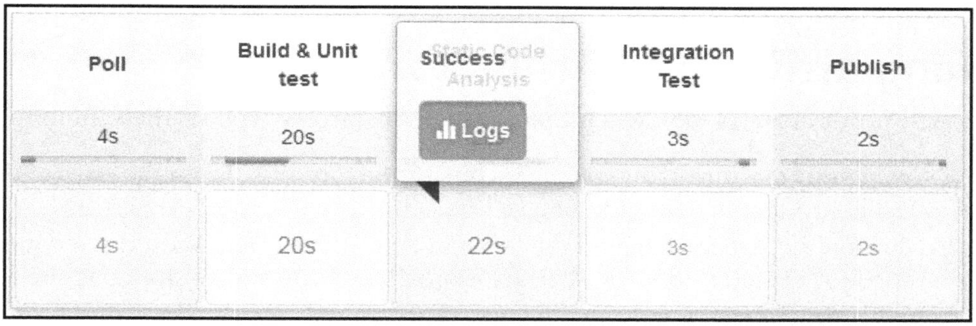

Fetching individual stage logs

3. In the resultant pop-up window named **Stage Logs (Static Code Analysis)**, scroll all the way down to the end. You should see a link to the SonarQube analysis page. See the following screenshot:

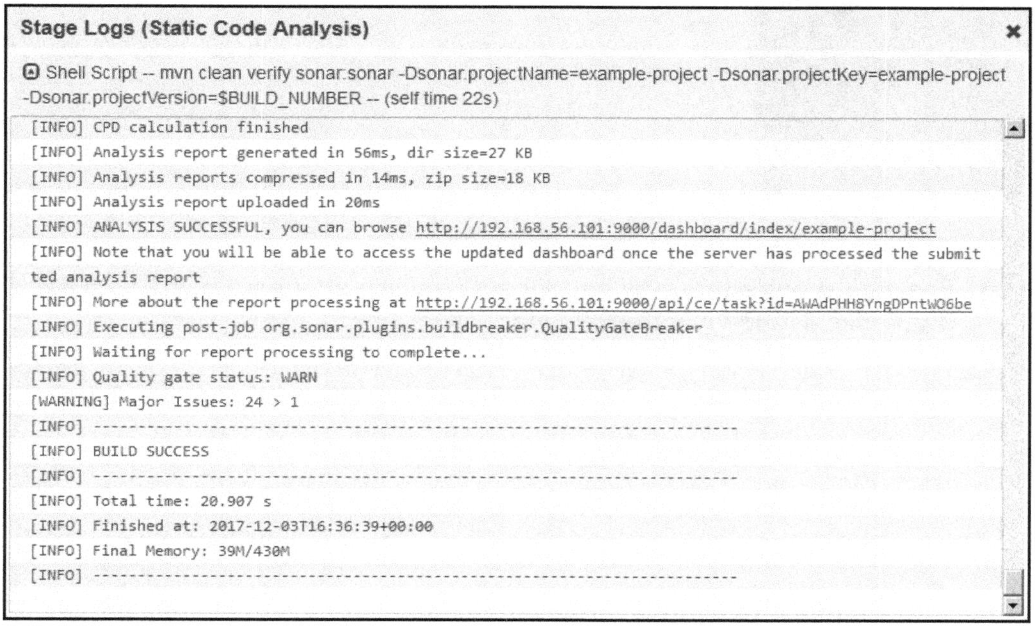

```
Stage Logs (Static Code Analysis)
Shell Script -- mvn clean verify sonar:sonar -Dsonar.projectName=example-project -Dsonar.projectKey=example-project
-Dsonar.projectVersion=$BUILD_NUMBER -- (self time 22s)
[INFO] CPD calculation finished
[INFO] Analysis report generated in 56ms, dir size=27 KB
[INFO] Analysis reports compressed in 14ms, zip size=18 KB
[INFO] Analysis report uploaded in 20ms
[INFO] ANALYSIS SUCCESSFUL, you can browse http://192.168.56.101:9000/dashboard/index/example-project
[INFO] Note that you will be able to access the updated dashboard once the server has processed the submit
ted analysis report
[INFO] More about the report processing at http://192.168.56.101:9000/api/ce/task?id=AWAdPHH8YngDPntWO6be
[INFO] Executing post-job org.sonar.plugins.buildbreaker.QualityGateBreaker
[INFO] Waiting for report processing to complete...
[INFO] Quality gate status: WARN
[WARNING] Major Issues: 24 > 1
[INFO] ------------------------------------------------------------------------
[INFO] BUILD SUCCESS
[INFO] ------------------------------------------------------------------------
[INFO] Total time: 20.907 s
[INFO] Finished at: 2017-12-03T16:36:39+00:00
[INFO] Final Memory: 39M/430M
[INFO] ------------------------------------------------------------------------
```

SonarQube analysis link from Jenkins logs

4. Clicking on the link, as shown in the previous screenshot, will take you straight to the SonarQube dashboard of the respective project.

Viewing artifacts in Artifactory

Let us see how our artifacts look when uploaded to Artifactory. Follow these steps:

1. From your favorite browser, access the Artifactory link. From the Artifactory dashboard, log in using the **Log in** link.
2. Click on the **Artifacts** tab on the left-hand side menu. You should see your repository listed under the **Artifact Repository Browser**, as shown in the following screenshot:

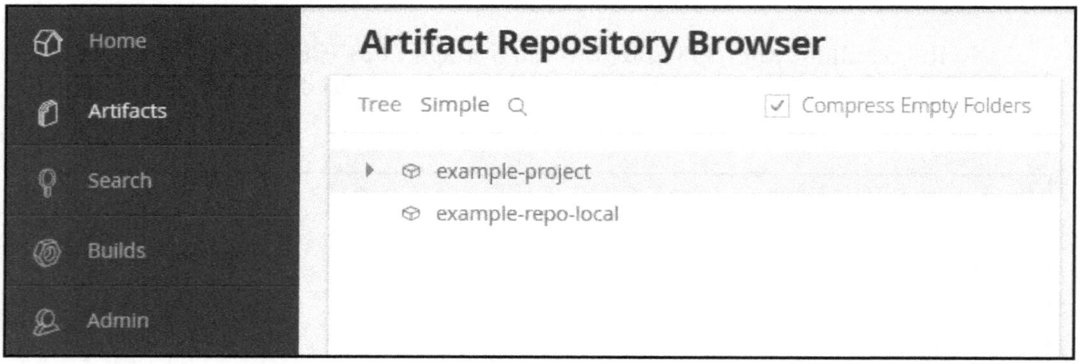

Artifact Repository Browser

3. Expand the repository, and you should see the built artifact along with the properties, as shown in the following screenshot:

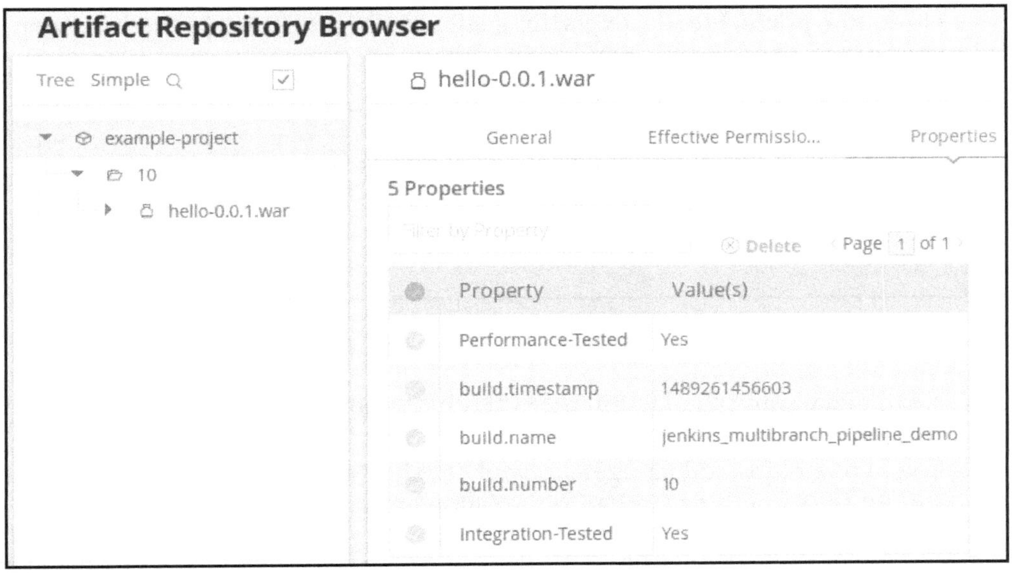

Artifact generated by the CI pipeline

Failing the build when quality gate criteria are not met

In the following section, we will tweak the SonarQube quality gate that we created in the previous chapter, such that it should fail the Jenkins CI pipeline. Follow these steps to simulate this scenario:

1. Log in to your SonarQube server and click on **Quality Gates** from the menu bar.
2. From the left-hand side menu, click on the quality gate: `example-quality-gate` that we created in the previous chapter.
3. Now, change the value of the **ERROR** field from `50` to `3`.

4. Click on **Update**. Finally, everything should look as shown in the following screenshot:

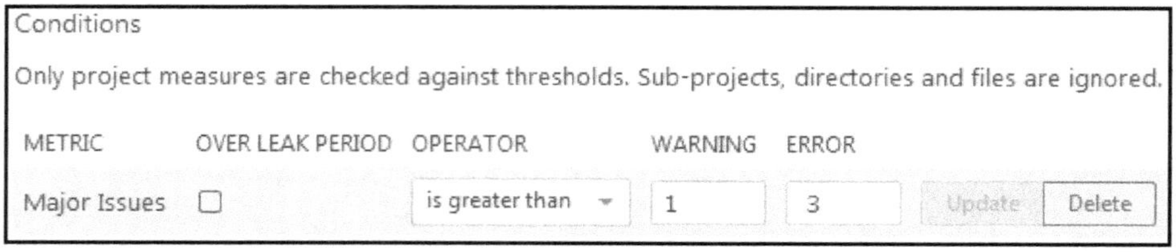

Updating the SonarQube quality gate

5. Next, make some changes on the GitHub repository to trigger a CI pipeline in Jenkins.
6. Log in to Jenkins and navigate to your Jenkins Multibranch CI Pipeline. You should see something similar to the following screenshot:

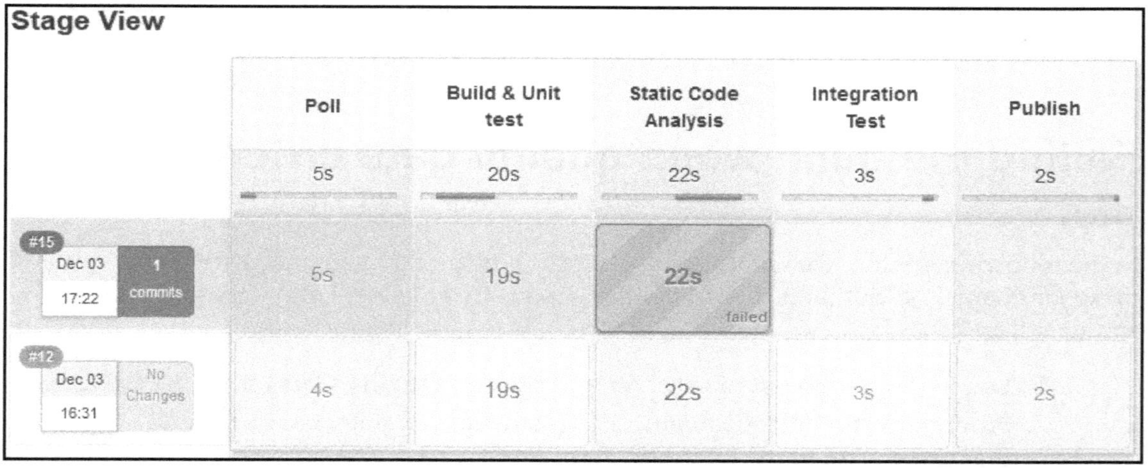

Failed CI pipeline

7. Click on the failed stage of the respective pipeline to fetch its logs. In the pop-up window, scroll all the way down. You should see the reason for the pipeline failure, as shown in the following screenshot (arrow):

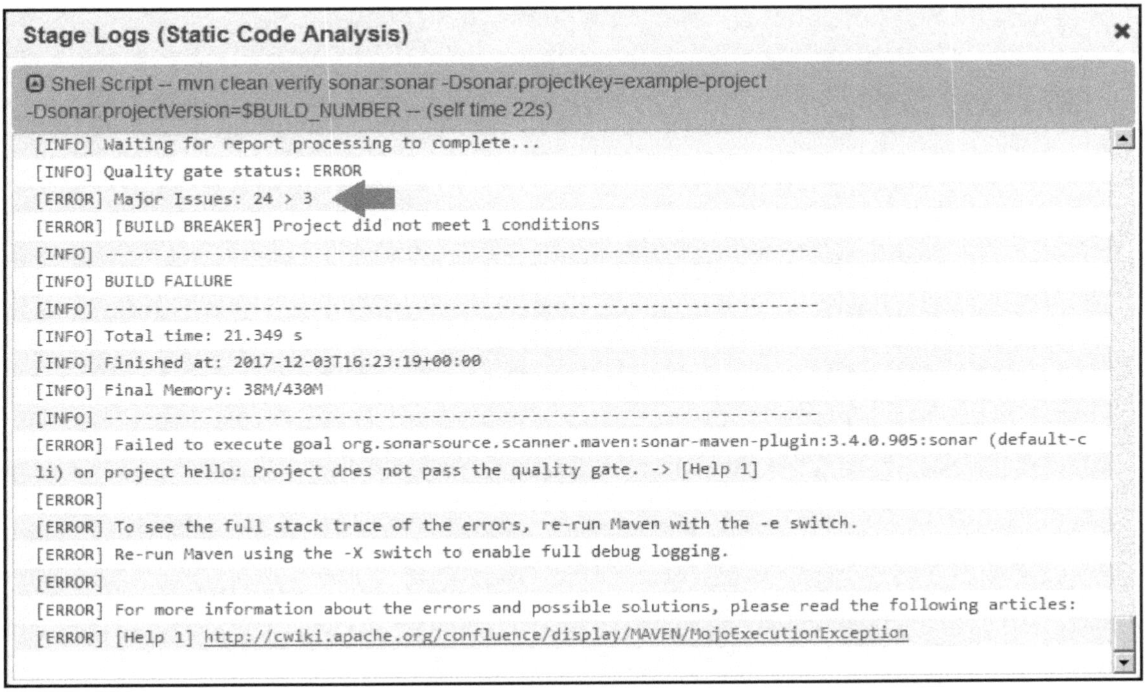

SonarQube logs with quality gate status

Summary

In this chapter, we learned how to create a Multibranch CI Pipeline that gets triggered on a push event, performs build, static code analysis, integration testing, and uploads the successfully tested binary artifact to Artifactory. Lastly, we saw the whole CI pipeline in action from the perspective of a developer.

The CI design discussed in the book can be modified to suit the needs of any type of project; the users just need to identify the right tools and configurations that can be used with Jenkins.

In the next chapter, we will extend our CI pipeline to do more in the area of QA.

8

Continuous Delivery Using Jenkins

We will begin this chapter with a Continuous Delivery design that covers the following areas:

- Branching strategy
- A list of tools for Continuous Delivery
- A Jenkins pipeline structure

The **Continuous Delivery** (**CD**) design will serve as a blueprint that will guide the readers in answering the how, why, and where of the CD being implemented. The design will cover all the necessary steps involved in implementing an end-to-end CD pipeline.

The CD design, discussed in this chapter, should be considered as a template for implementing CD, and not a full and final model. All the tools used can be modified and replaced to suit the purpose.

Jenkins CD design

In this section, we will go through a very general CD design.

Branching strategy

In `Chapter 7`, *Continuous Integration Using Jenkins*, we followed a branching strategy for the CI that included the following:

- The master branch
- The integration branch
- The feature branch

This branching strategy is a slimmer version of the *GitFlow workflow* branching model.

While CI can be performed on integration/development branches or feature branches, CD is carried out only on the integration and release branches.

The release branch

Some teams go with the strategy of having a release branch. A release branch is created after a successfully-tested code goes live in production (distributed to customers) from the master branch. The purpose of creating a release branch is to support bug fixes on the respective release:

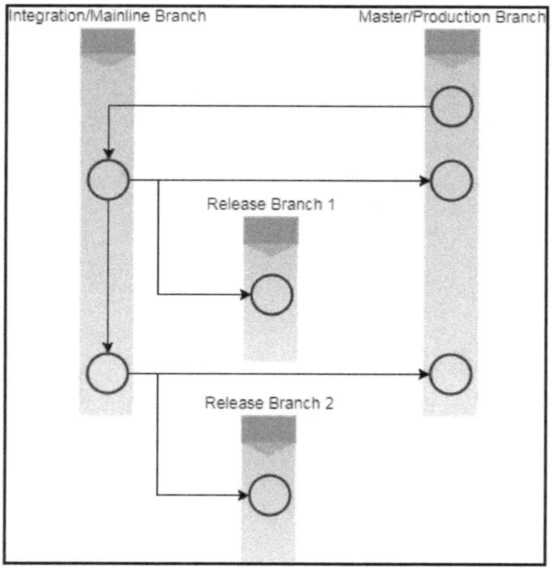

Branching strategy

CD pipeline

We are now at the heart of the CD design. We will not create a new pipeline; instead, we will build on the existing CI Multibranch Pipeline in Jenkins. The new CD pipeline will have the following stages:

1. Fetch the code from the **version control system** (**VCS**) on a push event (initialization of the CI pipeline).
2. Build and unit test the code; publish a unit test report on Jenkins.
3. Perform static code analysis on the code and upload the result to SonarQube. Fail the pipeline if the number of bugs crosses the threshold defined in the quality gate.
4. Perform integration testing; publish a unit test report on Jenkins.
5. Upload the built artifacts to Artifactory along with some meaningful properties.
6. Deploy the binaries to the testing environment.
7. Execute testing (quality analysis).
8. Promote the solution in Artifactory and mark it as a release candidate.

The purpose of the preceding CD pipeline is to automate the process of continuously deploying, testing (QA), and promoting the build artifacts in the binary repository. Reporting for failures/success happens at every step. Let us discuss these pipelines and their constituents in detail.

In the real world, the QA may contain multiple stages of testing, such as performance testing, user acceptance testing, component testing, and so on. To keep things simple, we will perform only performance testing in our example CD pipeline.

Toolset for CD

The example project for which we are implementing CI is a simple Maven project. Therefore, we will see Jenkins working closely with many other tools.

The following table contains the list of tools and technologies involved in everything that we will be seeing:

Tool/Technology	Description
Java	Primary programming language used for coding
Maven	Build tool
JUnit	Unit test and integration test tools
Jenkins	CI tool
GitHub	VCS
SonarQube	Static code analysis tool
Artifactory	Binary repository manager
Apache Tomcat	Application server to host the solution
Apache JMeter	Performance testing tool

Creating a Docker image – performance testing

In this section, we will create a Docker image for our **performance testing** (**PT**). This Docker image will be used by Jenkins to create Docker containers, wherein we will deploy our built solution and execute our performance tests. Follow the given steps:

1. Log in to your Docker server. Give the following command to check the available Docker images:

   ```
   sudo docker images
   ```

2. From the following screenshot, you can see I have three Docker images (`ubuntu`, `hello-world`, and `maven-build-slave-0.1`) already on my Docker server:

ubuntu@node4:~$ sudo docker images
REPOSITORY TAG IMAGE ID CREATED SIZE
maven-build-slave-0.1 latest 317fb6ec990f About a minute ago 298 MB
ubuntu latest f49eec89601e 3 weeks ago 129 MB
hello-world latest 48b5124b2768 4 weeks ago 1.84 kB
ubuntu@node4:~$

Listing the Docker images

3. We will build a new Docker image for running our PT using the Ubuntu Docker image.
4. Let us upgrade our Ubuntu Docker image with all the necessary application that we need to run our tests, which are as follows:
    - Java JDK (latest)
    - Apache Tomcat (8.5)
    - Apache JMeter
    - A user account to log in the Docker container
    - OpenSSH daemon (to accept SSH connection)
    - Curl

5. Execute the following command to run a Docker container using the Ubuntu Docker image. This will create a container and open up its bash shell:

```
sudo docker run -i -t ubuntu /bin/bash
```

6. Now, install all the required application as you would do on any normal Ubuntu machine. Let's begin with creating a `jenkins` user:
    1. Execute the following command and follow the user creation steps, shown as follows:

```
adduser jenkins
```

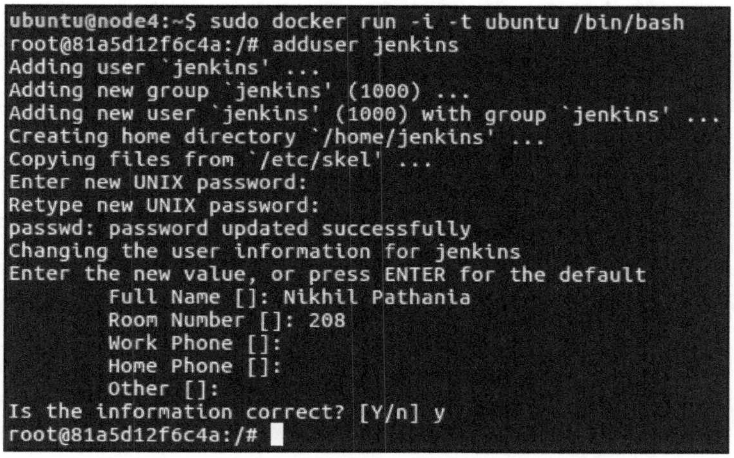
ubuntu@node4:~$ sudo docker run -i -t ubuntu /bin/bash
root@81a5d12f6c4a:/# adduser jenkins
Adding user `jenkins' ...
Adding new group `jenkins' (1000) ...
Adding new user `jenkins' (1000) with group `jenkins' ...
Creating home directory `/home/jenkins' ...
Copying files from `/etc/skel' ...
Enter new UNIX password:
Retype new UNIX password:
passwd: password updated successfully
Changing the user information for jenkins
Enter the new value, or press ENTER for the default
Full Name []: Nikhil Pathania
Room Number []: 208
Work Phone []:
Home Phone []:
Other []:
Is the information correct? [Y/n] y
root@81a5d12f6c4a:/#

Creating a user

2. Check the new user, using the switch user command:

```
su jenkins
```

7. Switch back to the `root` user by typing `exit`.
8. Next, we will install the SSH server. Execute the following commands in sequence:

```
apt-get update

apt-get install openssh-server

mkdir /var/run/sshd
```

9. Follow the given steps to install Java:
    1. Update the package index:

    ```
    apt-get update
    ```

    2. Next, install Java. The following command will install the **Java Runtime Environment** (**JRE**):

    ```
    apt-get install default-jre
    ```

10. The best way to install Tomcat 8.5 is to download the latest binary release and then configure it manually:
    1. Move to the `/tmp` directory and download Apache Tomcat 8.5, using the following commands:

    ```
    cd /tmp

    wget
    https://archive.apache.org/dist/tomcat/tomcat-8/v8
    .5.11/bin/apache-tomcat-8.5.11.tar.gz
    ```

    2. We will install Tomcat inside the `home/jenkins/` directory. To do so, first switch to the `jenkins` user. Create a `tomcat` directory inside `/home/jenkins/`:

    ```
    su jenkins

    mkdir /home/jenkins/tomcat
    ```

3. Then extract the archive to it:

```
tar xzvf apache-tomcat-8*tar.gz \
-C /home/jenkins/tomcat --strip-components=1
```

11. Switch back to the `root` user by typing `exit`.
12. Apache JMeter is a good tool to perform performance testing. It's free and open source. It can run in both GUI and command-line mode, which makes it a suitable candidate for automating performance testing:
    1. Move to the `/tmp` directory:

    ```
    cd /tmp
    ```

    2. Download `apache-jmeter-3.1.tgz`, or whichever is the latest stable version, from `http://jmeter.apache.org/download_jmeter.cgi`:

    ```
    wget
    https://archive.apache.org/dist/jmeter/binaries/ap
    ache-jmeter-3.1.tgz
    ```

    3. We will install JMeter inside the `opt/jmeter/` directory. To do so, create a `jmeter` directory inside `/opt`:

    ```
    mkdir /opt/jmeter
    ```

    4. Then extract the archive to the `/opt/jmeter/` directory and also give it the appropriate permissions:

    ```
    tar xzvf apache-jmeter-3*.tgz \
    -C /opt/jmeter --strip-components=1

    chown -R jenkins:jenkins /opt/jmeter/

    chmod -R 777 /opt/jmeter/
    ```

13. Follow the given step to install `curl`:

```
apt-get install curl
```

14. Follow the given steps to save all the changes that we made to the Docker image:
    1. Exit the container by typing `exit`.
    2. We need to save (`commit`) all the changes that we did to our Docker container.
    3. Get the `CONTAINER ID` of the container that we worked on recently by listing all the inactive containers, as shown in the following screenshot after the command:

```
sudo docker ps -a
```

```
ubuntu@node4:~$ sudo docker ps -a
CONTAINER ID   IMAGE    COMMAND        CREATED           STATUS
f8b14a252e77   ubuntu   "/bin/bash"    30 minutes ago    Exited (0) About a minute ago
81a5d12f6c4a   ubuntu   "/bin/bash"    2 weeks ago       Exited (0) 2 weeks ago
ubuntu@node4:~$
```

Listing inactive containers

4. Note the `CONTAINER ID`, and execute the following command to save (`commit`) the changes that we made to our container:

```
sudo docker commit <CONTAINER ID> <new name for
the container>
```

5. I have named my container `performance-test-agent-0.1`, as shown in the following screenshot:

```
ubuntu@node4:~$ sudo docker commit f8b14a252e77 performance-test-agent-0.1
sha256:5218edfb90a9d3391393e5b11a2188f6fe8e1f85fd7e92a12d9bac558cc33e41
ubuntu@node4:~$
```

Docker commit command

6. Once you have committed the changes, a new Docker image gets created.

7. Execute the following `docker` command to list images, as shown in the following screenshot after the command:

```
sudo docker images
```

ubuntu@node4:~$ sudo docker images
REPOSITORY TAG IMAGE ID CREATED SIZE
performance-test-agent-0.1 latest 5218edfb90a9 23 hours ago 720 MB
maven-build-slave-0.1 latest 317fb6ec990f 2 weeks ago 298 MB
ubuntu latest f49eec89601e 6 weeks ago 129 MB
hello-world latest 48b5124b2768 7 weeks ago 1.84 kB
ubuntu@node4:~$

Listing the Docker images

8. You can see our new Docker image with the name `performance-test-agent-0.1`. We will now configure our Jenkins server to use the `performance-test-agent-0.1` Docker image to create Jenkins slaves (build agents).

Adding Docker container credentials in Jenkins

Follow the given steps to add credentials inside Jenkins to allow it to talk to Docker:

1. From the Jenkins dashboard, navigate to **Credentials** | **System** | **Global credentials (unrestricted)**.
2. Click on the **Add Credentials** link on the left-hand side menu to create a new credential (see the following screenshot).
3. Choose **Kind** as **Username with Password**.
4. Leave the **Scope** field to its default value.
5. Add a username for your Docker image (`jenkins`, as per our example) under the **Username** field.
6. Under the **Password** field, add the password.
7. Add an ID under the **ID** field, and a description under the **Description** field.

8. Once done, click on the **OK** button:

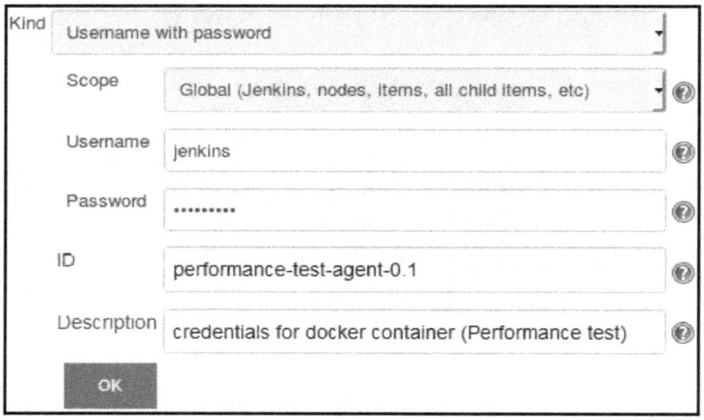

Creating credentials inside Jenkins

Updating the Docker settings inside Jenkins

Follow the given steps to update the Docker settings inside Jenkins:

1. From the Jenkins dashboard, click on **Manage Jenkins** | **Configure System**.
2. Scroll all the way down to the **Cloud** section.
3. Under the **Cloud** section, click on the **Add Docker Template** button and choose **Docker Template**.
4. You will be presented with a lot of settings to configure (see the following screenshot). However, to keep this demonstration simple, let us stick to the important settings.
5. Under the **Docker Image** field, enter the name of the Docker image that we created earlier. In my case, it is `performance-test-agent-0.1`.
6. Under the **Labels** field, add a label. The Docker container will be recognized, using this label by your Jenkins pipeline. I have added the `docker_pt` label.
7. **Launch Method** should be **Docker SSH computer launcher**.
8. Under the **Credentials** field, choose the credentials that we created to access the Docker container.
9. Make sure that the **Pull strategy** option is set to **Never pull**.
10. Leave the rest of the options to their default values.

11. Once done, click on **Apply** and then **Save**:

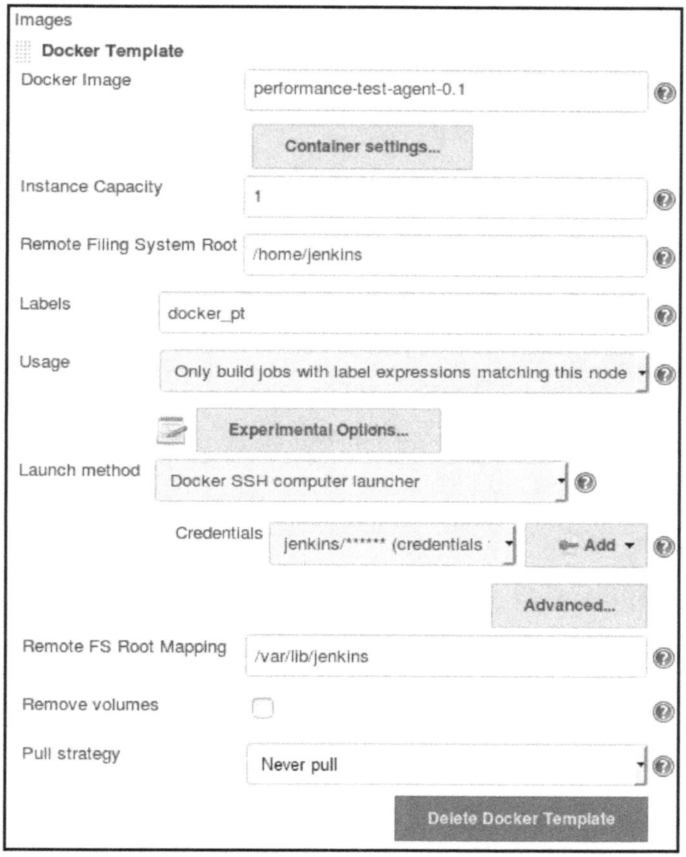

Creating a Docker Template for integration testing

Creating a performance test using JMeter

In this section, we will learn how to create a simple performance test using the JMeter tool. The steps mentioned should be performed on your local machine. The following steps are performed on a machine with Ubuntu 16.04.

Installing Java

Follow the given steps to install Java:

1. Update the package index:

```
sudo apt-get update
```

2. Next, install Java. The following command will install the JRE:

```
sudo apt-get install default-jre
```

3. To set the `JAVA_HOME` environment variable, first get the Java installation location. Do this by executing the following command:

```
sudo update-alternatives --config java
```

4. Copy the resultant path and update the `JAVA_HOME` variable inside the `/etc/environment` file.

Installing Apache JMeter

Follow the given steps to install Apache JMeter:

1. Move to the `/tmp` directory:

```
cd /tmp
```

2. Download `apache-jmeter-3.1.tgz`, or whichever is the latest stable version, from `http://jmeter.apache.org/download_jmeter.cgi`:

```
wget
https://archive.apache.org/dist/jmeter/binaries/apache-jmeter-3
.1.tgz
```

3. We will install JMeter inside the `/opt/jmeter` directory. To do so, create a `jmeter` directory inside `/opt`:

```
mkdir /opt/jmeter
```

4. Then extract the archive to it:

```
tar xzvf apache-jmeter-3*.tgz \
-C /opt/jmeter --strip-components=1
```

Starting JMeter

Follow the given steps to start JMeter:

1. To start JMeter, move to the JMeter installation directory and run the `jmeter.sh`, script using the following command:

```
cd /opt/jmeter/bin

./jmeter.sh
```

2. The JMeter GUI utility will open up in a new window.

Creating a performance test case

By default, you will see an example test plan. We will create a new test plan by modifying the existing template:

1. Rename the test plan to `Hello_World_Test_Plan`, as shown in the following screenshot:

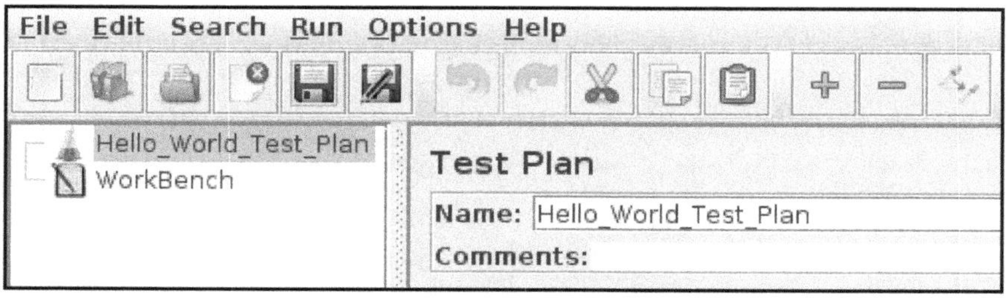

Creating a test plan

2. Save it inside the `examples` folder by clicking on the **Save** button from the menu items or by clicking *Ctrl* + *S*, as shown in the following screenshot:

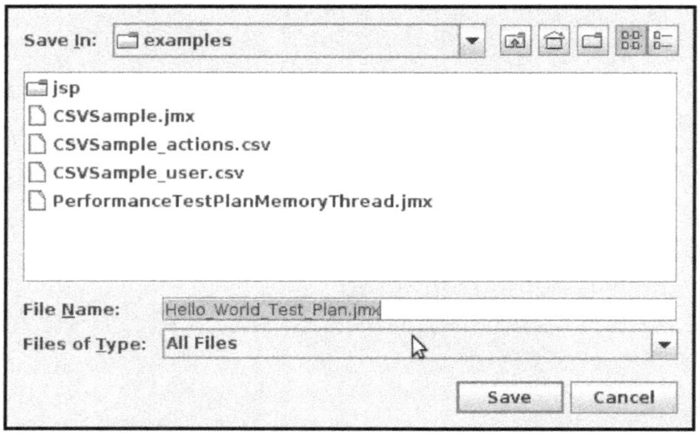

Saving the test plan

Creating a thread group

Follow the given steps to create a thread group:

1. Add a thread group. To do so, right-click on `Hello_World_Test_Plan` and select **Add** | **Threads (Users)** | **Thread Group**:

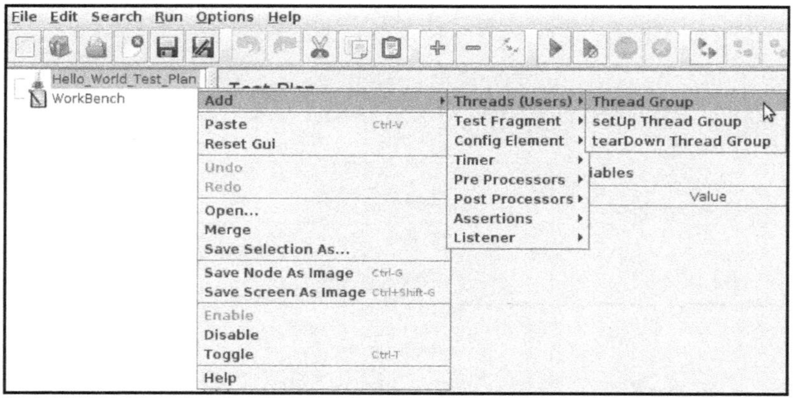

Creating a thread group

2. In the resultant page, give your thread group a name and fill the options as follows:
    1. Select **Continue** for the option **Action to be taken after a Sampler error**.
    2. Add **Number of Threads (users)** as `1`.
    3. Add **Ramp-Up Period (in seconds)** as `1`.
    4. Add **Loop Count** as `1`:

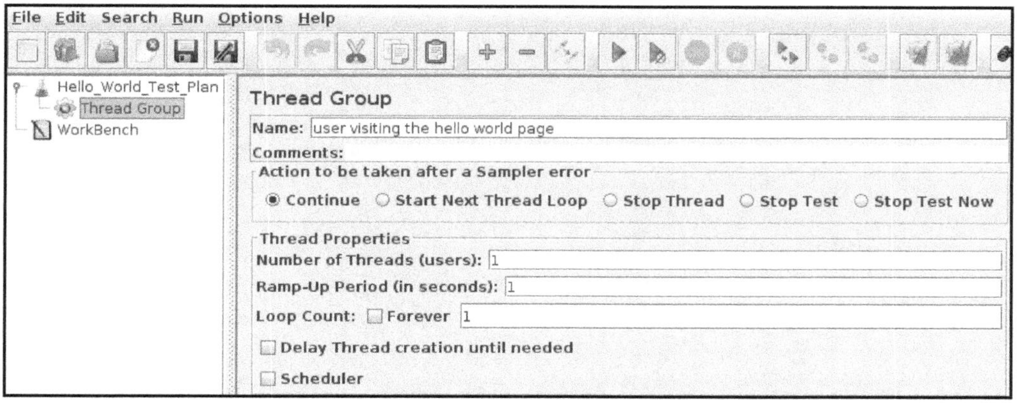

Configuring a thread group

Creating a sampler

Follow the given steps to create a sampler:

1. Right-click on `Hello_World_Test_Plan` and select **Add** | **Sampler** | **HTTP Request**:

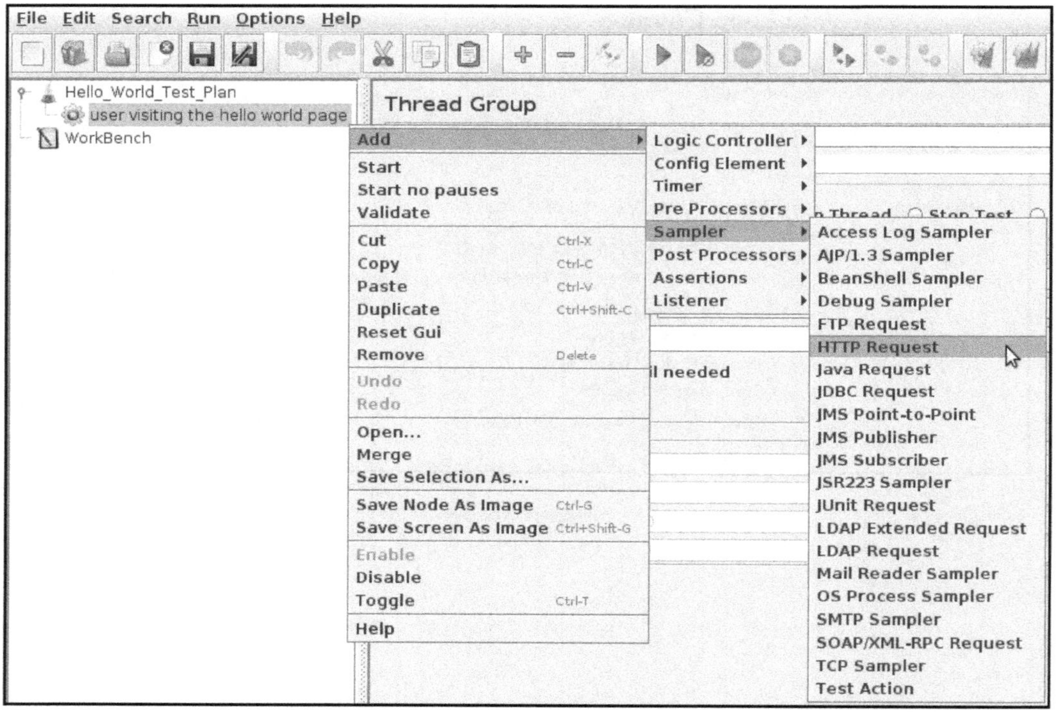

Adding a Sampler

2. Name the **HTTP Request** appropriately and fill the options as follows:
    1. Add **Server Name or IP** as `<IP Address of your Testing Server machine>`.
    2. Add **Port Number** as `8080`.
    3. Add **Path** as `/hello.0.0.1/`:

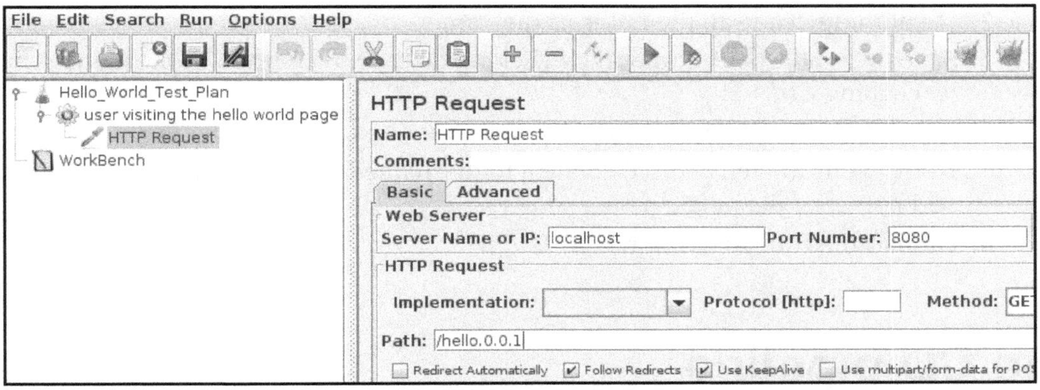

Configuring a sampler

Adding a listener

Follow the given steps to add a listener:

1. Right-click on `Hello_World_Test_Plan` and select **Add** | **Listener** | **View Results Tree**:

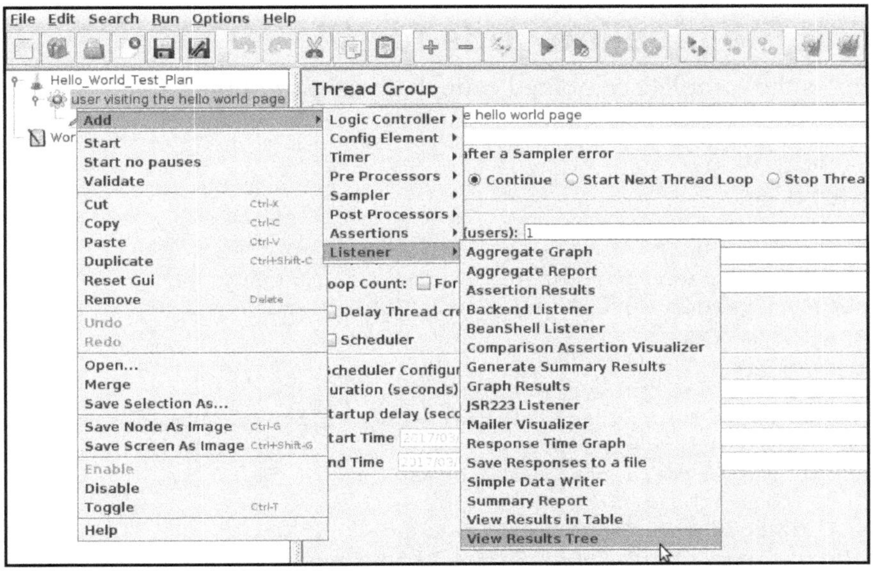

Adding a Listener

2. Do nothing; leave all the fields as they are.
3. Save the whole configuration by clicking on the **Save** button in the menu items or by clicking *Ctrl* + *S*.
4. Copy the `.jmx` file from `/opt/jmeter/bin/examples`.
5. Under your Maven project, create a folder named `pt` inside the `src` directory and add the `.jmx` file inside it.
6. Upload the code to GitHub.

The CD pipeline

We have all the required tools and the Docker image is ready. In this section, we will create a pipeline in Jenkins that will describe our CD process.

Writing the Jenkinsfile for CD

We will build on the CI pipeline that we created earlier. Let's first revisit our CI pipeline, and then we will add some new stages to it as part of the CD process.

Revisiting the pipeline code for CI

The following is the complete combined code that was part of the CI:

```
node('docker') {
  stage('Poll') {
    checkout scm
  }
  stage('Build & Unit test'){
    sh 'mvn clean verify -DskipITs=true';
    junit '**/target/surefire-reports/TEST-*.xml'
    archive 'target/*.jar'
  }
  stage('Static Code Analysis'){
    sh 'mvn clean verify sonar:sonar -Dsonar.projectName=example-project
    -Dsonar.projectKey=example-project
    -Dsonar.projectVersion=$BUILD_NUMBER';
  }
  stage ('Integration Test'){
    sh 'mvn clean verify -Dsurefire.skip=true';
    junit '**/target/failsafe-reports/TEST-*.xml'
    archive 'target/*.jar'
```

```
    }
    stage ('Publish'){
      def server = Artifactory.server 'Default Artifactory Server'
      def uploadSpec = """{
        "files": [
          {
            "pattern": "target/hello-0.0.1.war",
            "target": "example-project/${BUILD_NUMBER}/",
            "props": "Integration-Tested=Yes;Performance-Tested=No"
          }
        ]
      }"""
      server.upload(uploadSpec)
    }
  }
```

Pipeline code to stash the build artifacts

The Jenkins pipeline uses a feature called `stash` to pass build artifacts across nodes. In the following step, we will `stash` a few build artifacts that we wish to pass to the `docker_pt` node, wherein we will perform our performance test:

```
stash includes: 'target/hello-0.0.1.war,src/pt/Hello_World_Test_Plan.jmx',
name: 'binary'
```

In the preceding code:

- `name`: Name for the stash
- `includes`: Comma-separated files to include

Spawning a Docker container – performance testing

First, let us create a pipeline code that will create a Docker container (Jenkins slave) using the `performance-test-agent-0.1` Docker image for performance testing:

```
node('docker_pt') {
}
```

Where `docker_pt` is the label for the `performance-test-agent-0.1` Docker template.

We would like to perform the following tasks on the `docker_pt` node:

1. Start Tomcat.
2. Deploy the build artifacts to Tomcat on the testing environment.
3. Perform performance testing.
4. Promote the build artifacts inside Artifactory.

All the preceding tasks are various stages of our CD pipeline. Let's write the pipeline code for each one of them.

Pipeline code to start Apache Tomcat

The pipeline code to start Apache Tomcat on the performance testing agent is a simple shell script that will run the `./startup.sh` script present inside the Tomcat installation directory:

```
sh '''cd /home/jenkins/tomcat/bin
./startup.sh''';
```

Wrap the preceding step inside a `stage` called `Start Tomcat`:

```
stage ('Start Tomcat'){
    sh '''cd /home/jenkins/tomcat/bin
    ./startup.sh''';
}
```

Pipeline code to deploy build artifacts

The pipeline code to deploy build artifacts happens in two steps. First, we will un-stash the binary package that we stashed from the previous node Docker block. Then, we deploy the un-stashed files into the `webapps` folder inside the Tomcat installation directory on our testing environment. The code is as follows:

```
unstash 'binary'
sh 'cp target/hello-0.0.1.war /home/jenkins/tomcat/webapps/';
```

Wrap the preceding step inside a `stage` called `Deploy`:

```
stage ('Deploy){
    unstash 'binary'
    sh 'cp target/hello-0.0.1.war /home/jenkins/tomcat/webapps/';
}
```

Pipeline code to run performance testing

The pipeline code to execute the performance testing is a simple shell script that evokes the `jmeter.sh` script and passes the `.jmx` file to it. The test result is stored inside a `.jtl` file that is then archived. The code is as follows:

```
sh '''cd /opt/jmeter/bin/
./jmeter.sh -n -t $WORKSPACE/src/pt/Hello_World_Test_Plan.jmx -l
$WORKSPACE/test_report.jtl''';

step([$class: 'ArtifactArchiver', artifacts: '**/*.jtl'])
```

The following table gives the description the preceding code snippet:

Code	Description
`./jmeter.sh -n -t <path to the .jmx file> -l <path to save the .jtl file>`	This is the `jmeter` command to execute the performance test plan (the `.jmx` files) and generate a test result (the `.jtl` files).
`step([$class: 'ArtifactArchiver', artifacts: '**/*.jtl'])`	This line of code will archive all files with the `.jtl` extension.

Wrap the previous step inside a `stage` called `Performance Testing`:

```
stage ('Performance Testing'){
    sh '''cd /opt/jmeter/bin/
    ./jmeter.sh -n -t $WORKSPACE/src/pt/Hello_World_Test_Plan.jmx -l
$WORKSPACE/test_report.jtl''';
    step([$class: 'ArtifactArchiver', artifacts: '**/*.jtl'])
}
```

Pipeline code to promote build artifacts in Artifactory

The way we are going to promote build artifacts in Artifactory is by using the properties (key-value pair) feature. All builds that have passed performance testing will be applied a `Performance-Tested=Yes` tag. The code is as follows:

```
withCredentials([usernameColonPassword(credentialsId: 'artifactory-
account', variable: 'credentials')]) {
    sh 'curl -u${credentials} -X PUT
"http://172.17.8.108:8081/artifactory/api/storage/example-project/${BUILD_N
UMBER}/hello-0.0.1.war?properties=Performance-Tested=Yes"';
}
```

The following table gives the description the preceding code snippet:

Code	Description
`withCredentials([usernameColonPassword(credentialsId: 'artifactory-account', variable: 'credentials')]) { }`	We are using the `withCredentials` plugin inside Jenkins to pass Artifactory credentials to the `curl` command.
`curl -u<username>:password -X PUT "<artifactory server URL>/api/storage/<artifactory repository name>?properties=key-value"`	This is the `curl` command to update the property (key-value pair) on the build artifact present inside Artifactory. The `curl` command makes use of the REST API features of Artifactory.

Wrap the previous step inside a `stage` called `Promote build in Artifactory`:

```
stage ('Promote build in Artifactory'){
    withCredentials([usernameColonPassword(credentialsId: 'artifactory-
account', variable: 'credentials')]) {
        sh 'curl -u${credentials} -X PUT
"http://172.17.8.108:8081/artifactory/api/storage/example-project/${BUILD_N
UMBER}/hello-0.0.1.war?properties=Performance-Tested=Yes"';
    }
}
```

Combined CD pipeline code

The following is the complete combined code that will run inside the `docker_pt` node:

```
node('docker_pt') {
  stage ('Start Tomcat'){
    sh '''cd /home/jenkins/tomcat/bin
    ./startup.sh''';
  }
  stage ('Deploy '){
    unstash 'binary'
    sh 'cp target/hello-0.0.1.war /home/jenkins/tomcat/webapps/';
  }
  stage ('Performance Testing'){
    sh '''cd /opt/jmeter/bin/
    ./jmeter.sh -n -t $WORKSPACE/src/pt/Hello_World_Test_Plan.jmx -l
    $WORKSPACE/test_report.jtl''';
    step([$class: 'ArtifactArchiver', artifacts: '**/*.jtl'])
  }
  stage ('Promote build in Artifactory'){
    withCredentials([usernameColonPassword(credentialsId:
      'artifactory-account', variable: 'credentials')]) {
        sh 'curl -u${credentials} -X PUT
        "http://172.17.8.108:8081/artifactory/api/storage/example-project/
        ${BUILD_NUMBER}/hello-0.0.1.war?properties=Performance-
Tested=Yes"';
      }
  }
}
```

Let us combine the preceding code with the pipeline code for CI to get the complete CD pipeline code, shown as follows:

```
node('docker') {
  stage('Poll') {
    checkout scm
  }
  stage('Build & Unit test'){
    sh 'mvn clean verify -DskipITs=true';
    junit '**/target/surefire-reports/TEST-*.xml'
    archive 'target/*.jar'
  }
  stage('Static Code Analysis'){
    sh 'mvn clean verify sonar:sonar -Dsonar.projectName=example-project
    -Dsonar.projectKey=example-project -
Dsonar.projectVersion=$BUILD_NUMBER';
  }
```

```
    stage ('Integration Test'){
      sh 'mvn clean verify -Dsurefire.skip=true';
      junit '**/target/failsafe-reports/TEST-*.xml'
      archive 'target/*.jar'
    }
    stage ('Publish'){
      def server = Artifactory.server 'Default Artifactory Server'
      def uploadSpec = """{
        "files": [
          {
            "pattern": "target/hello-0.0.1.war",
            "target": "example-project/${BUILD_NUMBER}/",
            "props": "Integration-Tested=Yes;Performance-Tested=No"
          }
        ]
      }"""
      server.upload(uploadSpec)
    }
    stash includes:
  'target/hello-0.0.1.war,src/pt/Hello_World_Test_Plan.jmx',
    name: 'binary'
  }
  node('docker_pt') {
    stage ('Start Tomcat'){
      sh '''cd /home/jenkins/tomcat/bin
      ./startup.sh''';
    }
    stage ('Deploy '){
      unstash 'binary'
      sh 'cp target/hello-0.0.1.war /home/jenkins/tomcat/webapps/';
    }
    stage ('Performance Testing'){
      sh '''cd /opt/jmeter/bin/
      ./jmeter.sh -n -t $WORKSPACE/src/pt/Hello_World_Test_Plan.jmx -l
      $WORKSPACE/test_report.jtl''';
      step([$class: 'ArtifactArchiver', artifacts: '**/*.jtl'])
    }
    stage ('Promote build in Artifactory'){
      withCredentials([usernameColonPassword(credentialsId:
        'artifactory-account', variable: 'credentials')]) {
          sh 'curl -u${credentials} -X PUT
          "http://172.17.8.108:8081/artifactory/api/storage/example-project/
          ${BUILD_NUMBER}/hello-0.0.1.war?properties=Performance-
  Tested=Yes"';
        }
    }
  }
```

CD in action

Make some changes on your GitHub code or just trigger the Jenkins pipeline from the Jenkins dashboard:

1. Log in to Jenkins, and from the Jenkins dashboard click on your Multibranch Pipeline. You should see something like the following:

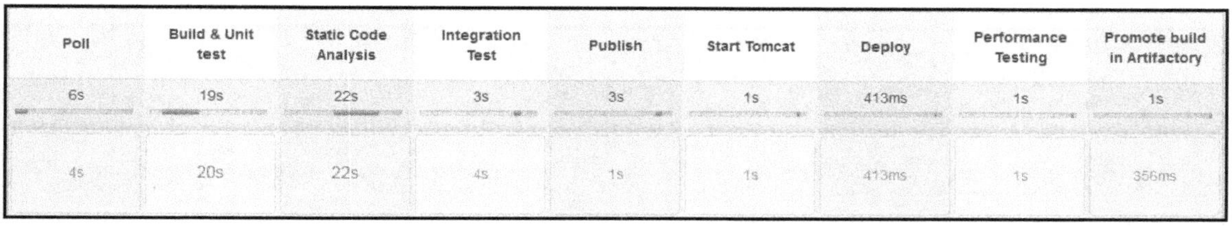

Poll
Build & Unit test
Static Code Analysis
Integration Test
Publish
Start Tomcat
Deploy
Performance Testing
Promote build in Artifactory
6s
19s
22s
3s
3s
1s
413ms
1s
1s
4s
20s
22s
4s
1s
1s
413ms
1s
356ms

Jenkins CD pipeline in action

2. Log in to the Artifactory server and see if the code has been uploaded and promoted using the properties, shown as follows:

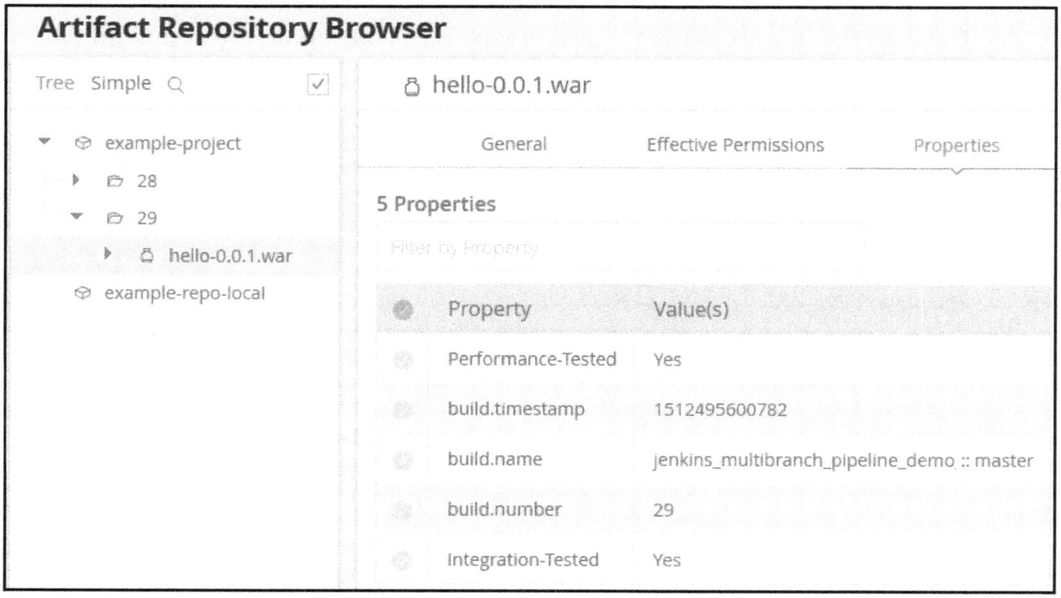

Build artifacts being promoted inside Artifactory

3. Let us see our CD pipeline in Jenkins Blue Ocean. To do so, navigate to your Jenkins Multibranch CD pipeline (`<Jenkins URL>/job/<Jenkins multibranch pipeline name>/`).
4. On the pipeline page, click on the **Open Blue Ocean** link available on the left-hand side menu.
5. You will be taken to your Multibranch Pipeline page in Blue Ocean, as shown in the following screenshot:

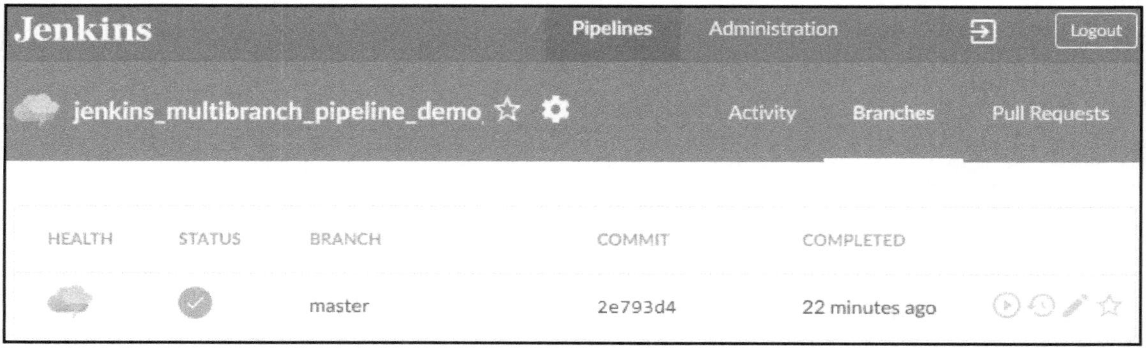

6. Click on the **master** branch to see its pipeline. You should see something like the following:

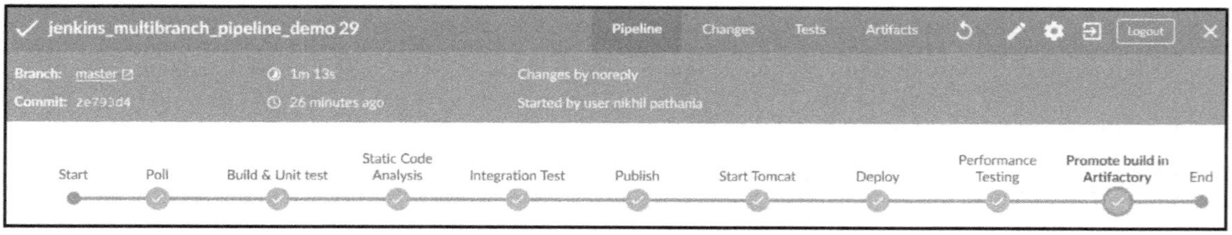

Summary

In this chapter, we learned how to create an end-to-end CD pipeline that gets triggered on a push event, performs builds, static code analysis, and integration testing, uploads the successfully tested binary artifact to Artifactory, deploys the code to the testing environment, performs some automated testing, and promotes the binaries in Artifactory.

The CD design discussed in the book can be modified to suit the needs of any type of project. The users just need to identify the right tools and configurations that can be used with Jenkins.

In the next chapter, we will learn about Continuous Deployment, how different it is from Continuous Delivery, and more.

9

Continuous Deployment Using Jenkins

This chapter begins by defining and explaining Continuous Deployment. We will also try to differentiate between Continuous Deployment and Continuous Delivery. Continuous Deployment is a simple, tweaked version of the Continuous Delivery pipeline. Hence, we won't be seeing any major Jenkins configuration changes or any new tools.

The following topics will be covered in the chapter:

- Creating a production server
- Installing a Jenkins slave on a production server
- Creating a Jenkins Continuous Deployment pipeline
- Continuous Delivery in action

What is Continuous Deployment?

The process of continuously deploying production-ready features into the production environment, or to the end user, is termed as **Continuous Deployment**.

Continuous Deployment in a holistic sense means, *the process of making production-ready features go live instantly without any intervention*. This includes building features in an agile manner, integrating and testing them continuously, and deploying them into the production environment without any breaks.

Continuous Deployment in a literal sense means, *the task of deploying any given package continuously in any given environment*. Therefore, the task of deploying packages into a testing server and a production server conveys the literal meaning of Continuous Deployment.

How Continuous Deployment is different from Continuous Delivery

First, the features are developed, and then they go through a cycle, or Continuous Integration, or through testing of all kinds. Anything that passes the various tests is considered as a production-ready feature. These production-ready features are then labeled in Artifactory (not shown in this book) or kept separately to segregate them from non-production ready features.

This is similar to the manufacturing production line. The raw product goes through phases of modifications and testing. Finally, the finished product is packaged and stored in the warehouses. From the warehouses, depending on the orders, it gets shipped to various places. The product doesn't get shipped immediately after it's packaged.

We can safely call this practice Continuous Delivery. The following illustration depicts the **Continuous Delivery** life cycle:

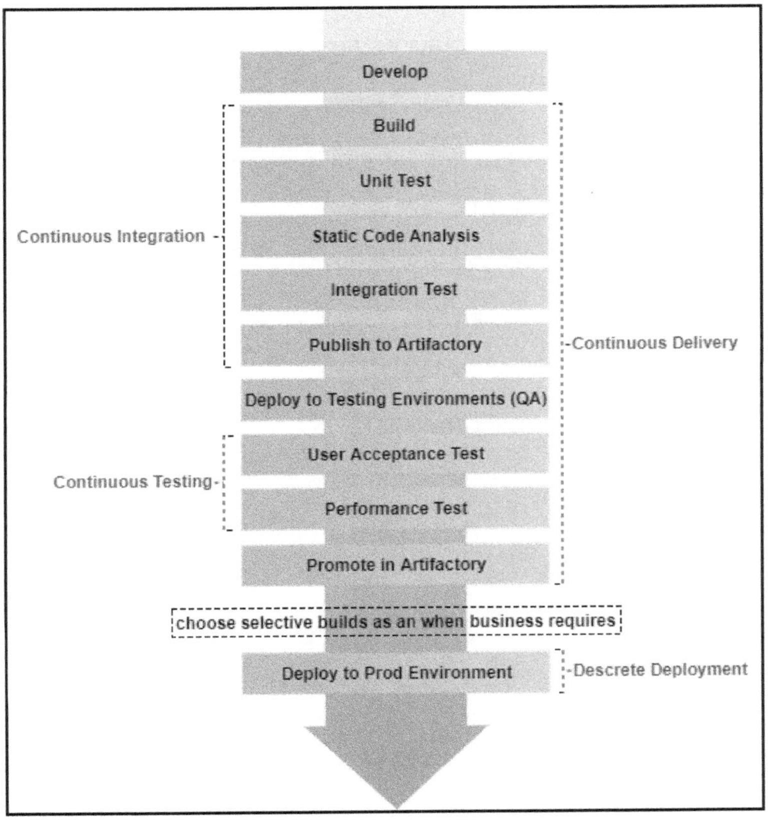

Continuous Delivery pipeline

On the other hand, a **Continuous Deployment** life cycle looks somewhat as shown in the following illustration. The deployment phase is immediate without any break. The production-ready features are immediately deployed into production:

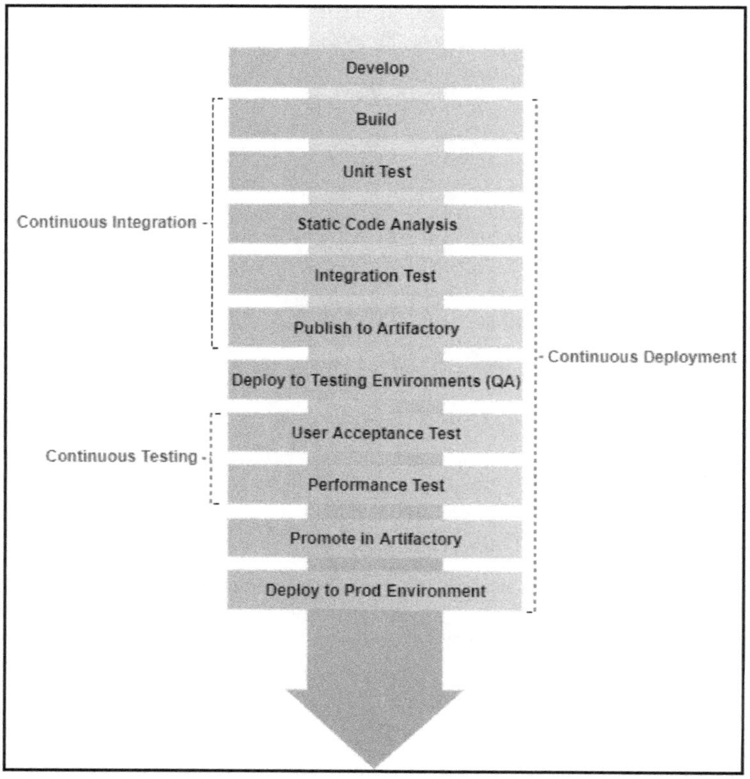

Continuous Deployment pipeline

Who needs Continuous Deployment?

One might have the following questions rolling in their minds: *how can I achieve Continuous Deployment in my organization, what could be the challenges, how much testing do I need to incorporate and automate?* The list goes on.

However, technical challenges are one thing. What's more important to decide is whether we really need it. Do we really need Continuous Deployment?

The answer is, *not always and not in every case*. Since, from our definition of Continuous Deployment and our understanding from the previous topic, production-ready features get deployed instantly into the production environments.

In many organizations, it's the business that decides whether or not to make a feature live, or when to make a feature live. Therefore, think of Continuous Deployment as an option, and not a compulsion.

On the other hand, Continuous Delivery; which means creating production-ready features in a continuous way, should be the motto for any organization.

Creating a production server

In the following section, let us create a production server that will host our *hello world* application. We will later extend our Continuous Delivery pipeline to automatically deploy fully testing binary artifacts on our production server.

In the following example, our production server is a simple Tomcat server. Let us create one using Vagrant.

Installing Vagrant

In this section, we will install Vagrant on Ubuntu. Make sure you perform these steps as a `root` user or with an account having root privileges (`sudo` access):

1. Open up a Terminal and type the following command to download Vagrant:

```
wget
https://releases.hashicorp.com/vagrant/1.8.5/vagrant_1.8.5_x86_
64.deb
```

Or, you can also download the latest Vagrant package from the Vagrant website at `https://www.vagrantup.com/downloads.html`:

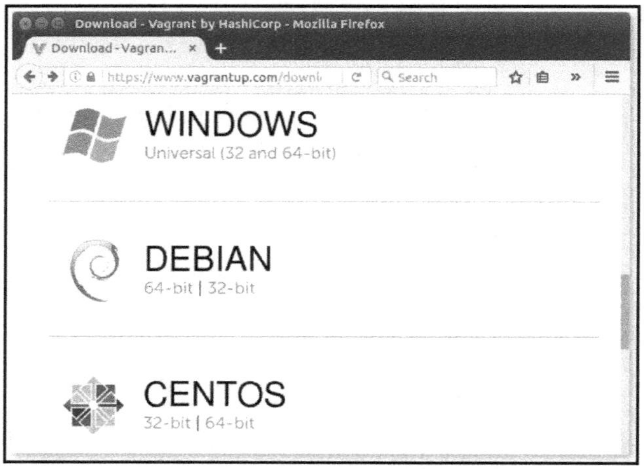

Vagrant download webpage

Use the latest version of Vagrant and VirtualBox available. Using an older version of Vagrant with a newer version of VirtualBox or vice versa may result in issues while creating VMs.

2. Once the download is complete, you should see a `.deb` file.
3. Execute the following commands to install Vagrant using the downloaded package file. You may be prompted to provide a password:

```
sudo dpkg -i vagrant_1.8.5_x86_64.deb

sudo apt-get install -f
```

4. Once the installation is complete, check the installed version of Vagrant by executing the following command:

```
vagrant --version
```

5. You should see a similar output:

```
Vagrant 1.8.5
```

Installing VirtualBox

Vagrant needs Oracle VirtualBox to create virtual machines. However, it's not limited to just Oracle VirtualBox, you can use VMware too. Follow the given steps to install VirtualBox on your machine:

> To run Vagrant with either VMware or AWS, visit `https://www.vagrantup.com/docs/getting-started/providers.html`.

1. Add the following line to your `sources.list` file present inside the `/etc/apt` directory:

```
deb http://download.virtualbox.org/virtualbox/debian \
xenial contrib
```

> According to your Ubuntu distribution, replace `xenial` with `vivid`, `utopic`, `trusty`, `raring`, `quantal`, `precise`, `lucid`, `jessie`, `wheezy`, or `squeeze`.

2. Download and register the keys using the following commands. You should expect a output: `OK` for both the commands.

```
wget -q \
https://www.virtualbox.org/download/oracle_vbox_2016.asc -O- |
sudo apt-key add -

wget -q \
https://www.virtualbox.org/download/oracle_vbox.asc -O- |
sudo apt-key add -
```

3. To install VirtualBox, execute the following commands:

```
sudo apt-get update

sudo apt-get install virtualbox-5.1
```

4. Execute the following command to see the installed VirtualBox version:

```
VBoxManage --version
```

5. You should see a similar output:

```
5.1.6r110634
```

Ubuntu/Debian users might want to install the `dkms` package to ensure that the VirtualBox host kernel modules (`vboxdrv`, `vboxnetflt`, and `vboxnetadp`) are properly updated if the Linux kernel version changes during the next `apt-get upgrade`. For Debian, it is available in Lenny backports and in the normal repository for Squeeze and later. The `dkms` package can be installed through the Synaptic package manager or through the following command:
sudo apt-get install dkms

Creating a VM using Vagrant

In the following section, we will spawn up a VM that will act as our production server using Vagrant and VirtualBox.

Creating a Vagrantfile

We will create a Vagrantfile to describe our VM. Follow the given steps:

1. Create a new file named `Vagrantfile` using the following command:

```
sudo nano Vagrantfile
```

2. Paste the following code into the file:

```
# -*- mode: ruby -*-
# vi: set ft=ruby :
Vagrant.configure(2) do |config|
config.vm.box = "ubuntu/xenial64"

config.vm.define :node1 do |node1_config|
node1_config.vm.network "private_network", ip:"192.168.56.31"
node1_config.vm.provider :virtualbox do |vb|
vb.customize ["modifyvm", :id, "--memory", "2048"]
vb.customize ["modifyvm", :id, "--cpus", "2"]
end
end
end
```

Choose the IP address, memory, and number of CPUs accordingly.

3. Type *Ctrl* + *X*, and then *Y* to save the file.

Spawning a VM using Vagrant

In this section, we will create a VM using the `Vagrantfile` that we created just now:

1. Type the following command to spawn a VM using the preceding `Vagrantfile`:

   ```
   vagrant up node1
   ```

2. It will take a while for Vagrant to bring up the machine. Once it is done, execute the following command to log in to the new VM:

   ```
   vagrant ssh node1
   ```

   The output is as follows:

   ```
   Welcome to Ubuntu 16.04.2 LTS (GNU/Linux 4.4.0-83-generic
   x86_64)

    * Documentation:  https://help.ubuntu.com
    * Management:     https://landscape.canonical.com
    * Support:        https://ubuntu.com/advantage

     Get cloud support with Ubuntu Advantage Cloud Guest:
       http://www.ubuntu.com/business/services/cloud
   0 packages can be updated.
   0 updates are security updates.

   ubuntu@ubuntu-xenial:~$
   ```

3. We are now inside the VM. We will upgrade our VM with all the necessary applications that we need to run our application:
   - Java JDK (latest)
   - Apache Tomcat (8.5)
   - A user account to log in to the Docker container

- Open SSH daemon—`sshd` (to accept SSH connections)
- Curl

4. Now, install all the required applications as you would do on any normal Ubuntu machine. Let's begin with creating a `jenkins` user:
   1. Execute the following command and follow the user creation steps:

      ```
      adduser jenkins
      ```

      The output is as follows:

      ```
      Adding user `jenkins' ...
      Adding new group `jenkins' (1001) ...
      Adding new user `jenkins' (1001) with group
      `jenkins' ...
      Creating home directory `/home/jenkins' ...
      Copying files from `/etc/skel' ...
      Enter new UNIX password:
      Retype new UNIX password:
      passwd: password updated successfully
      Changing the user information for jenkins
      Enter the new value, or press ENTER for the
      default
              Full Name []: Nikhil Pathania
              Room Number []:
              Work Phone []:
              Home Phone []:
              Other []:
      Is the information correct? [Y/n] Y
      ```

   2. Check the new user using the switch user command:

      ```
      su jenkins
      ```

5. Switch back to the root user by typing `exit`.
6. Next, we will install the SSH server. Execute the following command in sequence (ignore if the `openssh-server` application and the `/var/run/sshd` directory path already exist):

   ```
   sudo apt-get update

   sudo apt-get install openssh-server

   sudo mkdir /var/run/sshd
   ```

7. Follow the given steps to install Java:
    1. Update the package index:

    ```
    sudo apt-get update
    ```

    2. Next, install Java. The following command will install the JRE:

    ```
    sudo apt-get install default-jre
    ```

8. The best way to install Tomcat 8.5 is to download the latest binary release, then configure it manually:
    1. Move to the `/tmp` directory and download Apache Tomcat 8.5 using the following commands:

    ```
    cd /tmp

    wget
    https://archive.apache.org/dist/tomcat/tomcat-8/v8.5.11
    /bin/apache-tomcat-8.5.11-deployer.tar.gz
    ```

    2. We will install Tomcat inside the `$HOME` directory. To do so, create a `tomcat` directory inside `$HOME`:

    ```
    mkdir $HOME/tomcat
    ```

    3. Then, extract the archive to it:

    ```
    sudo tar xzvf apache-tomcat-8*tar.gz \
    -C $HOME/tomcat --strip-components=1
    ```

9. Exit the VM by typing `exit` in the Terminal.

Adding production server credentials inside Jenkins

In order to make Jenkins communicate with the production server, we need to add the account credentials inside Jenkins.

We will do this using the Jenkins **Credentials** plugin. If you have followed the Jenkins setup wizard (discussed at the beginning of the chapter), you will find the **Credentials** feature on the Jenkins dashboard (see the left-hand side menu):

Follow the given steps:

1. From the Jenkins dashboard, click on **Credentials** | **System** | **Global credentials (unrestricted)**.
2. On the **Global credentials (unrestricted)** page, from the left-hand side menu, click on the **Add Credentials** link.
3. You will be presented with a bunch of fields to configure.
4. Choose **Username with password** for the **Kind** field.
5. Choose **Global (Jenkins, nodes, items, all child items, etc)** for the **Scope** field.
6. Add a username under the **Username** field.
7. Add a password under the **Password** field.
8. Give a unique ID to your credentials by typing a string under the **ID** field.
9. Add a meaningful description under the **Description** field.
10. Click on the **Save** button once done:

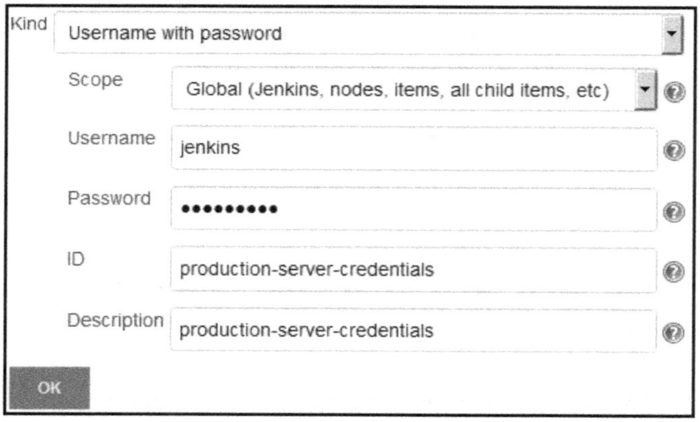

Adding credentials inside Jenkins

Installing a Jenkins slave on a production server

In this section, we will install a Jenkins slave on the production server. This will allow us to perform deployment on the production server. Execute the following steps:

1. From the Jenkins dashboard, click on **Manage Jenkins** | **Manage Nodes**.
2. Once on the **Node Manager** page, from the left-hand side menu click on **New Node**.
3. Give your new Jenkins slave node a name, as shown:

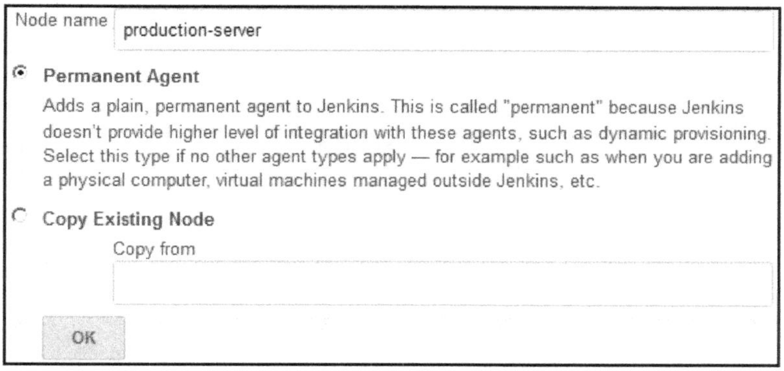

Adding a new Jenkins slave

4. On the resultant page, you will be presented with a large number of options. Let us see them one by one.
5. For the **Remote root directory** field, add the value `/home/jenkins`.
6. For the **Labels** field, add the value `production`.
7. For the **Usage** field, choose **Use this node as much as possible**.
8. For the **Launch method** field, choose the option **Launch slave agents via SSH**.
9. Under the **Host** field, add the IP address of the production server.
10. Under the **Credentials** field, choose the credentials that we created in the previous section.

11. Leave the rest of the options as they are.
12. Once done, click on the **Save** button:

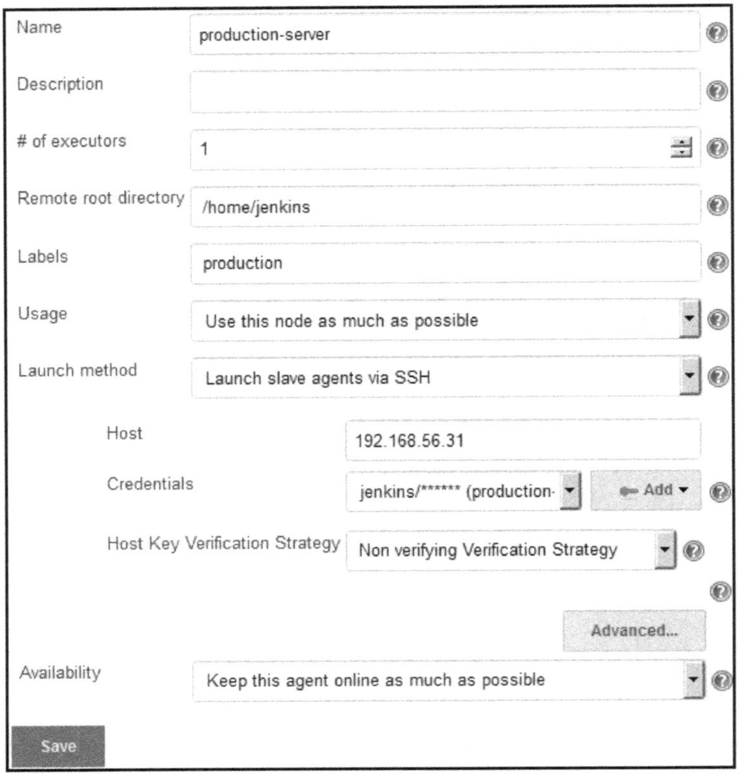

Configuring the Jenkins slave

Creating a Jenkins Continuous Deployment pipeline

In the following section, we will extend our Continuous Delivery pipeline to perform deployment.

A revisit to the pipeline code for CD

The following is the complete combined code that was part of the CD:

```
node('docker') {
  stage('Poll') {
    checkout scm
  }
  stage('Build & Unit test'){
    sh 'mvn clean verify -DskipITs=true';
    junit '**/target/surefire-reports/TEST-*.xml'
    archive 'target/*.jar'
  }
  stage('Static Code Analysis'){
    sh 'mvn clean verify sonar:sonar -Dsonar.projectName=example-project
    -Dsonar.projectKey=example-project
    -Dsonar.projectVersion=$BUILD_NUMBER';
  }
  stage ('Integration Test'){
    sh 'mvn clean verify -Dsurefire.skip=true';
    junit '**/target/failsafe-reports/TEST-*.xml'
    archive 'target/*.jar'
  }
  stage ('Publish'){
    def server = Artifactory.server 'Default Artifactory Server'
    def uploadSpec = """{
      "files": [
        {
           "pattern": "target/hello-0.0.1.war",
           "target": "example-project/${BUILD_NUMBER}/",
           "props": "Integration-Tested=Yes;Performance-Tested=No"
        }
      ]
    }"""
    server.upload(uploadSpec)
  }
  stash includes:
   'target/hello-0.0.1.war,src/pt/Hello_World_Test_Plan.jmx',
  name: 'binary'
}
node('docker_pt') {
  stage ('Start Tomcat'){
    sh '''cd /home/jenkins/tomcat/bin
    ./startup.sh''';
  }
  stage ('Deploy '){
    unstash 'binary'
```

```
      sh 'cp target/hello-0.0.1.war /home/jenkins/tomcat/webapps/';
    }
    stage ('Performance Testing'){
      sh '''cd /opt/jmeter/bin/
      ./jmeter.sh -n -t $WORKSPACE/src/pt/Hello_World_Test_Plan.jmx -l
      $WORKSPACE/test_report.jtl''';
      step([$class: 'ArtifactArchiver', artifacts: '**/*.jtl'])
    }
    stage ('Promote build in Artifactory'){
      withCredentials([usernameColonPassword(credentialsId:
       'artifactory-account', variable: 'credentials')]) {
        sh 'curl -u${credentials} -X PUT
        "http://192.168.56.102:8081/artifactory/api/storage/example-project/
        ${BUILD_NUMBER}/hello-0.0.1.war?properties=Performance-Tested=Yes"';
      }
    }
  }
```

Pipeline code for a production Jenkins slave

First, let us create a node block for our Jenkins slave, production-server:

```
node('production') {
}
```

Where `production` is the label for the Jenkins slave node, production-server.

We would like to deploy the build artifacts to Tomcat on the production server on the `production` node.

Let's write the pipeline code for it.

Pipeline code to download binaries from Artifactory

To download the build artifacts from Artifactory, we will use the File Specs. The File Specs code looks as follows:

```
"files": [
    {
      "pattern": "[Mandatory]",
      "target": "[Mandatory]",
      "props": "[Optional]",
```

```
        "recursive": "[Optional, Default: 'true']",
        "flat" : "[Optional, Default: 'true']",
        "regexp": "[Optional, Default: 'false']"
      }
    ]
```

The following table describes the various parameters used:

Parameters	Description
`pattern`	`[Mandatory]` Specifies the local filesystem path to artifacts that should be uploaded to Artifactory. You can specify multiple artifacts by using wildcards or a regular expression as designated by the `regexp` property. If you use a `regexp`, you need to escape any reserved characters (such as `.`, `?`, and so on) used in the expression using a backslash `\`. Since version 2.9.0 of the Jenkins Artifactory plugin and version 2.3.1 of the TeamCity Artifactory plugin, the pattern format has been simplified and uses the same file separator `/` for all operating systems, including Windows.
`target`	`[Mandatory]` Specifies the target path in Artifactory in the following format: `[repository_name]/[repository_path]` If the pattern ends with a slash, for example, `repo-name/a/b/`, then `b` is assumed to be a folder in Artifactory and the files are uploaded into it. In the case of `repo-name/a/b`, the uploaded file is renamed to `b` in Artifactory. For flexibility in specifying the upload path, you can include placeholders in the form of `{1}, {2}, {3}...` which are replaced by corresponding tokens in the source path that are enclosed in parentheses. For more details, please refer to the *Using Placeholders* document at `https://www.jfrog.com/confluence/display/RTF/Using+File+Specs#UsingFileSpecs-UsingPlaceholders`.
`props`	`[Optional]` List of `key=value` pairs separated by a semi-colon (`;`) to be attached as properties to the uploaded properties. If any key can take several values, then each value is separated by a comma (`,`). For example, `key1=value1;key2=value21,value22;key3=value3`.

`flat`	`[Default: true]` If `true`, artifacts are uploaded to the exact target path specified and their hierarchy in the source filesystem is ignored. If `false`, artifacts are uploaded to the target path while maintaining their filesystem hierarchy.
`recursive`	`[Default: true]` If `true`, artifacts are also collected from subdirectories of the source directory for upload. If `false`, only artifacts specifically in the source directory are uploaded.
`regexp`	`[Default: false]` If `true`, the command will interpret the pattern property, which describes the local filesystem path of artifacts to upload, as a regular expression. If `false`, the command will interpret the pattern property as a wildcard expression.

The following is the File Specs code that we will use in our pipeline:

```
def server = Artifactory.server 'Default Artifactory Server'
def downloadSpec = """{
  "files": [
    {
        "pattern": "example-project/$BUILD_NUMBER/*.zip",
        "target": "/home/jenkins/tomcat/webapps/"
        "props": "Performance-Tested=Yes;Integration-Tested=Yes",
    }
  ]
}"""
server.download(downloadSpec)
```

Wrap the preceding step inside a `stage` called `Deploy to Prod`:

```
stage ('Deploy to Prod'){
  def server = Artifactory.server 'Default Artifactory Server'
  def downloadSpec = """{
    "files": [
      {
        "pattern": "example-project/$BUILD_NUMBER/*.zip",
        "target": "/home/jenkins/tomcat/webapps/"
        "props": "Performance-Tested=Yes;Integration-Tested=Yes",
      }
    ]
```

```
    }"""
  server.download(downloadSpec)
  }
```

Wrap the `Deploy to Prod` stage inside the `production` node block:

```
node ('production') {
  stage ('Deploy to Prod'){
    def server = Artifactory.server 'Default Artifactory Server'
    def downloadSpec = """{
      "files": [
        {
          "pattern": "example-project/$BUILD_NUMBER/*.zip",
          "target": "/home/jenkins/tomcat/webapps/"
          "props": "Performance-Tested=Yes;Integration-Tested=Yes",
        }
      ]
    }"""
    server.download(downloadSpec)
  }
}
```

Combined Continuous Deployment pipeline code

The following is the combined Continuous Deployment pipeline code:

```
node('docker') {
  stage('Poll') {
    checkout scm
  }
  stage('Build & Unit test'){
    sh 'mvn clean verify -DskipITs=true';
    junit '**/target/surefire-reports/TEST-*.xml'
    archive 'target/*.jar'
  }
  stage('Static Code Analysis'){
    sh 'mvn clean verify sonar:sonar -Dsonar.projectName=example-project
    -Dsonar.projectKey=example-project
    -Dsonar.projectVersion=$BUILD_NUMBER';
  }
  stage ('Integration Test'){
    sh 'mvn clean verify -Dsurefire.skip=true';
    junit '**/target/failsafe-reports/TEST-*.xml'
    archive 'target/*.jar'
  }
  stage ('Publish'){
```

```
      def server = Artifactory.server 'Default Artifactory Server'
      def uploadSpec = """{
        "files": [
          {
            "pattern": "target/hello-0.0.1.war",
            "target": "example-project/${BUILD_NUMBER}/",
            "props": "Integration-Tested=Yes;Performance-Tested=No"
          }
        ]
      }"""
      server.upload(uploadSpec)
    }
    stash includes:
     'target/hello-0.0.1.war,src/pt/Hello_World_Test_Plan.jmx',
    name: 'binary'
  }
  node('docker_pt') {
    stage ('Start Tomcat'){
      sh '''cd /home/jenkins/tomcat/bin
      ./startup.sh''';
    }
    stage ('Deploy '){
      unstash 'binary'
      sh 'cp target/hello-0.0.1.war /home/jenkins/tomcat/webapps/';
    }
    stage ('Performance Testing'){
      sh '''cd /opt/jmeter/bin/
      ./jmeter.sh -n -t $WORKSPACE/src/pt/Hello_World_Test_Plan.jmx -l
      $WORKSPACE/test_report.jtl''';
      step([$class: 'ArtifactArchiver', artifacts: '**/*.jtl'])
    }
    stage ('Promote build in Artifactory'){
      withCredentials([usernameColonPassword(credentialsId:
       'artifactory-account', variable: 'credentials')]) {
        sh 'curl -u${credentials} -X PUT
        "http://192.168.56.102:8081/artifactory/api/storage/example-project/
        ${BUILD_NUMBER}/hello-0.0.1.war?properties=Performance-Tested=Yes"';
      }
    }
  }
  node ('production') {
    stage ('Deploy to Prod'){
      def server = Artifactory.server 'Default Artifactory Server'
      def downloadSpec = """{
        "files": [
          {
            "pattern": "example-project/$BUILD_NUMBER/*.zip",
            "target": "/home/jenkins/tomcat/webapps/"
```

```
          "props": "Performance-Tested=Yes;Integration-Tested=Yes",
        }
      ]
    }"""
    server.download(downloadSpec)
  }
}
```

Update the Jenkinsfile

A Jenkins Multibranch CD Pipeline utilizes a Jenkinsfile. In this section, we will update our existing Jenkinsfile. Follow the given steps:

1. Log in to your GitHub account.
2. Navigate to the forked repository.
3. Once on the repository page, click on the `Jenkinsfile`. Next, on the resultant page click on the **Edit** button to edit your `Jenkinsfile`.
4. Replace the existing content with the following code:

```
node('docker') {
  stage('Poll') {
    checkout scm
  }
  stage('Build & Unit test'){
    sh 'mvn clean verify -DskipITs=true';
    junit '**/target/surefire-reports/TEST-*.xml'
    archive 'target/*.jar'
  }
  stage('Static Code Analysis'){
    sh 'mvn clean verify sonar:sonar
    -Dsonar.projectName=example-project
    -Dsonar.projectKey=example-project
    -Dsonar.projectVersion=$BUILD_NUMBER';
  }
  stage ('Integration Test'){
    sh 'mvn clean verify -Dsurefire.skip=true';
    junit '**/target/failsafe-reports/TEST-*.xml'
    archive 'target/*.jar'
  }
  stage ('Publish'){
    def server = Artifactory.server
      'Default Artifactory Server'
    def uploadSpec = """{
      "files": [
```

```
          {
            "pattern": "target/hello-0.0.1.war",
            "target": "example-project/${BUILD_NUMBER}/",
            "props": "Integration-Tested=Yes;
              Performance-Tested=No"
          }
        ]
      }"""
      server.upload(uploadSpec)
    }
    stash includes:
     'target/hello-0.0.1.war,src/pt/Hello_World_Test_Plan.jmx',
    name: 'binary'
  }
  node('docker_pt') {
    stage ('Start Tomcat'){
      sh '''cd /home/jenkins/tomcat/bin
      ./startup.sh''';
    }
    stage ('Deploy '){
      unstash 'binary'
      sh 'cp target/hello-0.0.1.war
/home/jenkins/tomcat/webapps/';
    }
    stage ('Performance Testing'){
      sh '''cd /opt/jmeter/bin/
      ./jmeter.sh -n -t
$WORKSPACE/src/pt/Hello_World_Test_Plan.jmx
      -l $WORKSPACE/test_report.jtl''';
      step([$class: 'ArtifactArchiver', artifacts: '**/*.jtl'])
    }
    stage ('Promote build in Artifactory'){
      withCredentials([usernameColonPassword(credentialsId:
       'artifactory-account', variable: 'credentials')]) {
        sh 'curl -u${credentials} -X PUT
        "http://192.168.56.102:8081/artifactory/api/storage/
         example-project/${BUILD_NUMBER}/hello-0.0.1.war?
         properties=Performance-Tested=Yes"';
      }
    }
  }
  node ('production') {
    stage ('Deploy to Prod'){
      def server = Artifactory.server
       'Default Artifactory Server'
      def downloadSpec = """{
        "files": [
          {
```

```
                "pattern": "example-project/$BUILD_NUMBER/*.zip",
                "target": "/home/jenkins/tomcat/webapps/"
                "props": "Performance-Tested=Yes;
                   Integration-Tested=Yes",
              }
           ]
        }"""
        server.download(downloadSpec)
      }
    }
```

5. Once done, **Commit** the new file by adding a meaningful comment.

Continuous Delivery in action

Make some changes to your GitHub code or just trigger the Jenkins pipeline from the Jenkins dashboard.

Log in to Jenkins, and from the Jenkins dashboard click on your Multibranch Pipeline. You should see something similar to the following screenshot:

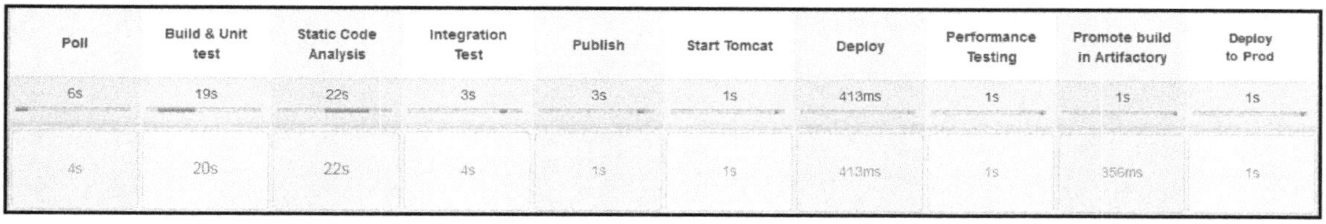
Poll
Build & Unit test
Static Code Analysis
Integration Test
Publish
Start Tomcat
Deploy
Performance Testing
Promote build in Artifactory
Deploy to Prod
6s
19s
22s
3s
3s
1s
413ms
1s
1s
1s
4s
20s
22s
4s
1s
1s
413ms
1s
356ms
1s

Jenkins Continuous Deployment pipeline in action

Summary

This marks the end of Continuous Deployment. In this chapter, we learned how to achieve Continuous Deployment using Jenkins. Also, I hope the confusion between Continuous Delivery and Continuous Deployment is clear. There were no major setups or configurations in the chapter, as all the necessary things were achieved in the previous chapters while implementing Continuous Integration and Continuous Delivery.

I really hope this book serves as a means for you to go out there and experiment more with Jenkins.

Until next time, cheers!

Supporting Tools and Installation Guide

This chapter will take you through the steps required to make your Jenkins server accessible over the internet. We will also cover the steps required for installing Git on Windows and Linux.

Exposing your localhost server to the internet

You are required to create Webhooks on GitHub in order to trigger a pipeline in Jenkins. Also, for the GitHub Webhooks to work, it is important that the Jenkins server is accessible over the internet.

While practicing the examples described in this book, you may feel a need to make your Jenkins server accessible over the internet, which is installed in your sandbox environment.

In the following section, we will use a tool named ngrok to achieve this feat. Perform the following steps to make your Jenkins server accessible over the internet:

1. Log in to the Jenkins server machine (standalone Windows/Linux machine). If you are running Jenkins using Docker, log in to your Docker host machine (most probably, Linux).
2. Download the ngrok application from `https://ngrok.com/download`.
3. What you download is a ZIP package. Extract it using the `unzip` command (to install the ZIP utility on Ubuntu, execute `sudo apt-get install zip`).

4. Run the following command to unzip the ngrok ZIP package:

```
unzip /path/to/ngrok.zip
```

5. To run ngrok on Linux, execute the following command:

```
./ngrok http 8080
```

   Alternatively, run the following command:

```
nohup ./ngrok http 8080 &
```

6. To run ngrok on Windows, execute the following command:

```
ngrok.exe http 8080
```

7. You should see a similar output, as shown as follows; the highlighted text is the public URL of `localhost:8080`:

```
ngrok by @inconshreveable (Ctrl+C to quit)
Session Status online
Version 2.2.8
Region United States (us)
Web Interface http://127.0.0.1:4040
Forwarding http://8bd4ecd3.ngrok.io -> localhost:8080
Forwarding https://8bd4ecd3.ngrok.io -> localhost:8080
Connections ttl opn rt1 rt5 p50 p90
0 0 0.00 0.00 0.00 0.00
```

8. Copy the preceding public URL.
9. Log in to your Jenkins server. From the Jenkins dashboard, navigate to **Manage Jenkins** | **Configure System**.
10. On the Jenkins configuration page, scroll all the way down to the **Jenkins Location** section and add the public URL generated using ngrok inside the **Jenkins URL** field.
11. Click on the **Save** button to save the settings.
12. You will now be able to access your Jenkins server using the public URL over the internet.
13. While creating Webhooks on GitHub, use the public URL generated using ngrok.

Installing Git on Windows/Linux

The steps mentioned in the following sections are required to install Git on Windows and Linux:

Installing Git on Windows

To install Git on Windows, follow these steps:

1. You can download Git from `https://git-scm.com/downloads`:

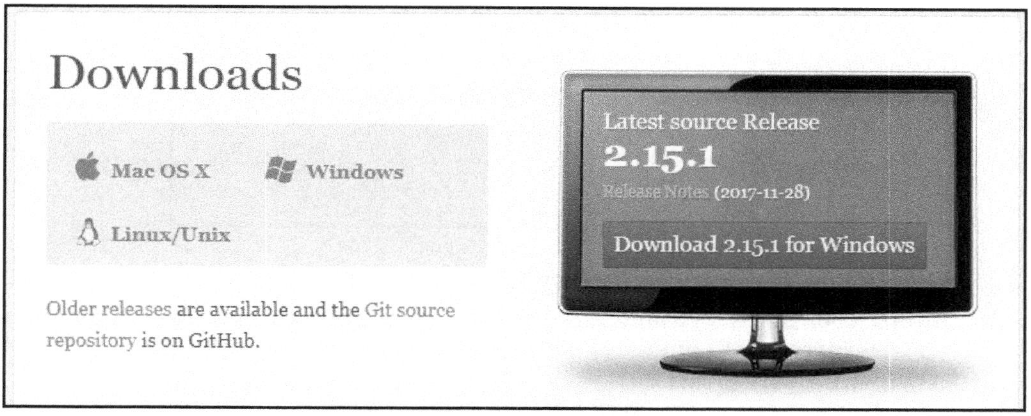

2. Click on the downloaded executable and proceed with the installation steps.
3. Accept the license agreement and click on **Next**.

4. Select all the components and click on **Next**, as shown in the following screenshot:

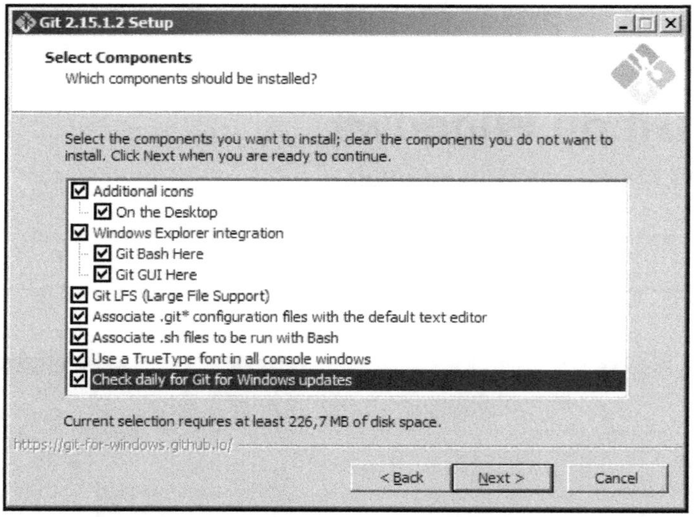

5. Choose the default editor used by Git, and click on **Next**.
6. Adjust your path environment by selecting the appropriate environment and click on **Next**, as shown in the following screenshot:

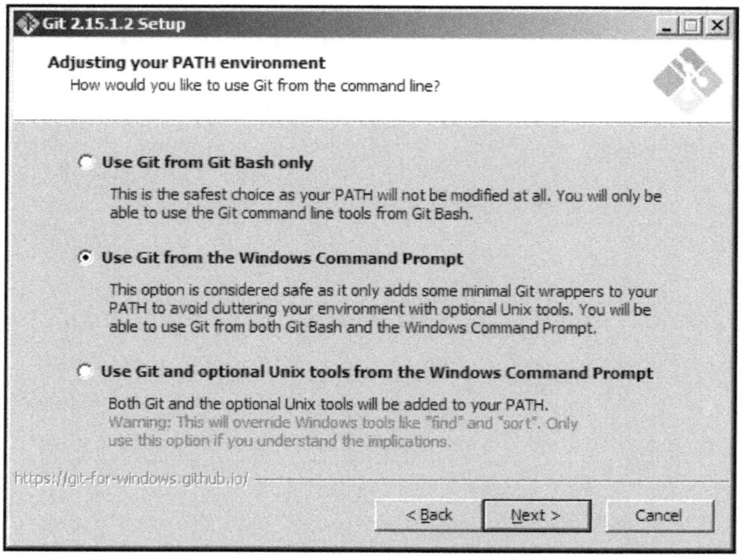

7. Choose **Use OpenSSH** as the SSH executable and click on **Next**:

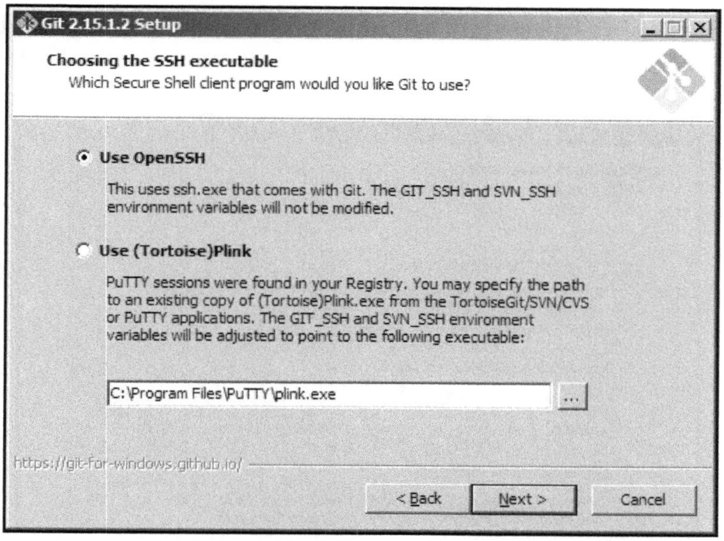

8. Select **Use the OenSSL library** as the HTTPS transport backend and click on **Next**:

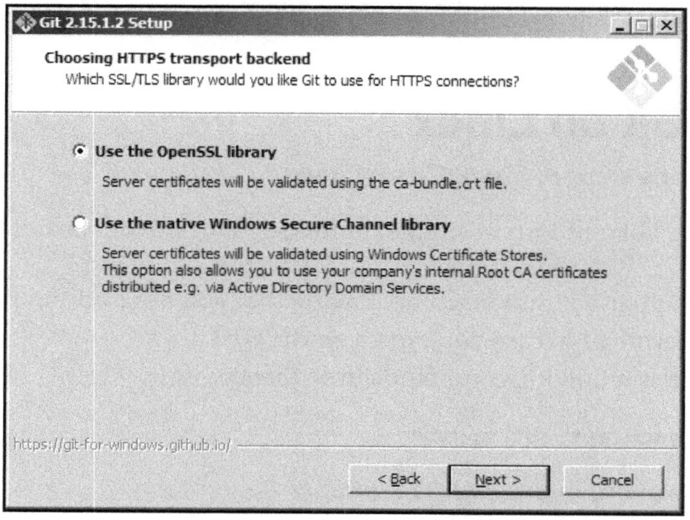

9. Choose the line ending conversion that suits you the best and click on **Next**.
10. Choose the terminal emulator and click on **Next**.
11. Select the **Enable file system caching** and **Enable Git Credentials Manager** options, as shown in the following screenshot, and click on **Install**:

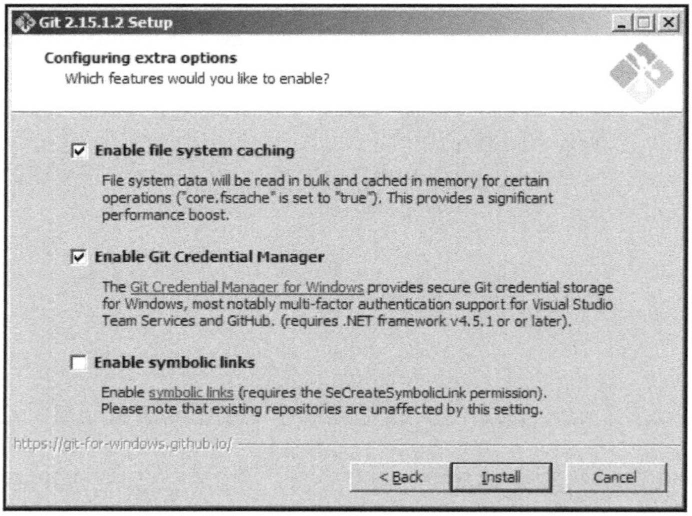

12. The Git installation should begin now. Once it's complete, click on **Finish**.

Installing Git on Linux

Perform the following steps to install Git on Linux:

1. Installing Git on Linux is simple. In this section, we will install Git on Ubuntu (16.04.x).
2. Log in to your Ubuntu machine. Ensure that you have admin privileges.
3. Open a terminal in case you are using the GUI.
4. Execute the following commands in sequence:

```
sudo apt-get update

sudo apt-get install git
```

5. Execute the following command to check the Git installation:

```
git --version
```

6. You should get the following result:

```
git version 2.15.1.windows.2
```

Index

.

.deb package
  download link 78

A

Agile
  about 12
  principles 12
  software development process, advantages 14
  software development process, working 13
Apache JMeter
  installing 290
Apache Tomcat server
  configuring 40
  installing 37
  Jenkins alone, installation 43
  Jenkins, installing 42
  realms, reference 173
Artifactory application
  running 238
Artifactory package
  download link 236
Artifactory plugin
  configuring 245
  installing, in Jenkins 245
Artifactory Pro
  reference 236
Artifactory
  API key, generating 240
  configuring 234
  credentials, adding inside Jenkins 244
  default credentials, resetting 240
  installing 234
  Java, installing 235
  package, downloading 236
  repository, creating 241
authentication methods
  delegating, to servlet container 173
  LDAP 175
  Unix user/group database 176
  user database 174
authorization methods
  about 179
  control option 179
  legacy mode 179
  logged-in users 179
  matrix-based security 180
  Project-based Matrix Authorization Strategy 181
automated testing 29

B

benefits, Continuous Integration (CI)
  issue catch 32
  metrics 32
  no long integrations 32
  rapid development 32
  time consumption, for adding features 33
binary repository tools 30
branching strategy, Jenkins CI design
  about 250
  feature branch 250
  integration branch 250
  master branch 250
build breaker plugin
  installing, for SonarQube 226
  reference 226

C

CD pipeline
  about 296
  Jenkinsfile, writing 296
Certificate Signing Request (CSR) 63

CI pipeline
creating 252
Jenkinsfile, using 261
Jenkinsfile, writing 254
multibranch pipeline, creating 263
repository, creating on GitHub 253
SonarQube scanner, using for Maven 253
Webhooks, re-registering 264
Common Name (CN) 64
Continuous Delivery (CD)
about 149, 279
lifecycle 308
using 303, 329
Continuous Deployment
about 308
audience 310
differentiating, with Continuous Delivery 308
lifecycle 310
Continuous Integration (CI)
about 7, 18, 149
agile, running 19
artifacts, viewing in Artifactory 274
benefits 32
elements 21
projects 20
quality gate criteria fail scenario 275
SonarQube analysis, accessing 272
static code analysis, viewing 270
using 266

D

data volume
testing 82
used, for running Jenkins container 81
Declarative Pipeline
reference 109
structure 106
syntax 106
development and staging instances, Jenkins
creating 85, 87
data, copying between data volumes 86
empty data volume, creating 85
prerequisites 85
development process, Scrum
Daily Scrum meeting 17
retrospective 18
review 18
Sprint cycle 17
Sprint Planning 17
Sprint progress, monitoring 17
distributed build and testing 185, 186
Docker container
credentials, adding in Jenkins 287
Jenkins, upgrading 169
Docker host
installing 76
installing, from package 78
repository, setting up 75
setting up 75
Docker image
creating 282
reference 212
Docker remote API
docker.conf file, modifying 208
docker.service file, modifying 209
enabling 207
Docker server
installing, .deb package used 207
installing, apt-get used 206
repository, setting up 205
setting up 205
Docker
Jenkins, running 75
settings, updating inside Jenkins 288

E

elements, Continuous Integration (CI)
automated packaging 31
automated testing 29
binary repository tools 30
branching strategy 21
code coverage 26
code coverage, tools 27
self-triggered builds 25
static code analysis 27
version control system 21

F

Fully Qualified Domain Name (FQDN) 64

G

Git
  download link 333
  installing, on Linux 333, 336
  installing, on Windows 333

I

Internet
  localhost server, exposing 331

J

Java Network Launch Protocol (JNLP) 191
Java Runtime Environment (JRE) 36, 284
Java Web Start
  Jenkins slave, launching 201
Jenkins backup
  creating 159
  logs, restoring 161
  logs, viewing 161
  restoring 160
Jenkins Blue Ocean plugin
  features 132
  installing 132
  pipeline, creating 136, 144
  viewing 133
Jenkins CD design
  about 279
  branching strategy 280
  branching, release branch 280
  CD pipeline 281
  toolset 281
Jenkins CI design
  about 249
  branching strategy 250
  pipeline 251
  toolset 252
Jenkins Continuous Deployment pipeline
  code 321
  code, for downloading binaries from Artifactory 322
  code, for production Jenkins slave 322
  Combined Continuous Deployment pipeline code 325
  creating 320
  Jenkinsfile, updating 327
Jenkins Manage Nodes page 187, 189
Jenkins pipeline job
  about 96
  creating 97
  Global Tool Configuration page 101
  prerequisites 97
  Stage View 103, 105
Jenkins pipeline syntax utility
  about 109
  Pipeline Maven Integration Plugin, installing 110
  prerequisite 109
  used, for creating Jenkins pipeline 111, 117
Jenkins pipeline
  creating, with Jenkins pipeline syntax utility 117
  creating, with pipeline syntax utility 111
Jenkins Plugin Manager
  about 149
  Available tab 151
  downgrading 152
  Jenkins plugin, manual installation 154
  Jenkins plugin, uninstalling 152
  proxy settings, configuring 153
  updating 151
Jenkins setup wizard
  about 91
  prerequisites 92
Jenkins slave
  about 195, 197
  adding, prerequisites 204
  Docker container credentials, adding 215
  Docker containers, adding 204
  Docker image, creating 212
  Docker plugin, configuring 210
  Docker plugin, installing 210
  Docker remote API, enabling 207
  Docker server, setting up 205
  Docker settings, updating 216
  environment variables, passing 192
  installing, on production server 319
  launching, via Java Web Start 201, 204
  launching, via SSH 194
  standalone Linux machine, adding as 189
  standalone Windows machine, adding as 199
  tools' location, passing 193

Jenkins, running behind reverse proxy
and nginx running on same machine 73
firewall, configuring on nginx server 59
Jenkins server, configuring 70
nginx server, restarting 62
nginx server, securing with OpenSSL 63
nginx server, starting 62
nginx server, stopping 62
nginx, configuring 58
nginx, installing 58
prerequisites 58
reverse proxy setting, adding to nginx configuration 71
Jenkins, running inside servlet container
Apache Tomcat server, configuring 40
Apache Tomcat, installing 37
firewall and port 8080, enabling 39
home path, setting up 44
Java, installing 36
prerequisites 36
Jenkins, running on Docker
data volume, using 81
Docker host, setting up 75
prerequisites 75
steps 78
Jenkins
backup and restore 156
on Docker container, upgrading 169
reference 163
running, behind reverse proxy 58
running, inside servlet container 35
running, on Docker 75
setup wizard 91
upgradation, running on Tomcat Server 163
upgrading 162
Jenkinsfile, creating for CD
combined CD pipeline code 301
Docker container, spawning 297
pipeline code 296
pipeline code, for deploying build artifacts 298
pipeline code, for performance testing execution 299
pipeline code, for promoting build artifacts 300
pipeline code, for starting Apache Tomcat 298
stash feature, for passing build artifacts 297
Jenkinsfile, writing for CI
combined CI pipeline code 260
Docker container, spawning 254
latest source code, downloading from VCS 255
pipeline code, for performing build and unit test 255
pipeline code, for performing integration testing 256
pipeline code, for performing static code analysis 256
pipeline code, for publishing built artifacts 257
JMeter
used, for creating performance test (PT) 289

L

labels 186
Linux
Git, installing 333, 336
localhost server
exposing, to Internet 331
Long Term Support (LTS) 47

M

mainline branch 250
multibranch pipeline
about 118
creating, in Jenkins 126
prerequisite 119
using 129

N

nginx, securing with OpenSSL
changes, enabling 68
configuration, modifying 65
setup, testing 68
SSL certificate, creating 63
strong encryption settings, creating 64
ngrok application
download link 331

P

packaging 31
People page
about 177

user information and settings 177
Perfect Forward Secrecy (PFS) 64
performance test (PT), creating
case, creating 291
Java, installing 290
JMeter, installing 290
JMeter, starting 291
JMeter, using 289
listener, adding 295, 296
sampler, creating 294
thread group, creating 292
Periodic Backup plugin
configuring 157
installing 157
prerequisites, multibranch pipeline
GitHub credentials , adding inside Jenkins 120
Jenkinsfile, using 125
new repository, creating on GitHub 124
testing, with new feature branch 130
Webhook, configuring on GitHub 121
Webhooks, re-registering 127
production branch 250
production server
creating 311
credentials, adding inside Jenkins 317
Jenkins slave, installing 319
Vagrant, installing 311
VirtualBox, installing 313
VM, creating with Vagrant 314

R

Red Hat Linux
standalone Jenkins server, installing 54
remote shell (RSH) 191

S

Scrum framework
about 15
Development Team 16
increment 15
Product Backlog 15
Product Owner 16
Scrum Master 16
Sprint 15
Sprint Backlog 15
working 16
servlet container
Jenkins, running 35
setup wizard
first admin user, creating 96
Jenkins, customizing 93, 95
Jenkins, unlocking 92
Software Development Life Cycle (SDLC)
about 7
design 8
evolution 9
implementation 9
requirement analysis 8
testing 9
software development
Waterfall model 9
SonarQube application
executing 222
SonarQube
build breaker plugin, installing 226
configuring 219
configuring, in Jenkins 233
default credentials, setting 223
default quality profile, updating 230
installing 219
installing, in Jenkins 232
Java, installing 220
package, downloading 221
project, creating 224
quality gates, creating 227
static code analysis, viewing 270
token, generating 223
standalone Jenkins server installation, on Red Hat Linux
Java, installing 55
latest version, installing 56
prerequisites 55
restarting 57
stable version, installing 56
starting 57
stopping 57
standalone Jenkins server installation, on Ubuntu
Java, installing 51
latest version, installing 52

prerequisites 51
restarting 54
stable version, installing 53
starting 54
stopping 54
standalone Jenkins server installation, on Windows
Java, installing 46
latest stable version, installing 47
prerequisites 45
restarting 47
starting 47
stopping 47
standalone Jenkins server
installing, on Red Hat Linux 54
installing, on Ubuntu 50
installing, on Windows 45
standalone Jenkins
upgrading, on Ubuntu 167
upgrading, on Windows 165
standalone Linux machine
adding, as Jenkins slaves 189
static code analysis 27
structure, Declarative Pipeline
directives 107
node block 106
stage block 106
step element 107

T

Tomcat Server
Jenkins, upgrading 163

U

Ubuntu
standalone Jenkins server, installing 50
standalone Jenkins, upgrading 167
user administration
about 171
authentication methods 173
authorization methods 178
global security, enabling/disabling 172
new users, creating 176
People page 177
user credentials remember option, enabling/disabling 172

V

Vagrant
download link 312
installing 311
used, for creating VM 314
used, for spawning VM 315
version control system (VCS) 281
VirtualBox
installing 313
URL 313
VM
creating, with Vagrant 314
production server credentials, adding inside Jenkins 317
spawning, Vagrant used 315
Vagrantfile, creating 314

W

Waterfall model
advantages 11
disadvantages 11
of software development 9
white-box testing 27
Windows
Git, installing 333
standalone Jenkins server, installing 45
standalone Jenkins, upgrading 165

CPSIA information can be obtained
at www.ICGtesting.com
Printed in the USA
BVHW01s1212260418
514515BV00006B/39/P

9 781788 479356